Jim Jordan's wife
Kathleen in my Callawassie
Book Group. We've
had him speak to us.
2019

The Slave-Trader's Letter-Book

The Slave-Trader's Letter-Book

Charles Lamar,
the *Wanderer*, and Other Tales
of the African Slave Trade

Jim Jordan

The University of Georgia Press
ATHENS

A Sarah Mills Hodge Fund Publication

This publication is made possible, in part, through a grant from the Hodge
Foundation in memory of its founder, Sarah Mills Hodge, who devoted her life
to the relief and education of African Americans in Savannah, Georgia.

To my wife,
Kathleen Cullen Jordan

Contents

Abbreviations

NEWSPAPERS

AG	*Alexandria* (Virginia) *Gazette*
AC	*Augusta Chronicle*
ADC	*Augusta Daily Constitutionalist*
BL	Boston *Liberator*
BT	*Boston Traveler*
CC	*Charleston Courier*
CM	*Charleston Mercury*
DG	*Daily Georgian*
LT	*The Times of London*
MT	*Macon Telegraph*
NYCA	*New York Commercial Advertiser*
NYE	*New York Emancipator*
NYEP	*New York Evening Post*
NYH	*New York Herald*
NYJC	*New York Journal of Commerce*
NYS	New York *Spectator*
NYT	*New York Times*
NOB	*New Orleans Bee*
NOD	*New Orleans Delta*
NOTP	New Orleans *Times-Picayune*
DMN	*Savannah Daily Morning News*
SG	*Savannah Daily Georgian*
SMN	*Savannah Morning News*
SR	*Savannah Republican*
WDNI	*Daily National Intelligencer* (Washington, D.C.)
WDU	*Daily Union* (Washington, D.C.)

COLLECTIONS

G. B. Lamar Papers, GHS — James Jordan Collection of Lamar family papers, MS 2549, Georgia Historical Society, Savannah, Georgia

> G. B. Lamar letter book. G. B. Lamar letter book 1854–1858, Vol. 20, Box 15, G. B. Lamar Papers, GHS
>
> G. B. Lamar Estate letter book. Lamar Estate copy correspondence December 1854–1860, 1860–1878, Vol. 19, G. B. Lamar Papers, GHS
>
> Slave-Trader's Letter-Book, GHS. Charles Lamar letter book 1855–1863, Vol. 24, G. B. Lamar Papers, GHS
>
> G. B. Lamar daybook. Gazaway Bugg Lamar daybook 1836–1848, Vol. 1, G. B. Lamar Papers, GHS

G. B. Lamar Papers, UGA — G. B. Lamar Papers, Special Collections, Hargrett Rare Book and Manuscript Library, University of Georgia, Athens

Charles Lamar Papers, G.A. — Charles Lafayette Lamar Papers, AC 1973-504M, Georgia Archives, Morrow

C. A. L. Lamar Papers, Emory — Charles A. L. Lamar Papers, Stuart A. Rose Manuscript, Archives, and Rare Book Library, Emory University

Gardner Papers — James Gardner Papers, AC 1951-0003M, Georgia State Archives, Morrow

U.S. Attorney Letters — Letters Received by the Office of the United States Attorney, National Archives, College Park, Md.

JOURNALS

GHQ   *Georgia Historical Quarterly*
JMH   *Journal of Mississippi History*
JNH   *Journal of Negro History*

OTHER CITATIONS

Circuit Court Minutes	Minutes of the U.S. Circuit Court of Savannah, Georgia, March 1857– November 1860, Federal Records Center, Morrow, Ga.
C. A. L. Lamar's Estate	Estate of Chas. A. L. Lamar, Folder L-155, Records Department, Chatham County Probate Court, Savannah, Ga.
G. B. Lamar Civil War Copy Books	Personal Press Copy Books of G. B. Lamar, National Archives, Division of Treasury Department Archives, Civil War Records of the Fifth Special Treasury Agency
"Log of *Wanderer*"	"The Log of the *Wanderer*," *Wanderer* Records, Stuart A. Rose Manuscript, Archives, and Rare Book Library, Emory University
Message from the President	*Message from/of the President of the United States*, all volumes
OR	*The War of the Rebellion: A Compilation of the Official Records of the Union and Confederate Armies* (Washington, D.C.: Government Printing Office, 1900)
OR-N	*Official Records of the Union and Confederate Navies in the War of the Rebellion* (Washington, D.C.: Government Printing Office, 1899)
"Slave-Trader's Letter-Book," NAR	"Slave Trader's Letter-Book," *North American Review*
U.S. vs. the "Wanderer"	*The United States of America, by Information, Versus the Schooner* "Wanderer," *and Cargo* (Boston: Prentis & Deland, 1860)
Wanderer Folder	*Wanderer* Folder, Slave Papers, Manuscript Division, Library of Congress, Washington, D.C.

OTHER ABBREVIATIONS

GHS   Georgia Historical Society

Acknowledgments

WHEN I STARTED READING about the Lamar family and the *Wanderer* thirteen years ago, I had no idea that a novel, journal article, and non-fiction book would come of it. During my research on these projects, I have had the privilege of working with many people who have provided me with invaluable support and assistance.

I could not have written *The Slave-Trader's Letter-Book* without the help of the people at the Georgia Historical Society—my home away from home. In 2009 the head archivist at the society—aware of my interest in the Lamars—notified me that she had spoken to a woman from New Jersey who had three steamer trunks of papers belonging to nineteenth-century businessman Gazaway Bugg Lamar that she wanted to sell. That set the wheels in motion. If the papers were authentic, I had to make sure that they wound up in the proper home. I worked closely with Dr. W. Todd Groce, president and chief executive officer of the Georgia Historical Society, and Dr. Stan Deaton, its senior historian and managing editor of the *Georgia Historical Quarterly*, and within several months, that goal became a reality. Lynette Stoudt, director of the Research Center, and I spent months sorting through and organizing the collection. Archivists Katharine Rapkin and Lindsay Sheldon helped me photograph the brittle pages of the various letter-books, including "The Slave-Trader's Letter-Book."

I am honored that I have been able to contribute in some small way to this institution, which, since its founding in 1839, has accumulated such a significant and rich collection of records detailing and illustrating the history of the state of Georgia.

Of course, I am deeply indebted to Rosemary Jerome, who knew to keep the Gazaway Lamar collection from the auction houses. She allowed me, a total stranger, access to her house for three days to examine and inventory the papers. She and her son Jack have become good friends to me, and I visit them whenever I travel to New Jersey.

I owe special thanks to my editor, Steve Hoffius, for making my writing more readable and offering valuable suggestions for presenting the narrative. My wife, Kathleen, was indispensable in helping me with the arduous task of transcribing the letters. Dr. John and Ginger Duncan of V & J Duncan of Savannah, with an incredible collection of antique maps, prints, books, and portraits, furnished me with research material and photographs.

I owe special gratitude to Gordon Burns Smith, a Savannah historian who passed away in 2013. A fixture at the Georgia Historical Society, Gordon could tell me where to find an elusive source of information, and he always gave me encouragement to carry on when "researcher frustration" set in. It is still difficult walking into the society library, knowing that Gordon won't be there.

My sincerest appreciation goes to all the institutions that store and maintain the treasures from the past. I received courteous and helpful treatment from all, including the Georgia Historical Society in Savannah, the Augusta Genealogical Society, Armstrong University Lane Library in Savannah, Georgia Southern University Zach S. Henderson Library in Statesboro, Georgia Regents University Reese Library in Augusta, University of South Carolina, Columbia's Thomas Cooper Library and South Caroliniana Library, University of South Carolina's Bluffton and Beaufort libraries, the Charleston County Public Library, the National Archives at Morrow, Georgia, and College Park, Maryland, the Library of Congress, the Hargrett Rare Book and Manuscript Library at the University of Georgia, and the Manuscript, Archives, and Rare Book Library at Emory University. I also want to thank Tony Pizzo, director of the Ships of the Sea Maritime Museum in Savannah, for allowing me access to the museum's records, and friend and neighbor Bill Julavits for making nautical terms understandable. I greatly appreciate the time that several descendants of Gazaway Lamar gave me.

Introduction

The Journey of the Slave-Trader's Letter-Book

In 1858 Savannah businessman Charles Augustus Lafayette Lamar and a group of associates committed one of the most brazen crimes of the century when they smuggled more than four hundred Africans into the United States on the luxury yacht the *Wanderer*. It was the first known successful importation of Africans to U.S. soil in decades. Reports of the landing sparked outrage and condemnation throughout the North and even in some editorial pages in the South. Authorities soon arrested three of the crew and tried them and several of the partners, including Lamar, in federal district court in Savannah. The trials drew national attention, but the prosecutors could not gain one guilty verdict related to the importation.[1]

Historians who have written about the illegal slave trade, and especially the expedition of the *Wanderer*, invariably reference an article titled "A Slave-Trader's Letter-Book," which appeared in the November 1886 issue of the *North American Review*, a political journal. Written by an unnamed author, the article presents extracts of correspondence by Charles Lamar from 1855 to 1861, reportedly taken from his letter-book. The selected passages describe his slave-trading exploits and involvement in the Cuban filibustering movement of the 1850s.[2]

These letters have attracted the interest of scholars because they were written by a member of one of the most prominent and wealthy families in the South, who claimed that he entered the trade to uphold southern rights and defiantly announced his intentions to the world. His family name and involvement in many businesses gave him a reputation as a savvy, successful entrepreneur and deeply principled rebel. "Given young Lamar's keen business spirit," wrote Ronald T. Takaki of the University of California Berkeley, "it should not be surprising to find him viewing his African slave-trade enterprises in terms of profitability. . . . But for Lamar, the African slave-trade was much more than a moneymaking scheme: it involved Southern honor." Pulitzer Prize winner Don E. Fehrenbacher of Stanford University echoed that sentiment when he noted, "Thirty-three-year-old Charles Augustus Lafayette Lamar of Savannah, a mixture of shrewd businessman and southern romantic, decided to vindicate the

1

morality of slaveholding society while turning a good profit in the process." Tom Henderson Wells, in a book on the *Wanderer*, praised Lamar's ability to spot opportunities and turn them into thriving businesses: "Like his father [Gazaway Bugg Lamar], he had the vision and the nerve to undertake the unusual and see it through."[3]

Over the years the motives behind the publication of the article in the *North American Review* have been questioned. Historian Harvey Wish speculated in 1941 that "its publication may have been due to a partisan desire to discredit [President Grover] Cleveland's administration which included the former Confederate general, L. Q. C. Lamar [Charles's cousin], as secretary of the interior." In 1963 Warren S. Howard, in his book *American Slavers and the Federal Law, 1837–1862*, also suggested that the article was intended to embarrass L. Q. C. Lamar. In addition, he questioned the authenticity of the letters, claiming that they "raise further suspicions. . . . Many of the individuals named . . . were unquestionably engaged in the slave trade, but anyone well acquainted with the history of the trade could have written up any of the actions described for the *Review*. . . . This questionable document adds nothing of value to other source materials." Four years later, Tom Henderson Wells wrote *The Slave Ship "Wanderer"* and challenged Howard, contending that the letters read like others that Lamar had written and were indeed genuine. However, since Howard's book the issue of legitimacy has hovered over any scholarship referencing the article in the *North American Review*.[4]

To be sure, the letter-book was discovered under suspicious circumstances. The journal author claimed, "It was my fortune, during my summer's vacation, to rescue from the obliterating maw of a New England paper-mill, a letter-press copy-book, containing impressions of a series of remarkable letters, written by a prominent 'Southern gentleman.'. . . It must have been confiscated during 'Sherman's march to the sea,' and brought North." He never explained his presence at the pulp mill nor how he happened to pick out that one book from what must have been a considerable mound of rubbish.[5]

———————

While researching Charles Lamar for a novel about antebellum Savannah and a subsequent article for the *Georgia Historical Quarterly*, I located close to eighty of his letters, mostly in collections at Emory University, the Georgia State Archives, the University of Georgia, and the National Archives, but the letter-book could not be found.

In the autumn of 2009, about the time that the *Georgia Historical Quarterly* published my article, "Charles Augustus Lafayette Lamar and His Efforts to Reopen the African Slave Trade," the director of archives at the Georgia Historical Society informed me that her organization had been contacted by a woman living in New Jersey. The woman wanted to sell three steamer trunks filled with documents of Charles's father, Gazaway Bugg Lamar, a successful and politically connected cotton merchant, banker, and shipper during the antebellum, Civil War, and Reconstruction years.

The woman and her husband had purchased a house in Upper Montclair, New Jersey, in 1969. They inspected the attic after moving in and found the trunks, which were packed with accounting books, bound letter-books, and thousands of loose pieces of paper. The husband, a history buff, understood their importance and resisted his wife's temptation to discard them. Over the years he occasionally ventured into the attic to read the contents. In the 1980s he offered to sell or donate the papers to the Georgia Historical Society, but a transfer never materialized.

The documents remained in the attic until 2009, when the husband passed away. Before his widow sold the house to relocate to smaller quarters, she contacted a few auction houses about the collection. After several meetings she realized that a buyer of this type probably would sell the contents in pieces, which would diminish their historical significance. She moved the trunks to her new residence and contacted the staff of the Georgia Historical Society, and they, aware of my interest in the Lamars, alerted me.

I called the woman from my home in South Carolina, explained my work as a researcher, and asked if I could evaluate the collection on behalf of the Georgia Historical Society. She consented and welcomed me into her house in New Jersey a few weeks later. After serving her son and me lunch, she led me upstairs to an unfurnished but freshly painted, white-carpeted room with a large black tarp spread on the floor. Three dark-colored, dust-covered steamer trunks with broken front latches sat in the middle. "There you go," she said.

I stepped up, kneeled, and opened them one by one. I remember saying, "Wow!"

The woman allowed me access to the documents and use of a study for three days. Under the watchful eye of her cat Shadow, I got to work. Since I was familiar with Gazaway Lamar's personal history and handwriting, I immediately realized that I had come across a treasure of long-lost documents of an important nineteenth-century southern businessman. The trunks contained various accounting records from the 1830s to the 1870s; his letter-books from the 1850s, the late 1860s, and early 1870s; and letter-books of his son Gazaway DeRosset (known simply as DeRosset or Derry) from the 1870s and early 1880s, when he served as the executor of his father's estate. The loose papers included letters from family, friends, politicians, business associates, and lawyers, as well as legal documents, pamphlets, cancelled checks, cotton-warehouse receipts, and much more. For example, there was a presidential order from Andrew Johnson written on Executive Mansion stationery and signed "The President," releasing Lamar from a bail-bond obligation; letters to Lamar from Secretary of War John B. Floyd of Virginia, confirming a highly questionable sale of muskets from a federal arsenal in New York to the state of Georgia on the eve of the Civil War; and passports issued to Lamar from Union generals after the Civil War, allowing him to travel to certain places inside and outside of Georgia.

Toward the close of the second day of my visit, bleary-eyed from sifting through so many documents, I opened a volume about nine by eleven inches, almost an inch thick, with a black cover and red binding, and saw that it contained copies of letters. I read one and got a feeling of déjà vu—I had seen it before. The correspondence bore the signature of C. A. L. Lamar. Another letter also sounded familiar and was signed by Charles Lamar. Then I realized that these were verbatim from the article in the *North American Review*. The book that I held was the actual "Slave-Trader's Letter-Book," not seen by anyone for perhaps 125 years. The article was not a fraud. A minute later, my host walked into the room. She asked, "Is everything all right?" I guessed that I had verbalized my thoughts and she heard me. When I explained the significance of the book, she smiled, said, "Sounds good," and left. My bleariness disappeared and I sat to study the letters, transfixed by revelations of this southern fire-eater.

At the end of my visit I thanked the woman for her hospitality and assured her that she would hear from me soon. I returned home and reported the substance of my trip to the executive director of the Georgia Historical Society. The society does not typically purchase collections— they are donated—and we mulled over the value of this one and how to raise the funds to make an offer. But, as impatient as a child in a candy store, and not wanting to let this collection go to another archive or library, I decided to purchase it myself and donate it to the Georgia Historical Society.

A few weeks later, as I was driving from New Jersey to my home near Beaufort, South Carolina, with the long-lost collection in the back of a rented SUV, I wondered how the papers had ended up in an attic in New Jersey, so far from Gazaway Lamar's home, and so long after his death. During the years researching and writing this book, I came up with some answers.

Soon after General Sherman's army had occupied Savannah in late December 1864, U.S. treasury agents seized, among other things, Gazaway's business and personal papers and sent them to Washington, most likely to find evidence to charge the well-known rebel. Lamar immediately started petitioning the government to return them, but his requests were denied. After Gazaway died in 1874 in New York, where he had lived his final two years with his daughter and filed his last will, his son DeRosset became the estate's executor. DeRosset tried to get the courts to force the government to turn over his father's papers, which he needed to defend the estate in the many lawsuits brought against it. He failed and the probate process dragged on.[6]

DeRosset died in 1886 and, with Gazaway's estate still unsettled, the court appointed his sister Harriet and her husband Frank Jones Sr., also living in New York, as co-administrators. In 1909 Harriet died when she was run over by a vehicle while crossing Fifth Avenue in Manhattan, and Frank took over as sole administrator. Two documents in the Georgia Historical Society's Lamar Collection are legal motions by Frank Jones Sr. calling on the Treasury and War Departments to release Lamar's private papers. While these documents are in draft form and dated "191_," it is clear that the estate still did not have possession of the records fifty years after they were confiscated. Jones died in 1918 and his son Frank C. Jones Jr. succeeded him as administrator.[7]

The estate was finally settled in the 1920s and the government released most of Lamar's papers, which included Charles's letter-book, to Frank Jones Jr., who stored them, along with the letter-books and papers of his uncle DeRosset, in the attic of his house in Upper Montclair, New Jersey. Jones Jr. died in 1949 and his widow, Helen Griffith Jones, moved from the house about 1950, leaving behind the trunks in the attic. Fortunately, so did the subsequent residents of the house, probably because the trunks were so heavy to move and were tucked out of the way. Then the thoughtful couple bought the house in 1969, and the rest, as they say, is history.[8]

How the author of the article in the *North American Review* gained access to the letter-book requires some guesswork. The article appeared in

1886, when either the Treasury or War Department had possession of the papers. A government employee of the same political persuasion as the author might have come across the letter-book and allowed him access to it. One way or another, the story of finding it in a trash heap at a New England paper mill was a subterfuge.

More undiscovered Gazaway and Charles Lamar documents probably still exist—perhaps stored in other attics—as gaps can be found in the available collections. For example, there are no Gazaway Lamar letter-books prior to 1855 or accounting records prior to 1836, and surely this fastidious businessman maintained them. Also, Charles wrote many letters that he never copied. Some of them, as well as his personal possessions, must have been saved by family members or friends.

The government did not return four of Gazaway Lamar's letter-books, which include his correspondence from 1861 to 1866, and a letter-book that Charles maintained during a trip to Europe in 1863. They are available to researchers at the National Archives in College Park, Maryland. Unfortunately, the binders are fragile and the onionskin pages are falling apart. Also, the National Archives has a folder of newspaper clippings from Gazaway's trial before a military commission after the war, and several cotton books belonging to Lamar and the Importing and Exporting Company of Georgia, a blockade-running concern. The University of Georgia's Hargrett Rare Book and Manuscript Library has a large collection of Gazaway Lamar papers.

Many of Charles's letters dated between 1858 and 1861 that he never copied in his letter-book are found at the Georgia Archives and Emory University and are referenced here to help explain his life and exploits. One can only surmise why he never pressed them, other than his haphazard nature in record keeping—the polar opposite of his meticulous father. Charles's sloppiness is illustrated in the Slave-Trader's Letter-Book by his recording some letters upside-down and others on the reverse side of the page.

—————

The Slave-Trader's Letter-Book contains seventy letters written between 1855 and 1861. The article in the *North American Review* excerpted thirty-one of them. Charles pressed another 145 letters in the book in a six-week period in 1863 when he worked with his father in the cotton and guano businesses and the Importing and Exporting Company of Georgia. As these letters do not deal with Charles's filibustering and slave-trading activities, they are not transcribed in this volume. However, several are cited in chapter 19 during the discussion of his involvement in blockade-running.

The letter-book, along with other documents found in various collections, reveals many new facts and calls for an updated account of Charles Lamar and his illegal activities. While the landing of the *Wanderer* Africans and the resulting trials shocked the nation, there have been few books and articles written about the episode, and much of what has been recorded is incomplete or inaccurate. Perhaps the most egregious mistake made by authors is the portrayal of Lamar as a successful, wealthy, principled businessman driven to defend southern rights, specifically the right to import African slaves. In fact, Lamar was broke when he began participating in the trade and failed at almost every business venture—both legal and illegal—that he entered.[9]

While the circumstances around the outfitting of the yacht in New York, its departure from Charleston, the landing in Georgia, and the arrest of three of the crewmembers are well known through newspaper reporting and trial testimony, the letter-book shows that the rest of the operation was a disaster. Lamar claimed that he could sell slaves for $650 as soon as they stepped off the ship, yet his agents sold them for much less, and for risky notes instead of cash, causing Lamar to admit that he lost money on the venture. The letters show Lamar's frustration with his partners, whom he accused of abandoning their responsibilities after the crime was exposed, and leaving him to do all the work and bear all the associated costs.

The correspondence exposes more than just the 1858 *Wanderer* expedition. Before the *Wanderer* trials in November 1859, a stranger appeared in Savannah, partnered with Lamar in a commercial voyage, stole the yacht and hijacked the crew, and headed for Africa on a slaving expedition. Lamar's letters describe the incident and how he was fooled by the stranger. Others who witnessed the theft felt that Lamar wasn't hoodwinked at all but played an integral part in it.

The letter-book brings to light several episodes in U.S. history that have been largely ignored by chroniclers of Lamar and the *Wanderer*, yet must be explored to understand Lamar's actions. The first is his connection to the Cuban filibustering schemes of the 1850s, where factions within the United States attempted to overthrow Spanish rule of the island with the intent to bring it into the Union as a slave state to increase southern representation in Congress. Through these letters Lamar reveals his involvement in recruiting volunteers and raising money for one of the expeditions, and his perspective on the chances for the operation's success. Lamar's participation in the illegal venture portends his entry into the slave trade.

Lamar's letters expose his exploitation of the little-known African apprentice movement of the mid-nineteenth century, as conducted by the British and French in their colonies in the West Indies, to legitimize his slave-trading ventures. Although Lamar failed to convince the government that African apprentices were persons acting on their own rather than slaves, he opened a national debate on the practice.

Lamar also expressed an interest in the Chinese "coolie" trade, another little-understood effort of the mid-nineteenth century to sell people into bondage. Although he never sent any ships to China, Lamar considered it and cited the involvement of northern shippers in that commerce as yet another example of Yankee hypocrisy in condemning the African slave trade.

Before the *Wanderer*, Lamar entered into the slaving business with a bark named the *E. A. Rawlins*. Lamar names his partners and admits to losing $80,000 on two failed expeditions. Nonetheless, he used this experience as a selling point to attract investors to new slave-trading ventures.

One is struck by the characters with whom Charles corresponded— significant men such as U.S. treasury secretary Howell Cobb, Mississippi governor John Quitman, U.S. senator Robert Toombs of Georgia, *New York Tribune* editor Horace Greeley, and *New York Times* publisher and editor Henry J. Raymond—all of whom helped shape the American political terrain in the 1850s. He also wrote to others who represented the fringe of American politics—men such as John Thrasher, George N. Sanders, and Leonidas Spratt.

Throughout the letter-book, the shadow of the South's coming secession looms large, and Charles's activities in the slave trade certainly played some role in exacerbating the tension between the North and South. Lamar did not hesitate to take credit for the split in the Union. He wrote to his father, "I hope Lincoln may be elected. I want dissolution & have I think contributed more than any man South for it."[10]

The letters offer much new information about the life and times of one of the more colorful, flamboyant, and dangerous southern men of the mid-nineteenth century. Contrary to Warren S. Howard's assertion, the letter-book adds significantly to our understanding of Lamar and his participation in the African slave trade. And Howard errs when he says that many of the individuals named in the article were known to be engaged in the trade. Only two of the men mentioned in the letters had previously participated in the trade, and one of them used a false name, so Howard would not have been able to identify him.

―――――――

The book is arranged in two parts. The first is a narrative of Lamar's life. To provide context, a brief history of the various events in which Lamar was involved—namely Cuban filibustering, the African slave trade, and the African apprentice movement—is presented. While the narrative is not fictional, in chapter 1 I sometimes infer from historical documents thoughts, emotions, and scenes that likely played out. The second part contains the Lamar letters from the letter-book from 1855 to 1861, sixty-three of which are fully annotated. Seven of the letters, which are extraneous to Lamar's life as a slave trader or filibuster, are included at the end with minimal annotations.

Because of the condition of the paper and an occasional sloppy pen and lack of an ink blotter, some of the words are illegible, in which case [_?] has been inserted. Charles rarely used paragraph breaks when jumping to new subjects. He seldom used periods to end sentences and was inconsistent with his use of capitalization and other punctuation. In order to assist the reader, paragraph breaks and proper punctuation have been inserted where necessary.

CHAPTER 1

The Last Laugh

December 2, 1858

Charles Lamar's jaw dropped when he arrived at the camp off the Jekyll Island beach and saw four hundred black people—the blackest he'd ever seen—sitting in groups on the pine needle–covered ground. They huddled under a roof made of ship sails tied to trees and were wearing blankets or old, torn, ill-fitting clothes to keep warm in the early December morning air. They talked to each other in words he couldn't understand.

He had done it. After being lectured incessantly by his father and publicly insulted by the U.S. secretary of the treasury—a relative, no less—he was having the last laugh. His men had outsmarted U.S. port officials and the mighty British and U.S. naval squadrons. No one had successfully smuggled Africans into the United States for close to forty years until Charles Lamar came along.

Lamar smiled and nodded his approval to one of his partners and the captain of the voyage, William C. Corrie. He patted the supercargo John Egbert Farnum on the back and shook the hand of sailing captain Nicholas Danese. While Charles had helped plan the expedition and organized the syndicate, these three men actually made the trip to Africa, which began five months earlier, on July 3, 1858. Lamar couldn't wait to hear about their experiences. But first he had to distribute the Africans as quickly as possible before the authorities got wind of the scheme, collect his cash, and pay off his mountain of debt. Then he could plot the next voyage. The South would have its slaves, as was its constitutional right, and he would get rich furnishing them.

He also wanted to see his beloved yacht, the *Wanderer*, the fastest sailing ship on the high seas, which had carried the Africans across the Atlantic Ocean. But some of the crew had taken the ship up the Little Satilla River, away from snooping eyes, to clean it, replace all the bulkheads, and return it to preslaver condition. Charles knew he was taking a risk by keeping the *Wanderer*. Most slave traders, after unloading their human cargo on the shores of Cuba or Brazil, burned and sank their vessels, as they could be highly incriminating evidence. The immense profits from the venture made the cost of the ship insignificant. But Lamar would not allow that. The *Wanderer* was like no other. Nothing could catch the ship. Nothing could compare to it.

Charles walked among the Africans. Many looked up with blank stares, some smiled at him, while about ten others lay on their backs, their eyes and cheeks sunk deep into their heads, with their boney arms and legs lying in random directions like fallen twigs. Lamar could tell that they wouldn't make it more than another day or two. Such were the costs of doing business in the trade. Pack as many as possible in the yacht's hold in Africa and hope that most would survive. On the trip down to Jekyll the previous day, Danese had told him that they started with 487 and landed 409. A loss of seventy-eight, with about ten or fifteen more bound to die—20 percent in all—was acceptable. Plenty were left for a huge profit.

Charles returned to his men and made certain that they all understood their roles in sending the slaves to their destinations. Lamar could hear the money rolling in. He could also hear his fellow southerners praising him while abolitionists cursed his name. He laughed to himself as he considered his legacy as a fierce and tireless defender of southern rights. Now it was time to get to work.

CHAPTER 2

"You Are a Noble Boy"

June 1838

As Charles Lamar stood at the railing of the ss *Pulaski* on a sunny Wednesday morning in mid-June 1838, watching the skyline of Savannah slowly shrink from view, he had to know that he was a child of privilege, even though he was just fourteen years old and a student at the Chatham Academy. Few surnames in the South commanded more respect. The Lamar dynasty gave rise to a cadre of prominent planters, merchants, lawyers, jurists, and politicians who were ambitious, wealthy, and admired. It was Charles's birthright to follow in their footsteps. Even his baptism in Christ Episcopal Church in Savannah foretold that the infant had a special destiny; it was attended by the French hero of the American Revolution, the Marquis de Lafayette, who was in town during his heralded tour of the United States.[1]

Few Lamars were more successful than Charles's own father, Gazaway Bugg Lamar. One could hardly walk the streets of downtown Savannah and not pass by some company or tract of land in which he had an interest. His businesses included shipping, wharfage, factoring, banking, and insurance. As the *Pulaski* chugged from the harbor, Charles would have seen the Eastern Wharves, a prime riverfront property that his father had recently purchased with several partners, sealing yet another deal in a remarkable string of commercial successes.[2]

In fact, Gazaway was part owner of the side-wheeled steamer taking Charles and his family to Baltimore. When Gazaway started building his empire in the 1820s and 1830s, no business attracted him more than shipping—primarily between Savannah and Augusta. In 1836 several men from South Carolina and Georgia formed the Savannah and Charleston Steam Packet Company to carry passengers and goods between those two cities and any other port on the Atlantic seaboard. Lamar envisioned large profits, invested in the company, and soon became a director. In 1837 the company built the ss *Pulaski* for the passenger trade. The wood-hulled ship measured 206 feet long, with a 25-foot beam, a depth of 13 feet 7 inches, and a 225-horsepower engine, and could accommodate about two hundred passengers and crew in comfort. However, the ship proved to be one of Lamar's few unsuccessful ventures. In early 1838 he tried to sell the vessel to the Republic of Texas, presided over by his cousin Mirabeau Buonaparte Lamar, but the struggling country couldn't afford it. The ship carried a large loan and Gazaway's partners were not inclined to satisfy the indebtedness to accomplish a sale. Lamar had little choice but to put her back on the Savannah-to-Baltimore run, hoping that the other investors would accept a lower price after the boat lost even more money.[3]

In the meantime Gazaway tried to make the best of the situation and had the steamer totally refurbished. The *Pulaski* represented the first-class travel of the day. Passengers could not help but be impressed the moment they boarded. The open, spacious promenade, or top deck, covered all of the main deck except for the bow and contained the pilothouse, two sailing masts, and two smokestacks. Four lifeboats were located at the stern, two on hoists covered with tarp and two lying top down, uncovered. The deck had ample space for passengers to enjoy refreshments, stroll, mingle with each other, relax on settees, and gaze at the shoreline and endless ocean. Two aft and fore companionways led to the main deck and the sleeping quarters. The ladies' cabin was located at the stern of the main deck, while the mid and fore sections housed several staterooms, the captain's room, the dining room, and a gentlemen's cabin. A stairway led to the lower deck and another men's cabin directly beneath the ladies' cabin. Gazaway's wife, two youngest daughters, youngest son, and nurse occupied one stateroom, while Rebecca Lamar, Gazaway's twenty-six-year-old sister; Martha, Gazaway's oldest child; and Eliza, the daughter of Gazaway's brother John, slept in another. Rebecca first declined her brother's invitation to join him because of her dread of the sea, but he wrote to her in Augusta, "Were you to see the boat, you would not refuse." Gazaway's reassuring words and her desire to be with his family changed her mind.[4]

As the *Pulaski* reached the mouth of the Savannah River and turned north for Charleston, the only stop on the way to Baltimore, Charles and his family passed the time on the top deck relaxing and marveling at the sights all around them. The *Pulaski* reached Charleston later that afternoon of June 13 and docked overnight. This itinerary enabled the owners to advertise a voyage to Baltimore with only one night at sea, a big selling point, since ship disasters were not uncommon. The previous October, the *Home* had sunk in a storm while traveling from New York to Charleston, resulting in the loss of 90 of the 135 passengers and crew, an event that surely must have been on many of the *Pulaski* travelers' minds.[5]

The ship departed Charleston at six o'clock Thursday morning. The folks enjoyed another peaceful day at sea and retired to bed after dark. At eleven o'clock, thirty miles off the North Carolina coast, the second engineer attempted to fill a white-hot boiler that had burned off all its water, causing an explosion that tore a hole in the starboard side of the ship. It also blew to pieces the pilothouse on the promenade deck above the boiler room, killing instantly the second engineer and captain.[6]

Lamar awoke, gathered his boys, and rushed to the staterooms to find the rest of his family. Certain that the ship would soon sink, he told them to wait on the main deck while he crawled over the mangled forward companionway to the promenade deck. He went to the stern and secured one of the two exposed lifeboats. With the help of some other men, Gazaway prepared to launch the boat over the side. He then fetched his family, who had been joined by Mrs. William Mackay of Savannah, her two children, and their nurse. They climbed one by one onto the promenade deck as other passengers began to emerge in their nightclothes, trancelike, confused by the loud noise followed by total silence.

Gazaway and the other men lowered the boat into the water, but before the group could descend into it, two crewmen jumped in, claiming they had to evaluate the damage to the ship, and rowed away.[7] Furious at the confiscation, Lamar and the men prepared to launch the second uncovered lifeboat. To prevent it from being taken by other passengers, he told his family and the Mackays to sit in it, expecting that the *Pulaski* would sink horizontally and enable the lifeboat to float off. He would then clear it from the side of the ship and jump in. But seawater filled the hold, and, in a deafening crash, the *Pulaski* broke in two. The stern floated for a few moments and then pitched forward as it sank, causing the lifeboat to slide off bow first, hit the sea at a steep angle, and fill with water. A huge swell caused by the sinking of the stern washed Gazaway and many others into the ocean. As passengers screamed and slapped at the water, trying to stay afloat, Lamar swam to an exposed part of the stern and grabbed onto the promenade deck railing. In the bright moonlight he spotted nearby two of his children, Martha, sixteen years, and Thomas, seven, and snatched them up. Charles swam to them on his own.

As Gazaway made sure that his three children were safe, he looked about at the very moment the lifeboat carrying the rest of his family and the Mackays flipped over, throwing them all into the sea. Gazaway was helpless as he watched his family drown, unable to try to save them without forfeiting the lives of the three children in his care.

Twenty to thirty other people who were hanging onto the stern climbed to its apex. Gazaway saw the larger bow section floating about a hundred yards away. Believing it was more stable, he urged Charles to swim to it. Just then the stern rolled over, throwing everyone into the water. Gazaway floated to the surface to the cries and thrashings of drowning passengers, but he did not see his two sons or daughter. Exhausted and devastated by the loss of his entire family, he grabbed hold of a floating object and waited to die.

Suddenly, the promenade deck over the ladies' cabin separated from the stern and rose to the surface, directly underneath Gazaway, and he found himself standing on a veritable raft. Within minutes Rebecca appeared next to him. He greeted her, "Oh, my sister, do we meet again once more?"[8]

Over the next several hours, other passengers swam or drifted on ship debris to the raft, including Robert Hutchinson of Savannah. A while later a man came aboard carrying a little girl who looked around and cried, "Papa, Papa!" Corinne Hutchinson was placed in her father's arms. Yet another man with a young boy reached the wreck. Thomas Lamar sloshed to his aunt Rebecca and cried inconsolably in her arms. Still, the reunions brought a sliver of joy amid the horror.[9]

One man snared a basket floating in the water. It contained two bottles of wine—one quart and one pint—and two vials, one filled with peppermint and the other with laudanum. Rebecca was given charge of these items.

It is not known how long Charles swam after being thrown from the stern, but he eventually found temporary safety on a piece of debris with Reverend and Mrs. Jonathan L. Woart of Tallahassee, Florida. The three survived through Thursday night when they spotted the raft. Miraculously, Charles was reunited with his father, brother, and aunt. He wept as he embraced Rebecca and fell asleep against her side as soon as they sat. When he awoke, he asked, "Oh, Aunt Rebecca, what do you think has become of Mother and the children?"[10] She replied that she did not know but urged him to hope for the best and keep his strength.

Based on Rebecca's memoir, twenty-three people, including the four Lamars, reached the raft between Thursday night and Friday. There were three children: Corinne Hutchinson, Charles, and Thomas; two female slaves; four white women, including a younger and an older Mrs. Smith; and fourteen men. Also, one man reached the raft early Friday but soon died, and the corpse of Samuel Parkman, a business associate of Gazaway from Savannah, drifted onto the raft. Lamar refused to cast off the two bodies.

The top of the promenade deck, while buoyant, floated under a few inches of water, keeping everyone constantly soaked. The deck did have a cable box about four feet high where three people at a time alternated sitting out of the water. In a touch of good fortune, the survivors secured the two lifeboats that Gazaway had tried to occupy after the explosion. One drifted by empty, and the other carried two men. Both boats had to be caulked with rags and handkerchiefs to seal the many leaks.

The Friday morning sunrise revealed an ocean surface littered with debris from the *Pulaski*—countless pieces of jagged wood, chairs, clothing, towels, luggage, bottles, drinking glasses. The folks gathered any items they thought could be useful. The men began debating whether to pack everyone into the lifeboats and head to the coast. Gazaway favored this plan, but several other men felt that the small vessels would be crushed in the surf and even the strong swimmers would drown. Lamar prevailed and the people boarded the boats. They had no oars and after one hundred yards, for some unexplained reason, returned to the raft. That night, Thomas and Charles slept against Rebecca's sides, depriving her of rest.[11]

On Saturday Captain Hubbard, a sailor and passenger on the ship, convinced the group that the six most capable swimmers should take the smaller, sturdier boat to shore, brave the breakers, and summon local fishermen to save the other seventeen. Before leaving, they opened the quart bottle of wine and everyone took one sip. The rest was saved for the children. Rebecca finally persuaded Gazaway, one of the six to leave, to cast off the two dead bodies.

As the men completed making a sail out of a tablecloth and a rudder from a piece of plank, Gazaway decided to take Thomas with him and called the boy's name. But before the youngster could reach the rowboat, the other five men pushed away, leaving Thomas standing by the edge of the raft, waving goodbye to his father.

The raft dwellers could only wait and pray for their rescue. Charles and Rebecca watched as many of the other survivors, who hadn't eaten or drunk for two days other than a few drops of wine, slowly dehydrated, drifted into delirium, and died. One man could no longer stand the thirst and drank seawater. He started to wretch uncontrollably and not even a dose of laudanum eased his agony. The younger Mrs. Smith lapsed into a coma. Reverend Woart approached Rebecca, keeper of the wine, and begged for a drop. Rebecca hesitated, explaining that it was for the children. Woart persisted, even sticking out his tongue, which looked like a brown brick. Charles, sitting next to his aunt, told her to give the man his share. Woart replied, "You are a noble boy."[12] Soon after that incident, the younger Mrs. Smith died.

A storm blew over on Saturday night. A few of the survivors held empty bottles under the corner of a small makeshift sail to collect the rainwater as it streamed off. They drank till they were satiated. Other than the roar of nature, the only noise came from an old female slave, who chanted in an unknown language.

Sunday morning brought high winds and heavy seas. The survivors sat in a circle and clung to each other for safety. Reverend Woart dragged his barely conscious wife from a salvaged settee to the group. One man panicked and ran to the lifeboat. Mr. Hutchinson, with his daughter in his arms, jumped up to stop him, tripped, and lost hold of Corinne, who splashed onto the submerged floor. Hutchinson retrieved her, returned to his seat in the circle, and cradled the girl, whose head rolled back, her neck unable to support it. The child soon died in his arms. Then a wave washed over the raft, taking Woart and his wife with it.

The storm eased by late afternoon, but the suffering didn't. Three men, thinking they were in Florida, walked off the raft and plunged into the sea, only to regain their senses and swim back. However, their mirage soon reappeared and they again strode into the ocean. This time they didn't return.

By Sunday night, three full days into the living nightmare, there were no more than eleven people alive, and the agony continued. Mr. Smith claimed he saw a ship on the horizon, tied two pieces of wood together in the shape of a cross, jumped in the water, straddled his vessel, and began paddling with his hands. Not even his wife made an effort to stop him, claiming that he was too stubborn to be persuaded to return. Mr. Smith soon disappeared.

On Monday afternoon Charles thought he saw his dog Boatswain drowning in the ocean and rushed to save him, only to trip. Mr. Hutchinson returned him to Rebecca. Charles made several more attempts before losing consciousness and collapsing against his aunt. That night Thomas began to writhe as he slept on Rebecca's lap and slipped to the deck. It was all a sapped Rebecca could do to lift him back up and keep him on her. Soon the boy stopped breathing and his body went limp. Rebecca sobbed as she held her nephew in her arms. Fortunately, Charles slept through the death of his little brother.

When Rebecca awoke on Tuesday morning she started to babble and asked Mr. Hutchinson and Mrs. Smith when the carriage was coming to take her to Savannah. She then lapsed into unconsciousness. At noon she awoke with Mrs. Smith shaking her arm. Rebecca looked up and squinted at the bright, billowing white sails of a ship heading toward her. She cried, "Oh, how beautiful! Oh, how beautiful!!" before blacking out again.[13] The crew of the *Henry Camerdon* fished the seven survivors from the raft, dressed them in dry clothes, and laid them in berths. On the trip to Wilmington, North Carolina, after she regained consciousness, Rebecca learned from another *Pulaski* survivor that the *Henry Camerdon* had previously rescued him and twenty-two others from the bow section of the *Pulaski*. They told the captain of the *Camerdon* that they had seen another raft bobbing in the ocean and convinced him to continue his search until they found Rebecca and the others.[14]

When the ship reached Wilmington, Rebecca, Mrs. Smith, and Charles, still unconscious, were taken to a private house where Dr. Armand John DeRosset Sr. looked after them.[15] The physician informed her that Charles might not live. But by Wednesday the boy showed improvement, and on Thursday the doctor declared that he was out of danger.

On Thursday Gazaway arrived in Wilmington and was overjoyed to be reunited with his son and sister, both of whom he thought had died, but devastated to learn that Thomas had not survived. He revealed to Rebecca his experiences after he left the raft. The six men approached land between one and two o'clock on Saturday afternoon. The rowboat was demolished in the surf, but they all reached shore safely. They lay exhausted on the beach for an hour before walking to the nearest village, New River Inlet. Lamar offered the owner of the only fishing boat at the inlet at the time $5,000 each to rescue his sister and two children, and $1,000 each for anyone else. The fisherman declined, claiming that it was far too dangerous to go out in such a fierce gale. Lamar paid another man to ride to Wilmington to tell the authorities that other survivors were on a raft at sea. He and the five other men were then taken in by local families. Gazaway awoke the next day to learn that the village fishermen had convinced the messenger not to make the treacherous trip to Wilmington for a lost cause. Over the following days three more vessels came into the inlet. Lamar made the same offer to each and received the same rejection. With no rescue attempted, he assumed his remaining family had perished.[16]

Gazaway soon learned the extent of the disaster. Of the 195 passengers and crew, 136 died. Word reached Savannah on Thursday, June 21, and a pall blanketed the town. The city council cancelled the July 4 celebration for the first time in memory. On June 23 a public meeting was held at the

City Exchange, which gave rise to several resolutions, including selecting a clergyman to deliver an address to the city suitable to the melancholy occasion and asking the residents to suspend their usual activities during the sermon and to wear crepe on the left arm as a token of respect for the deceased.[17]

Several Lamar relatives from Augusta rushed to Wilmington. They convinced Gazaway to allow Charles to return with them and Rebecca while he endured the painful process of closing the affairs of his family.

It would be impossible to determine the effect of the *Pulaski* disaster on young Charles Lamar. He would never mention it in any of his surviving letters.

CHAPTER 3

"Young as You Are, You Are Failing Already in Mind"

1838–1854

The clanging bell in the City Exchange building at three o'clock in the morning woke most people in town. The subsequent ringing of the bells in the First Presbyterian Church and the guardhouse raised the rest. The policemen, known as "the watch," fired muskets in the air and shook rattles. In less than a minute Savannah was awash in noise, a cacophony that filled the residents with dread, for it signaled an event that they feared almost more than any other—a fire that might devour the town. At the very first gong, the city firefighters—free men of color, male slaves, and white men—leaped from their beds, donned their uniforms, and dashed from their homes.[1]

By the time the men reached their engine houses, they knew the general area of the fire. The city was divided into five sections, or beats. Once the watchman in the cupola of the City Exchange determined the location of the conflagration, he rang the bell from one to five times to signify the beat. That April 1852 night, the single gong told the entire city that the fire was on the east side, somewhere between the river and South Broad Street. As the companies pulled their hand-drawn, hand-pumping engines to Bay Street, they saw the sky glowing orange over the eastern end of the harbor and headed down one of the several ramps to River Street. In minutes they approached Charles Lamar's cotton press and warehouse, which were engulfed in flames and beyond saving. The chief ordered the firefighters to direct their efforts at preventing the fire from spreading to the adjoining structures and the ships anchored in the river in front of the Eastern Wharves. With the white firemen keeping their distance from the blacks, the companies dropped their suction hoses into the harbor, grabbed the bars on either side of the engine, and started pumping for dear life, trying to generate a stream of water that could reach the roofs of the buildings and riggings of the ships. Men alternated on the bars to continue pumping at maximum power.

Twenty-eight-year-old Charles, who was running the Lamar businesses since his father had moved to New York, lived only blocks from the facility. He undoubtedly watched with dread the hundreds of men gathered around their engines, trying to extinguish the fires. He would have to tell his father not only of the destruction but also of his failure to insure the cotton press or warehouse, valued together at $50,000. It was unthinkable for any sensible businessman not to cover a structure that housed one of the most flammable products imaginable—cotton. Gazaway would be enraged, even though the loss was Charles's to bear.[2]

It wasn't supposed to turn out this way. Charles had striven to follow in his father's footsteps, yet he didn't seem to have learned anything from Gazaway. The elder Lamar made his mark in business by working hard, forming strong relationships with his peers, weighing business decisions carefully, and limiting his risk. Not even personal tragedy derailed him from his track to success.

———————

Fourteen years had passed since the *Pulaski* tragedy. Gazaway Lamar hadn't wasted any time picking up the pieces of his shattered life. Although the horror of the accident and the grief of losing a wife, two sons, three daughters, and a niece must have been devastating, he had to move on. He couldn't ignore his many business interests, and he needed to be a father again to Charles. Those who knew Gazaway were not surprised at the speed of his rebound. Accomplishment had always been the man's trademark.

Gazaway Lamar was born on October 2, 1798, the third of eleven children of Basil and Rebecca Kelly Lamar. Basil owned a plantation on the Savannah River a few miles below Augusta, on which he raised cattle and hogs and grew wheat and corn. He owned a small fleet of pole boats, which he likely used for shipping services along the Savannah River and to carry his plantation products to the Augusta market. In 1817 he and thirty-four other men received a charter from the state to organize the Steam Boat Company of Georgia, with an exclusive, twenty-year right to operate steam vessels on all rivers and other waters of the state.[3]

Gazaway's articulate, grammatically correct letters and meticulous accounting records indicate that he received a formal education, probably at a private school in Augusta or with a private tutor. He then set out to make his own way in life. In November 1817, at age nineteen, he was elected assistant clerk of the Branch Bank of the United States in Augusta. A few months later he was selling shipping services and other goods as an agent for the Steam Boat Company.[4]

At age twenty-one, Lamar took up part-time residence in Savannah, where he worked as a commission merchant, selling consigned cotton and other merchandise of Augusta planters. In October of that year, he and an Augusta man formed a partnership for the purpose of transacting a general commission business in Savannah. It would last little more than two years.[5]

On October 18, 1821, at the age of twenty-three, Gazaway formed another partnership when he married Jane Meek Creswell, herself a member of a prominent Augusta family. Over the next seventeen years the couple gave birth to six children, with Charles, born in 1824, the second oldest.[6]

During the 1820s Gazaway became deeply involved in Savannah's business community. He sold products such as molasses, prime Georgia lard, Saint Domingue coffee, lime, and corn from Bolton's Central Wharf on the west side of the harbor. In 1824 he started booking freight and passage on ships running between Augusta and Savannah, and by 1825 he owned the steamboat *Enterprise*. Also in 1825, Gazaway teamed with his brother John T. Lamar of Macon to provide freight services from Macon and Milledgeville direct to Savannah.[7]

Lamar soon added banking to his portfolio of successes. In December 1825 the Georgia State House of Representatives elected the twenty-seven-year-old to be a director of the Planter's Bank. A year later he and several other men formed the Bank of Macon with Lamar as the first president. In 1831 he was elected a director of the Mechanic's Bank of Augusta while his brother-in-law, John Phinizy, served as president.[8]

By the early 1830s there was hardly a segment of Savannah commercial life that Lamar did not influence, but shipping remained his major interest and required prime waterfront property. In 1830 he purchased Bolton's Wharf. He sold it a few years later and, with several local men and the fledgling Central Railroad and Banking Company, acquired a joint interest in the Eastern Wharves on the other end of town.[9]

Lamar continued to procure ships, and by the early 1830s he owned and operated the *Governor Taylor, Free Trade*, and *Basil Lamar*. He also solved a major problem that had long plagued Savannah River commerce, delays due to low tides and sandbars, by introducing iron-hulled ships, which required less water in which to float than wooden ones. At that time only one or two iron-hulled ships existed in America, and there were no commercial builders of them. In 1833 he traveled to England and ordered one such ship from Birkenhead shipbuilder John Laird. He also hired noted Savannah shipping entrepreneur William Scarbrough to supervise the construction. In 1834 Laird sent the ship to Savannah in pieces, individually marked, with assembly instructions. John Cant's shipyard put together the vessel in three months.[10]

On July 9, 1834, the *John Randolph*, named for the deceased U.S. senator from Virginia and champion of states' rights who reflected Lamar's political bent, made a test run. The local paper heaped praise on the ship and its owner: "She glided into the water with an easy and graceful motion, amid the cheers of a vast concourse of spectators who had assembled to witness the novelty of an Iron Boat. . . . If this boat succeeds . . . the people of Georgia will be indebted to the enterprise and public spirit of Mr. Lamar."[11]

In 1835 Lamar and several other Augusta and Savannah men formed the Iron Steamboat Company, to which Lamar transferred several of his ships, including the *John Randolph*. The company went on to play a major role in Savannah River commerce.[12]

By the mid-1830s Savannah's merchant community, including Gazaway Lamar, buzzed with excitement at the prospect of another venture, one that promised to be as lucrative to the city as the shipping industry—the Central of Georgia Railroad. The plan proposed to link Savannah with Macon, a distance of almost two hundred miles; it would allow cotton planters in the Georgia interior to move their products to Savannah in one day, as opposed to two to four by ship. Savannahian William Washington Gordon spearheaded the project, and Lamar served as a commissioner overseeing the company stock subscription books. In late March 1836 Lamar was elected by shareholders to be one of nine directors.[13]

When the company announced a plan to build the terminus on the west side of town, about one mile from the river, where the incoming cotton would be shipped to northern and European ports, Lamar suggested to the city council that much time and expense could be saved by building extension tracks from the terminus, across town, and along River Street, eliminating the need to unload the cotton twice, or cart it in heavy wagons over the town's sandy streets. He even offered to pay for the tracks in exchange for an exclusive, twenty-five-year contract, charging customers no more than four cents a bale. The city tabled the resolution, saying it didn't have the authority to make the deal. This issue may have soured Lamar on the railroad company, as he did not serve as a director after the first year.[14]

Lamar's sixth sense for profitable opportunities led him back to his old hometown. In May 1838 he purchased the Augusta Toll Bridge for

$70,000; when he sold it two years later, he made $40,000 in the process.[15] The future could not have looked brighter for the entrepreneur. Then came the ill-fated trip on the *Pulaski*.

A few months after the disaster, Gazaway uprooted Charles from Augusta and sent him to A. Bolmer's private school for boys in West Chester, Pennsylvania. Charles's stay at the school was brief. On July 11, 1839, forty-year-old Gazaway married twenty-one-year-old Harriet Cazenove of Alexandria, Virginia. After a honeymoon at Niagara Falls, the couple moved to Alexandria and enrolled Charles in Benjamin Hallowell's local private school, which Robert E. Lee had attended.[16]

In 1840 the Lamars moved back to Savannah where Gazaway continued his involvement in cotton factoring, wharfage, towing services on his ship the *DeRosset* (he had divested his interest in the Iron Steamboat Company), and selling lime and hay. During this period Gazaway got involved in local politics. In 1841 he was appointed as the city commissioner of pilotage, and in 1845 he was elected a city alderman and served on the committee of docks and wharves.[17]

Seventeen-year-old Charles moved to Charlottesville in July 1841 to attend the University of Virginia. But the regimented world of academia could never hold his attention. It is not known if he ever attended classes, as he was back in Savannah in the fall forming a partnership with his cousin William Sims "for the purpose of transacting a general grocery and commission business in this city." In December 1842 the partners opened a grocery store. Over the next two years Charles and William sold iron, steel, nails, groceries, bagging, and rope to the public. They also offered towing and freight services and passenger travel on the *De-Rosset*. The endeavor lasted only two years. In February 1844 the young businessmen advertised the liquidation of their inventory of groceries, but Charles remained close with his cousin and would name his first son after him.[18]

Charles then worked as a general commission merchant, advertising products such as English parlor coal, eastern hay, and Thomaston lime for sale at the Eastern Wharves, undoubtedly under his father's eye. In anticipation of Charles becoming more deeply involved in cotton trading, Gazaway sent him with his brother John for three months to Liverpool, the center of England's knitting mills.[19]

In early 1846, due to his wife's poor health, Gazaway, Harriet, and their three children, Charlotte, DeRosset, and Anthony, moved to Brooklyn, New York, and the elder Lamar started trading commodities, primarily cotton, in New York City. He placed twenty-one-year-old Charles in charge of the Savannah operations while Gazaway's brother George Washington Lamar ran the business in Augusta.[20]

Father and son worked together closely in acquiring cotton for the northern U.S. and European markets. Charles also ran the wharfage operations, acted as a general commission merchant, and booked freight and passage on the *DeRosset* and freight on the *Richard Cobden,* a ship that Gazaway purchased for the transatlantic route. In 1850 Charles expanded the family operations by building a large cotton press and warehouse on the Eastern Wharves property. A local newspaper hailed the facility: "The press is one of Devall's patent and has tremendous power. Mr. Lamar has also erected a large warehouse in connection with his press. The whole establishment is on a scale of magnitude and liberality highly creditable to our city." Charles helped form and personally invested in a company to lay a plank toll road from Savannah south over the Ogeechee Road. In early 1853 Charles became the agent for the *State of Georgia* and *Keystone State* steamships, which carried passengers from Savannah to Philadelphia. The younger Lamar seemed to be developing into a clone of Gazaway—an aggressive, creative businessman who invested in a wide array of enterprises. Few could doubt that he would honor the name Lamar.[21]

As Charles honed his business skills, he assimilated easily into Savannah society and civic life. On February 11, 1846, he married Caroline Agnes Nicoll, daughter of the judge of the U.S. District Court in Georgia, John C. Nicoll, forming a rich and influential union. The couple lived in the Lamar family house in Warren Ward.[22]

Charles joined the Savannah Rifle Club and served on the committee of invitations for the club's annual soiree. He entered his horses in the January races at the Oglethorpe racetrack, one of the major social and sporting events in Savannah. Like his father years before, he was appointed by the mayor to be the health officer for his ward.[23]

Few organizations were held in higher esteem by Georgians than the local militia companies, composed of men ready to drop everything at their governor's call to defend their country. Charles joined the Georgia Hussars, who in December 1851 elected the twenty-seven-year-old as its captain, the highest rank in the unit. Whenever the city held a parade to celebrate a historic event—such as Washington's birthday, May Day, or the anniversary of the Battle of New Orleans—Charles, in uniform and atop his favorite horse, Black Cloud, led his men in a procession around the city's fabled squares. Always the sportsman, Charles helped form the Aquatic Club of Georgia, which sponsored rowboat races in Savannah.

He was a judge at the annual state agricultural fair and helped organize
the Chatham and Effingham County Agricultural Club. Because of his involvement in these activities, his business interests, and the prominence
of his father, there probably wasn't a person in Savannah who hadn't
heard of Charles Lamar.[24]

One so prominent was destined to enter politics. In late 1852 Charles
ran for city council and appeared on both tickets, the Citizens' and the
Democratic—the only candidate to do so. He emerged victorious with
the latter. Alderman Lamar offered several pieces of legislation during
his tenure. One of the more popular was a motion to appoint a committee to petition the state legislature to pass an act prohibiting vessels with
free black crewmen from calling at Savannah, lest those sailors entice
local slaves to run away. It passed by a vote of nine to zero. Charles, a
future member of the nativist, anti-Catholic American Party, also offered
a motion "that all resolutions and ordinances relating to that portion of
Laurel Grove Cemetery set apart for Catholics be . . . repealed and declared non-effect." The other aldermen didn't support it and Charles's
vote was the only one in the affirmative.[25]

Then came the fire at the wharves. Despite Lamar's early successes,
the disaster—especially Charles's failure to insure for it—displayed a
crack in his armor. The privileged son was not infallible after all. The
traits that made Gazaway so successful were strangely lacking in his son,
despite the father's attempts to pass them on. Perhaps Gazaway's wealth
made Charles overconfident—he knew he could withstand almost any
financial loss, so insurance may have seemed unnecessary. Or maybe his
near-death experience on the *Pulaski* made him feel invulnerable—if
he could survive that, he could survive anything. Whatever the cause,
Charles eschewed Gazaway's business conservatism. He was becoming
careless at best and reckless at worst.

The bad news did not end on the night of the fire. Charles soon
learned that his prize horse, stabled at the wharves and valued at $1,500,
burned to death. Also, the cotton on one of the ships anchored by the
cotton press got soaked during the effort to save it and was subsequently
laid out in a nearby field to dry. A few days later it mysteriously caught fire
and was completely destroyed. Although the cotton was insured, Charles
was convinced that the fires were no accident. He offered a reward of
$1,000 for information leading to the capture and conviction of the cul-
prits. There is no record that anyone collected it.[26]

Not long after the fire, Charles began to display a nasty temper. In
1853 he was indicted in superior court for assault and battery, but he

settled the case before it went to trial. Months later he was back in court, this time for assault with the intent to murder, though the grand jury reduced the charge to assault and battery. A petit jury found him guilty and fined him fifty dollars and court costs, a remarkably light sentence considering the crime. Charles had shown that he would not hesitate to resolve disagreements with violence, especially when he perceived no threat of legal consequences.[27]

Perhaps because of these problems, Charles resigned from the Georgia Hussars and declined to run again for city council, which must have delighted his father. Gazaway wanted his son to devote all his time to the family operations. But by the end of 1854, Gazaway began questioning thirty-year-old Charles's behavior, writing to him, "You don't appear to be thinking, considering your business. . . . It is all haphazard with you." A week later, he asked, "Your business movements don't partake of your energetic character—are you worn out or enfeebled in any way?" In his next letter he wondered, "But young as you are, you are failing already in mind. There is something the matter with you—tell me what it is."[28]

Gazaway had read his son well. Charles did have more than business on his mind. He was helping plan an invasion of Cuba.

CHAPTER 4

"I Have No Fears of the Consequences"
1851–1856

At seven o'clock on the morning of September 1, 1851, General Narciso López, under guard and covered by a white shroud, walked from a prison in Havana's Punta Castle to an adjacent courtyard crammed with thousands of spectators and about one hundred American prisoners. He was led to a makeshift wooden structure with a single flight of steps, which he climbed to a ten-foot-high landing. A man dressed in black guided López to the center, turned him toward the crowd, and removed the shroud, revealing a fully ornamented general's uniform. The executioner ripped away all semblances of rank and honor, including his coat, sash, and cravat, and tossed them like garbage to the side of the platform. López, with his hands bound in front of him and his chin held high, addressed the crowd. He forgave those who revealed him to the Spanish army, thanked his followers, and said goodbye to his beloved Cuba. The executioner grabbed his arm, sat him in a chair in front of a fourteen-inch-thick wooden post, and placed the metal collar of the garrote, which extended from the post, around López's neck. A priest wearing a black robe and holding a silver cross stepped in front of the condemned man and delivered the last rites. The holy man then placed the cross in López's hands and bent to kiss the general's forehead. The executioner turned the large screw that controlled the garrote. López's neck snapped and his head dangled forward. The crowd groaned.[1]

In that one motion, the hopes of thousands of Americans, including Charles Lamar, and an undetermined number of Cubans also died. López's failure to conquer Cuba was the latest in a string of attempts to overthrow the ruling Spanish, and it wouldn't be the last.

Cuba had always been coveted by the United States since the republic's earliest days. The island's appeal lay in her fertile soil and strategic location, sitting between the southern tip of the Spanish-held Florida territory and the northern edge of the Yucatán Peninsula. Ships could not travel the sea-lanes connecting the Atlantic Ocean and the Gulf of Mexico without passing the Spanish colony. The country that possessed Cuba could control those waters and have ready access to North America, making the island especially attractive to the main U.S. adversaries, Great

Britain and France, that jockeyed for power in the region. But Spain, the largest landholder in the Western Hemisphere at the end of the eighteenth century, played the part of a protective father who believed that no suitor deserved his beautiful daughter's hand.[2]

President Thomas Jefferson dealt with Spain's intransigence by declaring that if the United States could not have Cuba, no one else would, either. His cabinet drafted a resolution that was communicated to the island's governor, known as the captain general: "If you remain under the dominion of the kingdom and family of Spain, we are contented; but we should be extremely unwilling to see you pass under the domination or ascendance of France or England."[3]

Spain fared poorly in the first third of the nineteenth century. By the 1830s, through wars, revolutions, and treaties, only Cuba and Puerto Rico remained in its empire in the Western Hemisphere, but the Spanish showed no signs of loosening their grip on either of them. Cuba's thriving economy, based on sugar, tobacco, and coffee plantations, depended on slave labor. Although Spain had bowed to British pressure in 1817 and banned the African slave trade, to take full effect by 1820, thousands of Africans still landed illegally in Cuba every year, thanks to the country's long, rugged coastline with hidden coves and dishonest captains general. By 1840, of the island's million inhabitants, 58 percent were black.[4]

In 1840 the British inflamed a sore in the Cuba-U.S. relationship by appointing outspoken abolitionist David Turnbull as its consul. Southern politicians feared that Turnbull would apply pressure to the Spanish to abolish slavery, just as the British had done in 1834 in its colonies in the West Indies. Proslavery forces couldn't allow an island to exist with a free black population and free labor economy just ninety miles from its shores, especially in light of the black-controlled government in Haiti, and they protested the appointment. Although Captain General Jerónimo Valdés eventually expelled Turnbull, a fear had been planted in the minds of many Americans—a black military republic in Cuba, inspired by the British.[5]

The start of the Mexican War in 1846 temporarily pushed Cuba from Americans' consciousness. But Cuban planters, known as Creoles, who detested the heavy-handed Spanish rule wielded by the captains general, still feared that Madrid might cave to British pressure and abolish slavery. The planters formed the Havana Club to press for annexation by the United States and, if that failed, to raise funds to hire a mercenary army—known as filibusters—to overthrow the Spanish regime.[6]

Cuban expatriates living in the United States, especially in New York, also wanted the Spanish expelled from their homeland. They used their U.S. allies to pressure President James Polk to purchase Cuba or take it by force. The president, who believed that the British wanted to annex the island and disrupt American commerce, consented to try to buy Cuba. Polk authorized the U.S. minister to Spain to offer up to $100 million. The Spanish foreign minister rejected the proposal, claiming that Spain would rather see the island sunk in the ocean than have it transferred to another power. With the Jefferson doctrine still the controlling policy, the U.S. government had no choice but to suspend plans to acquire Cuba.[7]

The spoils of the Mexican War created another problem for the United States—resolving the status of the land acquired in the Treaty of Guadalupe Hidalgo of 1848. Politicians in the North wanted to prohibit slavery in all new territories, while those in the South demanded that it be allowed below the 36/30 line, the boundary above which no new slave states could enter the Union, according to the Missouri Compromise of 1820. In 1848 there were fifteen free and fifteen slave states. Southerners knew that if states formed from the territories entered the Union as free, the slaveholding states would be cast into a permanent minority status in the Senate. But there was another way to maintain their power—have the United States acquire territories where slavery already existed—just as it had done with Texas. Cuba became more crucial than ever to the South.[8]

Of course, gaining control of Cuba was not so easy, with Spain refusing to sell the island and the U.S. government unwilling to take it by force. Many thought a revolution was needed, and a tenacious adopted son of Cuba was the first to try to incite one. Narciso López was born in Venezuela in 1799 when that country was part of the Spanish Empire. He enlisted in the Spanish army as a teenager and fought in the uprising led by Simón Bolívar, which eventually liberated the country. López relocated to Cuba, married a local woman, and then moved to Spain where he served in a number of military positions before being elected a senator to the Cortes, the legislative body of the Spanish government. When Spain expelled Cuba from the Cortes, López became disgusted and returned to the island, where he invested, quite poorly, in several businesses. His revulsion at the oppressive rule over the island, which stifled political dissent, freedom of speech, and commerce, convinced him that the Spanish had to go.[9]

In mid-1848 López and a group of Creoles planned to incite an uprising of the Cuban people. But the operation had to be postponed, and in the intervening weeks someone revealed the plot to the government. When the Spanish authorities started to arrest the suspected conspirators, López, with his son and a servant, caught a ship to Rhode Island, barely escaping his pursuers. He immediately made his way to New York and contacted the leaders of the expatriate Cuban community.[10]

During this time the Havana Club tried but failed to recruit an American general, William Worth, to raise a mercenary force to invade Cuba.[11] General López assumed responsibility for expelling the Spanish. He enlisted a few aides, including Ambrosio José Gonzales, an American-educated Cuban, and with money likely donated by Cubans in New York and Havana, they set about trying to raise a "patriotic junta" of several thousand American fighters, confident that on their landing, Cubans would rally to their side. By August 1849 close to eight hundred men had gathered on Round Island, Mississippi, near New Orleans. This action violated the Neutrality Act of 1818, which prohibited any person residing in the United States from participating in any hostile action against a country with which the United States was at peace. President Zachary Taylor learned of the plot and sent in the navy, which blockaded Round Island and prevented supplies from being delivered and ships from departing. The expedition soon fell apart, though no one was prosecuted.[12]

López would not be denied. He moved to New Orleans, the center of Cuban revolutionary activity in the South, and befriended Laurent I. Sigur, the wealthy owner of the *New Orleans Delta* and an annexationist, who supported the general financially and editorially. López planned his next expedition and sought Mexican War hero and Mississippi governor John A. Quitman, an advocate of states' rights and slavery, to take command. Although Quitman sympathized with the cause, he told López that he had to devote all his time to fighting the federal government's encroachment on the rights of the southern states.[13]

Once again López took the reins and set about raising money and men. For the former, he sought contributions from individuals and issued "Cuban Bonds," to be repaid from the public lands, public property, and fiscal resources of Cuba. Recruitment efforts resulted in an army of about six hundred soldiers, significantly less than the two thousand he thought he needed. In order to avoid violating the Neutrality Act of 1818 and interference from U.S. port officials, López shipped the recruits from New Orleans to islands off the Yucatán Peninsula before launching the invasion. President Taylor learned of the scheme and ordered the navy to stop it, but López's ships had already left for the Yucatan.[14]

The transport ship *Creole* landed the filibusters at Cárdenas, Cuba, in the very early hours of May 19, 1850. After a battle with Spanish forces, the rebels gained control of the town, but López had to order a retreat

when the locals showed no interest in joining them. They returned to
Key West with a Spanish warship in hot pursuit. The soldiers scattered
while López and several of his aides caught a steamship to Savannah. The
U.S. district attorney there learned of López's arrival and arrested him
under a warrant issued by district court judge John C. Nicoll, Charles
Lamar's father-in-law. Nicoll then acted in a way that seemed to support
the cause of the annexationists. He granted López's request for a hearing that night. As the district attorney could not produce any witnesses
on such short notice, Nicoll dismissed López, who boarded a train for
New Orleans the next morning. Surely, Lamar knew of—and probably
observed—the excitement.[15]

Despite Judge Nicoll's actions, the federal government pressed its case
against López and fifteen others associated with the plot, including Governor Quitman, who had to resign his office in light of the scandal; former U.S. senator John Henderson of Mississippi; López's friend Laurent
Sigur; and Ambrosio Gonzales. As a first step to test the legal waters,
the district attorney of Louisiana decided to try just one of the suspects,
Henderson, for violating the Neutrality Act of 1818. His efforts resulted
in three mistrials in January and February 1851. The district attorney
concluded that he would never get any convictions and dropped the
charges against Henderson and all the others, leaving López free to plan
the next invasion.[16]

At this point, in March 1851, Charles Lamar's name first surfaces in
relation to the movement. López's top aide, Ambrosio Gonzales, wrote
to his friend Mirabeau Buonaparte Lamar, former president of the Republic of Texas and first cousin of Gazaway Lamar, for assistance: "I need
very especially your moral influence . . . with your cousin Charles in Savannah." López's men clearly knew of Charles Lamar's interest in the
scheme.[17]

When word of a new expedition reached Washington, President Mil-
lard Fillmore issued a warning to the filibusters. López ignored it as his
new recruits made their way to the rendezvous points in southern Georgia, Jacksonville, and New Orleans for a late August 1851 departure.
In July López, still headquartered in New Orleans, heard that uprisings
were erupting across the island. Wanting to join the action and provide
support, he left Louisiana early with about 450 men, mostly Americans
but also some Cubans and Hungarians, on the steamer *Pampero*, which
had been purchased by his friend Laurent Sigur. They had planned to go
to Jacksonville and Georgia to pick up more fighters, but López changed
his mind at Key West and opted to go directly to Cuba, land with his men,

and send the ship back for the others. On August 12 they came ashore east of Havana and learned that the rumors of widespread revolts were untrue. Worse yet, the locals still had no interest in joining them. López and his small army had to face a Spanish force of several thousand until the *Pampero* could return with reinforcements, but due to many delays, the ship never made it back. The expedition quickly turned into a rout as the Spanish army chased López and his men through the countryside and mountains. Within a few days of landing, a company of fifty men, mostly Americans, was separated from López. The group retreated to the coast, took several small boats, and headed for Key West, but they were captured by a Spanish steamer. All were executed by firing squad the next day. On August 29, seventeen days after the start of the operation, and with his remaining army scattered into small bands, López was apprehended near San Cristóbal and sent immediately to Havana. He was executed on September 1. Cuba's liberation would have to wait.[18]

Southerners were shocked by the executions of López and the American soldiers, but their interest in Cuba remained strong as annexation was considered crucial to the security of slavery at home. Also, Cuban exiles such as Ambrosio José Gonzales kept up the campaign condemning Spanish oppression on the island and insisted that the revolutionary spirit there was still alive. Within months, U.S. supporters of the cause started the Order of the Lone Star, named for the Cuban flag. Chapters of the society formed in southern cities, including Savannah, and in the North as well. Charles Lamar joined one of the two Savannah divisions.[19]

John Quitman, free from his legal problems, joined the order and began negotiating with the Cuban community in New York about leading another filibuster mission. Around this time, September 1853, Spain appointed Juan M. de la Pezuela, known for his abolitionist views, as captain general of Cuba, reviving American slaveholders' concerns that he would liberate the slaves and create a free black republic with the backing of Great Britain and France. An "Africanized" Cuba without slavery would be useless to the South and, they feared, would cause unrest among American slaves.[20]

In April 1854 the New York Cuban community and Quitman finally agreed to terms. He received the authority to manage the next Cuban expedition, including enlisting recruits and raising funds by issuing bonds. Quitman wanted a minimum of 3,000 men and $800,000 for the mission.[21]

Inevitably, the effort of organizing another invasion, with so many people involved, could not be kept secret, and word reached Washing-

ton. On May 31, 1854, President Franklin Pierce issued a proclamation
warning that any attempt to invade Cuba would be prosecuted by the U.S.
government. In July a grand jury in New Orleans ordered Quitman and
two associates, John S. Thrasher and A. L. Sanders, to post a $3,000 bond
for nine months to ensure they would obey the Neutrality Act of 1818.[22]

The order did not prevent these men from raising volunteers and
money for an invasion. In late 1854 Thrasher, based in New Orleans,
recruited Charles Lamar to be one of the expedition's agents in Georgia. Lamar told him that he wanted to communicate directly with Quitman, and in early January 1855 the general wrote to Charles, explaining
that the invasion would proceed "with from three to four thousand well
armed and well provided men, embarked in swift and safe steamers. . . .
We must move within sixty days or forfeit a half million already invested.
To complete this formidable enterprise, we want yet about $50,000. . . .
The want of money is the obstacle in the way of prompt and quick action. . . . Will you help us? If so act at once."[23]

Lamar agreed to help. He tried to raise money by selling Cuban bonds
with a face value of three times the amount of cash paid in, at an interest
rate of 6 percent. Despite an effective interest rate of 18 percent, Charles
only managed to raise $2,000—and that from himself and his friend Nel-
son Trowbridge—on the condition that Quitman lead the expedition.
Charles sent some of the bonds to his associates around Georgia, but they
were unable to sell any. A local chapter of the Order of the Lone Star
pledged a meager $500, which was never fulfilled.[24]

Charles was equally unsuccessful in finding volunteers, in part because
of obstacles created by Quitman. The general required recruits to pay
fifty dollars for the privilege of joining the mercenary army. In exchange,
they would receive $150 worth of Cuban bonds. When Lamar tried to en-
list men on the "fifty-dollar principle," he hit a brick wall. Also, Quitman
would not commit to a launch date, which created uncertainty that the
mission would ever take place.[25]

At Thrasher's suggestion, Lamar met with another Georgia supporter
of the filibuster movement, Dr. Henry A. Ramsay of Atlanta, who had
made wild claims that unlimited funds and men could be raised in the
state. After the meeting, Lamar complained to Thrasher that Ramsay was a blowhard who wouldn't commit to raising one dollar or one
man. He told Thrasher that unless a specific launch date was named
and the fifty-dollar principle lifted, very few Georgians would join the
movement.[26]

Lamar also offered advice to Thrasher about a safe place near Savannah from which to launch the expedition, as it could accommodate ships with a deep draft, and a port official who could be bribed. Charles was personally unconcerned about being prosecuted. "I have no fears *myself* of the consequences of an Infringement of the Neutrality Laws. Gen'l [Franklin] Pierce & his whole cabinet, were they *here*, could not convict me or my friends—that is the great advantage of a small place—a man of influence can do as he pleases."[27]

Spanish authorities in Cuba had many spies in the United States, particularly New Orleans, and word of a pending invasion soon reached Captain General José Gutiérrez de la Concha in February 1855. He declared the island to be under a state of siege and ordered a complete blockade of its coast. Meanwhile, Quitman learned of an uprising about to take place in Cuba and wanted to coordinate his invasion with it. However, Cuban authorities uncovered the plot and executed the leader and one hundred followers. President Pierce, who Quitman had claimed gave him assurances that he would not interfere in the expedition, summoned the general to a private meeting in Washington. As a result Quitman, who had won a seat in the U.S. House of Representatives in March 1855, submitted his resignation to the Cuban Council on April 30, 1855.[28]

On learning that the mission was cancelled, Lamar wrote to Quitman for a refund of the $2,000 he and his friend had invested, citing the terms of their deal. The former governor did not respond. Charles sent several more letters but never heard back. A year later, with his patience exhausted, Lamar wrote to Quitman by way of U.S. senator Robert Toombs of Georgia, demanding a refund of his investment or he would publish all the "Strictly Private & Confidential" correspondence that he had received from the congressman. In a letter to Toombs, Charles wrote, "You will see something rich if he don't reply."[29] Quitman finally answered, though no record could be found explaining the resolution of the matter. As Lamar never published the correspondence, Quitman may have paid him, or perhaps a mediator achieved a compromise.[30]

Thus ended Charles Lamar's filibustering career. His involvement distracted him from running the family businesses, and he never fully regained an interest in them. Instead, he showed a willingness to ignore national laws to support the spread of slavery. After all, as "a man of influence" in "a small place," he felt he could do as he pleased. And in the next few years he would do just that.

CHAPTER 5

"I Never Was So Hard Up in My Life"
1855–1857

As Charles Lamar hounded John Quitman for money in 1855, Gazaway Lamar chided his son for mishandling the family businesses. He no longer asked Charles what was on his mind, knowing that he wouldn't get an answer. Instead, he criticized Charles for a wide range of management failures: operating on impulses, not sending money or bills of lading in full sets, not quoting cotton prices, not communicating with customers, not supervising employees, not supplying financial reports, and not controlling expenses on the *Richard Cobden*.[1]

The elder Lamar also put Charles on notice about future borrowing by reminding him that he had not repaid one dollar of a loan from the previous fall. "If you don't pay up promptly I will not credit you, so take fair notice for the future. I have sacrificed $35,000 to keep you easy." On August 1, 1855, Gazaway prepared a financial schedule listing the items he had given Charles since he departed for New York in 1846. It included the Eastern Wharves with attached land, nineteen slaves, cows, silverware, a carriage, the pew at Christ Church, the house and lots in Warren Ward, and cotton, all totaling $54,816. Gazaway added, "But in consideration of your misfortune by the [cotton press] fire, I charge you no interest on what you have had as patrimony." Gazaway expected to collect all his receivables and was not about to let his irresponsible son off the hook.[2]

Despite the growing tension between the two, they still maintained a family relationship. Gazaway sent his then thirteen-year-old son, DeRosset, to live with Charles and attend school in Savannah. A month earlier, on October 22, 1855, Charles and Caro gave Gazaway his third granddaughter, Caroline Nicoll Lamar.[3]

And Gazaway still offered his thirty-one-year-old son business advice, hoping that something might sink in. "Remember always, that in all partnerships you are bound for the whole tho you own but ⅛ or less & must make up all deficiencies of your partners." He also urged Charles never to endorse notes for anyone. As usual, Charles ignored his father. By then he had reentered politics. In the fall of 1855 he ran for the U.S. House of Representatives as a member of the American Party, also known as the Know-Nothings, because when secretive members were asked about their political affiliation, they responded that they knew nothing. The party aimed at keeping Irish and German Catholics out of the United States and limiting the influence of those already in the country. Charles lost, which pleased his father, who wrote to his cousin Thomas B. Lamar, "I do not sympathize with you . . . on Charles's defeat. I am unalterably opposed to all secret societies, but more especially to those in political matters . . . and I am very glad of Charles being left at home . . . to attend to his business."[4]

Of course, Charles didn't attend to the family business. In 1855 he entered into a partnership with two Augusta men—his friend and fellow investor in Cuban bonds, Nelson C. Trowbridge, and James Gardner. Trowbridge was a constant presence in Charles Lamar's adult life. He did some trading in cotton but devoted most of his efforts to buying, selling, and renting out slaves. James Gardner was a planter, owner of the *Augusta Constitutionalist*, and an acquaintance of Gazaway. The three partners and several other Augusta men invested in the Parks and Co-lumbia Gold Mine companies in Columbia County, near Augusta, even though many experienced mine workers had left the area for the Califor-nia gold rush. The operation had problems from the start. In December 1855 Trowbridge, who had given power of attorney to Charles Lamar for his interest in the mines, offered advice to Gardner on running the business and begged for help in getting out of debt. Similarly themed letters followed during the ensuing year as the partners' losses continued to mount. Lamar's original cash infusion of $15,000 would soon grow to $50,000 without generating a dividend.[5]

Though battered by the losses, Charles still chased opportunities in new areas. He built a flour mill despite Gazaway's warning: "I can get you the plans for the mill but if you take my advice you'll have nothing to do with it. Flouring mills have ruined more people & merchants in particu-lar than cotton ever did."[6]

The partnership of Lamar, Trowbridge, and Gardner soon ventured into the legal business of buying and selling slaves domestically at Trow-bridge's urging. In January 1857 Trowbridge informed Gardner, "I be-lieve I wrote you I had made an arrangement with a gentleman in New Orleans to engage in the negro trade for two years. The party stands as high as any man in the [state] and commands unlimited means. A friend of ours has arranged for me to get 50 thousand [dollars] to carry out the arrangement and I have bought a large lot of negroes and shall commence at once to make money." The gentleman in New Orleans was Theodore Johnston, and the friend who arranged the financing must have been Charles Lamar. Johnston would turn out to be a clone of Trowbridge—incompetent, unreliable, and always mired in debt.[7]

Within weeks Trowbridge transported the slaves from an estate in Beaufort, South Carolina, to New Orleans. Johnston eventually sold them but did not distribute all the proceeds to the partners, sinking Charles deeper into a financial hole. In February 1857, in order to satisfy a debt, Lamar sent three notes totaling $8,500 to Gardner signed by Trowbridge and himself. He asked in desperation, "Can't you tell me how I can make some money?"[8]

Charles could no longer turn to his father, who was struggling as well at the onset of a recession. Gazaway had even asked his son to send him $100,000 if he were flush.[9] Charles, however, was far from flush. He was broke and needed to make money fast. He focused on a business that promised huge profits in a short period of time—the illegal African slave trade, most likely encouraged by Nelson Trowbridge. Lamar was also influenced by a few southerners who were campaigning to repeal the laws banning the slave trade, claiming they were unconstitutional.

Although the movement to reopen the slave trade started in the early 1850s, it didn't gain momentum until the 1855 Southern Commercial Convention in New Orleans. These annual gatherings of southern businessmen were held to discuss ways to reduce dependence on the North in banking, commerce, and education, and they were not meant to be political. But in 1855 a delegate recommended that representatives from slaveholding states in Congress introduce a bill to repeal all laws suppressing the trade. The convention never acted on it, as most delegates were against reopening the traffic. At the 1856 convention in Savannah, a Georgia delegate proposed to reintroduce the resolution. After much debate the committee voted sixty-seven to eighteen to table it indefinitely. However, its supporters vowed to continue the fight at the following year's convention.[10]

Charles received further inspiration from South Carolina governor James H. Adams, who, in his annual message to the legislature in November 1856, called for the reopening of the trade, declaring that the South must have cheap labor to prosper. Charles was all too happy to jump on the bandwagon.[11] But he was too impatient to wait for politicians to debate the merits of the issue and pass new laws. He understood the

history of the commerce, and he had no doubt as to his right to participate in it.

═══════════

The Portuguese started capturing Africans and bringing them back to
their country as slaves in the middle of the fifteenth century. Spain soon
followed the practice. But it wasn't until 1517 when the transatlantic African slave trade officially began. In that year King Charles V of Spain, with
his empire in the West expanding, granted several individuals the exclusive right to import four thousand Africans annually to the islands of
Hispaniola, Cuba, Jamaica, and Puerto Rico. Over the following century,
other European nations gained territory in the Western Hemisphere and
established sugar, coffee, tobacco, and cotton plantations, all of which
needed large amounts of cheap labor to prosper. Accordingly, the slave
trade continued legally for about three hundred years, and about ten
million Africans were landed in the Americas.[12]

In 1619 a Dutch ship delivered the first twenty slaves to North America at Jamestown, Virginia. Over the next hundred years shipments to
the British North American colonies trickled in, but they expanded rapidly in the mid-eighteenth century as settlers populated the agricultural
South. By the start of the Revolutionary War, when the Continental Congress stopped all imports from Great Britain, about 250,000 Africans had
been landed on colonial shores. The trade to North America resumed
after the Treaty of Paris was signed in 1783; about 28,000 Africans survived the Middle Passage to the states between then and 1790. It was
during this latter period that opposition to the trade started to take hold
in some of the northern states.[13]

In August 1787, during the Constitutional Convention in Philadelphia,
the slave trade took center stage as the delegates considered its future in
the new Union. Luther Martin of Maryland argued that "slaves weakened
one part of the union which the other parts were bound to protect. . . . It
was inconsistent with the principles of the revolution and dishonorable
to the American character to have such a feature in the Constitution."
John Dickenson of Delaware added that "the true question was whether
the national happiness would be promoted or impeded by the importation, and this question ought to be left to the National Gov't., not to
the States." But a northern delegate, Oliver Ellsworth of Connecticut,
thought the decision should be left to the individual states. "The old
confederation had not meddled with this point," he proclaimed, "and

neither should the new one." John Rutledge of South Carolina made clear the position of three southern states, that admission into the Union depended on the legality of the Atlantic slave trade: "If the convention thinks that N.C.[,] S.C.[,] and Georgia will ever agree to the plan, unless their right to import slaves be untouched, the expectation is in vain." The delegates compromised by allowing the African slave trade to continue but only for twenty years, to December 31, 1807. Congress could then revisit the issue.[14]

In fact, the states started taking independent action even before the convention had begun, and by 1798 all had banned the trade through either legislation or their state constitutions. However, in 1803 the South Carolina legislature, concerned about the upcoming federal ban and the increased need for enslaved labor in the rich lands acquired in the Louisiana Purchase, allowed the trade to resume to its shores. During the four-year period of 1804 through 1807, 39,075 Africans arrived in South Carolina. No other state followed South Carolina's lead.[15]

While the Constitution gave the trade a twenty-year extension, it said nothing of the involvement of Americans in it, so Congress acted quickly to limit their role. It passed laws in 1794 and 1800 that prohibited U.S. citizens or residents from building, equipping, or loading ships at any port or place in the United States to carry on a trade in African slaves; holding an interest in any vessel used to transport slaves from one foreign place to another; and working on board a slave ship. U.S. government vessels were given the authority to seize any ship employed in the trade.[16]

As the end of the twenty-year grace period neared, President Thomas Jefferson urged Congress to pass an anti–slave trade law before January 1, 1808, and make it effective on that date. After a lengthy debate, on March 2, 1807, that body passed and Jefferson signed the act outlawing the African slave trade to the United States.[17]

Great Britain enacted a similar law later in 1807, ending a bitter, twenty-year battle in Parliament that pitted the shipping, planter, and mercantile interests in England and the West Indies against the slave-trade abolitionists. Within a period of months, two world powers had banned the trade, giving hope that others might soon follow.[18]

The British also tried to shut down the international trade conducted by other countries. In 1808 they formed the West Africa Squadron to patrol the African coast in search of slave ships and established a prize court in Freetown, Sierra Leone, a British colony, to try cases of captured slavers. Despite having to cover two thousand miles of coastline, the squadron captured nine Cuba-bound ships between 1809 and 1810 and twenty-four Portuguese and Brazilian slave ships between 1810 and 1813.[19]

Spain and Portugal protested the seizures, arguing that the high seas were common territory, open to all nations, and British cruisers had no right to search and seize ships of countries that considered the trade legal. Great Britain heeded the protest, but her ambassadors pursued another course. They lobbied the other major seafaring nations to ban the trade and allow a mutual right of search of each others' ships suspected of being involved in it and, if the ships were found to be slavers, a right of seizure. The diplomatic approach worked. By 1830 the French, Dutch, Spanish, Portuguese, and Brazilian governments had also banned the trade, making it illegal worldwide for the first time. These countries agreed with Great Britain to some form of a right of search and, with the exception of France, the establishment of courts with representatives from both contracting countries to adjudicate the fate of captured vessels.[20]

The British also attempted to strangle the supply of slaves by pressuring African tribes to stop attacking, capturing, and selling their countrymen. Between 1826 and 1827 the headmen of seven tribes signed treaties in exchange for annual payments of fabrics, gunpowder, tobacco, rum, and other products. By the 1850s the British had enlisted more than forty tribes.[21]

But the British fight against the slave trade faced a major, insurmountable hurdle—the United States. During the Napoleonic Wars in the early nineteenth century, Great Britain's cruisers routinely stopped and boarded U.S. merchant ships and took away British-born crew members, even if they had become U.S. citizens. The practice led, in part, to the War of 1812. After that, the United States would never again trust another nation to stop, no less search, its ships, and certainly not Great Britain. Instead, to combat the trade, the United States enacted more laws. Congress passed the Act of 1818, which required defendants charged with holding recently imported Africans to prove that those persons of color had been in the United States for at least five years before the charge was made. The Act of 1819 authorized the president to protect illegally imported Africans and return them to Africa as well as send armed vessels to cruise any area where he thought U.S. citizens or residents were carrying on the trade. Accordingly, President James Monroe sent five ships to the African coast between 1820 and 1821. They liberated 573 Africans before being recalled in 1823. The Act of 1820 designated participation in the trade as piracy; conviction resulted in the death sentence.[22]

Although all the major powers had banned the slave trade by 1830, slavery was still legal in most of the Western Hemisphere and an illegal traffic persisted. Great Britain took another giant step in its quest by ending slavery in the British West Indies. By an act of Parliament, effective August 1, 1834, and an amendment to it, all slaves (except those five years old or younger, who were freed immediately) became apprenticed laborers, to work for their masters for four years, after which they became fully emancipated on August 1, 1838.[23] Despite these efforts, Great Britain saw little success in reducing the illegal trade. Other countries simply did not have the desire or resources to fight it.[24]

Slave traders were quick to take advantage of the United States' refusal to allow any country the right to stop its vessels. Slavers began carrying two sets of ownership papers and flags—one from the United States and one from another country. Whenever the captain spotted a British cruiser or one from any other country except the United States, he simply raised the Stars and Stripes to avoid capture. If he saw an American cruiser, he ran up the colors of the alternate country.[25]

The British soon got wise to the ploy and, as the United States had no patrol ships on the coast at the time, began stopping and searching ships flying Old Glory. It didn't take long for them to find slavers, including some of U.S. origin, and in 1839 they started seizing them—even escorting a few to New York to hand over to authorities. The U.S. public was outraged at the British actions, but President Martin Van Buren realized the extent of the abuse of the U.S. flag. He ordered the New York district attorney to prosecute the owners of the slavers and, for the first time since 1823, sent two cruisers to patrol the coast of Africa.[26]

The British knew they needed U.S. support to make progress against the trade, so they proposed a meeting to resolve a number of mutual problems, including the slave trade. The countries negotiated the Webster-Ashburton Treaty of 1842, which provided for a joint cruising operation along the African coast with each nation supplying a fleet with no fewer than eighty guns that would act independently but cooperate to carry out the objective of the treaty. The British would no longer stop ships flying the U.S. flag, and suspected slavers could be searched only by their own country's cruisers. Progress had been made, but it fell far short of granting the right of search.[27]

During this time the United States became embroiled in two high-profile slave-trading incidents. The first occurred in 1839 when several recently imported African slaves being transported on the *Amistad* from Havana to Principe, Cuba, mutinied. They killed the captain and a mixed-race cook and attempted to sail back to Africa with the help of the two Cuban slave owners on board. Each night, while the slaves slept, one of the Cubans changed course and steered the ship toward the United States until they reached Montauk Point, Long Island, about six weeks later. A navy ship seized the *Amistad* and towed her to Connecticut. Spain demanded the return of the vessel, the Cubans, and the Africans. The U.S. authorities refused to send back the Africans until their status could be resolved legally. The case made its way to the U.S. Supreme Court, which decided in March 1841 that the Africans were not property but were free, as they had been kidnapped in Africa against the laws of Spain, which had banned the slave trade in 1820. The thirty-five surviving Africans were transported home to Africa.[28]

The second case occurred in late October 1841. A group of 135 slaves was being shipped from Virginia to New Orleans on the brig *Creole*—a legal, interstate conveyance—when nineteen of them mutinied, killed a white passenger, wounded several others, and ordered the captain to take the ship to Nassau. When they arrived on November 8, British authorities took control of the vessel, detained the white passengers and crew, jailed the nineteen men, and freed the rest of the slaves. On November 19 the governor of Nassau finally released the ship to the crew and white passengers, who immediately departed for New Orleans. In April 1842 the nineteen suspects were tried in Nassau. The judge declared that he could not rule on the murder charge as a British court had no jurisdiction to try a foreigner for an offense against another foreigner on the high seas, except for piracy, which this crime was not. As for the status of the mutineers, he ruled that subjects held in bondage have a right to recover their freedom when they have the opportunity to do so and set them free. All of this happened during negotiations of the Webster-Ashburton Treaty. After the signing of the treaty, U.S. secretary of state Daniel Webster wrote to Special Envoy Lord Ashburton, protesting the British action in the *Creole* incident. The hostility between the two countries regarding the rights on the oceans of the world still boiled.[29]

The illegal trade continued to thrive in the 1840s, especially to Brazil, by far the largest importer of Africans over the history of the commerce, where local officials could easily be bribed. In March 1845 Brazil terminated its 1826 treaty with Great Britain. The British retaliated and passed the Aberdeen Act of 1845, which gave their navy the unilateral right to seize Brazilian ships suspected of participating in the trade.[30]

In 1850 the British navy started seizing Brazilian vessels in Brazilian waters. The Brazilian government and emperor finally relented and abolished the slave trade on September 14, 1850. Within a few years, the trade to Brazil had all but died. It was a great victory for the British—and for an untold number of Africans.[31]

Cuba became the only major destination for slave ships, but importations were relatively light due to the rule of Captain General José Gutiérrez de la Concha, reputed to be one of the few Spanish officials who could not be bribed. Also, many slaves were transferred from dying coffee plantations to thriving sugar fields. In fact, with the reduced activity in the trade, the British cut their African squadron from twenty-six ships in 1851 to twelve by 1855.[32]

However, as world demand for Cuba's inexpensive sugar grew, so did Cuba's requirement for labor. A cholera epidemic in 1853 that killed thousands of enslaved laborers exacerbated the need. By the mid-1850s the demand for slaves on the island grew to match the record levels of the 1830s.[33] Clearly, the Spanish were not living up to their 1835 treaty—there was too much money involved. Spain was reaping much-needed revenues from the Cuban sugar industry; Cuban officials were getting rich from slave traders' bribes; and slave-trade syndicates were making fortunes on slaving expeditions.[34]

While Cuba remained the main destination of the slave ships, the ports of New York and New Orleans became the major points of embarkation, with abundant ships available for purchase, slaver crews available for hire, port officials who looked the other way, vague laws, and sympathetic judges. By the early 1850s New York had become the undisputed headquarters for the illegal trade.[35]

The British squadron again grew frustrated by suspicious-looking vessels flying the U.S. flag, and their captains began overstepping their authority by searching and, in some cases, firing at and seizing them, even in the waters surrounding Cuba. Until U.S. and British diplomats could resolve their differences and fight the slave traders together, fortunes could be made by lawless men willing to take the risk of outsmarting and outrunning the African squadrons. Charles Lamar was such a man.[36]

―――――

Lamar's entry into the African slave trade shouldn't have surprised anyone. As shown in his involvement in the filibuster movement, he wasn't concerned with breaking federal law. Also, he believed in the institution of slavery and felt that the federal government had no right to ban the trade in the first place. He was already involved in the legal, interstate sale of enslaved humans. It made little difference to him whether those blacks came from Africa or another state. Most important, by 1857 Lamar was broke. The slave trade offered the lure of huge profits in a relatively short amount of time, and he needed cash to pay off his mounting debts. The odious commerce seemed like a natural fit for a man of Charles's character, beliefs, and financial condition.

As Lamar planned his first expedition, he recruited six other investors: Nelson Trowbridge, his similarly broke friend and associate; Theodore Johnston of New Orleans, one of Charles's partners in the failed interstate slave-trading business, and in debt to Charles and James Gardner; W. W. Cheever of Albany, Georgia, Gazaway Lamar's cotton agent there; Jonathon S. Montmollin, a Savannah businessman; Roger Lawson Gamble II, a lawyer in Jefferson County, Georgia; and Dr. Eldridge C. Williamson II of Bibb County, Georgia.[37]

Lamar needed a fast ship that could sail long distances and haul hundreds of humans in its hold. The vessel of choice for slave traders was the speedy Baltimore Clipper, and Charles purchased the *E. A. Rawlins*, which carried coffee from Brazil to cities along the East Coast of the United States, including Savannah, since its launch in 1854.[38]

The *Rawlins* arrived in Savannah on June 29, 1857, under Captain A. Grant Jr., and Lamar started loading supplies for his first slaving venture. On July 9 Lamar filed a manifest with the customhouse for a commercial voyage to Africa. The Savannah port collector, John Boston, considered the cargo suspicious as many of the items were typical provisions for a slaving expedition, including 13,000 feet of lumber (for the construction of a slave deck), 200 bricks (to build an oven on deck to cook large quantities of food), 115 barrels of pilot bread or hard tack, 40 tierces or large barrels of rice, and 2 cases of firearms and cutlery. Boston seized the ship as a slaver.[39]

A furious Charles Lamar wired U.S. treasury secretary Howell Cobb, Boston's boss. Cobb was married to Gazaway Lamar's first cousin Mary, making Cobb Charles's cousin once removed, and he clearly knew Charles. Charles used the relationship to his advantage. He told Cobb that Boston created the problem. "He said the manifest was an '*unusual one*'—so it was—but he was the occasion of it. He directed me to put on it, the ship stores, & the Captain & officers' private stores, & to attach to each & every article, its cost. I protested against it, as unusual—but he insisted and I did it—and he then makes *that* a justification for his proceedings." Lamar also claimed that "John Boston had her detained because he said he knew she would be engaged in the trade, & he heard that from men who confessed that they were eavesdroppers who hung around my windows to listen to all communications that took place."[40]

Cobb wired Boston on July 16 and ordered him to "lay the papers & facts before the district attorney" to determine probable cause to institute legal proceedings and, if none existed, to release the vessel and give it clearance. The next day the U.S. marshal in Savannah inspected the cargo and found nothing suspicious. The *Rawlins* finally received clearance.[41]

The U.S. marshal happened to be Daniel Stewart, who knew Lamar well. Both had been members in the Order of the Lone Star; both were part of a group calling for a town meeting in 1856 regarding the Kansas situation; and in that same year both were committeemen for an agricultural fair. Their relationship would prove invaluable to Charles.[42]

The departure of the *Rawlins* did not end Charles's dispute with Boston. He claimed that he had incurred extra costs of $1,320 for docking, wharfage, and storage fees during the eight days of unwarranted seizure and sought compensation from the government. Boston denied Lamar's claim, saying he had "detained" and not "seized" the ship. Lamar again sought Cobb's intervention in the matter, though it couldn't be determined if Charles ever collected anything.[43]

After the *Rawlins* departed, Charles played verbal games with Cobb regarding the true purpose of the voyage and prepared the treasury secretary for the inevitable: "I did not in my other communications disclaim any intention of embarking in the Slave Trade, nor did I say anything to warrant you supposing I would not engage in it. . . . I will now say, as the vessel is 1,000 miles from here, that she was as unfit for a voyage to import negroes, as any vessel in port—she was not fitted up *in any way* & there was nothing on board to warrant the suspicions. What she may hereafter do is another matter, which don't concern the present issue."[44]

The voyage of the *Rawlins* turned out to be a fiasco. Captain Grant lost his nerve and on August 14 sailed into the port of Funchal, Madeira, having never visited Africa. The ship departed on August 20 for the West Indies, where Grant sold some of its outfit and cargo.[45] He then went to New Orleans, found Trowbridge, returned all but $1,800 of the $18,000 in gold coins he had been given to purchase Africans, and disappeared. Lamar fumed when he heard of Grant's actions. "He has acted *badly* & sacrificed our interests *most shamefully*. His clearance papers would have taken him any where he wanted to go, unmolested. Why did he not return directly to Savh? What took him to the West Indies? Why did he sell any of the outfit? He knew the vessel was fitted for nothing else but *the trade*, & ought to have known we would want to send her back. Port her up for freight for Savannah and send her here. I will send her [on] a trip to Cuba, & in the mean time consummate arrangements for another go." Lamar couldn't let go of his rage against the captain. "Grant ought to receive no pay—refund what he got & make good all the deficiencies. . . . Why did he not go to the Coast. He knew, before he undertook the command that there were armed vessels on the coast, and a number of them. He ought have known, that *he was running no risk*, that the Captain & crew are always discharged."[46]

Lamar never received any answers to these questions. His first foray into the slave trade failed. He ordered Trowbridge to get the ship ready for another voyage. Now even deeper in debt and with notes falling due that he couldn't pay, he admitted to Trowbridge, "I never was so hard up in my life."[47] Charles needed a big score more than ever.

CHAPTER 6

"An Expedition to the Moon Would Have Been Equally Sensible"

October 1857–July 1858

While Charles planned his next slaving expedition, he had to carry on with his other responsibilities, including dealing with his father, who still lived in New York. When word of the failed *Rawlins* mission reached Gazaway, he berated his son. The younger Lamar readily explained his actions.

> You need give yourself no uneasiness about the Africans and the Slave Trade. I was astonished at some of the remarks in your letter. . . . For example, you say "*an expedition to the moon would have been equally sensible, and no more contrary to the laws of Providence and of the Seward doctrine. May God in his mercy forgive you. . . .*" Did the negroes not all come originally from the coast of Africa? What is the difference between going to Africa & Virginia for Negroes and if there is a difference, is not that difference in favor of going to Africa? You need not reproach yourself for not interposing with a stronger power than argument & persuasion to prevent the Expedition. There was nothing you or the government could have done to have prevented it. Let all the Sin be on *me*. I am willing to assume it all.[1]

In reasoning that no difference existed between going to Virginia or Africa for slaves, Charles ignored the deadly tribal wars fought to capture the victims and the horrors of the Middle Passage to bring them across the Atlantic Ocean. Of course, the illegality of the trade did not concern him.

In that same letter to Gazaway, Charles downplayed the rumor that he was broke. Charles explained that he was merely short of cash, and not because of himself, but because of those who owed him money. This became the favorite excuse for his problems: it wasn't his fault. And he informed his father that he didn't intend to pay back the thousands of dollars Gazaway demanded, as Charles didn't recognize the debt. Charles knew that he could push his father around and never hesitated to do it.[2]

Still, to most Savannahians, Charles gave the appearance of a successful businessman and happy family man. In September 1857 his six-story flour mill was completed and hailed as a major contribution to the commerce of the city. He continued to run the rebuilt Lamar cotton press and warehouse and serve as a director of the Bank of Commerce, which he helped found. He fulfilled his civic duty by sitting as a committeeman for the Chatham-Effingham Counties Agricultural Fair, which was held at his Ten Broeck racetrack. And he doted over his three daughters, Eliza, age ten, Jane, nine, and Caroline, two.[3]

However, his hope for quick riches still lay in the African slave trade. The first *Rawlins* venture taught him that he needed an experienced and fearless captain, but he still hadn't found one for the next expedition. So he tried to subcontract the pickup and delivery of the Africans to the United States, where he would take charge of selling them. He wrote to José da Costa Lima Viana, a Portuguese man long associated with the trade, who ran his operation from New York. "I am anxious to have you interested in the next expedition & wld [would] be pleased to have you say what interest you would like. . . . I would like you to say too, what number you would contract to land at a designated point by your own or other's vessels, the price per head and the time of probable delivery—I to take all the trouble, expense and *risk* after they are safely landed—or, if you would prefer it, make some proposition of the nature of the joint a/c speculation. I think I can manage two or three cargoes to much profit."[4] Viana apparently wasn't interested in Charles's proposal, as no such expedition took place. By the end of 1857, Lamar still lacked a captain for his next *Rawlins* voyage, and his prospects looked bleak.

Lamar was desperate for funds as he entered 1858. He had thousands of dollars in notes due to James Gardner that he couldn't pay and money owed to him by Nelson Trowbridge and Theodore Johnston that he couldn't collect. On January 18, 1858, he wrote to Gardner, "I have had nothing from Trowbridge in some time. He has drained me perfectly dry." Two days later he reported, "I have written Trow time and again to sell out and return [from New Orleans] with the proceeds of his [legal slave] sales to Georgia. I am suffering incredible inconsequence of some of his and Johnston's paper laying over, on which to my name I paid and paid until I was exhausted and I was forced to the mortification of a protest." Charles had ignored his father's advice against endorsing notes of others and was paying for it—literally.[5]

In addition, Charles entered into another disastrous business deal with a man he met through his father. He confessed to Gardner, "A damned rascal in NY took me for $45,000 and no prospect of ever getting a dollar from him, unless I take it out of his hide. . . . I am annoyed to death with the state of my affairs. It will take two years of hard work to make me right, provided I lose nothing of consequence with Johnston and Trow."[6]

The gold mines were faring no better, with distrust among the partners, disappointing production, and no dividends. Charles told Gardner, "If we find that the Columbia [mine] won't pay, let us stop operations and hire out or sell the Negroes. I am unwilling to involve myself any further for the mines. I have yet to receive the first dime from my investment up there." In the same letter Lamar claimed that he was done with "fancy speculations" until his finances improved. Nonetheless, two paragraphs later he admitted that he was thinking of going to Africa for a cargo of camels to sell to the U.S. government.[7]

Desperate for funds, Lamar borrowed $10,250 from the Marine Bank of Georgia and $26,900 from the Merchants and Planters Bank. For security, he put up most of his personal assets, including the racetrack, seventy-five acres of land in Chatham County, two houses in Savannah, ten enslaved people, one-eighth interest in the *Richard Cobden*, and thousands of acres of land in Lowndes and Baker counties, Georgia.[8]

Lamar's private life suffered as well. The highlight of the winter social season in Savannah centered on horse-racing week at the Ten Broeck track in early January. Charles had a special interest in the event as he owned the track and was the president of the Savannah Jockey Club, the sponsor of the event. At the end of the last day of the 1858 races, after the women had left the venue, Charles's friend Henry Dubignon, whose family owned Jekyll Island on the Georgia coast, started to argue with him over an unknown matter. Dubignon became aggravated and charged Lamar with a knife, but bystanders apprehended him and ejected him from the premises. Fifteen minutes later, as Lamar and his entourage sat to eat, Dubignon returned with the knife in hand and resumed his attack. John Phinizy, Charles's uncle, grabbed hold of Henry and begged him to stop, but the enraged man threatened him. Charles drew his pistol and warned Dubignon, who struck Phinizy with a bottle and threw an inkstand at Lamar. Charles fired, hitting Dubignon in the eye. The wounded man was rushed to a hospital in town, with two doctors who were at the track in attendance. By the next morning Dubignon was declared out of danger, although the doctors couldn't find the musket ball. The two men soon reconciled, but the incident left Charles shaken.[9]

Charles had one achievement during the early months of 1858—he hired a captain and supercargo for the *Rawlins*. He wrote to the latter, William Ross Postell, a Savannahian whom he handpicked, telling him to go to New Orleans and report to either N. C. Trowbridge or Theodore Johnston, or in their absence, Captain Gilley at the bark. "You, as Supercargo, are to take charge as such of money & cargo, & see that it is properly . . . applied to such purposes as intended." After the Africans boarded, Postell was to see that the *Rawlins* returned to the coast of Georgia as instructed. For his services Postell would receive two Africans for every one hundred landed, plus eighty dollars per month to his family for the four months of his absence. The ship left New Orleans for the African coast on February 11 under the command of Captain C. W. Gilley. Charles no doubt hoped that his money problems would soon be over.[10]

With Johnston still delinquent on his notes, Lamar and Gardner paid him a visit in New Orleans at the end of February. Johnston swore he had no funds and couldn't pay. A frustrated Gardner soon returned to Augusta, but Lamar remained to apply more pressure. A few days later he extracted a small payment, but he remained pessimistic and wrote to Gardner, "I am very much afraid he will not settle. If so, our fat is in the fire & away goes your printing press—sure." He closed by saying, "Trow is in a good humor & says he will pay us all out in less than one year. He has just seen in the evening paper, the passage of the Bill by the Louisiana legislature for the importation of 2,500 Africans. . . . He swears it will pass the Senate, & if it does, he is in the Company & means to go himself to the coast." Charles didn't comment further on Trowbridge's opportunity, but he and Trowbridge would soon be consumed with importing African "apprentices." They just might be the pot of gold Lamar had been looking for.[11]

———————

The African apprentice movement began after the British banned slavery in its colonies effective August 1, 1838. Many of the freed slaves immediately deserted the Caribbean plantations and sugar production plummeted. By 1840 sugar output in Jamaica, British Guyana, and Trinidad declined 58, 24, and 38 percent, respectively, from 1834. Planters desperately needed labor and started importing East Indian workers, called "coolies." However, abolitionists in England raised concerns about their treatment, and in 1838 the colonial governments of Bombay, Madras, and Bengal began withholding permits for vessels carrying emigrants to the West Indies. The planters appealed to their governments for help finding workers. Slaves were not possible, so an alternative labor source had to be found.[12]

Once again the British turned to Africa. When the West African Squadron cruisers seized ships packed with Africans, or suspected of planning to pick up Africans, they escorted them to the nearest port with a mixed commission court—presided over by representatives from Great Britain and the other treating country—usually in Freetown, Sierra Leone, or, after 1840, Saint Helena Island. These courts ruled on the legitimacy of the vessel's mission. If the seized ship carried Africans, they were immediately liberated. The freed slaves, called "recaptives," were handed over to the Liberated African Department, which, in the early years, housed and fed them until they could be relocated to nearby villages.[13]

However, Sierra Leone and the recaptive program turned out to be a disappointment to the British. "[The country's] affairs were riddled with waste and corruption. The labor of Europeanizing liberated Africans had not succeeded," notes William A. Green; "recaptives were settling with fellow tribesmen, asserting their independence from European control . . . rejecting European education, and resisting Christian worship." British authorities eventually came up with what seemed to be a perfect solution—send the recaptives to the West Indies for a few years of employment. For the African, employment on a plantation offered better pay, housing, and medical care than was available in Africa, and he or she theoretically would be free and have the option to return to Africa after the indenture. For the planter, it provided a sorely needed workforce. And for the British government, it saved an estimated £14,000 a year that otherwise would have supported the recaptives in Sierra Leone.[14]

The British were concerned, though, that other countries might view the relocation plan as an attempt to circumvent their own slave-trade treaties and accuse the British squadron of seizing ships to supply British colonies with labor. At the same time, hopes mounted in England that if the experiment of a labor system of free workers on plantations proved successful, it would convince the United States, Brazil, and Cuba to abandon slavery and adopt such a policy.[15]

In 1840 Parliament authorized the exportation of Africans, both residents of Sierra Leone and recaptives, to Jamaica, British Guyana, and Trinidad, the colonies with the greatest need for workers, under the auspices of the Colonial Land and Emigration Commission. Emigration agents were sent to Freetown, Sierra Leone, to supervise the operation. Potential emigrants were interviewed to ensure that they understood the arrangement and that the decision to relocate was theirs alone. Ship transportation, provided by the colonies, had to meet the standards of the Colonial Passengers Act in terms of space per passenger, food rations, and medical care. In April 1841 the first ships left Sierra Leone. Over the ensuing year, approximately 2,600 Africans emigrated to the three colonies; authorities had hoped for more.[16]

In 1846 Parliament terminated a tariff that gave a price advantage to free-grown over slave-grown sugar in the British market. British West Indies planters lost a critical advantage against Brazilian planters, and Brazilian sugar production soared, as did that country's demand for slaves, which increased the number of illegal slave ships crossing the Atlantic. This in turn boosted the number of seizures by the West African Squadron, which increased the number of recaptives and the pool of potential African emigrants to the West Indies. In other words, the British colonies benefited from a flourishing illegal slave trade to other countries.[17]

However, when the Brazilian and British governments signed a slave-trade suppression treaty in 1850, this labor source soon dried up. The population of recaptives at Freetown and Saint Helena all but disappeared, and the planters once again turned to India, which had reopened emigration in 1845. Despite the best efforts of the home and colonial governments, the free African emigration movement to the British West Indies never met expectations, although it would temporarily revive with the growth of the Cuban slave trade in the mid-1850s.[18]

Like the British, the French faced similar labor problems after they banned slavery in their West Indies colonies in 1848, and they also decided to investigate the use of apprentices. But France had no mixed commission courts in Africa nor a pool of potential emigrants. So after several years of calls for assistance from her planters, Emperor Napoleon III allowed a French company to ship ten thousand African apprentices to work on plantations in the French West Indies. The indenture lasted ten years, during which time the Africans would live as free men and women. Afterward, they could opt to remain or return to Africa, at the expense of the colonial government.[19]

France's action sparked a three-week debate in Parliament over the propriety of African apprenticeship, despite the fact that the British had been practicing it for years. Anti–slave-trade members thought that France wanted to revive the slave trade. However, as France had abolished slavery in its colonies, most in Parliament acknowledged that Africans sent there could not legally be enslaved. Still, the British wanted assurances from France that the emigrants would have proper accommodations and medical care on the vessels and would be returned to their native land if they became dissatisfied with their new environment.[20]

At a subsequent session, one lord argued that even if the Africans received these guarantees, they would have to be procured, and deadly tribal wars could not be avoided. "The danger," he announced, "lies in exciting the cupidity of the chiefs of the interior by establishing a demand for an article in which they would unhesitatingly deal—the bodies of their subjects, or their neighbours. If it were once known that Negroes were in request for shipment to the West Indies, they would be brought down to the coast, after having been captured or coerced, without a will of their own, and, as far as regards this stage of the proceedings, the consequences would be as bad as if the vessel waiting to embark them were a genuine slaver. Traffic in human flesh would be revived." He also noted that the legitimate trade the African tribes had developed since the suppression of the slave trade—such as palm oil, ground nuts, lumber, gold dust, and ivory—would be sacrificed for the immoral and deadly trade in humans.[21]

A few days later a British citizen who had lived in Africa for nearly fifty years publicly criticized the apprentice scheme. "To talk of a contract with [African] men in their condition is absurd; they do not know what they are bargaining for even if the truth were told them. How the negroes are to be obtained by France is clear enough from the locality selected for the operation. Whydah [a port in the country of Dahomey] and its neighborhood were till lately the focus of the contraband slave trade."[22] Several members of Parliament also worried that France's plan might induce nations that had abandoned the slave trade to renew it in the French model.[23]

But others saw a positive side to African emigration. One lord said that the issue should be discussed as millions of acres of rich land then lay uncultivated because of a lack of African labor. A London newspaper opined that, "as regards the emigrants themselves, it will be a positive benefit to be removed to a locality where they will be protected by equal laws, and where they may eventually acquire independence." The paper added that emigrants returning to Africa would bring with them the knowledge and habits of the industry of their European masters.[24]

While the British defended their recaptive scheme and the French their African apprentice ploy, many observers in the United States, North and South, saw them as thinly veiled revivals of the African slave trade. Some condemned them, others saw opportunity.

In fact, France's plan caught the eye of legislators in Louisiana. On March 2, 1858, when Charles Lamar was in New Orleans trying to collect from Theodore Johnston, a state representative introduced a bill authorizing Louisianan James H. Brigham to import into the state 2,500 free Africans to work as apprentices in agriculture and other projects for at least fifteen years. After the indenture, the Africans would be returned to their homelands. No discussions were held about the contracts with the apprentices, their pay, shipping arrangements, living conditions, or any other rights. On March 3, after a short debate, the bill passed the house by a convincing vote of forty-six to twenty-one.[25] Passage seemed assured in the state senate, and this, along with his connections to James Brigham, caused Trowbridge's upbeat mood.

Initially, Trowbridge's plan didn't seem to interest Lamar, who was more concerned about collecting money from Johnston, but those efforts failed. On March 4 Charles wrote Gardner, "The fat is in the fire sure enough. . . . I went to see [Johnston] and he refused to do anything with me, when I exploded and opened on him, and such a talk and cursing a man never got before. Trowbridge even begged for him. . . . I go home tomorrow afternoon. I can do nothing by remaining here."[26]

Lamar returned to Savannah empty-handed. Shortly afterward, he learned that the Louisiana senate voted fifteen to thirteen to postpone indefinitely action on the African apprentice bill.[27] Yet again, Trowbridge's optimism turned out to be ill founded. But something about the bill captured Lamar's attention. If France, which had abolished the slave trade, could employ African apprentices, why couldn't Louisiana—or any other slave state? In that case he could hire legitimate captains and crews to transport the Africans. And since his cousin, Howell Cobb, was U.S. secretary of the treasury, he could obtain preauthorization for the importation, guaranteeing its success.

Lamar took pen to paper. He wrote to E. Lafitte and Company, his shipping agent in Charleston, asking Lafitte to apply to the local port collector for clearance for his ship the *Richard Cobden* "to the coast of Africa for the purpose of taking on board African emigrants in accordance with the United States passenger laws, and returning with the same to a port in the United States."[28] Lamar knew that the port collector would have heart palpitations on reading the application and would forward it to Cobb. If Cobb rejected it, Lamar would turn the issue of the federal slave-trade laws into a national debate at the highest level of government for the entire country to witness. He couldn't wait.

CHAPTER 7

"Let Your Cruisers Catch Me If They Can"

April–July 1858

Charles Lamar waited impatiently for a response to the application made in late March by his Charleston agent Edward Lafitte for clearance of the *Richard Cobden.* On April 20 port collector William F. Colcock forwarded the application to Secretary of the Treasury Howell Cobb. When Lamar did not hear back from Cobb in what he deemed a reasonable amount of time, he wrote to his cousin directly and confidentially, explaining in detail the true purpose of the application—to land Africans near New Orleans and have the matter resolved in the courts—and urging a prompt decision.[1]

While Cobb still took his time to reply, Lamar began planning another African venture. On May 24 and 25 he wrote to four men, offering them an opportunity to invest in an expedition that would use a steamer to import 1,200 African apprentices who would be sold for $650 each "as fast as landed." Lamar needed $300,000 to finance the mission: half to purchase the steamship *Vigo,* and the other half for repairs, guns, small arms, and coal ($50,000); supplies ($25,000); and the purchase of Africans ($75,000). The gross receipts of $780,000 would generate a net profit of $480,000. With his usual blind overconfidence, Charles boasted to one of the men, Leonidas Spratt, a Charleston lawyer, the editor of the *Charleston Standard,* and an African slave-trade advocate, "There is nothing short of an interposition of Divine Providence that can prevent her success."[2]

Lamar's weakness as a businessman can be seen in his unrealistic financial projections. While there is no doubt that successful slaving expeditions yielded enormous profits, Charles's estimates were vastly overblown. For example, he assumed that all the Africans, costing an average of $62.50 each, would survive the transatlantic journey. That would be highly unusual. The average death rate during the Middle Passage ranged between 15 and 20 percent. A 15 percent loss would reduce receipts and profits by $117,000. Also, Lamar didn't specify wages for the crew, often paid in part with Africans, as evidenced in his earlier agreement with William Ross Postell.

Charles planned to outfit the ship with six Paixhan guns—which fired exploding shells—and hire "as good men as are to be found in the South." Even though Lamar felt that fighting would be unnecessary because the steamer could easily outrun the government cruisers, the captain might choose to defend the ship if he were caught in a creek or river while loading the cargo. The fact that Lamar prepared for an armed confrontation with the superior guns of the British and U.S. navies displayed reckless judgment.[3]

Lamar stated in these letters that he had a ship ready to sail for the coast of Africa to place an order for one thousand slaves—two hundred fewer than he used in his profit projection—to be ready on September 1. This would allow the steamer to pick up its cargo immediately on arrival on the coast without having to wait up to one month for a slave dealer to accumulate the human cargo at his barracoon, or holding pen. It is uncertain which ship Lamar had in mind to deliver the order. The *Rawlins* was involved in another slaving expedition, and the *Richard Cobden* was sitting in Charleston harbor waiting for clearance from the port collector to pick up a cargo of African apprentices.

In any event, the *Vigo* mission never got off the ground, likely due to a lack of investors, and Lamar's thoughts were quickly diverted back to the *Cobden* situation. On May 22 Cobb finally replied to Colcock, and although he knew that Lafitte had made the application on behalf of Lamar, Cobb's reply only referred to the agent. His letter was published by the *Charleston Mercury* on June 1 for the country to see. Cobb emphatically rejected the application. He reasoned that a cargo of African apprentices landed in the United States could only be disposed of in one of two ways: as slaves bound to labor or as emigrants to be treated as freemen. Regarding the former, Cobb explained how Congress had passed legislation over the years to suppress American involvement in the slave trade and, after 1807, to prohibit the importation of slaves into America, making the first possibility clearly illegal. He went on, "Whether or not the wisdom of our fathers foresaw at that early day that efforts would be made, under a pretended apprentice system, to renew the slave trade under another name, I cannot undertake to say; but the language of the law which they have left to us on the statute book, leaves no doubt of the fact that they intended to provide, in the most unequivocal manner, against the increase of that class of population by immigration from Africa." Cobb added that the states themselves had passed laws prohibiting the importation of Africans.[4]

In addressing the second possibility, Cobb wrote that the implication by Lafitte that African immigrants would be entitled "to all the rights and privileges of free men . . . upon its face is so absurd that it is hardly worthy of serious refutation." But he still explained why he rejected the notion. He questioned which states would accept the Africans. "It cannot be the one from which it sails, nor any other port in the State of South Carolina, as the introduction of free negroes into that State is wisely prohibited. . . . It cannot be the port of any other slaveholding state as similar laws in each of those states alike forbid it." He wondered if Lafitte intended to carry the Africans to non-slaveholding states, a few of which might not have laws prohibiting such immigrants. "I am not aware of a single State where these newcomers would receive a tolerant, much less cordial welcome; whilst, by stringent laws and constitutional provisions, some of them have provided for their unconditional exclusion." Cobb pointed out that all the states, for various reasons, were taking measures to provide for the removal of free blacks—"this most unfortunate class." Finally, Cobb questioned the motive for importing free Africans. "It cannot be the profits of the voyage. There are no African emigrants seeking passage to this country; and if there were, they would have no means of remunerating Messrs. Lafitte & Co. for bringing them. The motive cannot be mere philanthropy for it would confer no benefit upon those negroes."[5]

Cobb couldn't help but take a swipe at Charles, who had used him for getting clearance for the first *Rawlins* expedition. "To believe . . . that there is a bona fide purpose on the part of Messrs. Lafitte & Co. to bring African emigrants to this country to enjoy the rights and privileges of freemen, would require an amount of credulity which would justly subject the person so believing to the charge of mental imbecility." He closed by admitting that it was unwise for a government officer to act on a suspicion that a citizen intended to violate the laws of the United States, but in this instance there could be no doubt as to the objective. He rejected the application.[6]

Lafitte and Lamar were incensed at Cobb's letter. Lafitte wrote a lengthy response to the editors of the *Charleston Mercury* expressing his disgust. "We think the proper bounds of official duty and decorum have been transgressed, and no little violence done to candor, in the manner in which this application has been discussed by the Secretary, coming as it did from private citizens, and constituting a simple question. . . .

There was nothing in the letter of our correspondent, well known as a highly respectful merchant of Savannah, which could lead us to suppose that any violation or evasion of the law was intended. . . . We had a right to expect, if deemed conformable to law, that it would be granted; and if deemed otherwise, that the refusal would be couched in respectful terms. . . . [Cobb] was aware that we were acting as mere agents for the real applicant, one of his own constituents . . . who had addressed him in his official capacity, avowing himself as the principal in this transaction, and giving him full information of his intentions and designs."[7]

Lafitte's response was polite compared to what Lamar had planned. Being called an imbecile did not sit well with him. On June 2 Charles wrote to business partner James Gardner, "I want to open on him myself. He will catch the Devil sure." On June 6 he told Lafitte, "Get [Leonidas] Spratt [editor and publisher of the *Charleston Standard*] & other Southern men to toast him up. I have not had the time to prepare anything myself but will & open upon him then in the papers."[8]

Charles soon responded to Cobb in a letter published in the Charleston papers, telling the secretary that his objection to the application was "groundless." Lamar reasoned, "You virtually admitted the right to land such emigrants in some of the non-slaveholding States, but added that 'you were not aware of a single State where these newcomers would receive a tolerant, much less a cordial reception.' Has Northern public opinion, then, acquired the force of law?" Charles claimed that Cobb's opinion was "unsupported by a single quotation from the law, either State or Federal. Nay, you admit that no law exists by which they can be excluded." Charles suggested that as the application had not named the U.S. port of destination, which was not an unusual practice, Cobb assumed that the *Cobden* would return to a southern port, "which interpretation you [Cobb] had no right to make." Lamar then revealed publicly what he had asked privately of Cobb: "[to] grant the vessel protection on the coast of Africa from molestation." If Cobb would do so, Lamar "would land the cargo on the levee at New Orleans, and test the legality of the matter in the courts of the United States."[9] Cobb, of course, did not accept Lamar's proposal.

Once again, Charles played word games with Cobb, throwing up a confused argument in which he claimed that he might land Africans at a port in the North, where it might be legal, when all the while he intended, as he had admitted to Cobb, to land the Africans in New Orleans, where it was illegal, and have the courts decide the matter.

At the end of the letter, Charles told Cobb, "From your course, it would appear that the exception to this rule should exist only as a bar to Southern enterprise, as Northern vessels are constantly employed in the transportation of coolies, who are persons of color, held to service or labor."[10]

Charles was referring to the traffic in Chinese workers, under the guise of contract laborers, to the West Indies, particularly Cuba and Peru, which rivaled the African slave trade in inhumanity. It was conducted in part by U.S. shippers, many of whom were of northern origin. Although some congressmen protested against the "coolie" trade, little action was taken against it by the U.S. navy or in the courts. Lamar questioned why Cobb would hold southern shippers in violation of the law for transporting "African apprentices" but not northerners for transporting Chinese "contract laborers."[11]

Charles concluded his letter by reminding Cobb that he had submitted a second application for clearance for the *Cobden* on a similar voyage to return to a port in Cuba and requested an immediate answer to it, "and let the South know whether she has any rights in the Union or not."[12]

Cobb responded more quickly this time. On June 18 he wrote to Colcock, the port collector: "I have no hesitation in saying that the clearance should not be granted. . . . It would seem that the present application is made upon a supposed difference between the slave trade . . . and the slave trade under the name and form of apprenticed Africans. This government does not recognize that distinction." Undeterred, Charles filed yet another application, this time asking for clearance for the *Cobden* to Africa without specifying a destination port. This application was similarly turned down.[13]

Charles had run out of patience. On July 5 he published an eleven-page manifesto attacking Cobb's interpretation of the slave-trade laws and abuse of his office. He maintained that the rights of citizens could not be withheld because a government official feared they might be abused, as Cobb had even admitted he did in his letter of May 22. Lamar also claimed that shipping African apprentices to other countries violated no American law, specifically the Act of 1794, nor the law of nations, as France and England had been doing it openly for years. He questioned the constitutionality of the Act of 1808, contending that the clause preventing Congress from prohibiting the importation of persons bound to labor before 1808 did not expressly give Congress the right to outlaw it afterward—it only implied it. Lamar again accused Cobb of making decisions based on northerners' popular sentiment to gain favor with them. The fact that Cobb betrayed the land of his birth made his position worse.[14]

However, a few southerners openly supported Howell Cobb's interpretation. John Cunningham, the editor of the *Charleston Evening News*, was especially unimpressed by Lamar's argument for reopening the slave trade. He wrote in his paper, "But [Lamar's] appeal to the passions of sympathy, show, that in case he is caught, he had rather be regarded as a martyr than a convict, as a hero than a freebooter." Lamar quickly responded to Cunningham, saying that he found the statement offensive and asked if it were meant to be so, implying that if it weren't withdrawn, he would challenge the editor to a duel. Four days later Cunningham responded to the thin-skinned slave trader, disavowing any intention to wound or offend. Charles accepted the clarification and looked forward to the editor becoming a warm advocate for legalizing the trade.[15]

In closing his attack on Cobb in his published manifesto, Charles got personal. He said the way Cobb handled the response, to dance around the issue and to conciliate the North by taking a stand against slavery, was "the work of a little man to a little object." Lamar informed Cobb that while he didn't intend to engage in the slave trade with the *Cobden*, he would with other ships, and he laid down a challenge. "I intend to violate [the law,] if that shall be the only way by which the South can come to right upon this question, and I will re-open the trade in slaves to foreign countries, let your cruisers catch me if they can."[16]

Cobb, well aware of Lamar's many failures as a businessman and slave trader, probably laughed at the boast. But by the time Charles issued his manifesto threatening to violate the law, he already had set another slaving voyage on its way, one that would shake the conscience of the nation.

CHAPTER 8

"As Near Perfection as Anything of the Kind"

March–September 1858

During Charles Lamar's trip to New Orleans in February and March 1858 the city had another visitor, the luxury yacht *Wanderer*, owned by former Louisiana planter and current Long Island resident John D. Johnson. The craft had left New York in late December 1857 and made stops in Charleston, Brunswick, Key West, and Havana, before anchoring in Algiers on the west bank of the Mississippi River. Its beauty set the town abuzz. The vessel had been built the year before on Long Island by John Rowland under the supervision of Captain T. B. Hawkins at a reported cost of $25,000. A New York reporter raved, "She is 243 tons burden, is 95 feet length of keel, 10½ feet depth of hold, and 26½ feet beam . . . her bow is concave . . . and her run is so sharp and clean that one would be at a loss to tell where the water would touch it after it passes her midship lines. Her decks . . . are so scrupulously white that one instinctively looks for a mat on which to wipe his feet. . . . The sides of the gangway ladder are ornamented with brass work representing harps. Portions of the steering apparatus are also made of the same material, the whole being kept perfectly bright. No expense has been spared to make the cabin and staterooms all that could be desired for comfort and luxury." The *Boston Herald* was equally impressed: "The model of the yacht is as near perfection as anything of the kind ever produced."[1]

Within days of the *Wanderer*'s arrival Johnson started receiving guests. Although Lamar never acknowledges in his correspondence if he visited the ship, subsequent events indicate that he did, and that he fell in love with it. In early March, after returning to Savannah from his visit to New Orleans, Lamar enlisted seven other investors for an African expedition using the yacht. Based on the individuals he cites in his letters as having received Africans from the venture, the eight partners were Charles Lamar, William Corrie, Nelson Trowbridge, John Tucker, Richard Akin, Theodore Johnston, John Montmollin, and William Brailsford.[2]

Lamar does not reveal who thought of using a yacht to import slaves, nor who brought together the main players—Lamar, William C. Corrie, experienced slave trader Nicholas Danese, and supercargo John Egbert Farnum. However, some facts can be pieced together. Corrie had been targeted by Lamar and his friends as a potential partner in a slaving expedition the year before. On July 21, 1857, four days after the *Rawlins* embarked on her first mission, N. C. Trowbridge of New York, T. Johnston of Louisiana, and W. C. Torrie of South Carolina registered at Brown's Hotel in Washington, D.C. "Torrie" is either a misprint or a weak attempt at faking a name. It is too much of a coincidence to think that the three just happened to check in to the same hotel on the same day. One can safely assume that they talked about a voyage to Africa. They might have discussed using the *Wanderer* at that time, but the ship had only recently been christened and was little known. It is more likely that they talked in general about joining together in an expedition. Lamar, Trowbridge, and Johnston were in New Orleans when the *Wanderer* arrived on March 1, 1858, and one of the three may have come up with the concept at that time. Johnston, being from Louisiana, may have known John D. Johnson and approached him, which would have given Lamar time to return to Savannah, contact Corrie about the plan, and find other investors. Lamar probably raised his portion of the investment by selling the one remaining asset that he had not already mortgaged, the flour mill, on April 6 to his father and Andrew Low, a wealthy Savannah cotton factor, for $26,500.[3]

There is no record of Corrie having previous experience in the slave trade, but he was known to be a sailor and, most important, a smooth talker. Born in Charleston in 1817, "he received a good English school education, and then entered upon commercial pursuits, many of his contemporaries well remembering the time when he was a first class salesman in a dry goods store on King Street." Corrie partook in many important social and civic events in Charleston. In 1850 he served as a special guard of honor attending to the remains of South Carolina political legend John C. Calhoun when they were shipped from Washington to Charleston. The next year, Corrie joined the Charleston Southern Rights Association.[4]

Soon after, Corrie made his way to Washington, where he worked as a lobbyist and "wielded an influence among members of Congress so potent, that he was regarded as one of the chiefs of the 'lower house.'" Corrie did not impress everyone. The British consul in Charleston, Robert Bunch, noted "that Captain Corrie had been for years a lobbyist at Washington where, according to one of the South Carolina congressmen, 'he had more power than all the South Carolina Delegation put together'; he was . . . a vulgar fellow 'habitually boasting of his power in Congress and fond of specifying the exact sum for which each member is to be purchased.'"[5]

A New York newspaper described him more kindly, as "belonging to Charleston, S.C. and he is said to be connected with the most respectable and wealthy families of South Carolina. He has resided for five years at Washington, and has recently succeeded in a grant of some $200,000 in favor of his family founded upon some revolutionary claim. His manners are those of a well-bred gentleman."[6]

In early April the *Wanderer* sailed back to New York, arriving on April 11 and three days later continuing to Port Jefferson, Long Island. Soon afterward Johnson sold the yacht to William C. Corrie of South Carolina for a reported $22,000. It appears that Charles Lamar was in New York at the time and would have taken part in the negotiations. After the deal was finalized, Corrie, with Johnson's reference, became a member of the prestigious New York Yacht Club.[7]

Events transpired quickly after Corrie purchased the *Wanderer*. The vessel remained in Port Jefferson and "the whole business of fitting her out was entrusted to a friend of the Colonel's who was supplied with . . . a check for $6,000 . . . to get her in readiness for the sea." That friend was Nelson Trowbridge. Also, William V. Brooks of New Orleans checked into a Port Jefferson hotel and immediately took charge of the yacht as the sailing master. The surveyor at Port Jefferson, Sidney S. Norton, heard through the grapevine that Brooks's real name was Seth Briggs, and he had worked on a whaler in the South Seas about ten years earlier. He also learned from local residents that Briggs had been telling people that the ship was going on a twelve-month cruise. Norton became suspicious and kept a close eye on things.[8] While Trowbridge and Briggs got the *Wanderer* ready, Corrie returned to Washington, where on May 25 he applied for and received a passport, which described him as five feet, eight and one-half inches tall, with a full forehead, grey eyes, and mixed grey hair.[9]

In late May Surveyor Norton observed the arrival of four foreign sailors and a delivery to the yacht of casks of hams, barrels of onions, and several iron water tanks whose capacity far exceeded the requirements of a normal voyage with an average-sized crew. Such a huge amount of water would only be necessary for a large number of passengers, either soldiers on a filibustering mission or a cargo of Africans. Norton went to New York and informed U.S. marshal Isaiah Rynders and assistant U.S. district attorney Theodore Dwight. They agreed that the circumstances sounded suspicious, and Norton made out an affidavit on which a warrant was issued and placed in the hands of U.S. assistant marshal Maurice O'Keefe. Norton and O'Keefe returned to Port Jefferson to monitor the situation. The lighter *Charter Oak*, loaded with more provisions, sailed into the harbor and anchored near the *Wanderer*. A few days later, six more non–English-speaking sailors arrived by stage under the charge of Nelson Trowbridge and boarded the vessel. That night, William Corrie and John Egbert Farnum, a Mexican War veteran and filibuster, arrived at Port Jefferson and went on the ship. Norton and O'Keefe had seen enough. O'Keefe sent a messenger to New York to request a revenue cutter to seize the yacht and the lighter.[10]

Farnum, who was often referred to as "Captain Farnum," likely because of a military rank, and Charles Lamar traveled in similar circles. Farnum was born in New Jersey on April 1, 1824, the same day as Lamar. He was raised and educated in Pottsville, Pennsylvania. In 1846, at the age of twenty-two, he enlisted as a sergeant major in the First Pennsylvania Regiment and fought in the Mexican War. Afterward, like many former soldiers, he joined one of the filibuster movements and participated in some way in Narciso López's Cárdenas expedition of 1850. In May 1855, as John Quitman's Cuban filibuster movement was falling apart, Farnum helped organize the Worth Legion, a military unit founded in New York to enlist one thousand men to fight in Cuba in case of a war with Spain. A few years later he served under filibuster William Walker in Nicaragua in his losing war with Costa Rica and then returned to the United States. When Walker was in New Orleans for a trial in early March 1858 and toured the *Wanderer*, he was accompanied by several of his officers. Though Farnum is not identified as one of them, he was reportedly living in New Orleans at the time and getting involved in slaving expeditions. Farnum and Lamar almost certainly crossed paths during their associations with the filibuster and slave trade movements. Also, Nelson Trowbridge had spent months in New Orleans, dealing with the *Rawlins* after it returned from the first mission and organizing the second, as well as working with Johnston in the sale of slaves. He may well have made Farnum's acquaintance then.[11]

On June 7 Corrie applied for and received a temporary register and port clearance for Charleston. He had planned to load the *Wanderer* with provisions and proceed to sea by way of Montauk Point to Charleston, bypassing New York harbor. However, he had heard local gossip that O'Keefe had been watching the movements about the yacht and ordered it and the *Charter Oak* to sail to New York harbor to transfer the provisions under the eyes of the authorities to allay any suspicions. Just as the two ships got started, the revenue cutter *Harriet Lane* arrived, took possession of both, and towed them to New York, arriving on Wednesday, June 9. Corrie, who had several prominent (unidentified) guests with him, complained bitterly to the authorities on reaching New York harbor.[12]

Surveyor Norton came under pressure to explain his actions. He stuck by his decision and gave his grounds for the seizure: "That [the *Wanderer*] was undergoing repairs of a singular character; that an unusual number of water tanks were going on board; that she was receiving from the lighter, the *Charter Oak*, a very large supply of provisions; that on Wednesday night she shipped a crew of foreign sailors of uncouth appearance; that she was clearing at Port Jefferson for Charleston, and paying for the transportation of her provisions from New York, instead of going to the city at once and clearing at [that] port; and that John Egbert Farnum, a well-known filibuster, had come down and taken passage."[13]

The decision to include Corrie as the captain paid dividends immediately as the lobbyist easily fended off the meddling officials after the towed vessels reached New York. He explained the circumstances to the authorities: "That he was going on a pleasure trip to the West Indies; that he preferred to go round Montauk Point to going through Hell Gate [a dangerous tidal strait separating Queens from Randall's Island], and did not care for the expense of the lighterage; that the *Wanderer* had delicacies in her stores which, with the costliness of her outfit, would show that she was not destined for the slave trade; that she could not carry ten niggers, and that the water tanks were intended for ballast."[14]

The next morning, Thursday, June 10, U.S. district attorney Dwight and U.S. marshall Rynders inspected the yacht. Farnum assisted the authorities, turning his trunks inside out and opening all the lockers and drawers on the ship. The officers removed the water tanks to inspect beneath them but found nothing suspicious. The *New York Times* reported, "There were several small pieces of ordnance about deck, and below one of the staterooms which was fitted up as an armory by her former owner still contains muskets, pistols, boarding pikes and heavy cutlasses, enough to arm 30 men." Apparently, light weaponry on a ship in those times was not unusual.[15] The officials also inspected the *Charter Oak*, which carried ample supplies of beef, pork, hams, vinegar, potatoes, bread, rice, Champagne, brandy and other kinds of liquors, olives and olive oil, cigars, preserved meats, and condiments, enough to feed a ship's crew for a year.[16]

Corrie would not have wanted any official other than Marshal Rynders to perform the inspection. In 1861 the *New York Times* said of Rynders and an associate, "There are two of Mr. Buchanan's appointees in this city whose instant removal is demanded alike by humanity and justice. We refer to Marshal Isaiah Rynders and District-Attorney Roosevelt, two officials under whose benignant and fostering protection the Slave-trade has established itself amongst us as a secure and influential business-interest."[17]

Dwight released the ship and even allowed the yacht, under guard of a government revenue cutter, to be moved to a more secure location in the harbor where the provisions on the *Charter Oak* could be transferred under the supervision of Rynders and O'Keefe. One day during a rain shower, Corrie invited the officials below for a meal. He sat at the head of the table and toasted, "If thine enemy hunger, feed him, and if he thirst, give him drink." The guests laughed. Had Charles Lamar witnessed the performance, he would have stood and applauded.[18]

The *Wanderer* remained in New York harbor for a week before departing for Charleston with Corrie, Farnum, a guest named Mr. Brent, and the rest of the crew as identified by a newspaper reporter: "W. V. Brooks, sail-master; Antonio Barber, Italian; Joseph Williams, Greek; John Mikes, Russian; Nicholas Barras, Trieste; Frank Raymond, English, (doubtful;) John Smith, Italian; Demetrius Nichols, Greek; and Joseph Conaffe, Italian. They are an orderly and intelligent set of men, and apparently good sailors." Of course, the sailors did not give their real names—slaver crewmen never did—and they seemed to be quite casual in matching their fake names to their fictional nationalities.[19]

The yacht left New York on June 18 and entered Charleston harbor one week later. Corrie got right to work. On June 26 he obtained a permanent certificate of registry for the ship. The next day he and Farnum checked into the Moultrie House on Sullivan's Island, a popular beach resort across the harbor from Charleston, where they met Charles Lamar and Nelson Trowbridge, who had arrived three days earlier. The group made final preparations for the expedition.[20]

Leonidas Spratt, the newspaper editor and slave trade advocate whom Lamar had invited to invest in the *Vigo* expedition, registered at the hotel on the same day as Charles, as well as William F. Colcock, port collector for Charleston, and his wife, and Nathaniel Levin, the port collector's clerk, and his wife. There is no proof that they were guests of Lamar or Corrie, or that they had any connection to the scheme, but the ship was cleared with no known inspection.[21]

Over the following days Corrie purchased more supplies from Hugh E.

Vincent, a Charleston ship chandler who supported the reopening of the slave trade. On June 30 the *Wanderer* crew ferried provisions from the mainland to the yacht anchored in the harbor, including "thirty 6 qt. pans, twenty 5 qt. pans, and fifty 1-pt. tin cups," standard equipment for feeding slaves. The next day Corrie hosted a large party on the ship.[22]

On July 2 Corrie filed the crew list with the port collector. It included Corrie, William Brooks, Frank Raymond, John Mike—the only names that appeared on the New York list—and Demetry Tomatte, Gisseppe Galaffa, Nicholas Paris, Manuel Bassett, John Temboraza, Annest Basset, Basseli Grisper, and George L. Lewis. Six of these last eight men were assuredly part of the crew that left New York but with new names. Two more men were added in Charleston. All claimed nationalities other than Spanish or Portuguese, the most common of slaver crewmen.[23]

The next day Corrie visited the British consul's office with supercargo Farnum and two British guests, Mr. Brent and Mr. Beman, to obtain passports. He also requested one for guest Nicholas Dennis, most assuredly Nicholas Danese, reportedly a native of Louisiana, who was unable to come to the office. H. Pinckney Walker, who was filling in for the absent consul, Robert Bunch, issued the "protections" to the men, although it was not customary for the consul to do so for U.S. citizens. However, as he was new at the job and Corrie was in a hurry, Walker complied.[24]

The *Wanderer*, with twelve crewmen and three guests, left Charleston harbor on July 3 for Africa by way of Trinidad. Charles Lamar waited impatiently in Savannah for the yacht's successful return. But he didn't remain idle. Two days after the *Wanderer*'s departure he released his manifesto attacking Cobb.[25]

No doubt, unloading on the treasury secretary gave Charles immense pleasure, but Lamar's joy didn't last long. A month later, on August 2, the *Rawlins* slinked back into Savannah harbor with nothing to show for its efforts. In late May, more than three months after the vessel left New Orleans, it had entered the Port of Saint Thomas and anchored. On June 18 Captain C. W. Gilley went ashore for clearance papers. After he entered the customhouse, supercargo William Ross Postell, Lamar's handpicked representative, sailed away, leaving Gilley on shore. The ship appeared six weeks later in Savannah. Unsubstantiated rumors swirled that the *Rawlins* deposited a cargo of slaves in Cuba or Texas. In reality, the mission failed, leaving Lamar in worse financial shape than ever.[26]

Nonetheless, Charles's reputation continued to grow. In early July the slaver *Echo* of New Orleans had taken on 450 captives along the African coast. On August 21, after about forty-five days at sea, the ship was seized in Cuban waters by the USS *Dolphin,* whose crew found 318 mostly starving and sick blacks. By the time the *Dolphin* escorted the slaver to Charleston harbor, only 300 souls survived, 260 men and 40 women. One observer described their arrival. "Many were reduced to walking skeletons, and some evidently in a dying condition." The federal authorities in Charleston placed the *Echo* crew of eighteen in jail and sent the captain to Boston for trial. The liberated slaves were housed in the nearly completed Fort Sumter in the middle of the harbor.[27]

The arrival of pure Africans created immense local interest, drawing residents to the fort to see them. The question of their disposition created even greater excitement. Many southerners wanted them to remain in America, and an article in the *Charleston Mercury* reflected a common attitude of supporters of slavery:

> But there are also many who would like them upon any terms that the most solicitous guardian could require, who would undertake to give them all the clothes they could ever need, all the food they could require, the education they would be capable of receiving, all the liberty they could ever use, the skill of the physician, the teachings of religion, the care and discipline of a master, and exact of them just that service which would be consistent with their best physical well being, and yet in the name of humanity it is required that they shall be sent to the dreary wild where there can be no hope of clothing, food, education, or regulated liberty—where they could never have the skill of the physician, the teachings of the pastor, or the regulation of a higher nature.[28]

In short, the life of the African as a slave in the hands of a merciful and caring master was far more humane than as a free person in their wild, godless homeland. But the federal law of 1819 mandated that the president should remove "all such negroes, mulattoes or persons of color" to an agent on the African coast.[29]

The American Colonization Society, which formed in 1816 to help free persons of color in the United States move back to Africa, offered to take the survivors to Liberia, the country founded by the society, where they would house them and teach them industrial pursuits—for the sum of $50,000. This was too much for Lamar, who had spent a fortune trying to bring Africans into the country. He wrote to the editor of the *Savannah Daily Morning News* in reaction to the society's offer: "Now, I desire to make this proposition to the Government: I will take them and give $50,000 for the privilege, and will guarantee to teach them 'industrial pursuits' without any charge, and keep them for a term of years.

Which proposition will the Government accept? They are much in want of money, but equally in need of popularity North, and I am inclined to think they will favor the Society. . . . We shall soon see."[30]

Lamar's offer was not accepted, if ever considered. Even if it were, he would have had a tough time coming up with the $50,000. On September 21, 1858, the steam frigate *Niagara* departed Charleston with the surviving 271 *Echo* Africans—29 having died since landing at Charleston—bound for Monrovia. On November 9 the 200 living souls from the original cargo of 450 stepped onto African soil, 71 having died on the voyage home.[31]

With the *Wanderer* well on its way and the second *Rawlins* mission having ended in failure, Lamar felt the need to have more pokers in the slave-trade fire. He opened a correspondence with Henry C. Hall, an American living in Matanzas, Cuba, who would become a U.S. consul at Matanzas and Havana during and after the Civil War, about African expeditions with landings in the United States.[32] As Lamar negotiated with Hall, the *Wanderer* entered the mouth of the Congo River.

CHAPTER 9

"The Degraded Children of Africa"

July–November 1858

There never had been a slave ship like the *Wanderer*, a vessel built for opulence and comfort, and enough speed to set a record by sailing from New Orleans to New York in nine days and fifteen hours. The Baltimore Clipper, which could outrun government cruisers, even with a hold stuffed with humans, had been the ship of choice for slave traders since the trade became illegal.[1]

While the use of a yacht was unique, the duties of the *Wanderer* crew were the same as on other slavers. Supercargo John Farnum handled the business transactions and finances, including purchasing the slaves, acquiring supplies, and paying the crew. Nicholas Danese, who used the name Nicholas Brown throughout the venture, including the subsequent trials, and had previously owned a slaver and captained at least one other, probably acted as a guide in Africa. Sail master Seth Briggs, who went by the name William V. Brooks, had worked on Danese's slaver and had overall sailing responsibilities. The crewmen performed normal sailing duties on the outbound trip. However, on the return trip they also served as guards under the command of a boatswain, keeping the Africans tightly controlled and ensuring that they obeyed every order without hesitation. William Corrie's two English guests, Mr. Brent and Mr. Beman, likely were responsible for translating and providing medical attention to the slaves. Corrie played a special role—acting as a wealthy sportsman hosting an around-the-world adventure with friends, and charming every official and naval officer he met.[2]

Slaving expeditions needed certain stores and equipment to transport and feed hundreds of captives on an ocean journey of approximately six weeks. Water was critical, and tanks holding fifteen thousand gallons had already been installed in the *Wanderer*. The ship carried enough weaponry to arm thirty men, which failed to arouse suspicions among the New York authorities. They needed lumber to build a slave deck—a large shelf affixed to the port and starboard walls of the hold midway between the floor and ceiling after all the bulkheads had been removed—to pack in more humans; barrels of rice, farina, dried beans, hard biscuits, and perhaps some dried meat, the staples of an on-board slave diet; hundreds of bricks and lime to build a stove on the top deck; boilers and pots for cooking; wood to fuel the cooking fires; wooden cups, bowls, and spoons to serve the water and food; disinfectants to clean the ship; medicine to care for the sick; and perhaps cuffs or shackles to bind the slaves. Of course, hidden under lock and key, probably in the captain's stateroom, were thousands of dollars in gold coins to purchase the Africans.[3]

Loading these items and concealing them from port officials presented a challenge to slaver captains. Some hid the stores behind bulkheads. Others took on legitimate supplies at the port of embarkation and after departing met another vessel out of sight of the revenue cutters to take on the most obvious slaver equipment such as boilers, timber, bricks, and lime. Others obtained supplies in Africa from ships known as auxiliaries. Still other captains bribed port officials. Some bolder captains packed their ships with the necessary gear and, if challenged by the port collector, claimed that they were standard and necessary for a commercial voyage and sued in court to get clearance. Corrie purchased his slaving supplies from a Charleston ship chandler and suspected slave-ship owner, Hugh Vincent. No one saw items such as lumber and bricks being loaded onto the *Wanderer*, though Corrie counted many friends in Charleston and had no problem obtaining port clearance.[4]

The ship left Charleston on July 3 with all details taken care of. The first leg of the journey passed without incident. On July 22, after eighteen days, the yacht reached Trinidad, the British sugar colony near the northeastern coast of South America. It remained in port five days and took on 1,200 gallons of water. Corrie entertained visitors, including the governor and his sister, and told them that he was heading for Saint Helena Island, a remote spot in the South Atlantic Ocean where Napoleon had been exiled. For unknown reasons, the ship left on July 25 without obtaining port clearance. And instead of Saint Helena, Corrie set course directly for the coast of Africa.[5]

Although the *Wanderer* was a yacht and flew the Stars and Stripes and the burgee of the New York Yacht Club, there was no guarantee that it wouldn't be stopped by a British cruiser. With the sharp increase in slave-trade activity to Cuba in the mid-1850s, mostly in ships flying the U.S. flag, the British became more aggressive. In early 1858 Lord Francis Napier, the British minister to the United States, wrote several letters to Secretary of State Lewis Cass stating that the U.S. flag was being prostituted for the slave trade. Napier also claimed that Great Britain had a "right of visit," which allowed its officers to board and examine the registry and clearance papers of any suspicious ship to verify ownership.

If it were U.S. owned and the papers were in order, the British officer would leave the ship immediately, regardless of any evidence that it was a slaver. However, if the papers did not match the nationality of the flag, the British officer, according to Napier, had the right of search and, if circumstances warranted, seizure.[6]

Cass denied any right of the British navy to stop, no less search U.S. ships. He claimed that getting Spain to live up to her treaties was the real cure for the slave trade as all slave ships at the time were going to Cuba. Cass also claimed that the United States would never surrender the policing of the oceans to another country: "To permit a foreign officer to board the vessel of another power, to assume command in her, to call for and examine her papers, to pass judgment upon her character, to decide the broad inquiry whether she is navigated according to law, and to send her in at pleasure for trial, cannot be submitted to by any independent nation without injury and dishonor." He added, "Search, or visit, it is equally an assault upon the independence of nations."[7]

Despite the rebuke by Cass, British officers were reluctant to ignore ships that they thought to be slavers simply because they flew the U.S. flag. Besides, the crews of British cruisers received cash prizes for recaptured Africans, so the officers continued to exceed their authority. Charles Lamar had stressed to potential investors the importance of first sending a ship to Africa to preorder slaves to avoid waiting along the coast for three or four weeks and raising the suspicions of the squadrons. But he never did this for the *Wanderer*. The yacht would have to wait, as the demand for Africans by Cuba and the French colonies outpaced the supply.[8]

The trade continued to have a devastating impact on Africa. Tribes attacked each other to supply the slave marts, as they had done for hundreds of years. One missionary reported, "It is customary among the natives, whenever they take prisoners in war, to kill all the old people and small children—all who cannot be sold to slave-traders. The rest, both male and female, are generally sent to the slave marts on the coast, and sold to regular traders. And thus, for centuries have the degraded children of Africa been engaged in this abominable traffic, which has been the direct cause of most of the wars that have so extensively prevailed among the native inhabitants of this fertile and beautiful country."[9]

Another observer wrote, "I can testify, what no one can deny, that the battles and sieges which supply Europeans with slaves, or apprentices, *destroy from two to four persons* for every laborer who reaches the plantations in [the American hemisphere]. In one journey of sixty miles, viz: from

Badagry to Abbeokuta [in present-day Nigeria], I counted the sites of no less than eighteen towns and villages which have been laid in ruins to supply slaves for the markets of Brazil and Cuba. I found similar desolations in every country which I visited."[10]

Of course, neither Corrie, Farnum, Danese, the rest of the *Wanderer* crew, nor anyone involved in the trade cared about the decimation of Africa. They had business to conduct, and they needed to place an order and avoid the U.S. and British cruisers until they picked up their cargo.

———————

On September 16, 1858, two and a half months after departing from Charleston, the *Wanderer* entered the mouth of the Congo River, which had become the center of the African slave trade. The river had countless tributaries with banks covered in lush trees and bushes, making it impossible for the squadron ships to patrol them thoroughly. Slave dealers could easily hide their barracoons and canoes, and slave ships could anchor undetected while awaiting delivery.[11]

Not all slave dealers operated in secret, as any ship entering the Congo River in 1858 learned. A reporter traveling with the U.S. squadron observed "several large comfortable houses, over which floated the French flag. These houses are barracoons for the reception of the French emigrants, or rather slaves, which are brought down the river and delivered for embarkation at this point." The French did their trading in apprentices openly and in defiance of all, thanks to their agreement with Great Britain whereby the British ignored the French emigrant ships as long as the English could send East Indian laborers to the colonies in the West Indies.[12]

The *Wanderer* continued up the river for about thirty miles and anchored that evening off Pont du Lain, also known as Punta de Lehna, near a "factory." Although both legitimate businesses and barracoons were called factories, this was a well-known stop for slavers and was undoubtedly where Corrie placed an order with a Portuguese or Spanish slave dealer for about five hundred slaves. The dealer told him to return in four weeks to a specified location and wait for a message from shore for the time and place of delivery. After a glass of wine, the slave dealer sent his order to the interior. Within days tribal chiefs would gather their armies and continue to degrade the children of Africa.[13]

The ship remained at Pont du Lain for a week as the men rested and Corrie held parties for the white inhabitants of the area. They took on water and wood and on Thursday, September 23, moved down the river and anchored about fifteen miles from a town by Medova Creek. Soon, Corrie received a visit from the first lieutenant of the British frigate HMS *Medusa*, which was patrolling the river for slavers and curious about the presence of a yacht flying the flags of the United States and the New York Yacht Club. The officer extended an invitation to Corrie from Commander Charles Wise to visit the *Medusa* the next day.[14]

Corrie paid his respects to the commodore and, ever the gracious host, invited Wise and two of his officers to dine on the *Wanderer* that evening. During the meal, John Farnum suggested to the British officers that they might want to search the yacht to satisfy themselves that it wasn't a slaver. The British officers enjoyed the joke.[15]

Wise must have suspected the *Wanderer*'s true purpose—that was his job—but the yacht was flying the U.S. flag and gave no outward appearance of being a slaver. He couldn't justify searching the ship without causing another outrage as he had a few months earlier. Wise, as commander of the HMS *Vesuvius* in October 1857, boarded the merchant ship *Bremen*, which was flying the Stars and Stripes. He told the captain, whom he believed to be Portuguese, that he was seizing the vessel without examining the ship's papers. Wise gave the captain the choice of surrendering under the U.S. flag and being tried as a pirate in U.S. courts, or being taken without nationality, in which case he and his crew would be set free. The captain ordered the first mate to take down the flag and throw it and the ship's papers overboard. Wise deposited the captain and his men on shore to find their way home. On hearing of the incident, the commanding officer of the U.S. squadron sent a letter of protest to the commanding officer of the British station, and Secretary of State Cass formally complained to British minister Lord Napier. Although Wise was not reprimanded, he certainly would have been reluctant to seize the *Wanderer* without more evidence. However, word that the *Wanderer* was a slaver spread among the squadron, probably started by Wise.[16]

The next evening, September 25, Corrie and several of his men dined with Wise on the *Medusa*. The following day, with his social duties completed, Corrie ordered the *Wanderer* to sea to kill time and stay out of sight of cruisers. They sailed south and crossed paths with the schooner *Margate*. A challenge to a race was offered and accepted. It wasn't a contest as the *Wanderer* "passed her like the wind." Eight days later, on October 4, they reached Benguela, and sail master Briggs stopped recording entries in the yacht's log. The ship soon turned around to pick up its cargo.[17]

By mid-October the *Wanderer* arrived at the Congo River and signaled the slave dealer on shore, who sent a messenger to inform Corrie when and where to pick up the captives. The crew then removed the bulkheads in the hold and built a slave deck. Commodore Wise later reported that he could hear the hammering on the river at night, but he never explained why he didn't attempt to follow and capture the yacht after she took on Africans, which would have saved close to five hundred souls from the Middle Passage and earned his crew a considerable amount of prize money.[18]

On the morning of October 17 the *Wanderer* sailed to the designated area while the slave dealer's men scattered along the coast to watch for cruisers. When the *Wanderer* arrived, canoes emerged from behind sand banks and ferried 487 Africans to the yacht.[19]

The captives most likely wore ankle restraints to prevent an escape from the canoes. When they reached the ship, the manacles were removed to allow the slaves to climb a ladder to the deck. During the voyage, they may have been shackled to prevent a mutiny. However, not all slavers kept the captives bound. Some captains didn't like carrying cuffs because they were solid proof of slave trading if found by a squadron search party. One captain claimed that the slaves would die if bound for a long period of time and instead had the crew enforce rigorous discipline. Another captain stated that tribes from certain regions of Africa were more docile and less likely to rebel, so they didn't need to be shackled. Still other captains relied on a new invention, "a kind of small nail, so made that the points stand upright when thrown down, so that in case of revolt among the negroes aboard the ship, they are strewn thickly over the deck."[20]

Either the slaves arrived naked at the ship, or their clothes were taken from them as they boarded, presumably to prevent anyone from hiding weapons or other contraband. They were sent down the gangway stairs and directed by crewmen onto the slave deck and floor. They were bunched together as closely as possible and kept out of sight until the ship cleared the coast. An iron-grated hatch kept them from escaping and also limited the circulation of fresh air into the stifling hold.[21]

As the crew finished boarding the slaves—which probably took about four hours—and got the *Wanderer* under way, they realized that they had been spotted by a cruiser. The ss *Vincennes* had just rescued stranded crewmembers from a U.S. merchant ship that the British had burned because they deemed it a slaver when they came across the yacht. Corrie and his crew hardly broke a sweat. According to fleet flag officer Thomas A. Conover, "The *Vincennes* gave the *Wanderer* a hot chase, but the yacht being the faster vessel, she escaped." Corrie probably had a good laugh as the cruiser faded from sight. He had his cargo and was headed home.[22]

For certain, the Africans weren't laughing. An estimation of the space per person reveals some of the horrors of the Middle Passage. While the overall length of the schooner measured 114 feet, most of the excess space between that and the length on keel was occupied by the forepeak and lazarette—storage areas for the ship's sails and other equipment. Therefore, the total available space within the hold roughly equaled the length on keel of ninety-five feet. However, the captain's cabin was left intact, presumably for sleeping quarters for Corrie, his guests, and the crew, which would have taken up at least ten to fifteen feet of the length of the hold. Also, about five feet of open space around the aft gangway would have been needed, leaving about seventy-five feet for a slave deck.[23]

The hold at its widest point was 26½ feet, but it tapered toward the front and rear of the ship. Provision for an aisle the length of the hold had to be made for access to the fore gangway. Thus, the slave deck on the starboard and port sides could have been eight to ten feet wide, enough for each to hold two rows of people. In this manner, there could be eight rows, seventy-five to eighty feet long, available for 487 captives—two rows each on the port and starboard sides on the floor and slave decks—allowing for sixty-one people per row.

This would give each human about fifteen inches of deck space, not enough to lie flat on one's back to sleep. So the slaves had to lie on their sides (the right side being mandated by the crew, as it was considered best for blood circulation and heart function), pressed against the person in front, spoon-style. They slept on the hard plank floors in tropical heat with the sole ventilation coming through the iron-grated hatch. Sitting up during the day was slightly less confining, as the slave deck would have left about four feet of clearance for each level. Only the death of fellow captives provided more room.[24]

To keep order in the hold, the crew might appoint a few Africans "constables," arm them with whips, and pay them with a piece of clothing for their efforts. Women and children—a significant minority of the cargo—were usually separated from the older boys and men, either in a separate cabin, if one existed, or at the fore end of the hold, or on the top deck if no room existed between decks. In that case the crew would cover them with a tarp for protection in bad weather.[25]

Taking care of hundreds of captives for six weeks required a strict routine and absolute obedience. Since so many people could not fit on the top deck at the same time, they had to be brought up in groups for meals, a health inspection, and a little exercise, most likely dancing. During the morning shift each gang was hosed down with seawater and given a mouthwash of vinegar to prevent scurvy. They typically ate a breakfast of rice or farina with beans. The food, cooked in boilers on the brick stoves, was served in "kids" or wooden bowls shared by ten people using wooden spoons. After the meal each captive received between a half pint and a pint of water. Then they were examined by the "doctor" (in the *Wanderer*'s case, probably one of the two Englishmen) and given medicine if necessary. This process was repeated for each gang and took hours. At some point during the morning, healthy slaves carried up the sick and lifeless to the top deck, and the doctor decided who could be saved and who should be tossed overboard. If the Africans were well behaved, the crew allowed them access to the top deck in shifts during the day for fresh air. If any slave showed the slightest resistance to any order, the boatswain would whip him into submissiveness. The second and last meal of the day began at three to four o'clock, with the same serving routine and food, and with perhaps some scraps of dried beef. Before sundown, the slaves returned to their assigned places in the hold. The logistics of moving around so many people from one deck to another and feeding and otherwise caring for them seems daunting, yet crews of only ten to fourteen men had been doing it for hundreds of years with relatively few successful mutinies.[26]

Empty food barrels became toilets, which were placed on the top deck and in the hold, likely in the aisle. In the evening the barrels were emptied over the side and then sprinkled with chloride of lime, as were the decks where the barrels stood. The most common sicknesses on a slave ship were dysentery and diarrhea. At night the afflicted had neither the strength nor time to get to the barrels. Considering this, despite daily washings of the decks, the average death rate of 15 to 20 percent during the Middle Passage seems conservative.[27]

Such was the daily routine. Over the next six weeks, seventy-eight souls perished, about a 16 percent rate, and received watery burials. Losses of this size were considered acceptable to the slave trader—a cost of doing business—as the expeditions would still produce enormous profits if the survivors could be sold at $650 each, as Lamar planned.

Toward the end of the voyage the *Wanderer* suffered weather-related damage and needed repairs badly. After forty-three days, however, the crew finally spotted the coast of Georgia. Corrie had outsmarted the squadrons and brought home a cargo of Africans. All he had to do was land them. Then Charles Lamar would handle the distribution. In the late afternoon of November 28, 1858, Corrie brought the ship to anchor near the Little Cumberland Island lighthouse, across the Saint Andrews Sound from Jekyll Island. He waited for a pilot to take the *Wanderer* to the creek on the landward side of the island, hidden from view of passing ships. It was almost time to celebrate.

CHAPTER 10

"I Tell You Hell Is to Pay"

November–December 1858

Jekyll is one of a string of islands along the Georgia coast stretching from Tybee at the mouth of the Savannah River south to Cumberland near the Florida border. Immediately to the north of Jekyll is Saint Simons Island, which in 1859 was home to the largest Sea Island cotton plantations in the state and inhabited mostly by enslaved workers and their families. To the south, separated by the two-mile-wide Saint Andrews Sound, lies Little Cumberland Island, which at the time didn't have much more than a lighthouse. The Atlantic Ocean borders the eastern coast of Jekyll Island, and Jekyll Creek separates the western shore from Turtle Island and the mainland. The town of Brunswick, the only Atlantic port in Georgia other than Savannah, is about a ten-mile boat ride away. Jekyll was remote and desolate—a perfect place to land an illegal cargo.

The Dubignon siblings—John, Henry (whom Charles had shot in the eye in January 1858), and Katharine—owned Jekyll Island. John, the only one to live there, ran the plantation. Charles Lamar had anticipated the approximate arrival date of the *Wanderer* and had Henry and John place a notice in the *Savannah Daily Morning News* warning all persons "against landing on the Island of Jekyl, for the purpose of gunning, cutting wood, removing wrecks, or in any way trespassing on said island. . . . Captains of coasting vessels will pay particular attention."[1]

When no pilot came out to take the *Wanderer* across the sound to Jekyll Creek, William Corrie and Seth Briggs, with four oarsmen, took one of the yacht's rowboats to Little Cumberland Island. They met Horatio H. Harris, a pilot from nearby Brunswick who had stopped on the island on his way to Fernandina, and Corrie introduced himself as Captain Cook. He explained that he was escorting a group of men on a pleasure excursion and needed someone to take his yacht across Saint Andrews Sound. The three men walked to the beach so Harris could see the yacht, but, as it was dark, he refused the request. Corrie convinced Harris to take him and Briggs to Jekyll Island and the house of John Dubignon. During the trip Corrie said he wanted to engage Harris as a pilot the next day. Harris replied that he would go if the ship were not a slaver, a curious comment as it indicated that the landing site of the *Wanderer* was not a well-kept secret. Corrie joked that unfortunately the ship was not, as he would like to bring in forty thousand slaves. Harris then told Corrie that James Clubb, the regular Cumberland Island lighthouse keeper who was more experienced with Saint Andrews Sound, might bring in the ship. When they found Clubb, Corrie, still calling himself Cook, asked him to pilot the yacht that night as he was out of water and provisions. Clubb offered to do it the next morning. Corrie had no choice but to accept. From there the men went to the Dubignon house and met the Dubignon brothers and Nelson Trowbridge. Corrie then revealed to Clubb that the ship was the *Wanderer* and there were Africans on board—first calling them slaves and then referring to them as African apprentices. Clubb immediately backed out of the job. Corrie begged him, as without Clubb's help he would be forced to go to Port Royal, South Carolina, or Cuba. Clubb reconsidered, but he asked for $500 for the service, which normally cost $15. Trowbridge objected, but the Dubignons approved the charge.[2]

At five o'clock the next morning, Monday, November 29, Clubb started taking the *Wanderer* across the bar. On the way, he saw several crewmen throw a dead African overboard. At nine o'clock he anchored at the mouth of the Little Satilla River on the western side of the island, one to two hundred yards from shore. Using the yacht's two rowboats and one of John Dubignon's yawls, the crew ferried the Africans to land.

Harris, who was present at the landing, gawked at the sight of four hundred mostly naked Africans standing on the beach. Briggs told him that they had taken on 490 "savages" from the Congo River but lost about 80 on the voyage. Harris also had a brief conversation with Corrie's two English guests as they watched the crew, scruffy from not having shaved or had haircuts in weeks, move the Africans off the beach to a camp with a cover made of a vessel's sails tied to trees. Harris then joined Clubb aboard the yacht. It appeared to him that the Africans had access to the entire ship; he saw no evidence that they had been manacled or bound, but the boat was so filthy and smelled so bad that he couldn't remain. Corrie emerged from his cabin and the three men went ashore. Soon afterward, Clubb took the *Wanderer* and part of the crew a few miles up the Little Satilla River so the men could scrub and disinfect the yacht, replace all the bulkheads, and return it to a semblance of its original state. The rest of the crew remained at Jekyll and guarded the Africans.

Both Trowbridge and Nicholas Danese left Jekyll to alert Charles Lamar of the *Wanderer*'s return, although they didn't travel together. Danese caught a steamer at Jekyll Island Creek in the early morning hours of Tuesday, November 30, and reached Savannah late that night. It is unknown how Trowbridge got there.³ Lamar must have jumped for joy when the men arrived at his office and informed him of the *Wanderer*'s arrival. He had already chartered the steam tug *Lamar* (not owned by him or his father), and about two o'clock in the morning of December 1, he, Danese, Trowbridge, and Lamar's friend John F. Tucker began their trip to Jekyll Island. Piloted by Captain Luke Christie, they arrived that night after stopping at Brunswick to pick up Thomas Burke, another friend of Lamar. The men visited the camp the next morning. One can only imagine the look on Lamar's bearded face when he first saw the mass of black, mostly naked humanity. After failing twice with the *Rawlins* and fighting publicly with Howell Cobb over his "rights," he finally had his Africans. He knew his money problems soon would be over.⁴

On the morning of December 3 the crewmen who had remained on Jekyll packed three hundred Africans, now dressed in coarse clothing or blankets, onto the *Lamar*. At eleven o'clock, Lamar, Tucker, Danese, Farnum, and the crewmen boarded the tug for the return journey to Savannah.⁵

The *Lamar* entered the Savannah River late that night or the next, and no port employee thought to stop the familiar boat. The tug passed Savannah and dropped off Lamar at the Coleraine plantation six miles west of the city on the Georgia side of the river. Christie then piloted the ship ten more miles to a landing on the Carolina side of the river, opposite John Tucker's plantation. The white men led the Africans to a camp on Union plantation, owned by John Montmollin.⁶

Montmollin was a longtime Savannah resident deeply involved in the business community and civic life. Along with his South Carolina plantation, he owned a slave mart and an auctioneering business in town. He was the president of the Mechanics Savings Bank, for which his friend John Tucker served as a director, and was a board member of the Savannah Water Works. Despite all his success and prominence, he partnered with Lamar in the two *Rawlins* expeditions and then in the *Wanderer* venture, offering his plantation as a drop-off point.⁷

Another steam tug had arrived at Jekyll Island on December 2 and anchored near the *Lamar*. A few hours after the *Lamar* departed on December 3, the other tug headed up the Satilla River, carrying an estimated sixty Africans.⁸ About a week after the two tugs left, Henry Dubignon had his brother-in-law, Dr. Robert Hazlehurst, examine the remaining forty captives. Aided by two Jekyll Island slaves who understood the Africans' language, he treated several cases of diarrhea and skin disease, which were contracted during the voyage. This group would remain well hidden on Jekyll for three months.[9]

———————

After the crew scrubbed out six weeks' worth of waste, grime, and stink and restored the hold of the ship, the *Wanderer* returned to the mouth of the Satilla River. William Corrie, who had remained on Jekyll awaiting the yacht, had a decision to make. Slaver captains usually burned and sank their ships after they completed their missions in the Caribbean or South America, as the vessel could serve as evidence against the owners and crew in a trial. The dollar loss would be insignificant in light of the revenues generated. But Corrie, likely at the insistence of Lamar, who loved the yacht, didn't do this. Instead, he tried to get the schooner back to the safety of his home port of Charleston, where, with his contacts, he would have a much better chance of clearing customs and avoiding snooping inspectors. Corrie didn't think the damaged ship could make it to Charleston, so he opted to have it towed to the nearby port of Brunswick.[10]

On December 5, with Corrie and the remaining crew aboard, a hired pilot took the *Wanderer* to Brunswick harbor. Soon after anchoring, the crew departed, most likely for New York or New Orleans and another slaving voyage. Corrie checked in with port collector Woodford Mabry and explained that he was bound for Charleston but came into Brunswick due to weather-related damage. He told Mabry that he had just returned from Saint Helena Island, but the American consul wasn't there to clear the *Wanderer*. However, he produced clearance papers from Charleston to Trinidad, and Trinidad to Saint Helena, and the ship register and crew list from Charleston. Corrie requested clearance from Brunswick so he could have the ship towed to Charleston for repairs. Mabry knew the weather along the coast had been bad and, believing it to be the cause of the damage, gave Corrie clearance. Corrie immediately wired Lamar, asking him to send a steam tug to Brunswick to tow the *Wanderer*.[11]

During the rest of that day, Mabry heard rumors that the *Wanderer* had come in over the Saint Andrews bar and landed Africans. The next day he decided to perform a closer inspection of the yacht but still saw no evidence that she had carried slaves. He reexamined the ship documents and realized that there was no consular seal affixed to the Trinidad clearance papers. This, coupled with the lack of clearance from Saint Helena and the fact that the crew had disappeared, motivated Mabry to write to

U.S. district attorney Joseph Ganahl in Savannah and ask if he should seize the yacht. After he mailed the letter he decided to hold the *Wanderer* until he heard back from Ganahl.[12]

━━━━━━━

On December 7, with the Africans safely at Montmollin's South Carolina plantation and their duties completed, Nicholas Danese and two crewmen took a boat to Savannah to catch a ship to New York the next day. They arrived at the City Hotel on Bay Street sometime before three o'clock in the afternoon, dressed raggedly and unshaven. Danese registered them as Nicholas Brown, Juan Rajesta, and Miguel Arguirvi, all of New Orleans. That evening the three men entered Price's clothing store and bought genteel suits, for which Danese paid with gold coins, and left. Proprietor William O. Price had heard rumors of a cargo of Africans being landed somewhere on the Georgia coast and, knowing that these were seafaring men, became suspicious.[13]

U.S. district attorney Joseph Ganahl also had heard the rumors. He had been born in Savannah in 1828, the son of one of the first German cotton buyers to settle there. He studied medicine but eventually read law and became a lawyer. In 1852 he purchased an interest in the *Georgian* newspaper but only held it for a year. He was a staunch member of the Democratic Party and often served in an official capacity at their meetings. In 1856 he was appointed with John Montmollin and others to the committee to host the Southern Commercial Convention. In October 1857 Ganahl was appointed the U.S. district attorney for Georgia. He certainly knew of Lamar's undisguised public attempts to engage in the international slave trade.[14]

When informed on the morning of December 8, probably by the owner of the clothing store, of three sunburned, unkempt sailors who came to town the previous day, purchased stylish clothes with gold coins, and were due to sail to New York at noon that day, Ganahl commandeered U.S. marshal Daniel Stewart and confronted the three strangers at the City Hotel. Danese, the only one who spoke English, refused to answer Ganahl's questions, explaining that he was new in town and knew no one. Ganahl arrested the men and took them to the commissioner's office where he drafted an affidavit and a warrant. John Owens, a well-known criminal defense lawyer who often did work for the Lamars, walked in, claimed that he represented the men, and demanded bail. U.S. commissioner Charles Seton Henry refused the request and set hearings on the

Wanderer to begin in ten days, on December 18. Ganahl had no doubt that the rumors were true and that these men, along with Lamar and others, were involved in the importation of Africans. Stewart escorted the men to the jail, and Ganahl started gathering evidence.[15]

Five days later, on December 13, Ganahl received Mabry's letter regarding the *Wanderer*. He immediately wrote back, concerned that Mabry might have given the yacht clearance, and told him to seize it if it was still in port. Ganahl also informed Mabry of the arrest of the three men and that he was sending down a deputy marshal with open subpoenas ordering an appearance before Commissioner Henry. He asked Mabry to write in the names of any person who he thought might know about the landing of the Africans and deliver them. Ganahl also explained that he was dispatching the revenue cutter *Dobbin* to tow the yacht to Savannah.[16]

The deputy marshal arrived in Brunswick the next day, where he and Mabry confiscated the *Wanderer*'s logbook, charts, and other written memoranda, as well as a trunk of Corrie's personal effects, and had the yacht towed to Savannah. The deputy marshal then traveled to Jekyll Island with five crewmen from the *Dobbin*. They spent a day searching for Africans but returned to Savannah empty-handed.[17]

William Corrie did not witness the seizure of the yacht. Charles Lamar had sent a tug to Brunswick to tow the *Wanderer* to Charleston, but a guard refused to give it up. With the *Wanderer*'s port clearance withdrawn, Corrie left Brunswick and next appeared in South Carolina to pick up his share of the cargo—thirty-eight Africans—which, according to Lamar, he quickly sold before he proceeded to Charleston.[18]

Supercargo J. Egbert Farnum likely left Montmollin's plantation for Savannah on one of Montmollin's flat boats the day after he arrived—December 4 or 5—as he caught a ship to Charleston on December 6, the day before Danese, Arguirvi, and Rajesta arrived in town. He remained in Charleston one week before sailing to New York.[19]

By mid-December 1858 all of the *Wanderer* crew, other than the three in the Savannah jail, had disappeared, as had Corrie's two English guests, Brent and Beman. District Attorney Ganahl must have known that he would never find the other crewmen, and he didn't seem too concerned about Farnum. But he wanted in the worst way to lay his hands on Corrie and the man he knew to be behind the expedition, Charles Lamar.

By this time, news of the *Wanderer* began spreading beyond the Georgia coast. On Saturday, December 11, friends of Corrie, on hearing of the successful landing, held a party in his honor at Brown's Hotel in Washington, D.C. During his trip to New York, supercargo Farnum told a newspaper reporter about the highlights of the trip, including interactions with the officers of the *Medusa*, the race with a British yacht, and a tour of the African countryside, where they visited with "native princes in their palaces." The story was soon printed in newspapers around the country.[20]

An actual successful landing of Africans on U.S. soil—the first in decades—started to grab hold of the American conscience.

———————

On the morning of December 13, Captain Hillary Fraser piloted a steam tug from Savannah up the Savannah River with instructions to pick up a gang of blacks under the supervision of a white man on the South Carolina side of the river and take them to Hamburg, South Carolina, near Augusta. Before reaching the group, Fraser was flagged down by several men—one of them Charles Lamar—at Coleraine plantation. Fraser took them on and continued west until he saw a white man with a huge group of blacks. Fraser boarded them and returned to Coleraine to drop off the white men he previously took on there, except Lamar. Then he proceeded to Hamburg. On December 14 he deposited all the passengers at a woodyard owned by Charles's cousins, Thomas and Robert Lamar.[21]

Charles Lamar tried his best to conceal the landing in Hamburg, but on December 14, soon after they arrived, a man from Augusta sent Joseph Ganahl a letter describing a delivery of Africans in South Carolina on property belonging to Thomas and Robert Lamar. The next day an Augusta newspaper reported "that about two hundred and seventy of the wild Africans . . . are now on a plantation in South Carolina, two or three miles below this city . . . and we suppose will soon be offered for sale. Indeed, we are informed that sales have already been made of some of the cargo."[22] Despite the letter and the newspaper report, there is no record of any state or federal officers attempting to seize the Africans, or requests by Ganahl to those authorities to do so.

The effort to distribute the Hamburg Africans did not go well. Lamar's boast that he could sell them as fast as they landed for $650 each did not materialize, and he had to leave the unsold slaves in the hands of Tom Lamar so he could return to Savannah to deal with his mounting legal problems.[23] Charles arrived home on December 18, the first day of Commissioner Henry's hearings, and immediately wrote to Trowbridge—probably at Jekyll Island—with a bleak report. "I returned this morning from Augusta. I distributed the negroes the best I could but I tell you things are in a hell of a fix. No certainty about anything. The Government . . . are determined to press matters to the utmost extremity. The yacht has been seized, the examination commenced today, & will continue for 30 days, at the rate they are going on. They have all the pilots and men who took the yacht to Brunswick here to testify. *She will be lost certain and sure*, if not the negroes. . . . I don't calculate to get a new dollar for an old one—all of the men must be *bribed*. . . . Ganahl is doing his damndest, but I keep pretty well posted as to what he is doing." Lamar also commented on the status of the Africans. "Six of those left at Monts, who were sick, died yesterday. I think the whole of them will die that are now sick. They are too enfeebled to administer medicine to. I am paying 50c per day each for all those I took up the country—it was the best I could do. It won't take long at that rate for a large bill to run up." As was his style, Charles blamed someone else for all the problems. "I tell you Hell is to pay. I don't think they will discharge the men [Danese, Rajesta, and Arguirvi], but turn them over for trial. If so there's no telling when we can dispose of the negroes. If Danese had gone away as I told him to do all would have been well now."[24]

At some point during the trip to Hamburg, Lamar gave Captain Fraser an African boy as a gift. After Fraser returned to Savannah, word of the boy's presence spread about town. A local newspaper even reported it. Soon, crowds started appearing at Fraser's house to see a real African. The situation got so bothersome that Fraser asked Lamar to take back the gift.[25]

Sightings of the Africans were soon reported. One individual was spotted in Macon on the railroad traveling toward Columbus. Forty Africans were seen on a train in Atlanta, on their way to Montgomery. A correspondent for the *New York Times* saw a gang of Africans coming from Macon and passing through Montgomery, where they were put on a steamer to go down the Alabama River.[26]

In all likelihood Montmollin and Tucker kept for themselves the estimated thirty Africans left at Montmollin's plantation. Dr. W. H. Duke, John Tucker's physician at Drakies plantation, would testify that he examined fifteen or sixteen sick slaves for Montmollin in mid-December, probably after the Hamburg group had been shipped, but he wouldn't swear that they were Africans. He also attended to three slaves on Tucker's plantation who resembled the ones he saw at Montmollin's. He saw only the sick individuals, not healthy ones. Montmollin eventually sold most or all of the Africans left with him to an unnamed person in Florida.[27]

Just three weeks after the landing of the Africans, the scheme was un-raveling. Crewmen had been arrested, the yacht had been seized, sales of the slaves were going poorly, Lamar was spending much more money than he had planned, and the government lawyers were hot on his tail. His great triumph was turning into a personal hell.

CHAPTER 11

"She Could Not Possibly Accommodate More Than Half That Number"

December 1858–January 1859

As Joseph Ganahl gathered evidence, he acquired some valuable legal assistance. U.S. attorney general Jeremiah S. Black appointed highly respected Savannahian Henry Rootes Jackson as a special prosecutor to the case. Secretary of the Treasury Howell Cobb gave port collector John Boston, Ganahl, and Jackson the authority to enforce the law in the *Wanderer* case. Boston was named a special agent until a permanent one could be appointed.[1]

On Saturday, December 18, Commissioner Henry commenced hearings to determine if enough evidence existed to send the case of Brown (the name Danese gave to authorities), Rajesta, and Arguirvi to a grand jury. Attorneys Thomas Lloyd and John Owens defended the three crewmen and were in all likelihood paid by Lamar. There was an unwritten understanding between slave-ship owners and their crews: if apprehended, crewmen denied every allegation and never named names, and owners paid for the best legal defense and support during incarceration. It was policy at the Savannah jail to provide all the food, drink, and other provisions that a prisoner or his associates could pay for. After locking up the three men, jailor Charles Van Horn was ordered by U.S. marshal Stewart to give them every comfort, no doubt at the request of Lamar. Van Horn delivered to the prisoners claret, cigars, beef, bread, coffee, and other provisions and even had a new floor installed in the damp cell.[2]

The first four witnesses at the hearings spoke openly of their experiences with the *Wanderer*. However, Horatio Harris, the first person to see Corrie after the yacht's return, refused to answer questions on the grounds that he might "criminate" himself. The attorneys debated if Harris should be forced to testify. Commissioner Henry sided with the prosecution, but Harris still wouldn't talk. Jackson then requested a week's postponement, which the commissioner granted, giving Harris time to rethink his position and Ganahl and Jackson additional time to gather evidence.[3]

More than anything else, Ganahl had to prove that the *Wanderer* landed Africans on Georgia soil. He had Marshal Stewart deputize Edward Gordon, a Savannah policeman, to go to Jekyll Island to serve subpoenas to the Dubignons and find Africans. Gordon brought a friend. While walking on a dirt road, they saw in the distance a large group of blacks dancing around a fire. The blacks saw the white strangers and scattered. Gordon and his assistant searched the area and found a black boy who spoke no English. The men took possession of him and continued scouting. They eventually located John and Henry Dubignon, and Gordon handed them subpoenas. Then Gordon, his friend, and the boy returned to Brunswick to catch a steamer to Savannah. Gordon had an argument with the boat captain over the need for port clearance to bring the African to Savannah, which delayed them one day. The three finally arrived in town on the Gulf Railroad on Christmas Eve. Gordon took the boy to the Barracks, a former federal army facility where the Savannah police were quartered, and into the care of Marshal Stewart. Ganahl was ecstatic. He had his evidence.[4] On Christmas day Ganahl wrote to U.S. attorney general Black that an African boy had been seized and placed in the custody of Marshal Stewart. He added confidently, "The machinery of the land is just commencing to work and our prospects are brightening hourly. I believe I may promise the law will be practically enforced through much hard fighting and against a heavy tide of public opinion."[5]

Lamar knew that the evidence of an African in a trial would be damning. But Charles had friends, and it was time to call on them. As Ganahl celebrated the capture of the African, Marshal Stewart felt that the cell was too damp for a boy in such delicate health and, as a local newspaper explained, "From motives of humanity, placed him in the private lock-up of Mr. Geo. Wylly, where every necessary attention was given to his comfort." George Wylly, a friend and business associate of John Montmollin, was a slave broker. It was normal for men in that trade to have cells in their offices to hold slaves temporarily until they could be sold. Soon after the boy was transferred, the news of his existence spread through town, and Wylly decided to open his office for a public viewing. More than five hundred people filed past the smiling teenager, who repeated every word said to him. At eleven o'clock that night, Wylly went home, leaving Marshal Stewart and Simon, Wylly's trusted slave, in charge of the African. Stewart left shortly after Wylly. At midnight two white men and a black man knocked on the door. Simon called down from the second-floor window and asked their business. One of the white men said they wanted to lodge a slave for the night. Simon came downstairs, opened the door, and saw a pistol pointed at his head. Within minutes, the mysterious trio took possession of the boy and disappeared into the night.[6]

Ganahl and Jackson were incensed on learning of the loss of their evidence. They demanded that Secretary of the Treasury Cobb and Attorney General Black remove Stewart as U.S. marshal. Cobb replied to Jackson that James M. Spurlock, a fellow Georgian, had been designated as the replacement, but he first had to be confirmed by the U.S. Senate; until that happened, Spurlock should be employed as a special agent. For the time being, Stewart continued as the marshal.[7]

Ganahl and Jackson hardly had time to breathe after the loss of the young African as the commissioner's hearing restarted on December 29. Their problems continued. They first called pilot James Clubb, who also refused to testify for fear of incriminating himself. Judge Henry wanted to prevent more witnesses from claiming this defense and committed Clubb to prison until he agreed to talk. The next witness, Captain Hillary Fraser, testified about carrying blacks to a woodyard near Hamburg, South Carolina. Although he assumed that the boy given to him was an African, he could not judge the others.[8]

Luke Christie, who had piloted the tug *Lamar* from Savannah to Jekyll Island and back, also declined to testify for fear of incriminating himself. He worried that he might have broken the law by transporting slaves from one point in Georgia to another. Ganahl argued that this was not a violation of law and asked the court to instruct the witness to answer his questions. Christie still remained silent. An angry Ganahl glared alternately at him and the courtroom and declared, as a newspaper reported, "He should keep his eye on every one connected with this violation of the law of the land; and that as prosecuting officer of the Government, he would prosecute everyone connected with it, directly or indirectly, from the highest to the lowest. Witnesses might not be made to answer; juries might not give their verdicts; even the courts might not come up to the mark; but for him, thank God, he had taken an oath to perform his duty, and so help him God, so long as he had an arm to raise, or a voice to speak, he would perform it to the full extent of his ability."[9] The commissioner adjourned the court for the day.

Ganahl finally received some good news from the marshal in Macon, Georgia. Two Africans had been found unattended on a railroad car in Macon and taken into custody by a deputy marshal. The next day the deputy escorted the captives to Savannah, where they were met at the train station by ten officers dispatched by Stewart and John Boston. The Africans were taken to the Savannah jail and the care of jailer Charles Van

Horn. Ganahl had his living evidence again, and this time he wasn't letting go. He wrote to Van Horn to keep the Africans in custody, only to be
released on his order.[10]

———————

If Charles Lamar wanted the debate over reopening the slave trade to get
national attention, he succeeded. Newspapers throughout the country
covered the story of the *Wanderer*. Not surprisingly, most northern journals condemned the expedition and wondered if it prefaced a general
movement by the South. Several southern papers, including the *Georgia
Citizen, Macon State Press,* and *Savannah Daily Morning News,* hailed the
effort to reopen the trade. One reported, "This is only the 'beginning
of the end,' and we have not a word to say in condemnation of the act,
that will practically nullify an unconstitutional law against the South and
her institutions." Another echoed that sentiment and added, "The South
needs more slaves, and the General Government might as well attempt
to bridge the Atlantic as to try to prevent her from getting them. Our
anti-slave-trade laws must necessarily become a nullity; it is impossible
to enforce them." The Washington correspondent of the *Augusta Constitutionalist* opined, "The position of inequality which the people of the
South now occupy in the Union, under existing laws upon the subject
of slavery and the slave-trade, is beginning to be rather galling to the
Southern people. They must have an accelerated expansion of their peculiar institution."[11]

But many southern papers opposed the landing of Africans. The *Augusta Chronicle* editorialized that southern people "should not hesitate
to resort to any and all legitimate means to arrest at once and forever a
traffic so disastrous, if permitted, to the public [interest] of the South."
The *Montgomery Advertiser* asked, "But what would our readers think of
the destruction of a whole town by its neighbors in order to sell a rem-
nant of its inhabitants? . . . And yet it is by bloodshed and fire and rapine
that the slave ships of Africa are to be filled." The *Savannah Republican*
opined, "It is with much regret that we are compelled to believe that this
act has been perpetrated on Georgia soil. It has been our pride to know
that while the fanatics at the North were violent in their denunciation of
our 'peculiar institution,' and our Sister States of the South were trying
to lead us into favoring the extreme issues of the day, that Georgia stood
firm in her conservative principles; but we cannot now call upon other
States to do as we do, for we have broken the laws of our own land and
the laws of nations."[12]

There was one issue that most in the press, both North and South, agreed on—that a ship the size of the *Wanderer* simply could not have carried so many Africans as was being reported. The *New York Times* said of the rumored landing of hundreds of slaves: "They could not have been brought thither in so small a craft as a yacht." The paper went on to explain ways in which the yacht could have been used as a decoy for a larger vessel. A Charleston paper said, "We are authorized to state that the story about the yacht *Wanderer* bringing three hundred slaves to this country is simply ridiculous, from the fact that she could not possibly accommodate more than half that number. The truth of the matter, as we are informed, is that she had on board but eighty negroes."[13]

The outrage over the crime reached the highest level of government on January 7, 1859, when Senator William Seward of New York introduced a resolution in the U.S. Senate requesting that President James Buchanan release to the Senate any correspondence between Great Britain and the American minister in London "touching the abuses of the American flag in the prosecution of the African slave trade, on the coast of Africa, and especially touching the cruise of the *Wanderer* on that coast."[14] Buchanan replied that it was not yet compatible with the public interest to release such correspondence.

Lamar had certainly caught the nation's eye.

———

Captain Christie finally testified, as did ten other witnesses. On January 3, 1859, Commissioner Henry declared that based on the evidence presented, he had no hesitation in committing the prisoners to a grand jury of the U.S. district court.[15] Joseph Ganahl took comfort in the decision, but his work was just beginning. He had to build a case for a grand jury, a greater challenge than convincing the commissioner.

Lamar knew that Ganahl wanted his hide. He had written to Trowbridge that the government was "determined to press matters to the utmost extremity." He informed James Gardner, "The government is moving heaven and earth to execute the d—d infamous law." One wonders what Lamar expected from the district attorney once the crime became exposed, which it was bound to be.[16] But Lamar was a fighter, and he wasn't about to roll over. His first defensive ploy was to try to get southern opinion on his side. He asked Gardner, "Your paper [the *Augusta Constitutionalist*] could assist me . . . by boldly advocating the measure and counseling independent action upon the part of the people." He then wrote to his father in New York that a friend "advised the employment of prudence and no violence and the manufacture of public opinion by the employment of a man North to collate every act of injustice done to Southerners through their slave property in the last ten years and to crowd the Savannah papers with these extracts. Do you know where a man of that stamp can be found, and at what date?"[17]

Lamar needed much more than friendly editorials in the press. Soon he would have to take matters into his own hands.

CHAPTER 12

"I Am Afraid They Will Convict Me"

January–October 1859

Armed with the authority to take the *Wanderer* case to a grand jury, Joseph Ganahl petitioned the admiralty court to have the yacht declared a slaver and William Corrie extradited to face charges for his part in the crime. On January 8, 1859, Ganahl obtained a warrant for the arrest of Corrie, rumored to be in seclusion on Edisto Island, South Carolina, charging him with a violation of the Act of 1820. Five days later the warrant was presented to South Carolina district court judge Andrew Magrath, who, to Ganahl's amazement, refused to turn over Corrie, ruling instead that he should be tried in the district where he was arrested. Magrath did grant an order for Corrie's arrest and placed him in a Charleston jail.[1]

Corrie, however, did respond to a request for information through his lawyers and claimed that he had a one-eighth interest in the yacht; he did not name the other parties. The court directed U.S. marshal Daniel Stewart to publish a proclamation requiring all persons having or pretending to have an interest in the *Wanderer* to come forward and make their claim. Not surprisingly, no one did.[2]

Corrie's Georgia lawyers and Ganahl gave testimony to the clerk of the court. On February 25 admiralty court and U.S. district court judge John C. Nicoll, Charles Lamar's father-in-law, ruled that the *Wanderer* was employed in importing from a foreign country "negroes and persons of color" into the United States "to be held, sold and disposed of as slaves." He ordered the ship to be forfeited and sold by the U.S. marshal to the highest bidder at a public auction in front of the U.S. Custom House. Nicoll showed no favoritism to his daughter's husband. Charles was going to lose his beloved ship.[3]

Lamar was also facing prison time. Although he didn't make the trip to Africa, he faced many charges under the Act of 1818. The court ordered him to post bond to ensure his appearance at the grand jury hearings. Charles boasted to his father that he did not fear the trials, but later he admitted to Nicholas Danese, "I am afraid they will convict me, but my case is only 7 years & a fine. If I find they are likely to do so, I shall go to Cuba, until I make some compromise with the gov'mt. Matters look badly enough just now."[4]

Charles's creditors were unmoved by his problems. His partner in legal but equally unsuccessful businesses, James Gardner, kept hounding him to honor his debts. Lamar claimed, "If I can get through this venture with anything like luck and make anything, the same shall go towards the payment of my debts. I want it for nothing else. The government has pursued such a course that it has been impossible for me to realize any money." Tired of Lamar's excuses, Gardner presented $8,600 of his notes due at a New Orleans bank, but they were returned for nonpayment.[5]

As usual, Charles solicited his father's help. "I would like to be put into a position to make money enough to pay me out. Can't you devise some way—no retail business will do it." There is no record that Gazaway offered such an opportunity at that time.[6] Charles's money problems were compounded by troubles selling his share of the Africans. He had left them under the control of his thirty-two-year-old cousin Thomas Lamar in Hamburg, South Carolina. When Thomas had to leave town for several days, he entrusted them to a Mr. Tillman. Tillman charged Charles fifty cents a day each for upkeep and then refused to release them when Thomas returned. An enraged Charles told Thomas to deal with Tillman at once and look more carefully after his interests.[7]

Even after Tillman released the Africans, Charles had trouble making money, as Thomas was selling them for notes and not cash. Charles told him, "Don't sell any of the Negroes for anything but money. I would not give a damn for all the Notes that have been sent me. I want the money—*money* alone will pay my obligations. Keep the Negroes if they can't be sold for cash, & I will send them West." He also ordered his cousin to settle all other issues at once. "Don't let my interest suffer in the hands of these men—look after them." Two weeks later, Charles wrote again and in a more conciliatory tone assured Tom that he wasn't blaming him for the problems, but he claimed that the results of the African business had been disastrous. Charles also admitted to Theodore Johnston that he had yet to receive a dollar for any sales.[8] Tom finally sold the rest of the slaves, but not to Charles's satisfaction. Charles informed the incarcerated Nicholas Danese of his difficulties paying his obligations. "If I can do anything with the Notes, I can pay up, otherwise I cannot."[9]

Charles was particularly disturbed by the actions of his partners. He told Gardner, "My money, time and risks I have taken all gone to Hell, simply because parties in interest were too damned cowardly to stand up to their obligations. No one of them has come forward to pay up one cent of the moneys I have paid out, to take any of the responsibilities or to do any of the work." Similarly, Lamar wrote Danese, as recorded in the letter-book, "I have done all the work, taken all the responsibility & paid all the money, & shall make nothing, but on the contrary, shall lose a large portion of that I advanced for the Parties." As upset as Charles was with his associates, he had, of course, chosen them himself.[10]

———

As Lamar witnessed the *Wanderer* venture crumble around him, he still had enough self-confidence to pursue other slaving expeditions, though nothing ever came of them. On January 12, 1859, he responded to a request from John Scott, a retired lawyer and plantation owner from Virginia, with a proposal for a venture to the coast of Africa. In trying to sell his services, Charles admitted, "I know all the ins & outs of the matter . . . [from] my knowledge & experience which has cost me some $80,000 by making two unsuccessful [*Rawlins*] trips."[11] Surely, the *Wanderer* fiasco was adding to that total.

And Charles's current legal nightmare didn't prevent him from supporting fellow slave traders. In February 1859, in the midst of the first *Wanderer* grand jury, another grand jury considered the fate of the owners of the *Angelita*. On October 30, 1858, the ship arrived in Savannah. On January 19, 1859, port collector John Boston had the *Angelita* detained and charged owners Joachim Selvas, Charles Mares, and J. G. Cassimeras with fitting it out for the slave trade. On February 14 a grand jury returned indictments, called "true bills," against the defendants based on the testimony of the former master of the vessel. The next day Charles Lamar wrote a letter to the foreman of the grand jury, William H. Cuyler, a physician, former Savannah mayor and alderman, judge of the inferior court of Chatham County, and director of the Planters Bank. Charles claimed that the master had perjured himself, that the captain had offered him an interest in an expedition to Africa, but Charles, unhappy with the terms, turned him down. Lamar said that he subsequently discussed the *Angelita* venture with Messrs. Selves and Mares, who knew nothing about it. Not only was it highly unusual for a citizen to contact and give his opinion to a foreman of a sitting grand jury, but Lamar was perfectly candid in admitting that he tried to negotiate the terms of the illegal activity. A jury acquitted the defendants the following May.[12]

———

As Charles juggled all these issues, Joseph Ganahl forged ahead with the case. He impaneled a grand jury that, on February 13, 1859, found true bills against Corrie, Danese ("Brown"), Rajesta, and Arguirvi for piracy, which carried the death penalty. The prosecutors then began preparing their cases against the other participants, including Lamar, for an April grand jury.[13] With the government tightening the legal noose, Lamar started to fight back.

Soon after the February grand jury, Charles wrote to James Gardner that Trowbridge "left me to go after the Negroes on Jekyl Island—accompanied by Akin. He will have to wagon them all the way, as he is afraid to touch a Rail Road." The thirty-six Africans—thirty-five males and one female—had been living on Jekyll out of sight of the authorities for almost three months and were to be moved west. Richardson F. Akin, another Lamar friend and partner in the *Wanderer* scheme, shipped the Africans to the mainland, loaded them in three wagons driven by domestic slaves and started his trek.[14]

On March 1 word reached citizens in Jacksonville, Telfair County, southwest of Chatham County, that a white man was transporting a group of Africans westward across the state. Deputy Marshal John McRae raised a posse of four more men and caught up with Akin sixty miles farther west in Worth County, Georgia. McRae examined the blacks and, convinced that they were Africans, seized them. Akin protested, claiming that McRae had no warrant or any other authority to take them. The deputy marshal told Akin that he would hold the Africans until he got instructions from the U.S. marshal in Savannah. He took them back to Telfair County, put them in jail, and wired Marshal Daniel Stewart.[15] Akin camped outside of Jacksonville with the three domestic slaves while he waited to regain the property. On receiving McRae's request, Stewart wired Washington for instructions regarding the Africans. When he didn't receive a reply—it is not known how long he waited—he notified McRae to release the blacks. After a ten-day delay, Akin and his captives resumed their journey.[16]

Lamar fumed when informed of the actions of the posse, while Joseph Ganahl seethed on learning that Stewart had released the Africans. Still, the district attorney had five more witnesses of Africans in Georgia. He subpoenaed the Telfair County lawmen to testify before the next grand jury in April. Charles had one month to think of a way to silence them.

In the meantime, Lamar had other targets. On March 8 he and his friend John Tucker walked into magistrate John A. Staley's office and asked him to issue a writ of possession in favor of Lamar for the two Macon Africans sitting in the Savannah jail. Staley agreed and had a constable deliver the document. Marshal Stewart was at the jail when the constable presented the writ to jailer Charles Van Horn. Van Horn, who had been ordered by Ganahl not to release the Africans, asked Stewart and two other men to notify Ganahl that the Macon Africans were being taken and to come at once. If any of those men bothered to look for the district attorney, they didn't find him. Thirty minutes later, Stewart, Van Horn, and the two Africans, called Gumbo and Cuffee, sat with Lamar and Tucker in front of Justice Staley. The jailer asked Staley if he could have half an hour to find the district attorney. Staley gave him twenty minutes. Van Horn couldn't locate Ganahl in that time and returned to Staley's office.[17]

When the hearing began, Lamar claimed that the two black men were his slaves. Tucker, the only witness, swore that he knew the men to have been Lamar's property since December. Stewart acknowledged that he had no claim on them, and Staley awarded them to Lamar. Twenty minutes after the hearing began, Lamar and Tucker drove away with Gumbo and Cuffee. When Ganahl learned that he had lost his critical human evidence, he blamed both Van Horn and Stewart.

Four days later, on March 12, Lamar joined a huge crowd that turned out for the public auction of the *Wanderer* in front of the customhouse at Bay and Bull Streets. U.S. marshal Daniel Stewart, still in the job because James Spurlock hadn't yet posted bond for the position, stepped onto Captain Corrie's trunk, which had been seized with the yacht, waved his arms over his head, and quieted the crowd. He stepped aside and allowed Lamar to address the assemblage. Charles told the people that the yacht was rightfully his, taken away by the high hand of the law, and that no gentleman would allow the government to prevail by bidding against him. Lamar's public admission stunned one reporter for a northern newspaper, who wrote, "The statements made by Lamar at the sale . . . were amply sufficient if the law could but lay its 'high hand' upon him to convict him of piracy and to hang him therefore."[18]

The bidding began with Lamar offering $500. He awaited the striking of the gavel. To everyone's surprise, another man bid $800. It was Charles Van Horn, the jailer whom Lamar had recently humiliated in front of Justice Staley. Lamar bid $1,000, and from there the two men raised the stakes by $25 at a clip. When Lamar bid $4,000, Stewart struck the gavel, not giving Van Horn time to counter. Lamar then walked through the crowd and punched the jailer in the face, knocking him out, and drawing cheers from the crowd. Lamar had his yacht back, along with its tackle, apparel, furniture, and personal effects, though he paid $3,500 more than he had anticipated.

Lamar's performance made him the talk of the town, and he relished the attention. He wasn't finished. On Saturday, March 23, he took an

African boy, whom he kept for himself and called "Corrie," on a buggy ride around town. He made several stops and allowed the locals to gawk at the boy, who smiled, tipped his hat, and repeated the words that people spoke to him. Charles beamed at the youngster, who called him "Mass' Charlie." At one stop, port collector and Lamar foe John Boston approached the buggy and got a tip of the hat in the most accomplished manner. A reporter for the *Daily Morning News* gushed, "The rapidity with which this boy and his companions have learned the rudiments of civilization, plainly prove their native docility and amiability, and their entire capacity and willingness to acquire all that is necessary to render them valuable additions to our slave population."[19]

Lamar returned his focus to the grand jury, scheduled to begin on April 12. He knew that the members of the Telfair County posse who seized the thirty-six Africans in Worth County were among the subpoenaed witnesses. On April 13 he asked Magistrate Philip M. Russell to issue a warrant against the five men on the charge of larceny for unlawfully stealing and carrying away his slaves. Justice Russell agreed to Lamar's request but required him to post a bond of $3,000 to ensure his appearance at a trial during the October term of the Worth County superior court. When the Telfair County men stepped off the railroad car in Savannah, two constables presented them with the warrants, placed them under arrest, and escorted them to Russell's office. The men demanded to see Joseph Ganahl and Henry Jackson, who soon appeared. The lawyers told the men to protest the proceedings, waive rights to all examinations, and refuse to give security. Apparently, Ganahl and Jackson thought that these actions would resolve the matter for the time being and free the men, and they left. But Russell informed the five men that because of their stance, he had to commit them to jail. However, as it was two o'clock, Russell allowed them to go to a restaurant in the custody of one of the constables for their midday meal. When they returned to the courthouse at three o'clock, Russell announced that he had to hold a hearing to justify committing them to jail, even though they had waived that right. Russell then summoned two fellow justices of the peace.[20]

Lamar testified first, claiming that the men stole his property totaling $30,000 to $40,000, or about $1,000 a slave. The constable claimed that over their meal, the men confessed to having taken the blacks specified in the warrant as belonging to Lamar. Daniel Stewart, no longer U.S. marshal, testified that he had told McRae to seize any blacks who he thought to be Africans, and that he believed McRae had acted in good faith in this matter. The magistrates conferred and ruled unanimously that enough evidence existed to try the men for larceny and required each defendant to post security of $1,000 to ensure their appearance at the Worth County superior court in October. Lamar then had second thoughts about the matter and told Russell that he wanted to dismiss the case. The justice explained that once he made the ruling, he couldn't rescind it. Stewart volunteered to act as the men's security, and Staley discharged them. Despite not being allowed to negate his action, Lamar still had notched another victory over Ganahl.[21]

On April 15, with Judge Nicoll presiding, the grand jury returned true bills against Lamar and R. F. Akin for holding thirty-six Africans in Telfair County; against Lamar for holding an African boy named Corrie; and against Lamar for holding two Africans named Cuffee and Gumbo. In addition, the jurors returned a true bill against John Tucker for holding an African man.[22]

Ganahl and Jackson pursued the other suspects, and by the end of the hearings on May 3 they had obtained true bills against Nelson Trowbridge "for holding African Negroes," John and Henry Dubignon "for holding and abetting in the holding of African Negroes," Randolph L. Mott "for holding an African Negro as a slave," Nicholas Danese ("Brown") "for importing and holding and abetting of holding African Negroes," and William Corrie "for importing African Negroes." The grand jury returned "no bill" against John Montmollin.[23]

The government attorneys next turned their attention to trying Corrie, Danese, Rajesta, and Arguirvi for piracy in the May term. However, William Corrie was still in South Carolina. Ganahl asked associate Supreme Court justice James Moore Wayne, in town to preside over the grand jury, to order the South Carolina judge to extradite Corrie. Judge Wayne issued a bench warrant for Corrie's return to Georgia, but the South Carolina judge ignored the warrant and reaffirmed his prior decisions and claimed exclusive jurisdiction to try Corrie in South Carolina. Since Corrie was the main target in the group, Ganahl asked the court to postpone the trial to the November session while he continued his efforts to extradite the *Wanderer* captain. The court granted the request and ordered the three prisoners to remain in jail until the trial.[24]

———————

Henry Jackson had not forgotten about John Farnum, the supercargo of the *Wanderer* expedition and the other main player in the crime. On

March 25 he wrote to U.S. attorney general Jeremiah Black that Farnum was known to be living in New York and visiting Washington frequently and that Jackson, Joseph Ganahl, and the district attorney for the
southern district of New York wanted to charge and arrest him. Jackson
claimed they had enough evidence and witnesses to make a strong case.[25]

Not long after Jackson wrote the letter, he traveled to Washington and
met the attorney general. Black revealed that Farnum was at a Washington hotel and had made a confidential offer to supply Jackson "with the
log-book of the *Wanderer*, and with evidence enough to convict the men
you are now prosecuting, for seven thousand dollars, to be paid after conviction; himself [Farnum] of course, to enjoy immunity." Jackson rejected
the deal, saying he wouldn't convict any man based on such "infamous
testimony." Instead, Jackson proposed to "make out the requisite affidavit before Judge Wayne and have him [Farnum] arrested and taken to
Savannah for trial." Black wouldn't allow it, saying that Farnum's proposition had been made "in perfect confidence, and after I [Black] had given
a solemn pledge that, if it were not accepted, the whole matter would be
kept profoundly secret." Jackson returned to Savannah empty-handed.[26]

Fortunately for Charles Lamar, the November trials were a long way
off, affording him plenty of time to cause more trouble.

CHAPTER 13

"I Shall Simply Put an Indignity upon Him"

April–May 1859

More than any of his stunts, Lamar's actions at the auction of the *Wanderer* on March 12, 1859, caught the eye of the northern press. On March 21 the *New York Times* ran an editorial on Lamar titled "Chivalric Swindling." In it, founder, editor, and publisher Henry J. Raymond claimed that "the 'gentlemen of Georgia' . . . seem to take a special pride in being gazetted as knaves and liars; and after stealing the honorable flag of an honorable association [the New York Yacht Club] to cover the most dastardly tricks of the piratical peddler, flaunt their scandalous greed . . . by open and riotous violations of the laws even of their own peculiar society."[1]

Charles got hold of the article and wrote to Raymond, explaining that he found the remarks personal and offensive, and demanded a retraction. If one were not forthcoming, he wanted the opportunity to defend his honor in a duel.[2] Raymond responded by sending Lamar an article from the *Times* of March 22, the day after the original editorial. It began with an anonymous letter to the editor, requesting that the remarks made in the editorial be withdrawn, to "repair the injuries you have done [to Lamar]." The writer reasoned, "You may search the country in its whole length and breadth, and you cannot find one who stands higher in estimation of those who know him, as a high-minded, frank and fearless gentleman. His opinions on the Slave-trade may be wrong, but he honestly entertains them. They are the same that were generally entertained in Great Britain and America half a century ago."[3]

Raymond continued the article with an acknowledgment that the letter's author deserved respect, and that "we are . . . ready to add that the epithets employed in our article upon this subject in the TIMES of yesterday were not designed to have any application to Mr. Lamar's general character, or to be used towards him in any way outside of his connections with this specific transaction;—and even in that respect perhaps they were stronger and more sweeping than the occasion required."[4]

Lamar would have been satisfied if Raymond had ended the article at that point. However, Raymond continued, "Whatever [Lamar] may think of the Slave-trade in the abstract, he knows that it is in flagrant violation of the law. If he wishes to engage in it, his course, as a high-minded honorable gentleman, is, first of all, to seek a repeal of the laws which forbid it. . . . Instead of this he entered upon it—not openly, or even in frank defiance of the law—but in a clandestine manner . . . resorting throughout to subterfuges and concealments utterly at variance with the character he is reputed to bear. His conduct at the sale of the *Wanderer* was simply insolent."[5]

Lamar bristled at the comments and again wrote to Raymond to explain his actions. He said that waiting to change the slave trade laws would be fruitless as the North controlled the Congress. He claimed that he did indeed announce his intention to reopen the slave trade to foreign countries in his manifesto to Howell Cobb, and that the only subterfuge resorted to was not declaring the intention of the *Wanderer*, which would have stopped the expedition in its tracks. Charles revealed that he had asked Cobb in unpublished correspondence to send a navy officer with the *Wanderer* as it picked up the Africans and landed them on a levee in New Orleans, so that he, Lamar, could test the constitutionality of the slave trade laws of Congress. However, Cobb declined the offer. Lamar maintained that he concealed nothing—that he took the Africans from Jekyll Island to a plantation above the city on the Savannah River, transferred some of them to Hamburg, and made those actions public. (A review of Savannah and New York newspapers and other Lamar correspondence revealed no such public declaration.) Lamar also bragged that he recaptured all the Africans seized by U.S. officers and even paraded two African boys around the state, introducing them as "young wanderers." Charles finished his confession by noting that he hadn't intended to use the *Wanderer* as a slave ship but to place an order for Africans to be picked up by another vessel. However, in an effort to embarrass Howell Cobb, he informed the *Wanderer* crew as they were about to sail to take on as many slaves as the ship could comfortably accommodate. Charles concluded by stating that he expected a full and free withdrawal of all Raymond's charges.[6] Raymond responded, but Charles found it entirely unsatisfactory and wrote again to the publisher, asking, "Do you hold yourself responsible for the offensive matter published in your columns? As you decline further explanation, my future course will depend & be governed entirely by your response to the above Enquiry."[7]

Raymond corresponded with Lamar one last time, and Charles, disappointed with the content, replied, "You have taken the usual refuge of a coward, who, afraid to fight, undervalues his adversary. . . . When we meet I have determined upon my course." Charles then explained how he planned to handle Raymond to B. R. Alden, the author of the anonymous letter defending Charles in the *New York Times*. "I shall simply put an indignity upon him in a public moment such for instance as slapping his face and if he don't resent it, why I shall take no further notice of him."[8]

Bradford R. Alden graduated from West Point in 1831, served as an aide-de-camp to General Winfield Scott, and became commandant of cadets at West Point. He was wounded in the Indian wars in Oregon, resigned from the military, and got involved in oil drilling in western Pennsylvania. He lived in Manhattan when Lamar wrote to him. It is not known how Charles made the acquaintance of the man, or why Alden would intervene on Charles's behalf, although they could have met through Charles's father, who lived in New York between 1846 and 1861 and had high visibility in the city as a bank president.[9]

Charles wrote again to Alden on July 30, 1859, asking him to negotiate a deal with the editor. "In treating with Raymond demand nothing but what is *right* and then yield nothing. I am opposed to compromises. He shall make the amends, or he shall fight me." This is the last letter from Lamar to Alden, indicating that the New Yorker didn't meet with Raymond on Charles's behalf. But the slave trader would still not let go of the assault on his character.[10]

Charles knew that as a newspaper editor, Raymond visited Washington, D.C., frequently. In the winter of 1860 Lamar asked his cousin Lucius Quintas Cincinnatus Lamar Jr., a member of the U.S. House of Representatives from Mississippi, to telegraph him immediately on learning of Mr. Raymond's arrival in town so he could travel there and confront the editor face to face. Charles never heard back from Lucius, and Raymond's insult continued to fester.[11]

The *New York Tribune* also ran articles criticizing Lamar's behavior at the auction of the *Wanderer*. One written under the pen name of "Georgia" particularly disturbed Charles and prompted him to ask editor Horace Greeley for the real name of the author so that Charles might hold him legally and personally responsible. Lamar and Greeley exchanged several letters without Charles ever learning the reporter's name. The offending article of March 25 is particularly noteworthy in that the author must have been familiar with Savannah and Lamar. While all accounts of the day (and almost all since) describe Lamar as a wealthy businessman, "Georgia" correctly noted that Charles was "as insolvent in pocket as he is in character for some time past." The writer also mentioned several of Lamar's personal incidents, like the *Pulaski* disaster and the Henry Dubignon shooting.[12]

Charles had always been thin-skinned, and with his national notoriety and negative press in the North he became more so. When told that a northerner residing in Savannah had written an uncomplimentary letter to a Rhode Island newspaper about his behavior at the auction of the *Wanderer*, Lamar found the man, slapped his face with the back of his hand, and accused him of slander. The man explained to Lamar that he did not write the letter to the newspaper; he had written a private letter to a friend, and, based on it, the friend wrote the letter to the paper and added the offensive statement. Lamar apologized to the man and said that had he understood the circumstances he would not have acted as he did.[13]

Lamar, however, would not lose his sensitive nature, and more calls to defend his honor would soon follow.

CHAPTER 14

"Tell the People of Savannah They Can Kiss My Arse"

June–October 1859

The summer of 1859 turned out to be a long one for Nicholas Danese, Juan Rajesta, and Miguel Arguirvi, all of whom remained cooped up in jail during the steamy yellow fever season. Still, they fared better than John Montmollin, the *Wanderer* partner who wasn't charged by the April grand jury. On June 9, while he was traveling on the steamer *John G. Lawton* on the Savannah River, the boiler exploded, blowing him sky high. He was found the next day, "imbedded in marsh, head downwards, to the hips, some seventy or eighty yards from the spot where the explosion occurred. . . . A handkerchief, which he had in his hand at the time of the accident, was still tight in his grasp."[1]

Montmollin's death caused Charles Lamar considerable angst, as he had not paid Charles for twenty-seven of the Africans left at his South Carolina plantation the previous December. *Wanderer* partner John Tucker, who maintained Montmollin's administrative records after the fatal accident, couldn't substantiate Lamar's claim, although Charles said he had letters proving that the slaves were sent to Florida. Lamar, in yet another legal mess, enlisted the services of friend and lawyer Francis S. Bartow to negotiate a settlement with Montmollin's widow.[2]

Charles had other projects that kept him occupied over the summer. He appealed a lawsuit over a cotton press patent infringement which resulted in a judgment against him for $25,350—another huge loss for the insolvent businessman. The suit was first filed in Georgia but was subsequently moved to the U.S. Circuit Court in Charleston, as the Savannah district court judge was John Nicoll, Lamar's father-in-law.[3]

Charles also served on a five-man committee to make arrangements for a proper reception of his friend and ally Leonidas Spratt, whom he booked to give a speech in July on reopening the African slave trade. Spratt had been actively promoting his favorite subject. In May he attended the Southern Commercial Convention in Vicksburg, Mississippi, and presented resolutions to legalize the trade. However, few of the delegates wanted to touch that explosive topic, and former Mississippi governor Henry Foote accused Spratt of high treason. Undeterred, the Charleston lawyer gave a rousing speech on July 9 at the Masonic Hall in Savannah, no doubt further inspiring Charles.[4]

Gazaway worried that Charles's continued advocacy for reopening the African slave trade and other belligerent behavior would endanger his standing at the upcoming trials. As early as the grand jury hearings in February 1859, Gazaway had advised Charles, "Don't excite the prosecutors against you. The less ability they show the better for you and if you provoke them, they will be the more zealous." He reminded his son of past behavior: "I never knew any but a mad man going into an illicit trade to tell [off] the first officer of the government [Howell Cobb] & then exasperate him by every kind of provocation to make them active in prosecuting. But you have a way of your own. . . . You formerly ridiculed Judge Wayne which was disagreeable to his relatives who are your friends. I told you then you had better have his friendship & now time has proven it." In challenging Charles's assumption that the people of the South supported him, Gazaway scolded, "You must not calculate that 9 out of 10 are on your side. I wish you could be persuaded that conciliatory measures are better by 40 times than hostile measures."[5]

Gazaway also tendered legal advice. "Put off your trial if one be necessary & stave it off as long as you can till they tire out. You cannot rely on jurors unless bribed." He urged Charles to get good lawyers and jury counsel, adding, "The latter is the most important." The next month, the father wrote, "I fear you will have a tough time with the Wanderer. It is too late now, but you will remember how I foretold you all the difficulties." The statement suggests that Gazaway knew of Charles's plan to use the yacht as a slaver. The elder Lamar begged his son to break all ties with Nelson Trowbridge and presented him with an ultimatum. "You must give up Trowbridge or me—you can choose, but I cannot sail in the same company as him. From the time you commenced with him you have been going downhill in every respect, and I'm told Corrie is worse." Gazaway never followed through on the threat.[6]

More than anything, Gazaway tried to convince his son to get out of the slave trade. Before Charles reacquired the yacht, Gazaway wrote, "I hope you will have nothing to do with the Wanderer in any way—it will affect your interest in the trial. I shall be very glad if the E. Rawlins is gone, too." He would soon be disappointed to learn that Charles bought back the yacht. Gazaway continued to badger Charles over the summer. "If you prefer the slave trade, remove to some part of Cuba & get intimate with all the pirates, cutthroats & villains engaged in that line & also with the officials of the government & perhaps if none of them cut your throat you may make money." The sixty-one-year-old Gazaway even tried to play on Charles's sympathy—a futile strategy. "And I wish now you would listen to me and yield all your slave-trade notions to my peace in my declining years. I cannot live long and when I am gone you can do as you please, but until then I enjoin you to give it up."[7]

Charles ignored his father, as he had most of his adult life, and had little tolerance for the old man's lectures. However, he was broke. Failed business ventures, lost lawsuits, endorsed notes for insolvent friends, and disastrous slaving expeditions had taken their toll, and most of his assets had been pledged as security for his bank loans. Trading cotton and running the wharf, cotton press, and warehouse operations simply didn't pay him enough. So Charles had no choice but to reach out to the one person who always bailed him out. Gazaway, still residing in New York, signed a deal in September 1859 with the American Guano Company to be the sole distributor of its product in seven southern states. He made Charles his agent in Georgia, but the appointment came with more finger wagging. Gazaway advised his thirty-five-year-old son, who had been in charge of the Savannah businesses for twelve years, how to collect money, spend it, and balance his checkbook. He told Charles to run the guano business economically or not at all, and not ever to mix guano money with cash from other businesses.[8]

Charles wanted to do more than sell bird droppings and asked his father to make him president of the Bank of Commerce, over which Gazaway presided. The elder Lamar seemed to consider it, but he recognized the difficulties of putting a slave trader facing a trial at the helm of a prominent financial institution: "I cannot put you at the head of it until certain obstacles are removed. . . . Your going in as president of the bank would arouse the stockholders & they would make a fuss & injure the bank . . . to injure you and me." Still, Gazaway used the possibility as a carrot to try to get Charles to change his ways. "If you would restrain your temper, conciliate people rather than outrage their feelings, moderate your extremes, allow other people their rights of opinion & always think calmly before you express an opinion on questions exercising your judgment & not your feelings & impulses, you would soon recover [your credit] & stand above any of those who would injure you." Gazaway also told Charles that he had to control his spending and make sacrifices, such as selling his racehorses and yacht.[9]

Gazaway might as well have been talking to a barrel of guano. Charles wasn't about to start listening after so many years of ignoring and even taunting him. Besides, all business activities to Charles took a back seat to the African slave trade. Nothing else promised such huge returns, and after three failed attempts he considered himself an expert. He still had the perfect ship, the *Wanderer*, for the task. He claimed to one prospective partner, "She is the vessel of all others in the world." Since he reacquired the yacht in March, Charles had it overhauled and repainted and took it on a few trips to Havana and the fishing banks along the southern Atlantic coast. He docked at the Lamar wharf, where the ship loomed like a chained beast, waiting to break loose and create havoc at any moment. Port collector John Boston heard rumors that the yacht would soon be leaving for Africa or aiding in the escape of the *Wanderer* prisoners and stationed the revenue cutter *Dobbin* in the river to prevent her departure.[10]

Charles spent the rest of his time over the summer of 1859 trying to organize another slaving expedition. All he needed for success, he decided, were reliable partners and a captain. He told an interested party, William C. Cook, "You are aware that it is a risky business. I lost two out of 3. To be sure at first I knew not of the business. I have learned something since & I hope I can put my information to some a/c. I have been in for 'grandeur' & been fighting for a principle, *now* I am in for the dollars."[11]

With his growing national reputation, Charles received inquiries for slaving ventures from various points in the South—Mobile, Alabama; Blakely, Georgia; and Morehouse Parish, Louisiana. He made clear to all of his correspondents the requirements of prospective partners. "The Parties subscribing must agree to lose their interest if they, *after due notice be given them,* fail to be on the ground to take their property. I have lost money by the last voyage simply by my co-partners failing to come up & get . . . the negroes falling into the official's hands, which cost money to get them out, but worse than all, in falling into the hands of damned rascals, who will give but a meager account of them."[12]

Charles concentrated his sales efforts on the one man who had sent him cash, William C. Cook of Blakely County, assuring him that he put the $500 investment in a certificate of deposit, to be held for the venture. (Lamar may have subsequently received more funds, as Cook claimed he also sent a $2,000 draft.) Charles told his new partner on July 20 that everything was ready for an expedition to Africa except for securing the supplies and captain, and therefore he could not give a specific date of departure. Lamar did mention that the captain of his last expedition might be available, though he and the man were having a dispute over compensation. Since that captain, Nicholas Danese, was living in the Savannah jail, Lamar's plan to use him raises the possibility that Charles had been planning to free him.[13]

Lamar wrote to Danese the same day, offering him the captaincy in the next expedition, which would leave the following week—for China! Lamar confirmed this plan in a letter to Nelson Trowbridge the following day. It is unclear what Lamar had in mind by giving different destinations for the expedition. He wrote to Cook after Trowbridge, and this time he named Africa as the destination.[14] However, while Danese roasted in jail, Lamar still had no one to lead the voyage. He wrote to Lima Viana, the head of the slave trade syndicate in New York, asking him for the name of a captain experienced with the African coast, but came up empty. In early October Charles told Cook that he was still looking for a captain.[15]

Charles's involvement with planning an expedition and preparing for the *Wanderer* trials didn't leave time for managing the family businesses. He arranged with his cousins Gazaway Bugg Lamar Jr. and James H. ("Gov") Phinizy, both active in the operations, to take over his duties at the cotton press, effective October 5, while splitting the profits equally among the three of them.[16]

Around this time a man calling himself Captain David S. Martin arrived in town and approached Lamar about commanding the *Wanderer*'s next voyage and purchasing a 75 percent interest in the yacht for $20,000. The stranger boasted that he had recently landed cargoes of Africans in Cuba from the slavers *Niagara* and *Haidee*. Anxious for another expedition and some cash, Charles wrote to contacts in Havana and New Orleans for references on Martin. While he waited for replies, Lamar gave Martin access to the yacht until he came up with the money.[17]

Supposedly unbeknownst to Lamar, who rarely visited the cotton press after October 5, Martin immediately began planning a voyage. He asked the shipping master for the Port of Savannah to recruit a crew for him for a fruit run to Matanzas, Cuba. In a few days the shipping master and his assistant William Black had hired several men. On Friday, October 14, the crew filled the *Wanderer*'s water tanks from a fireplug at the cotton press. Then they anchored her in the river, clear of the wharf's operations.[18]

On Saturday the crew began removing the *Wanderer*'s sails from storage in the cotton press, ferrying them to the ship, and rigging and unfurling them. Gazaway Jr. informed Charles, who told his cousin to tell Martin to get his permission before taking anything else. That night Lamar departed for Worth County for the trial of the Telfair County posse. Before leaving he told his bookkeeper that Martin would be dropping off $20,000 at his office on Monday for his interest in the *Wanderer*.[19]

On Monday Martin hired more men. He had the crew remove the remaining sails as well as boxes of muskets and bayonets, tin pans, and jars of chloride of lime from the cotton press. If Gazaway Jr. was there at the time, he didn't stop them. The men rigged and unfurled the remaining sails during the day and loaded provisions at night. Martin never appeared at Lamar's office on Monday, but he visited the bookkeeper's house at ten o'clock that night to say he would have the cash the next morning.[20]

When Lamar reached Albany near the Worth County courthouse on Monday, he learned that the judge had become ill and postponed the trial. He returned to Savannah, arriving at his office on Tuesday morning. The bookkeeper told him that Martin hadn't delivered the funds. Lamar sent a message to Martin to come to the office right away and pay the money, but he never appeared. Charles looked for him at the cotton press and learned that he wasn't there or on the ship. Lamar must have seen the *Wanderer* in the river with her sails unfurled and the crew working on deck, but he didn't take any action other than to search the town—unsuccessfully—for Martin.[21]

Between seven and eight o'clock that night Lamar asked port collector John Boston to have the *Dobbin* prevent the *Wanderer* from leaving the river as he believed Martin might steal her. Boston explained that the *Dobbin* had left the port. Lamar took no other steps that night to find Martin.[22]

On Tuesday afternoon and evening the crew ferried provisions from a chandlery store to the *Wanderer*. Martin, Black, and Ned Talbot, an employee of the boardinghouse where many of the sailors stayed, arrived on the last supply boat at about ten o'clock. As the crew loaded the supplies onto the ship, Martin invited Black, who had once captained Lamar's ship, the *Richard Cobden*, and Talbot below for drinks. The two men were the only non–crew members on board.[23]

With the provisions finally loaded onto the yacht, the crew expected to return to shore, but the captain called them below and said that the ship had to leave that night. The men complained that they had no clothes with them. Martin went to his cabin and returned with a revolver in one hand and a pistol in the other, announcing that he would shoot any man who attempted to leave the ship. Martin then forced each crewman to sign a new agreement produced by Black, who had armed himself with a pistol and cutlass, for shipping on the *Wanderer* to Saint Helena Island on the way to Africa instead of Matanzas. After they signed, Martin poured them drinks. At midnight he ordered the crew topside and told Ned Talbot to take the helm for the fifteen-mile ride to the ocean. He also ordered two men to load the muskets and the two small cannons in case the *Dobbin* lay in the river and they had to fight their way past her.[24]

Ten minutes later the ship ran aground. Martin accused Talbot of doing it on purpose. He heard a few men talking about going ashore, walked up to them, pointed the pistol at each man's head, and asked, "Do you want to go ashore?" They all answered in the negative. Black said there was a steamer at a nearby wharf that could pull them off, and he, Martin, and two oarsmen took Black's rowboat to find it. They returned in fifteen minutes empty-handed. Despite having access to the loaded muskets and cannons, the shanghaied men made no attempt to prevent Martin from reboarding. The crew finally pulled the ship free with a cable and anchor. The first mate took over as pilot. At five o'clock in the morning, as they neared the mouth of the river, the ship grounded again. A cursing Martin decided to wait for the tide to float her off, and most of the crew caught some sleep.[25]

At about seven o'clock that morning, Wednesday, October 19, Gazaway Jr. and Gov Phinizy arrived at the cotton press to find the *Wanderer* gone. They notified Charles at his house. Lamar went to the customhouse and told John Boston to write to the American consuls at Havana and other cities about the theft and to seize the yacht if she appeared at their port. He then crossed the street and climbed to the cupola of the City Exchange building, which provided a clear view of the river all the way to the ocean. He saw that the schooner had grounded near the mouth and asked Boston to send a steamer after it. Boston replied that he didn't have the authority to incur that expense for a private matter, but if Lamar chartered a steam tug, he would send along several officers to make the arrest. Between ten and eleven o'clock, Lamar, a few friends, and two customs officers chugged down the river toward the *Wanderer*.[26]

By noon, with the steam tug approaching, the tide lifted the *Wanderer*, allowing the vessel to continue its escape. Once the yacht came abreast of the Tybee Island lighthouse, Martin let Black and Talbot take their rowboat back to shore. As they cast off, Martin yelled, "Tell the people of Savannah they can kiss my arse!" When the ship cleared land, Martin revealed to the crew the true object of the voyage: "We're going to the coast of Africa for a cargo of niggers!" From the river, Lamar watched his yacht shrink against the horizon.[27]

The ship had no clearance papers, supplies necessary for a slave voyage, crew experienced in handling a slave cargo, or, seemingly, gold to purchase Africans, all of which raised questions about the mission. The story of the theft of the *Wanderer* spread through town like a summer wind. Some residents were shocked at the brazenness of Captain Martin. Others doubted that he had acted alone and thought that Lamar's frenzied actions were just a ploy to cover up his part in another slaving expedition. A local resident, who said he had boarded the *Wanderer* several times "while she was . . . taking in her stores," described the incident. *"This was done openly, in broad daylight; hundreds of citizens looking on.* All her stores came through the Cotton Press, *which belongs to the owner of the yacht."* He wondered why the revenue cutter left the harbor just before the *Wanderer* departed. "It would have made you laugh," he wrote, "to see the owner, Charley Lamar, in chase of the yacht the next day. . . . He was like the Irishman looking for a day's work, and praying that he might not find it."[28]

Lamar's behavior during the days leading up to the heist certainly raises questions. It is hard to believe that he didn't learn about Martin's planned "fruit run" to Matanzas before the last minute. Martin began hiring a crew five days before Lamar left town for the trial in Worth County. Former *Cobden* captain William Black was hiring crew for Martin, friend William Hone owned the chandlery that was supplying provisions, and cousins Gazaway Jr. and Gov Phinizy witnessed the activity on the ship from the wharf. Surely one of them would have mentioned something to Charles, who had conveniently given up his duties at the cotton press, before Gazaway Jr. finally spoke up on Lamar's day of departure. And when Gazaway Jr. did tell him about the removal of the sails from the cotton press on that Saturday, surely Charles would have approached Martin instead of asking his cousin to do it.

It is even more difficult to believe that Charles would not have found Martin on Tuesday when he returned from Worth County and suspected that the stranger might steal his yacht. Lamar had lived in Savannah all his life and knew many residents. He could have learned of Martin's whereabouts within a few hours. And if he didn't, the Charles Lamar we have come to know would have fetched his rifle and revolvers, rowed out to the ship, told the crew to take down the sails before getting the hell off his yacht, and waited for Martin to return. But instead, Charles asked the port collector to have his revenue cutter guard the river. The *Dobbin*, of course, had already left port.

Charles had to inform W. C. Cook, his partner in the next expedition of the *Wanderer*, of the loss of the ship. He wrote, "The Wanderer is off. She went to sea this morning with a full complement of men, provisions & munitions of war etc. etc. But alas! She went without my knowledge or consent. . . . He [Martin] got his crew & provisions on board at night & put out. The Cutter had gone from her station. He has undoubtedly gone to the Coast of Africa for a cargo of negroes & if he is as smart there, as he has been here he will get one. . . . He must have had his plan well laid & for some time, so bold & daring [an] act has never before been committed." These words—praise for a man who had just stolen his beloved yacht—are totally out of character. A profanity-laced tirade describing how he would exact retribution once he got his hands on the rascal would have been more Charles's style.[29]

On the other hand, it is hard to believe that John Boston, Lamar's bitter enemy during the *Rawlins* and *Wanderer* incidents, would have cooperated with him to sneak the *Wanderer* from the river. Also, Lamar did make attempts to have Martin, after his capture, returned to Savannah to stand trial. If Charles had really been robbed, his reputation made it difficult for anyone to believe him.

In any event, the *Wanderer* was gone, and Charles began concentrating on the upcoming trials. His fate depended on the outcome.

CHAPTER 15

"Such Men as C. A. L. Lamar Run Riot without Hindrance"

November–December 1859

A surreal, almost paranoid atmosphere blanketed the town leading up to the piracy trial of Danese, Rajesta, and Arguirvi. On the first day, as locals gathered on the steps of the customhouse in hopes of getting a seat in the courtroom, a man in women's clothing paraded up and down Bay Street. Alarmed that he might be an abolitionist in disguise, the police took him to jail, to the jeers of the huge crowd.[1]

The trial started on Wednesday, November 16, in the U.S. district court on the second floor of the customhouse with Supreme Court justice James Moore Wayne and district court judge John Nicoll presiding. Charles Lamar chose not to attend. Another notable absentee was William C. Corrie. Joseph Ganahl had been unable to secure his extradition from South Carolina and had to move ahead without him. The proceedings began with the selection of twelve jurors, who would be sequestered for the trial. Joseph Ganahl read the indictment, and then the witnesses were called.[2]

Simply stated, the prosecution had to prove that the defendants worked on a ship that landed African slaves in the United States. The witnesses who could best testify to that were pilots Horatio Harris, James Clubb, and Luke Christie. They all saw the defendants on Jekyll Island at or near the time the Africans came ashore.

The government lawyers called Harris, who first met William Corrie and sail master Seth Briggs on their arrival at Little Cumberland Island. He described their initial meeting, being offered the job of bringing the yacht across the sound, and witnessing the landing of the Africans the next day. But he qualified identifying the defendants, saying that he thought he had seen them on the beach but could not swear to it as their physical appearance had changed so much since then. Nor could he swear that the blacks were Africans, though he acknowledged that Corrie and Briggs had told him that they were. Harris's hedging caused prosecutor Henry Jackson to announce to the court that the witness had been unduly influenced since the early stages of the hearings. This drew an angry protest from the defense, which claimed that there had never been such a charge made, and Jackson had no right to make it then.[3]

Luke Christie, pilot of the steam tug *Lamar*, testified the next day and gave a full account of taking Charles Lamar, Nelson Trowbridge, John Tucker, and Nicholas Danese, who was still recognized as Nicholas Brown by the court, to Jekyll Island and returning to the Savannah River. He thought he saw the two Spanish defendants help load the blacks onto the tug at Jekyll and unload them near Montmollin's plantation, but he wouldn't swear to it. However, he did identify Danese as being on Jekyll beach.[4]

James Clubb, who piloted the *Wanderer* across Saint Andrews Sound, gave a detailed account of his experiences, but he also claimed that he could not identify any of the crew of the *Wanderer* or any other person on the beach except Corrie and Briggs (who were not in the courtroom) and John Dubignon. He said he believed the blacks to be African.[5]

The testimony of these three witnesses unquestionably described a landing of black people in Georgia, but none of them would swear that the two Spanish defendants were on Jekyll beach at the time, and only one identified Danese. All three could only assume that the blacks were Africans.

Twenty-three other witnesses also testified. Some linked the defendants to the *Wanderer*, including Captain N. L. Coste, who saw them on the yacht in Charleston before they embarked. And Michael Cass of the City Hotel and William Price, owner of the clothing store, testified to the defendants' presence in Savannah eight days after the landing, looking as if they had just returned from months at sea, when they paid their bills in gold.[6]

Joseph Ganahl tried to prove that Africans had been landed in Georgia when he questioned Charles Van Horn, the city jailer, about the two men who were seized in Macon and placed under his care for several months. The district attorney still seethed at the loss of that evidence and asked Van Horn to describe the day when Lamar reclaimed them. The jailer stated that he had sent messengers to find Ganahl after being served with a writ of possession, and again after reaching Magistrate Staley's office, but they all told him that the district attorney was busy. Ganahl challenged Van Horn to think about what he had just said, and then tell the truth. Van Horn said he was telling the truth and if the district attorney didn't believe him, then he had nothing more to say. Ganahl countered that Van Horn had told him in a previous interview that he was prevented from sending anyone for him. The jailer denied it. The testimony, which should have been positive for the prosecution, was lost in the contentiousness between Ganahl and the witness.[7]

On Saturday, November 19, the fourth and final day of examinations, the prosecution called on Nelson Trowbridge, Henry Dubignon, John Dubignon, Richardson Akin, Charles Lamar, and John Tucker. The first four, who had attended the court sessions, refused to answer questions as they might incriminate themselves. Lamar and Tucker had not attended the trial and were not compelled to be brought before the court as their lawyers said they would answer in the same manner as the four others.[8]

On Monday, November 21, defense attorney John Owens and prosecutor Henry Jackson delivered their closing arguments. The next day Judge Nicoll read the minutes of the testimony and Judge Wayne charged the jury. At four o'clock, after a midday meal, the jury retired.[9]

The jury consisted of twelve seemingly responsible men with no ties to Charles Lamar or his *Wanderer* partners. The jury foreman owned a hat shop. The others included a physician, a pattern maker for the Central of Georgia Railroad, a cabinetmaker, a paint-shop owner, a ship captain, and an office clerk. One man owned the Union Steam Saw Mill located at Gazaway Lamar's Eastern Wharves, but there is no reason to believe that this relationship affected his vote.[10]

The prosecution delivered a strong case, and the jurors must have been impressed by the presence of Henry Jackson, who was deeply admired in Savannah. The jury sat through the night and took twenty hours to reach a decision, suggesting that unanimity on a verdict did not exist at the outset. However, the practice of deliberating nonstop without food or sleep until reaching a verdict could not have served justice well. We will never know how many men were sitting on the fence and changed their vote just to get out of the jury room. The inability of any witness to identify positively the defendants as being at Jekyll Island during the landing, with the exception of one man pointing out Danese, probably influenced the jurors.[11]

It is difficult to say if any of the jurors feared retribution from Charles Lamar. Although he was not on trial, everyone had to know that he headed the *Wanderer* syndicate after his public declaration at the auction. One Savannah resident saw the impact that Lamar had on the town after the landing of the Africans: "The tone of feeling in the city is to a great extent extremely at fault; and such men as C. A. L. Lamar, [John] Tucker, etc., run riot without let or hindrance. And this will continue until they are guilty of some flagrant outrage, at which the feelings of even their hangers-on . . . will revolt. Lamar is a dangerous man and with all his apparent recklessness and lawlessness, a cautious one too; for he never ventures in the presence of any save those whom he may regard as followers, or whom he may readily intimidate."[12]

At noon on November 23 the jury returned to the courtroom with their decision. They found the defendants not guilty. Charles Lamar must have been as elated as Ganahl and Jackson were deflated. Despite all the evidence and testimony, the prosecutors could not get a conviction for piracy. Judge Wayne remanded the defendants to jail to face other charges.[13]

Two days later a disappointed but determined prosecution tried Danese for "aiding and abetting in the landing of foreign Negroes in Georgia and holding the same." The case generated little interest as the prosecution examined the same witnesses and reviewed the same evidence from the first trial. Judge Wayne instructed a new jury at six o'clock on Saturday night. Twenty-one hours later, with the jury deadlocked, the foreman took ill. Wayne declared a mistrial and dismissed the jurors.[14]

Struggling against a riptide of apathy, Joseph Ganahl presented to a grand jury a bill of indictment against Rajesta and Arguirvi for "bringing in, holding, and disposing of Africans." The jurors returned "no bill" and Ganahl dropped all charges against the two sailors, who disappeared as soon as they were released.[15]

A dejected Jackson told Judge Wayne that the prosecution did not intend to try any other cases during the current term. Accordingly, the judge carried over all the open cases to the May 1860 session. The next day he released Danese on a $10,000 bond. Ganahl and Jackson left the courtroom with their heads bowed. So far they had lost every battle, but their fight for justice had not ended.[16]

There can be little doubt that most Savannahians welcomed the jury's verdict, not so much for their support of the slave trade, but because Charles Lamar had successfully thumbed his nose at the North. This feeling was especially true after October 16, one month before the trial, when abolitionist John Brown and a band of seventeen men seized the federal arsenal at Harpers Ferry and tried to incite the slaves in the area into rebellion. The slaves did not revolt, and two days later, under the command of Colonel Robert E. Lee, federal troops routed Brown and his men from the armory, culminating in Brown's capture and the death of five of his men. The act convinced many southerners that the North not only desired to abolish slavery but wanted their slaves to kill them in their beds. Southern newspapers hoped for a strong denunciation of Brown from their northern counterparts but felt they did not get it. The *Charleston Mercury* summarized the feelings of many in the region:

> The presses of the North . . . are pretty harmonious in representing it as a very light and trifling affair. . . . For twenty-five years the northern people have been keeping up a continual agitation in the Union concerning the institution of slavery. They have broken up our churches; they have run off our slaves; they have excluded us from our territory on the ground that the institution of slavery is too iniquitous to expand; and they have now organized a vast controlling party in the Northern States looking to the possession of the General Government to further their purposes of emancipation. . . . Here then is the great importance of the abolition [uprising] in Virginia. It shows to the people of the South the destiny which awaits them in this Union under the control of a sectional anti-slavery party in the Free States. . . . The Harper's Ferry invasion, therefore . . . [,] is of vast [significance], and should lead the people of the South to prepare for those future events, of which this is only the premonition.[17]

John Brown's trial began in Charles Town, Virginia, one week after his capture. The jury found him guilty and on November 2, 1859, the judge sentenced him to hang one month later, placating the South for the time being. He was executed one week after the dismissal of the first *Wanderer* case.

Given this intense anger at the North, it was not the best time for a trial against slave traders in the South. In fact, it was not a good time for anyone in the South to be suspected of having abolitionist sympathies. Unfortunately for Sewell H. Fiske, a native of Massachusetts who had lived in Savannah for several years running a boot and shoe shop, rumors swirled that he regularly invited slaves into his cellar at night and read abolitionist literature to them. Fiske's nephew and store clerk reportedly swore to a local magistrate that Fiske told slaves about John Brown and the advantages of freedom. The night before Brown's execution, a group of men visited Fiske in his apartment above his shop, bound and gagged him, threw him in the back of a wagon, and drove to a field on the east side of the city. They ripped off his clothes, cropped his hair, covered his body with a layer of tar and a coating of cotton, and drove off. Fiske hobbled to the hospital in town, and his apparition so frightened the security guard that he ran for help. No one was arrested. Fiske apparently fled from Savannah, as his name could not be found in the next year's city directory.[18]

The act made a lasting impression. One week later William Price, the owner of the clothing store where the *Wanderer* defendants shopped, and who notified Joseph Ganahl of their presence, wrote a letter to the editor of a local newspaper denying rumors that he sympathized with abolitionism. Soon, the town vigilantes, including Charles Lamar and Daniel Stewart, called for a public meeting to establish an association for the preservation of southern rights. Days later a large gathering assembled at Armory Hall, with Lamar in attendance. The group would ensure that no one spoke or acted out against slavery without suffering the consequences.[19]

The defeat in court angered Henry Jackson—not just because of the failure to convict, but also because so many government resources had been invested in the case against a few southerners while the slave trade operated virtually unopposed in the North, albeit landing the Africans in foreign countries. The ships were built there, the crews were hired there, and customs officials cleared the voyages from there, yet a bit player such as Charles Lamar garnered national headlines. After the trials, Jackson traveled to Washington and handed his resignation to Attorney General Jeremiah Black, claiming that he "could not consent to be longer engaged in helping to attract the attention of the world to the city of Savannah, as though it were the head center of the African slave trade, when [he] felt assured that it was in the North."[20]

The move shocked Black, and he arranged a meeting between Jackson and President James Buchanan. Jackson told Buchanan of his disgust that *Wanderer* supercargo J. Egbert Farnum roamed free despite all the charges made against southerners in the *Wanderer* case. Buchanan gave Jackson permission and the means to arrest Farnum, including the services of Lucien Peyton, a patent office employee whom Jackson knew to be an excellent investigator.[21]

The two men traveled to New York with a warrant for Farnum issued by the U.S. commissioner in Savannah. On December 9 they presented it to the Southern District of New York court judge, who issued a special warrant for Farnum's arrest. That night Marshal Isaiah Rynders and Deputy Maurice O'Keefe, who had been involved in the seizure and inspection of the *Wanderer* in June 1858, found the supercargo at the St. Nicholas Hotel. Owing to the hour, Rynders locked Farnum in the parlor of his own residence for the night. The next morning the New York judge told

Farnum of the charges against him, and by that afternoon Jackson, Peyton, Rynders, O'Keefe, and Farnum were on a train to Savannah by way of Washington, D.C.[22]

Jackson remained in Washington to persuade Attorney General Black to approve a large-scale investigation into the slave trade as conducted in the United States. Farnum and his guards reached Savannah on Friday, December 16. The prisoner was taken to the U.S. district court, where Judge Nicoll denied his application for bail and sent him to the city jail. Farnum settled down for a long stay, as the next court session would not begin until May, almost five months away.[23]

CHAPTER 16

"The *Wanderer* Bothers Me to Death"

December 1859–May 1860

Charles Lamar wasn't happy that another *Wanderer* participant had to endure a trial, which would extend his involvement in the matter and increase his legal bills, but there was nothing he could do about it. So he kept busy during the winter of 1860 by selling guano and cotton for his father. He maintained his visibility in town as he was reelected president of the Savannah Jockey Club and a director of the Savannah, Albany and Gulf Railroad. In addition, he rejoined the Democratic Party and remained a member of the Vigilance Association for the Preservation of Southern Rights.[1]

But Charles rarely experienced long periods without some kind of turmoil. Several days after Farnum landed in jail, Lamar learned of the fate of his missing *Wanderer*. The yacht had become a high-seas panhandler as it sailed toward Africa. During the voyage, David Martin stopped one vessel to hand the captain a letter addressed to William Black, with another letter to Lamar enclosed, and asked him to mail it when he reached the United States. He hailed two ships asking for provisions, but he received only two books and a chart from one and cabbages from the other. He stopped another and the captains exchanged longitudes. He chased two ships, firing the yacht's cannons at them and tearing the *Wanderer*'s mainsail in the process, but he failed to get them to heave to.[2]

After about fifteen days at sea the yacht approached Flores, a small island in the Azores. Martin had his men paint the name "William" over "Wanderer" on the stern. When they entered the port the British consul, a magistrate, and a pilot rowed out to greet them. Martin produced some fake clearance papers from Savannah and explained to the visitors that they were going to Smyrna, Turkey, to sell the ship for $35,000 and needed supplies, water, spars, and repairs to a sail. The local officials approved and left a customs officer and pilot on board for the duration of the *Wanderer*'s stay. The yacht remained for five days as Martin and a few of his men made trips to shore to purchase provisions. On the fifth night, Martin returned to the ship with two local women, who didn't leave, unbeknownst to the customs officer and pilot. On the sixth day, Martin went ashore with the carpenter to have a spar repaired. A few hours later the captain rushed back alone to the vessel and ordered the crew to raise the anchor and head for the ocean. It seems the supplies vendor had demanded payment from Martin, and the authorities wanted to question him about the two women—issues that the pirate didn't care to discuss. As the *Wanderer* got under way, one of the crew reminded Martin that the local pilot and customs officer were still on board. Martin ferried them to another ship in the harbor and made for the open seas, leaving his carpenter on shore. When the first mate asked the captain about the two women, the captain said that he would trade them for Africans on the coast.[3]

Nine days later they reached Funchal, the largest city in Madeira, but after spotting a British man-of-war in the harbor Martin decided to bypass the port. They flagged a ship from Bordeaux and asked for some provisions, but the captain couldn't supply them. Later that day they hailed the *Jeannie* of Marseilles, whose captain consented to help. Martin and three of the men rowed in a lifeboat to her with the intention of taking the crew by force and seizing all her stores. But when they boarded her, first mate Henry Welton, who remained on the *Wanderer*, ordered the crew to sail away. No one opposed him. They headed for the United States without Africans or their captain, who they left cursing into the wind on the *Jeannie*.[4]

Weeks later the crew skirted by Fire Island and continued northeast, finally anchoring in Boston, Welton's hometown, on December 23, 1859. The next day the U.S. district attorney for Massachusetts appeared before the U.S. district court judge and filed a motion for discovery. He claimed that the *Wanderer*, which he said was fitted out as a slave ship in Savannah for the purpose of procuring blacks from a foreign country to be transported to a place as yet unknown, had been seized and requested that all persons involved be cited to answer questions. The judge told the marshal to give notice to all persons concerned of an upcoming trial and to keep the *Wanderer* in custody. The crew and two women were housed in the jail, given clean clothing, and held for questioning.[5]

Charles Lamar had to recover his yacht once again from the federal government. This time he would require legal fees and connections in the North, which meant enlisting his father's help. Gazaway asked Joseph Story Fay, a New Englander who had lived in Savannah for many years but had recently returned to Boston, to represent Charles's interests and act as surety for the $1,000 bond required by the court to cover costs that might be awarded against Charles. On January 13, 1860, Fay appeared in court and claimed that Charles Lamar owned the *Wanderer*, that it had been stolen from him, and that he was requesting restitution of his property.[6]

In light of the size of the claims made against Lamar by the crew for wages and the vendor in Flores for supplies, the court ordered an appraisal of the *Wanderer*, which was given at $5,940. The judge increased the amount of the bond to that amount. Since Charles was in debt to his father, Gazaway felt he could get a bond more easily than Charles, and the court might be biased against his son for his previous activities, so he had Charles transfer ownership of the yacht to him. Gazaway had his lawyer Elijah Brigham and Fay act as his sureties.[7]

Gazaway now owned the ship that had given him so much grief. He wanted to send it to Havana to sell as soon as possible and wrote to Charles, "The *Wanderer* bothers me to death. I wish she was in the bottom of the ocean. I get one & sometimes two letters a day—every time with some new development—new obstacles, new expenditures & new risks & new demands. The collector will not clear her until he gets the register & your collector [in Savannah] will not give it up & I must write to Mr. Cobb." Finally, in early March Gazaway cleared all the legal hurdles, received the *Wanderer*'s register, and sent the yacht to Havana for Charles to sell. However, the hearings regarding the liabilities and the ship's status as a slaver continued, and the legal bills mounted.[8]

On April 23 the district court judge decreed that all crewmen, other than first mate Henry Welton, be paid wages by the owner for their work on board the *Wanderer*. This totaled about $800 plus costs. The judge delayed his ruling on the *Wanderer*'s status as a slaver, which meant more hearings and lawyers' fees.[9]

By the end of April, Charles still hadn't sold the ship, which enraged his father. The son's fumbling of the guano business intensified Gazaway's anger. On March 9 Gazaway wrote, "I had no letter from you since the 2nd & of course no money, which is of the utmost necessity. . . . You have $30,000 cost of guano & sales of at least $45,000 & yet you have not sent me one dollar." Three days later, his words exploded off the page as he scolded Charles for disobeying his order: "I protest against your using the guano money for any other purposes than those actually connected with it."[10] Charles couldn't care less. In fact, as his trial neared, his behavior grew more outrageous.

———————

The prosecution team underwent a major change when the beleaguered Joseph Ganahl resigned his position on December 30. A few weeks later

Attorney General Black appointed thirty-one-year-old Hamilton Couper to replace him. Couper had attended Yale and studied law in the North. In 1853 he settled in Savannah to establish his practice. Charles knew Couper's father well. James Hamilton Couper was a wealthy planter and the owner of Hopeton plantation in Glynn County. Like Charles, he too had survived the *Pulaski* disaster in 1838, and he and Charles cofounded the Savannah Aquatic Club in 1852. But the association wouldn't affect Charles's attitude toward the younger Couper.[11]

Hamilton Couper's first major task was to present the case against Farnum to a grand jury. He did so in April 1860 and obtained a true bill for piracy. The supercargo would face the death penalty.[12] Farnum had been in jail for four months when he learned of the charge against him, and he still faced another month before his trial. He was miserable and no doubt let Lamar know it. Charles had been angry with Farnum for not living up to his obligations after the *Wanderer* landed and then threatening to write a memoir about the *Wanderer* voyage. But Farnum never published any such account, and Charles felt badly about his incarceration. On May 1, with little more than a week before the court session, Lamar and several friends went to the jail undisguised and asked the deputy for the keys to Farnum's cell. The deputy thought the men, whom he must have known, were joking, until one of them ripped the keys from his jacket pocket and released the prisoner.[13]

Lamar and his friends drove Farnum to the Pulaski House bar for a party. Couper happened to be at the hotel on other business, and on hearing of the gathering, he confronted Lamar and the others, demanding that Farnum return to his cell. According to some reports, Lamar and his friends drew their revolvers. Lamar and Couper then negotiated a compromise—Farnum could remain with his friends until the next morning but then had to return to jail. His friends could then apply for bail.

By two o'clock the next day Farnum still hadn't turned himself in, so Couper asked the mayor of Savannah to have the city police arrest the escapee. Farnum then surrendered to the city jailer and the police were not summoned. Because Farnum did not meet his end of the bargain, he was not given bail. Yet again, Lamar's antics and the southern courts drew snarls of sarcasm from the northern press. The *New York Times* wrote: "We ought also to compliment Mr. Lamar on his forbearance in permitting the United States District and Circuit Courts to sit in Savannah as usual, considering the provocation he has received. We believe it is the only instance on record in which gentlemen in the position of Mr. Lamar and Capt. [Farnum] have permitted Courts of Justice to sit under their very noses when it was in their power to prevent them. Such moderation deserves more than a passing mention. Congress ought to reward it."[14]

On May 8 a grand jury returned true bills against Lamar and his three friends for freeing Farnum. Lamar's total disregard for the law started re-generating interest in the trials. It promised to be a fiery court session.[15]

CHAPTER 17

"The Most Strangely Constituted Piece of Human Nature"

May–December 1860

At first, after the government learned of the landing of Africans and arrested the *Wanderer* crewmembers, seized the yacht, subpoenaed witnesses, and held hearings, Charles Lamar seemed to panic. He complained about the prosecutors' zeal, thought about escaping to Cuba, worried about the money he was losing, and tried to start a public relations campaign portraying himself and the South as victims of northern abolitionists. But in a short time his fears were replaced by defiance. He publicly admitted that he owned the slave ship *Wanderer* when he bought it back. He claimed that he owned the Africans seized by law enforcement officers when he petitioned the justices of the peace to have them restored to him. He paraded an African boy around town in his buggy. He planned other slaving expeditions. And he even freed a prisoner from jail for a party. It seemed as if he was doing all he could to help the prosecution. Now, in the spring of 1860, Charles was finally going to have his day in court.

The sessions began on Monday, May 14, 1860, with James Moore Wayne and Charles's father-in-law John Nicoll presiding. Nelson Trowbridge and John Dubignon were the defendants in the first cases on the docket. Hamilton Couper and Henry Jackson had to convict these men not only as a punishment for their crimes but also to set a tone for the bigger Farnum and Lamar trials to follow.

The court called the case of Nelson Trowbridge for "holding African Negroes." The examination of the witnesses, most of whom had testified at the first *Wanderer* trial, took one and a half days, and the jury began deliberating at three o'clock on Tuesday afternoon. Lamar, who must have been hoping for a quick not-guilty verdict, agonized as the jury remained sequestered for the rest of that day. The next morning Charles awoke to learn that they still hadn't returned to the courtroom. And no one heard a word from them all through Wednesday. Finally, at seven o'clock that night, after twenty-eight straight hours in the jury room, the foreman told Judge Wayne that the jurors could not reach a decision and never would. Also, several members had taken ill. Judge Wayne declared a mistrial and Charles finally exhaled.[1]

Next up, on Thursday, May 17, John Dubignon faced the charge of "holding and abetting in the holding of African Negroes." The new jury got the case at two o'clock on Friday and before the day's end returned a verdict of not guilty. It undoubtedly added sunshine to Lamar's weekend but storm clouds to Couper's and Jackson's.[2]

On the following Monday John Egbert Farnum, the most infamous of the defendants except Lamar, faced the charge of piracy. Jury selection consumed the first day as the prosecution asked potential jurors if they had "any conscientious scruples against the infliction of capital punishment for the offences charged . . . against the prisoner." Anyone answering yes was rejected.[3]

The examination of the witnesses began on Tuesday. In the previous trials, no one had mentioned seeing Farnum on Jekyll Island during or after the landing, and he was unaccounted for until his appearance on a ship from Charleston to New York twelve days later. Without someone placing Farnum on Jekyll, Couper and Jackson would find it difficult to obtain a conviction, and Lamar must have known this. The prosecution called on the three crucial witnesses from the previous trials—Horatio Harris, James Clubb, and Luke Christie—who all testified meeting a man calling himself Farnum. Harris said Farnum boasted of fighting alongside famed filibuster General William Walker. Luke Christie said that Farnum got on the steam tug *Lamar* before the Africans were boarded for the trip back to Savannah. However, none of them could swear to the identity of the defendant sitting in the courtroom, as he looked so different from the time of the landing.[4]

To Farnum's and Charles's dismay, the district attorney produced two new witnesses who changed the complexion of the proceedings. The first, a lawyer named Marshall Bacon, testified that he had been asked by someone the prior year to propose a deal to the government on behalf of Farnum whereby the supercargo, for $5,000 to $7,000, would prove the ownership of the *Wanderer*, produce her log book, provide the real names of the people engaged in the expedition, and pinpoint the exact location where the three hundred Africans were landed. The lawyer refused to identify the mystery man, other than to say that he was an acquaintance of Farnum. Judge Wayne scolded Bacon for involving himself—a member of the legal profession—in such a disgraceful transaction and excused him.[5]

The next witness was more damaging. Edwin W. Moore, a former com-

modore in the Republic of Texas navy, testified that he had known Farnum since 1847, after the Mexican War, and met him again after the
Walker filibuster campaign in Nicaragua. Two or three months after the
Wanderer had landed her slaves, he ran into Farnum in a Washington,
D.C., hotel, and Farnum revealed his participation in the expedition.
Moore claimed that he warned the man not to speak so publicly about
his involvement, but Farnum said he was living in the North and had no
fear of being arrested. After Farnum had been apprehended and lodged
in the Savannah jail, and Moore was called as a witness, Moore visited
him, explaining that he regretted having to testify against him, but it was
Farnum's own fault for speaking so freely and openly. It was a bad day for
the defense—and Charles Lamar.[6]

As the fifty-year-old commodore left the courthouse, Lamar was waiting and insulted him. Moore took offense. A challenge to a duel was
issued, most likely by Moore, and Lamar accepted. The two immediately
selected seconds, the closest men they could find—defense lawyer John
Owens for Lamar and District Attorney Hamilton Couper for Moore.[7]

Though Charles had previously sought duels, there is no record that
he ever engaged in one. This would be his first. Duels were considered
affairs of honor, and gentlemen followed a formal set of rules. According to the code duello, the seconds negotiated the terms, such as the
date, time, and place; the weapons to be used, and, if guns, the number
of shots allotted to each man; and the number of paces to be taken.
Normally, the principals were given a day to put their affairs in order
and have a conversation with their families, as it might be their last. It
also gave the seconds a chance to attempt to broker a reconcilement.
As it was late Tuesday afternoon, Owens and Couper scheduled their
confrontation for early Thursday morning, before the start of the daily
legal proceedings.[8]

The seconds agreed to dueling pistols with one shot, most likely between five to ten paces each. Dueling had been banned in Georgia since
1809, but it was legal across the river in South Carolina. So on Thursday
Lamar and Moore, with their seconds, boarded separate rowboats and
traveled to the dueling ground at Screven's Ferry. In all likelihood, a
doctor and an independent referee attended the contest and went in a
separate boat. On arriving at the dueling ground the seconds normally
made one last attempt at reconciliation; if they tried in this case, they
failed. After the pistols were loaded, the seconds, doctor, and referee
stepped well to the side. Lamar and Moore stood back to back. At the

referee's command the men stepped off their paces and stopped. At a second command they turned, aimed, and fired. The blasts from the pistols were probably heard across the river by the crowd that had gathered on a Savannah pier.[9]

Both men remained upright and unharmed. Just like that, the affair ended. John Owens stepped forward and announced to Hamilton Couper, for all to hear, "I have a duty now to perform. I am authorized by Mr. Lamar to say to Commodore Moore that the language complained of was used by him under excitement and misapprehension, and that he now withdraws and regrets it." Couper replied that he welcomed Lamar's words. Charles and the commodore shook hands and parted as if they were old friends. Moore certainly knew Charles's cousin once removed, Mirabeau Buonaparte Lamar, the former president of the Republic of Texas. Although Lamar realized that his remarks to Moore were inappropriate, his pride would not let him apologize before the duel and end the matter.[10]

Acquaintances waited on a Savannah wharf to see whose rowboat appeared first, as it usually carried the victor. Both boats, however, returned in close proximity, indicating that no one had been injured or killed. The men were greeted with handshakes and then returned to the courthouse to continue the case. The attorneys finished their closing arguments. There is no record that the prosecutors brought into evidence the newspaper article in the *Albany Statesman* of December 15, 1858, in which Farnum described to a reporter his adventures during the *Wanderer* expedition to Africa. Judge Wayne delivered a defense of the constitutionality of the slave trade laws and then charged the jury at eight o'clock that night.[11]

The next day, Friday, while the Farnum jury deliberated, the court called the case of *U.S. vs. Charles Lamar, William Hone, James Mott Middleton, and Carey Styles* for rescuing J. Egbert Farnum from the county jail. Judge Wayne asked the men how they pleaded. They replied "guilty" and threw themselves on the mercy of the court. Wayne said that he would pronounce the sentence at the end of the court term.[12]

The prosecution then called the case of *U.S. vs. Charles A. L. Lamar* for "holding an African negro named Corrie." When Charles pleaded not guilty, ensuring a trial, his father-in-law, Judge Nicoll, recused himself.[13]

District Attorney Couper wanted to ask the prospective jurors if they "had any conscientious scruples against punishment by imprisonment for the offenses charged against the prisoner." John Owens objected as the death penalty was not involved. Wayne sustained Owens but gave the prosecution until Monday morning to cite precedents for its position. Wayne then dismissed the court for the weekend.[14]

At nine o'clock that night, Judge Wayne received a note from the jury foreman in the Farnum trial and reconvened the court. The foreman told him that the jurors had been without food for upwards of thirty hours and had been together for twenty-six of them. There was no chance they would ever agree on a verdict. Wayne called a mistrial, dismissed the jurors, and remanded Farnum to jail.[15]

On Monday morning Hamilton Couper failed to convince Judge Wayne that he should be able to ask prospective jurors if they had any objections to imprisonment based on the charge—a misdemeanor—against Lamar, and the lawyers proceeded to select a jury. The prosecution started examining the same witnesses from the previous trials. At the end of the morning session, Judge Wayne told the prosecutors that the indictment under the sixth section of the Slave Trade Act of 1818 required them to connect the defendant with the *Wanderer* and the importation of Africans; it was something they had so far failed to do.[16]

The midday meal must have been agonizing for Couper and Jackson, but they felt that they could produce no more evidence than they already had in trying to connect Lamar with bringing Africans into the United States from a foreign country or province. (There is no record suggesting that the prosecution presented Lamar's public admissions of ownership of the *Wanderer* at the ship's auction or of the Africans in front of Magistrate Staley.) At the start of the afternoon session Couper asked the court to be allowed to drop the case against the defendant in light of the interpretation by the court of the sixth section of the Act of 1818. Judge Wayne granted the motion. Then Couper requested permission to drop the cases against Lamar for holding the two Africans and against Lamar and Richardson Akin for holding thirty-six Africans, as well as several cases against other defendants. These requests were also granted.[17]

The cases against Nelson Trowbridge, Nicholas Danese, William C. Corrie (who still had not been extradited by the South Carolina district court judge), and J. Egbert Farnum were carried over to the November 1860 term. Justice Wayne granted bail of $5,000 to Farnum and lowered Danese's to $1,000.[18]

The next day, Judge Wayne sentenced Lamar and each of his three friends to thirty days in jail and a fine of $250, plus court costs, for their role in freeing Farnum from jail. The U.S. marshal allowed the prisoners to serve the sentences in Lamar's rooms above his office on Drayton

Street, be fed at government expense, and go home at night.[19] Charles finally had the weight of the legal system lifted off his back. Ultimately, no one would pay a price for importing the *Wanderer* Africans, or the approximately one hundred deaths that occurred as a result of the voyage.

Soon after Charles and his friends began serving their house arrest, he received an anonymous letter addressed to him in Savannah, "In Jail." Lamar exploded in indignation. He requested the post office to decipher the name of the sender. The post office either failed or refused to do so. Charles then sent the envelope to his cousin L. Q. C. Lamar Jr. in Washington, D.C., still serving Mississippi in the U.S. House of Representatives, to find out who sent the item to him, "& demand of him, in my name, if he intended in any way to reflect on me by addressing it 'In Jail.' If he did, challenge him peremptorily in my name, & telegraph me, & I will be there to meet the appointment." Charles explained what he found so offensive. "I am not in Jail, & the damned Government has not the power to put & keep me there. I am in my own rooms over my office, & go home every night & live like a fighting cock at the expense of the Government, for we notified the Marshal, at the beginning, unless he furnished us we would not stay with him, but dissolve all connection that exist or might exist between us. He submitted the same to the Judges, & they told him to supply us. I can whip the Gov'mt any time they make the issue unless they raise a few additional regiments." Charles also reminded his cousin that he wanted to be notified when Henry Raymond of the *New York Times* came to town, something that Lucius had not done since Charles's first request the previous winter.[20]

In New York, Gazaway kept abreast of his son's actions, many of which made the New York newspapers. On learning of Charles's freeing of Farnum, he wrote, "I am very much mortified that you should compromise yourself for such a fellow as Farnham [*sic*]. . . . Go into court & plead guilty. Make the best apology . . . & get off with as light punishment as possible. . . . Never make wine or stimulants an excuse for any misconduct for the balance of my life. . . . You are the most strangely constituted of any piece of human nature I ever saw or heard of." Gazaway didn't mince words when he learned of Charles's duel. "When I see my son risking his life for such a fellow as Farnham [*sic*] & with such a fellow as Com. Moore, I cannot but think he is mad—worse than a fool." Once the trials ended, Gazaway opined that "tho the imprisonment is longer than I expected, yet upon the whole you have got out altogether much better than you had any right to expect."[21]

With the *Wanderer* trials behind him, Charles got on with his life. But his personality and sense of honor didn't change. Sometime during or shortly after Lamar's incarceration, a twenty-three-year-old local man named Matthew Hopkins struck one of Charles's slaves on the street. Generally speaking, a white person did not hit someone else's slave, other than on his own property, or in self-defense. If a white found the behavior of another's slave objectionable, he or she would lodge a complaint with the owner, who would render punishment if he thought it warranted.[22]

However, the owner of a slave assaulted under other circumstances would not tolerate the violation of his property—certainly not Charles Lamar. When he learned that Hopkins had hit one of his "boys," whom Charles knew to be respectful and polite, for impeding Hopkins's passage through the street, he wrote to Hopkins demanding an explanation. Hopkins replied, commenting on the severity of the wording of Charles's letter, which indicated that, without a proper excuse, Hopkins would be challenged to a duel. Hopkins gave his side of the story, which Charles accepted, withdrawing his offensive words. Charles concluded by saying, "I think you would have done better to have put the boy out of the way & made complaint to [me.]"[23]

Charles's attention was soon diverted from the trials and assaults on his character to something much more significant—the breakup of the nation.

CHAPTER 18

"I Want Dissolution"

April 1860–December 1861

The outcomes of the May 1860 *Wanderer* trials hardly made a ripple beyond Savannah as the country started to unravel. At the end of April 1860 the Democratic Party held its presidential convention in Charleston, South Carolina. The frontrunner, Illinois senator Stephen Douglas, favored the policy of popular sovereignty to determine the issue of slavery in the territories. However, most delegates from the Deep South wanted to give slaveholders unfettered access to those lands. When the sides could not reconcile, all fifty-five Deep South delegates walked out of the convention. When Douglas could not garner the two-thirds majority of the total delegates invited, the meeting ended without a candidate. The party was hopelessly split.[1]

Both factions called for new conventions and invited delegates from all the states. The Deep South Democrats convened in Richmond on June 11 and selected Vice President John Breckenridge as their candidate, while the national Democrats met in Baltimore on June 18 and nominated Stephen Douglas.[2]

While the Democrats were feuding, some members of the defunct Whig Party, who did not want to see the country break up over the issue of slavery, formed the Constitutional Union Party and convened in Baltimore on May 9. They chose former senator John Bell of Tennessee as their candidate. Their platform was simple: maintain, protect, and defend the Constitution of the United States. It did not specifically address the burning issue of the day—slavery in the territories.[3]

The Republicans met in Chicago on May 16. They rejected favored senator William H. Seward and nominated little-known former U.S. representative Abraham Lincoln of Illinois. Most southerners couldn't make sense of the pick, though they knew they didn't like him, or any Republican, for that matter. Even northern Democrats scratched their heads. At least one newspaper predicted doom: "The defeat of Seward and nomination of Lincoln emasculates the Republican Party. . . . The Republican Party is struck with a paralytic stroke, especially in the State of New York, and with common prudence on the part of the Democracy, the latter will have an easy victory."[4] The Republican platform prohibited the expansion of slavery to the territories but did not call for abolition where it currently existed. The Democrats, especially in the Deep South, did not believe the Republicans would act with such restraint.

Charles Lamar hoped the contentious state of the country would lead to secession, but his father didn't think it possible. He told his son in late May, "As to secession, that is not to be had. Virginia & N Carolina, Kentucky, Delaware & Missouri would send troops to put it down. I know they would—so that is hopeless."[5] But the political tide started turning in the Republicans' favor during the summer of 1860, much to Charles's delight. On the day before the presidential election he revealed his sentiments to his father: "I hope Lincoln may be elected. I want dissolution & have I think contributed more than any man South for it."[6]

Charles got his wish on November 6. With only 40 percent of the popular vote but 59 percent of the Electoral College, Lincoln claimed victory. Charles sensed that war was inevitable. He immediately advertised for volunteers to form a cavalry company of one hundred men as authorized by Governor Joseph Brown. "Those of you who are anxious to attach yourselves to a military corp., ready to meet any call from the South, at a moment's notice, are invited to meet at my office, at 7½ o'clock, on Wednesday evening, the 7th November. None need come who cannot furnish his own horse." Charles had found a new purpose in life.[7]

Lincoln's election paid another dividend to Lamar. With emotions running so high over the issue of secession, District Attorney Hamilton Couper realized that prosecuting the remaining *Wanderer* cases against Corrie, Farnum, Danese, and Trowbridge would be a waste of time. On November 12 he asked the court for permission not to prosecute the defendants. The request was granted and the book officially closed on the *Wanderer* expedition.[8]

The election result that many southerners dreaded most, a victory by a "Black Republican" candidate, strangely caused jubilation across the section. States now had a reason to secede, to break away from northern abolitionists and govern their own destiny. Two days after the election, Savannahians gathered for a huge celebration in Johnson Square and raised the Georgia colonial flag on the General Nathanael Greene monument, a fifty-five-foot white marble obelisk. Charles's determination grew even greater as he wrote to Gazaway, who still opposed secession: "I do not agree with you . . . we must go out promptly. We have for ten years been calling upon the abolition states to repeal their laws & I am opposed to any further calls. . . . If Georgia don't act promptly we, the military of Savh, will throw her into Revolution & we will be backed by the Minute Men all throughout the state. . . . We know we are right & we'll act regardless of consequences."[9]

South Carolina, the angriest of the Deep South states, acted first. On December 20, 1860, six weeks after Lincoln's election, 169 delegates to a secession convention voted unanimously to leave the Union. Other states soon followed, and by the end of January 1861, Florida, Mississippi, Alabama, Georgia, and Louisiana had also seceded. The six states formed a new confederacy and had a provisional constitution by February 4, 1861. Texas joined them later in February.

The rush to join the new confederacy stopped abruptly at seven states, which had a total white population of 2,657,000. The other eight slave states, with a white population of 5,632,000, opted to remain in the Union and resolve their issues under the U.S. Constitution. This changed when the Confederate government could no longer tolerate the presence of a Union garrison of roughly seventy-five men at Fort Sumter in Charleston harbor and bombarded it on April 12. Civil war had begun. President Lincoln called on the states to supply their share of 75,000 soldiers needed for the federal army, forcing the eight slave states to make a decision on their future in the Union. Four of them—North Carolina, Virginia, Arkansas, and Tennessee—soon seceded, while four others—Maryland, Delaware, Kentucky, and Missouri—remained. On April 15, two days after the surrender of Fort Sumter, Charles paraded his newly formed company, the Mounted Rifles, through Savannah on the way to a drill.[10]

Gazaway found himself in a difficult position. While living in New York, he served as an agent for the state of Georgia in several capacities. The bank over which he presided, the Bank of the Republic of New York, sold state of Georgia bonds and paid the interest on the coupons, making the obligations easier to market. After Lincoln's election and with secession looming, he helped Georgia procure ten thousand muskets from the federal arsenal in Watervliet, New York. He helped free up another shipment of muskets that New York police had seized just before the ship carrying them left for Savannah. When these transactions were reported in the New York papers, Gazaway's support of the rebel states became public record, which led to hostility from some of his business colleagues as well as the local community.[11]

Although Gazaway wanted to return to Georgia after the state seceded in January 1861, his wife Harriet was very ill and unable to travel. As early as March 1860 he had told Charles, "My wife's tumor is very alarming." Two months later he admitted the inevitable: "I must shortly lose my best friend on earth." Gazaway remained in New York, not only after secession but also after the bombardment of Fort Sumter. Adding to his worries, Gazaway realized that he had overextended on the guano contract. He told Charles, "If we don't attend to the guano & sell it all, we have enough to ruin us." Gazaway's financial prospects rested on his inept son's ability to sell the product. He couldn't have slept easily.[12]

On May 6 Harriet Cazenove Lamar died at age forty-four, and by the end of the month, Gazaway arrived in Savannah with three of his five children. They lived temporarily with Charles, Caro, and their four daughters—Caro having given birth to Georgia Gilliam Lamar in January. Two days after he arrived, Gazaway was again elected a director and the president of the Bank of Commerce by the board of directors. He was home, back on his feet, and ready to resume control of the family business.[13]

———

Despite the historic breakup of the country and the rush to war, the African slave trade never strayed far from Charles's mind. After all, he still had possession of the *Wanderer* in Havana, and William C. Cook had agreed to be a partner in his next expedition, which had been delayed by the theft of the ship in October 1859.

In January 1861 Lamar wrote to Cook with good news. Captain David Martin had been captured. Somehow, he wound up in Liverpool after the shanghaied crew of the *Wanderer* left him stranded on a French ship in the Atlantic Ocean near Madeira in late November 1859. From there, Martin made his way to Key West, where the U.S. navy squadron brought captured slavers. In late summer 1860 Martin recruited a group of fellow thieves, stole the slave bark *William*, and headed for sea. A posse of sailors went after the ship, captured it, and returned it to Key West. Martin, who gave his name as Cummings, was arrested. When his true identity was revealed, Lamar got word of it and had the U.S. district court in Georgia issue an arrest warrant. After a jury acquitted Martin for stealing the *William*, authorities sent him to Savannah in January 1861 to be tried for the theft of the *Wanderer*.[14]

Lamar told Cook that he had taken care of all matters necessary to get the *Wanderer* cleared from Cuba to Savannah. He added, "She will then go immediately to the Coast—everything being arranged as far as can be, & I do hope we shall have no more troubles but land safely a cargo." Charles was not the least bit concerned that his father now owned the *Wanderer* and would face severe consequences if the yacht were again captured as a slaver.[15]

But the ship did have more troubles. As it lay anchored in Havana harbor, rumors swirled about its future. One said that the yacht had been sold to an American for $15,000. A second had it preparing for another expedition to Africa, with a Captain Brown in command. Yet another said that the ship had been purchased by the southern Confederacy. In May, one month after the fall of Fort Sumter, the ship left Havana under the cover of darkness but was seized off the Cuban coast the next day by the U.S. blockading squadron. She became a part of the Union navy, transferring supplies and acting as a patrol boat. Charles Lamar would never see her again.[16]

After the start of the war, thirty-seven-year-old Charles spent much of his time drilling his cavalry company and getting it into camp at Sunbury, Georgia. A sense of urgency hit the South on July 21. The Battle of Manassas, the first major armed conflict in the war, ended in a Confederate victory but with heavy casualties on both sides. The Oglethorpe Light Infantry of Savannah suffered more than most companies and lost its popular leader, Charles's friend Brigadier General Francis S. Bartow. The body was returned to Savannah, and the funeral on July 28 was one of the largest in the history of the city, with the entire population turning out. Bartow's widow, Louisa Greene Berrien Bartow, wanted to give away her husband's uniform hat as a symbol of passing on his legacy of love for and dedication to his native state. She chose Charles Lamar as the recipient.[17]

In August the Confederate secretary of war authorized Lamar to raise a cavalry of ten companies. Charles returned to Savannah and started recruiting for the Sixty-first Georgia Regiment. By the end of September he and several hundred men had encamped at the parade ground. At the end of October the regiment departed for a new location, and Charles left his business affairs, limited as they were, in Gazaway's hands.[18]

With southern confidence soaring after Manassas, Charles's men were itching to fight the Yankees. But any plans that Governor Joseph Brown had for his troops changed on November 7, 1861. The Union, looking to stop the South's ability to trade with foreign countries, sent an armada of more than seventy ships to the area and captured Hilton Head Island. The Union now controlled Hilton Head, Beaufort, and all the waters off the coast of South Carolina, Georgia, and Florida, and had the ability to attack rebel coastal positions at will. Charles Lamar was sent to defend an area with which he had some familiarity—Jekyll Island.

Instead of riding into battle on horseback with his sabre flashing in one hand and revolver blasting in the other, Lamar built batteries on the same island where the *Wanderer* had landed Africans three years earlier.

He hated the assignment and complained about everything, including his commanding officer and the quality of the men who served under him.[19]

Even though he was a soldier, ready to die for his fledgling country, some things never changed with Charles, such as getting into arguments with his father. This time, Charles refused a request from his stepbrother DeRosset, serving in the army in Virginia, to send up one of Charles's favorite slaves. When Gazaway told Charles that his harsh words had offended DeRosset and warned him of his eventual appearance at the judgment seat, Charles snapped and wrote to his father, "You ought to know by this time that I cannot be bullied or forced into your way of thinking & doing & that when an attempt of that kind is made, I am ready & willing to set everybody & everything on Earth, above & below, at defiance at any & every cost. . . . You need have no fears about my appearance at the 'Judgment Seat.' If it were optional with me, to appear or not, I should most assuredly decline the honor, as it is necessary to die before you can appear & it is the dying & not the appearance I have any dread of."[20]

At the end of 1861 the men of the Mounted Rifles elected officers of whom Charles didn't approve, and he declared that they "shall not control my horses, mules, etc. I shall take my black mares home." The officers beat Charles to it and had him thrown out of the regiment, although the reason was not explained. Charles returned to Savannah and rejoined his father selling guano and cotton. The military career of the fire-eating rebel concluded before the first year of the war had ended, without him firing a shot.[21]

CHAPTER 19

"He Was a Prime Mover in Secession"
1862–1864

In early 1862 Charles returned from the military to Savannah and his wife and four daughters. Gazaway welcomed him back to the business; Charles sold guano and traded cotton along with his father and William W. Cheever, Gazaway's new partner and an investor in the two failed *Rawlins* expeditions. But the family operations had never held Charles's interest before the war, and his attitude hadn't changed. He wanted to fight for his state and the Confederacy, even after the birth of his fifth daughter, Mary Stiles Lamar, in September. He asked his father to use his influence to get him back into the army. In late November Gazaway wrote to President Jefferson Davis,

> I have an older [son], who has raised a mounted Rifle Corps., & then a Battalion now the 61st Georgia Regt. from which he was thrown out, by what he considered unjust treatment to his command. He has no superior for energy & efficiency, & especially in Cavalry. I have asked the Hon. the Secy of War to give him a Colonel's commission & amass all the Cavalry from this to the southern line of Georgia into a Regiment for his command. He was a prime mover in secession, & is anxious to fight it to a conclusion. . . . Gen. Mercer recommended the arrangement to Gen. Lee last summer & the papers are on file on the War Department. . . . If you will accept a superior officer, he is at your command for that or any other service. . . . His name is Charles A. L. Lamar.[1]

Nothing resulted from the appeal. Soon after, Charles repeated his desire to rejoin the military to his friend Nelson Trowbridge: "If the war continues, I shall enter the service again, but I am in hopes the Yankees will soon find out their mistake & let us alone."[2]

While Charles pondered his future, Gazaway sought new opportunities. The Union blockade was strangling Savannah's commerce, and he recognized that blockade-runners were crucial to the South's war effort. The risks were huge, but so were the potential gains. A single successful expedition could deliver a profit of $100,000. In mid-1862 he and other investors purchased the steamer *Emma* with hopes of sneaking cargo from the Savannah River past the Union navy. On the night of August 30 the steamer barely got under way before grounding near the mouth of the river. The captain set the ship on fire to prevent capture by the enemy.[3]

In late October Gazaway purchased the *Nina*. It sailed with a cargo of cotton from Georgetown, South Carolina, destined for England by way of the Bahamas. Four months later Gazaway learned that the captain and mate had been found dead in a yawl at sea.[4]

It is not surprising that blockade-running captured Charles's interest, too. The operation involved sneaking property into the country by ship, promised huge profits, and included an element of danger. In early 1863 he and several partners, including his friend Lloyd Guyton ("L. G.") Bowers of Columbus, Georgia, purchased the steamers *St. Johns* and *Charleston*. The former vessel fared no better than his slave ships and was captured by the blockading squadron. As with his other failures, Charles was quick to blame someone else. "The St. Johns was lost by mismanagement. The fellow was drunk & 60 miles out of his reckoning. . . . I'll be damned [if] anything can have two heads. In [the] future I shall control or someone else shall."[5]

However, on April 24 Charles learned that the *Charleston* had arrived in Wilmington, having successfully carried out and brought back a cargo, though the ship grounded and suffered damage in the return. Initially elated at the news, Charles soon heard of problems with the handling of the vessel as it came into Wilmington. He told his agent in Charleston, "One of the engineers of the Charleston came in to see me this morning. He gives a bad account of the captain & pilots coming over—says they 'laid to' preparatory to surrendering to an unarmed steamer!!" It is unclear from Charles's letters if the cargo was salvaged and, if so, profitable.[6]

Gazaway realized that to make an impact on the needs of the South he required a fleet of fast blockade-runners operating continually, financed by a large amount of capital. He organized the Importing and Exporting Company of Georgia and, as with almost all his other ventures, included Charles in its operations. Gazaway immediately began promoting the company by advertising in southern newspapers. He wrote to Georgia governor Joseph E. Brown: "You may have seen in the papers a prospectus for an Importing & Exporting Company to be established in this city. We have about $200,000 subscribed . . . & I have just advertised to take subscriptions in the interior of the state & I have written to the government at Richmond to get them interested and would be pleased to have the enterprise promoted by your [Excellency]."[7]

The company needed ships that could make seventeen knots, draft in eight feet of water, and carry from three hundred to one thousand bales of cotton. With few if any vessels like that available in the South, Gazaway sent Charles, L. G. Bowers, and Captain Henry J. Hartstene to Europe to procure them. They left Wilmington, North Carolina, on June 30 and first called at Bermuda, a common stop for blockade-runners en route to England. From there they caught a British ship to Halifax and then another to Liverpool, arriving on July 20. Around the same time, Gazaway sent Captain David Martin—no relation to the man who stole the *Wanderer*—to Canada to purchase similar steamers, with the proviso that if he couldn't find any, he should sail for Europe to help Charles.[8]

Charles met with several contacts in Liverpool, the main destination for cotton shipments from the United States, and enjoyed a visit to the Southern Club, "a strictly southern institution. Many Englishmen are members but all sympathize with us. The portrait of Beauregard, full length adorns the parlor. They have . . . photographs of all our generals, and the new flag in every room."[9]

After two days, Charles traveled to London with Bowers and Hartstene for an emergency meeting with bankers arranged by former Savannah mayor John Ward, who was in Europe working to support the Confederacy and visiting his family in Switzerland. Charles set up a base of operations in his hotel and tried to secure cotton contracts and attract British investors to the blockade-running company. He encountered a brick wall as news of the Confederate defeats at Vicksburg and Gettysburg convinced the British that the South would soon surrender. He wrote his father after three weeks: "I have done nothing yet in the way of negotiating, farther than to feel the public pulse, which is very adverse to us at this time."[10]

Being away for so long made Charles homesick. He missed his wife and five daughters, and even his slaves. He asked Caro, "Remember me to all the servants, Nannie, Lucy, Nelson, Reuben, George and all the others who may be with you. Tell them if I get boats, I will bring them all something, clothing if nothing more." Charles's affection for his slaves was not uncommon among southerners. Close bonds often developed between master and servant. Yet Charles could not make the connection between his slaves and the Africans he had caused to suffer and die on the *Wanderer*.[11]

Having accomplished little in London, Charles went to Paris with Captain Hartstene to seek investors. At Gazaway's request, they also hoped to meet with the Confederate minister to France, James Slidell, and encourage him to discuss with the French government the possibility of making the Confederacy a French protectorate. While there, Hartstene visited his family in Munich, and Charles went to Geneva to see Gazaway's ten-year-old daughter Harriet, nicknamed Hattie, in the care of Gazaway's sister-in-law Paulina Fowle. Charles gushed over his little stepsister. "She is as pure & unselfish as Ma was & is as cheerful & merry as a cricket all the time. She attracts everybody to her, even strangers in the cars. I wish you could see her."[12]

Despite the excitement of visiting Europe and seeing family, Charles still wanted to be part of the rebellion, but on his terms. He wrote his father, "If I could get a brigade of state troops, I would go into the service again. Geo. and Carolina will be the coming winter the theatre of the war. I will be back & I hope to defend the old state." Charles also revealed something that must have made Gazaway's insides crunch into a knot. "I am engaged in a number of speculations, cotton, Confed. loan & powder. If the powder is the half they claim for it, it will enable us to whip this fight. It can be made out of simple plaster & a little hot water." One can envision Gazaway rolling his eyes at his son's latest get-rich-quick scheme.[13]

Disappointing news greeted Charles on his return to London in early October. He learned that Captain Hartstene, who was to pilot one of the newly acquired boats back to Wilmington, had an attack of paralysis in Munich and couldn't leave his bed. It was nearly impossible to hire pilots to deliver boats to Bermuda ever since British foreign secretary Earl Russell approved U.S. cruisers seizing British ships with Confederate-bound cargoes. Lamar also complained about the rapidly rising cost of ships and the purchasing environment. "It is impossible to make you conceive . . . the amount of swindling going on all the time & conducted by [Confederate] Gov'mt agents."[14]

Eventually, Charles made some progress. He purchased a boat in Sweden after getting a positive report from a captain and engineer who inspected her. The captain would sail her back to Wilmington. Also, Charles updated his father with what he considered good news on the magic gunpowder formula: "I purchased the secret to make powder out of plaster & hot water & the man is expected every day here to impart the secret. It will be worth millions to the Gov'mt & as much to me. It can be made in ten minutes & shoots wet almost as well as when dry. This I have seen. . . . But before I pay him the money, I am to make myself perfectly satisfied with its merits." Charles never revealed the steps he took to confirm the merits, but he handed over an unknown amount of cash for the formula.[15]

By late October, just before returning to Savannah, Charles wrote an associate in Paris that he had purchased two more ships (in addition to the one in Sweden) that were under construction, one to be finished by the end of January and the other by the end of February, each costing between £22,000 and £25,000. He closed by reporting on his failure regarding the magic powder formula: "See the powder man & tell him I have instructed Phinizy to institute proceedings against him for damages & he will go to Paris to attend to it before leaving for Bermuda." Charles had taken the bait—hook, line, and sinker—yet again.[16]

In early November Charles, along with L. G. Bowers and cousin L. Q. C. Lamar Jr., who was in Europe as the Confederacy's minister to Russia, sailed from Liverpool to Halifax to Bermuda on their journey home. There they boarded the *Ceres* to run the blockade back to Wilmington. In early December the ship grounded at night near the coast. The passengers and crew set the ship on fire, boarded lifeboats, and headed up the Cape Fear River to Wilmington, leaving behind most of their personal belongings and papers. The next morning two U.S. navy ships spotted the *Ceres* in flames. Navy sailors extinguished them, saved the ship, and recovered the personal papers, including copies of Charles's letters and those he received during the trip. Many would be published by the *New York Times* the following January, exposing Charles's and Gazaway's blockade-running activities, as well as their contacts in the United States and Europe.[17]

The Importing and Exporting Company of Georgia began receiving boats in early 1864 and immediately faced problems from an unlikely source. The Confederate government, badly in need of funds and wartime necessities, passed a law in February 1864 mandating that all blockade-runners, except those owned by the states, intending to sail from a Confederate port with a cargo of cotton, tobacco, rice, sugar, or naval stores had to allocate half their tonnage on outbound and inbound voyages to the Confederacy. To circumvent this restriction and keep the profits for the state rather than the Confederacy, Governor Joseph E. Brown chartered five of the Importing and Exporting Company's ships "to be used for the State in exporting cotton and other productions and commodities and importing supplies for the state." Brown appointed C. A. L. Lamar as agent to manage the operations, but the chartering ploy didn't work, and the company had to meet the government's set-asides. Gazaway Lamar's blockade-runners had moderate success, with the *Little Hattie* making eight successful round-trip voyages, and the *Little Ada, Mary*

Bowers, Lillian, Florie, and *Susan Bierne* making between one and three each. However, it is unclear how much profit, if any, the company made from its operations.[18]

By the time Charles had returned from Europe at the end of 1863 and the blockade-runners had been put into operation, it had become increasingly clear that the Union army amassing on the Tennessee border was going to make a move into Georgia. Charles Lamar had a decision to make about his future.

CHAPTER 20

A Sad Legacy
1864–1865

In the late fall of 1864, with Union major general William T. Sherman's army moving through Georgia, Charles Lamar entered the state military as a colonel. He joined the staff of the commanding major general of state troops, Howell Cobb, whom Lamar had publicly argued with and insulted over the dispute to import African apprentices.[1] Cobb's headquarters were in Macon, which the Union columns bypassed on their way from Atlanta to the coast.

On December 21 Sherman's troops entered Savannah and ended the war for thousands of Georgians. His soldiers immediately took control of all the town's warehouses, which contained 38,500 bales of cotton, including several thousand owned by Gazaway Lamar.

General John W. Geary addressed the residents from the steps of the City Exchange building. He declared that people who took the oath of allegiance to the Union and laid down their arms in accordance with President Abraham Lincoln's Proclamation of Amnesty and Reconstruction of December 8, 1863, would be entitled to keep all of their property except enslaved humans. Gazaway Lamar, then sixty-six years old and living in Savannah, could choose to defy the Yankee leaders, whom he despised, and maintain his pride but live his remaining days as a pauper, or bow in defeat before his conquerors, keep his cotton, and retain the means to support himself and his family in comfort. Lamar chose the latter, aware that by keeping his property, he would also deprive the federal government of his fortune.[2]

On January 6, 1865, Gazaway signed the oath. He also wrote letters to his sons Charles and DeRosset, encouraging them to surrender and come home, and he halted all his blockade-running operations. In late January or early February, Charles, while on duty, learned of his father's actions. He didn't show much sympathy for an old man trying to salvage his life savings from a lost cause. He wrote Caro, "Is father sane? I cannot believe it. . . . He has disgraced the name of Lamar. . . . I would not have taken the oath for all the cotton in the South. I would though, with reservations, to save my wife, children, and self. Nothing else would induce me to do so."[3]

In late February Charles traveled to Columbus to help defend the city and moved in with his friend, L. G. Bowers. As with his earlier stint in the military, Lamar wasn't thrilled with his assignment or his commanding officers. He was never one for taking direction from others. He told his wife: "I cannot serve under so many idiots who are Adjutant Generals, Major Generals, and Brigadiers."[4]

About this time, U.S. major general George H. Thomas ordered General James H. Wilson to lead five to six thousand mounted troops through Alabama and Georgia against the remaining rebel forces and destroy all war-manufacturing capabilities. Wilson began on March 22 and smashed through his targets like a bowling ball through pins. On March 31 Union troops occupied Ashbyville, Alabama. Three days later they took Selma, then Tuscaloosa, and on April 12 the advance guard accepted the immediate surrender of Montgomery from the mayor and city council.[5]

After resting his men for two days, Wilson headed for Columbus. The city's defenders were not aware of Wilson's whereabouts until shortly before his arrival. In fact, on April 10 General Cobb sent Charles Lamar to Savannah under a flag of truce to negotiate a prisoner exchange with Union officers. Charles asked to be allowed to enter the city to see his family, but the guards wouldn't even let him send a letter. He headed back to Columbus, arriving in time to encounter General Wilson's army.[6]

Columbus was a large manufacturing center with a population of twelve thousand inhabitants who supplied the Confederate army with clothing and other war materials. It was situated on the western border of Georgia, separated from Girard, Alabama (current-day Phenix City), by the Chattahoochee River. Three bridges connected the two towns. (A fourth bridge, three miles north of Columbus, had been destroyed.) Two redoubts with heavy artillery on the Columbus side of the river guarded the roads to the two northernmost bridges—one for pedestrians and the other for trains. The rebel military officer, Colonel Leon von Zinken, posted most of his two to three thousand soldiers in a defensive line on the Alabama side of the river. Around noon on April 16 Wilson's army gathered behind ridges on the western side of Girard. At two o'clock a detachment of Union soldiers attacked the bridge on the southern end of town but was repelled by the Georgians, who then set fire to the bridge. Von Zinken concentrated his troops in front of the two intact bridges.[7]

At about four o'clock General Wilson and General Emory Upton decided to launch an attack on the footbridge. However, because of a late arrival of one of the brigades, Wilson delayed the assault. It was dark by the time the tardy soldiers appeared. General Upton suggested attacking at night, a rarely employed tactic, and Wilson approved. At nine o'clock a force of three hundred Yankees charged the rebel lines. They broke through and pushed back the rebels to the Columbus side of the bridge. In the darkness they passed within ten feet of Howell Cobb, who was observing the action from his horse before deciding to retreat to Macon. The gunners in the redoubts held their fire as the soldiers merged together, fighting hand to hand.[8]

As the Yankees advanced, Charles Lamar charged on his horse into the fray, trying to rally his men. A Union soldier raised his rifle and fired. The shot blasted into Charles's head, just below his left eye, and he fell dead from his horse.[9]

Years later, Union colonel Edward F. Winslow recalled, "With the death of Colonel Lamar in Columbus, all serious resistance came to an end." By ten o'clock Union forces gained control of the town, taking fifteen hundred prisoners and a large quantity of guns and munitions. The next day Charles's body was recovered from under the bridge and turned over to the mayor of Columbus, who had him buried in the local cemetery. At some point after Charles was shot and before he was removed from the battlefield, a Yankee soldier stole his watch. Attempts by Howell Cobb to get it back through the Union chain of command failed.[10]

This brief encounter was the only known action that Charles Lamar saw in the war. To his credit, he probably could have retreated to Macon with Cobb and his staff, but he stood by his fellow soldiers to the end.

———————————————

On April 20, before Caro Lamar learned of her husband's death, the Yankees ordered her and her six daughters from their home. The family went to live with Charles's friend Seaborn Jones at Millhaven plantation in Sylvania, Screven County. There, on April 26, she learned that she had become a widow. Then on May 22 her new baby daughter Rebecca died. The wartime years had been especially hard for Caro. She lost her father, Judge John C. Nicoll, her mother-in-law, her husband, and a child. After six weeks at Millhaven, she was allowed to return to her house in Savannah. She wrote to Gazaway: "On the 2nd of June I arrived here and father my home is desolate, and I pine for him whose presence was sunlight, and joy to my soul."[11]

Over the course of the following year, whenever Mrs. Bowers and her children went for walks in Columbus, they gathered flowers and made wreaths to hang on the small cross on Charles's grave. She sent Caro a box with Charles's clothes and some leaves that had fallen on the ground where he was buried. "I had the woolen garments sunned during the summer," she wrote, "to prevent injury from moths, otherwise they are just as he left them. In the colored vest you will find his little pocket comb and knife. He wore the vest Saturday [the day before he died]."[12]

In late May 1866 Charles's remains were sent to Savannah under the charge of L. G. Bowers. They arrived on June 3 and were interred at Laurel Grove Cemetery, his final resting place. A local paper reported, "The funeral was attended by the relatives and friends of the deceased and a large concourse of our most respectable citizens."[13]

Charles Lamar left his wife with an estate laden with debt. Little wonder. Charles was a disaster as a businessman. He failed at almost every venture he entered and lost enormous amounts of money in the process. He admitted to investing $50,000 in underproductive gold mines, most of which would become worthless, without receiving any dividends. He was swindled out of $45,000 from a man named Lewin in New York. He incurred a $50,000 loss by not insuring his cotton press and warehouse. He claimed to have lost $80,000 on the two failed *Rawlins* missions, and he admitted to losing money on the *Wanderer* venture. Trowbridge and Johnston owed him thousands from the legal, interstate slave-trading partnership. He was constantly hounded by James Gardner to honor his notes. He lost $25,000 in a cotton press patent lawsuit. On his death his shares in a plank road company, one of his early investments, were worthless. He lost an unknown amount of money buying a magic formula for making gunpowder. Always a free spender, Charles owed his father more than $300,000, an amount that Gazaway, in debt himself to the tune of $350,000 after all his cotton had been seized, was not going to forgive. When Caro realized the financial abyss into which Charles had dropped her, she told Gazaway, "The indebtedness of dear Charlie's estate to you broods like a horrid nightmare over me, and I would like during your lifetime to have all things settled between us, for I know you love us."[14]

Charles died intestate and Caro had to apply to the court to become the administratrix of his estate. She had begged Charles to make a will, but "he laughingly told me . . . that whoever should have the winding up of his estate would have a very hard task to perform and I now find those words painfully verified."[15]

Gazaway had transferred the ownership of the Eastern Wharves to Charles in 1863, along with a mortgage of $82,000 from the Bank of the Republic. Caro didn't learn about the debt until a bank representative informed her a year after Charles died. The additional responsibility nearly destroyed her. "[The mortgage] distresses and harasses me to the degree that, but for my children, I could wish I were sleeping my last sleep beside my precious husband."[16]

Caro's next seventeen years were a constant struggle to pay the estate's debts. Yet she showed a discipline to manage money that her husband had never possessed. She rented the estate's property and slowly paid creditors while supporting herself and her five daughters. In 1883 she finally extinguished all the estate's obligations and the court granted her letters dismissory. Caro always wrote about Charles in cherishing words, and as a devoted wife she overlooked his criminal behavior, but one wonders if there were solitary times when she cursed him for leaving her with a crushing mountain of debt.[17]

One group of people who stood by Caro in her darkest hours were her former slaves, most of whom had departed after Sherman entered Savannah, but they later returned. "Nurse Lucy, Reuben, Old Will, and Missouri are with me, and are faithful and affectionate. . . . Phillis is also here, and offered to pay me rent for her room, but I told her all the pay I wanted was for her to help me with the children when Lucy was cleaning the nursery. She is true to her promise, and has now their little hearts."[18]

Caro died in August 1902 at the age of seventy-six. She is buried next to her husband in Laurel Grove Cemetery.[19]

―――――――

Gazaway didn't record when he learned of Charles's death. The *Savannah Republican* first reported the fall of Columbus on April 22, a delay caused by the destruction of so many telegraph lines as well as the extensive coverage of Robert E. Lee's surrender to Ulysses S. Grant on April 9 and President Lincoln's assassination on April 14. The *Daily Constitutionalist* of Augusta, published by Charles's business partner James Gardner, reported Charles's death on April 23. Surely Gardner would have sent word immediately to Gazaway. The *Savannah Republican* reported the death on April 29.[20]

The news must have hit Gazaway hard. The last member of his first family and his oldest son was gone. The two had a tumultuous relationship, to be sure, but Gazaway always came to Charles's rescue despite being continually disappointed by his son's lifestyle and his business and personal decisions, as well as embarrassed by his involvement in the slave trade.

Gazaway had to deal with other problems. Despite having taken the oath of allegiance to the Union, the U.S. treasury agents, headed by supervisor Albert G. Browne Sr., shipped all the stored cotton in the city—38,500 bales—to New York. Of that, about 3,200 bales belonged to Lamar personally, 790 bales to the Importing and Exporting Company of Georgia, and 400 to other individuals but held by him, altogether valued at close to $1 million. He had far fewer bales, numbering in the hundreds, stored in southern Georgia and Florida.[21]

Treasury agent Browne, whose son had performed legal services for Gazaway in Boston in the 1860 case involving the *Wanderer*, proved to be the elder Lamar's nemesis. He took possession of the Bank of Commerce, over which Gazaway presided, to use as his offices and persuaded Lamar to leave his books and papers in the building, where he claimed they'd be safe. Browne then seized them and sent them to Washington, probably to drum up charges against the well-known rebel. Lamar protested but never recovered his papers, which left him practically defenseless in his many lawsuits.[22]

With the death of his son, the defeat of the South, and the loss of his Savannah cotton and personal papers, Lamar probably thought that matters couldn't get worse, but they did. His open hostility toward the Yankees before the war came back to haunt him. In 1861, shortly before he returned to Savannah from his fifteen-year residency in New York, Gazaway challenged Charles A. Dana, a New York newspaper editor, to publish his letter decrying the incivility of the North in raising an army. He wrote,

> It will appear that the very first regiment that was armed, equipped and stimulated to make war upon the southern people was a certain 'Billy Wilson's Regiment,' every man in which from the colonel on down to the lowest private, was taken from the penitentiaries, as 'convicts' whom neither the laws of God or man could restrain from crime, except within the walls of a prison!!! [This] regiment was lauded by the Press, encouraged by the People, and egged on even by the Ministry of the Gospel of Jesus Christ (so called). [This] regiment was paraded through the streets—and on one occasion was assembled in Tammany Hall—where after politicians had addressed them, they were made to kneel down and take the most horrible & execrable oaths against the southern people.[23]

In 1862 Dana became an assistant secretary of war, and after Savannah fell he exacted revenge on Lamar. On April 28, 1865, twelve days after Charles had been killed, Dana had Gazaway arrested based on a rumor that a man named Lamar had been involved in the plot to kill Lincoln. Lamar was transported under guard eight hundred miles to the Old Capital Prison in Washington, D.C. His nineteen-year-old daughter Charlotte accompanied him as his nurse. Secretary of War Edwin M. Stanton not only forbade her from taking care of her father in prison but also ordered her from the city.[24]

Lamar spent three months in jail without ever being formally charged. He wrote several letters to President Andrew Johnson asking for a private meeting so he could plead his case. Johnson finally granted him an interview and released him on a parole of honor on the condition that he return to Savannah and travel only with a passport granted by the U.S. military authorities in Georgia.[25]

On August 1 Lamar arrived home and immediately set about trying to gain possession of the remaining cotton owned by him and the Importing and Exporting Company of Georgia, stored in warehouses and plantations in Thomasville, Georgia, and Tallahassee, Florida. In a bizarre sequence of events, Lamar eventually received written permission from the commanding general of Georgia to take possession of cotton personally owned by him in that state. However, when he attempted to ship the Thomasville cotton, Albert G. Browne Jr., who had replaced his ailing father as treasury agent, had his former client jailed.[26]

On December 26, 1865, Gazaway faced a military commission for defrauding the United States by stealing its cotton and attempting to bribe an official of the United States. After eight days of testimony, he was found guilty of all charges and sentenced to five years in prison and a $25,000 fine.[27]

On January 11, 1866, Lamar was incarcerated for a third time in less than a year. Three weeks later the commanding officer of the Savannah district ordered the sentence to be put on hold until President Johnson could review it. (Johnson rejected the military commission's findings days before he left office.)[28]

After his release, Gazaway, consumed with anger over his treatment by the Yankees, spent most of his time suing the government and any representative who he thought had anything to do with confiscating his cotton. His rage didn't serve him well. For years he had lectured Charles to be patient with people, let them express their opinions, and employ reason without insulting them. But Gazaway developed some of his son's objectionable traits, hurling epithets and making countless enemies along the way. In one letter to the U.S. secretary of war, asking for the return of his personal papers, he used such harsh language that he received the following response from a clerk in the office: "The terms of the letter are entirely unwarrantable, and are of such a character that he must decline answering them."[29]

Lamar still had to deal with the *Wanderer*, which the Union navy had seized in May 1861. Gazaway was the registered owner when the vessel was condemned by a prize court in 1863 and purchased by the United States. After the war it was sold at public auction for $6,000 to Israel L. Snow of Rockland, Maine, who invested another $7,000 for repairs. He employed it as a merchant ship, which made its first run from Maine to Savannah in November 1866 in a record six days. On December 28, 1870, soon after leaving Havana for Philadelphia with a cargo of fruit, the *Wanderer* wrecked on a reef and sank. Lamar put in a claim for compensation from the government for seized property.[30]

In 1872 Gazaway moved to New York to live with his daughter Charlotte Lamar Soutter as he continued his fight with the federal government for compensation for his cotton. In March 1874, after two favorable Supreme Court decisions regarding the rights of southerners who took the oath, he won a judgment for $579,343.51 in the court of claims. He had finally triumphed, thanks to the Constitution from whose protection he had been so willing to separate in 1861. He could pay off his debts of $325,000 and have enough left to live his remaining years in comfort.[31]

Gazaway didn't get much of a chance to enjoy his regained wealth. He died of natural causes six months later on October 5, 1874, at the age of seventy-six. He had outlived his two wives and eight of his eleven children. He is buried in Alexandria, Virginia, next to his second wife, Harriet. In his will, Lamar left $100,000 out of the residue of his cotton claims "to establishing and sustaining one or more hospitals for colored persons in [Savannah and Augusta] who have been slaves, and their descendants, giving preference to those which once belonged to or was hired by me."[32]

———————

In a letter to C. C. Cook on June 20, 1859, Charles Lamar claimed that he had originally entered the slave trade for "grandeur" and that he had been fighting for a principle. There is no doubt that Charles believed in the right of southerners to import Africans. But his actions suggest that his primary interest in entering the trade was financial. As early as 1855 Gazaway complained of having to support Charles. "I have sacrificed $35,000 to keep you easy," he wrote. Six months later he told Charles, "I hope $43,000 is not so small that you would be unthankful." Letters like this continued in the following years. The gold mines became a drain as early as 1856, and by 1857 the Lamar, Trowbridge, Gardner partnership was in debt for between $29,000 and $36,000. Charles had asked Gardner in February 1857 if he knew of ways to make money. Clearly, he was in financial trouble when he entered the trade in the summer of 1857.[33]

Perhaps most revealing of Charles's true intentions was his public attempt to import African apprentices in 1858. If he believed so much in his right to import slaves and wanted to challenge the law in the courts, why did he use the ploy of calling them apprentices? He had accused Howell Cobb of avoiding the issue of testing the legality of the slave trade in court, but it was Charles who ran from it. In his published manifesto to Cobb, Charles declared that he would reopen the trade in slaves to foreign countries. Charles might fatten his wallet by shipping slaves from Africa to Cuba, but the activity would do nothing for the southern planter whom Charles claimed he wanted to help.

During the *Wanderer* trials Charles finally had his long-sought-after opportunity to challenge the slave trade laws on a national stage. But instead of presenting his case in the courtroom, he used every ploy imaginable to cover up the importation and circumvent the law.

The author of the 1886 article in the *North American Review* understood Charles well. He wrote of Lamar's contention that he was fighting for a principle: "So queer a bulb is the human head that perhaps he thought he told the truth."[34]

The Slave-Trader's Letter-Book, along with other related materials, provides a portrait of one of the most flamboyant and reckless men of antebellum and Civil War Georgia. Had Charles Lamar been merely a rogue, a free-wheeling, free-spending, drinking, gambling, dueling sportsman who miraculously survived a ship disaster as a teenager to run the Union blockade and fight for his state and the Confederacy, he probably would have gained folk-hero status throughout the South and even beyond. But unfortunately he did more. He was largely responsible for cramming 487 innocent people into a ship under the most inhumane circumstances and carrying them on a six-week journey across an ocean. This act resulted in the deaths of about one hundred of them, and bondage for those who survived. It is this for which Charles Lamar should be remembered. It is a sad and tragic legacy.

Charles Augustus Lafayette Lamar (1824–65) as he
appeared in the *Roll of Officers and Members of the Georgia
Hussars* (Savannah, Ga.: The Morning News, 1906) when
he was about thirty years old. Lamar, who was elected
the company captain in 1851 at the age of twenty-seven,
resigned unexpectedly in 1854, the same time he became
involved in ex-Mississippi governor John Quitman's planned
invasion of Cuba. After his experience with the filibuster
movement and large losses in business investments, Lamar
began a career in the illegal international slave trade.

(Courtesy of the Georgia Historical Society, Savannah, Ga.)

Gazaway Bugg Lamar (1798–1874) accumulated
a fortune in cotton factoring, shipping, banking,
insurance, and wharfage. In 1838 he lost his first wife,
five children, and a niece in the sinking of the steamship
Pulaski off the coast of North Carolina. Of his family
members, only his sister and his fourteen-year-old son
Charles survived the disaster. As he grew into adulthood,
Charles tried to emulate his father's business success
but failed, and turned to filibustering and the African
slave trade. Gazaway chided his son for his involvement
in the trade, but the reprimands did no good.

(Photo from the *Georgia Historical Quarterly* 37 [June 1953].)

James Gardner (1813–74), of Augusta, Georgia, was a
planter and the publisher of the *Augusta Constitutionalist*
newspaper and in 1857 almost became the governor of
Georgia. He partnered with Charles Lamar and Nelson
Trowbridge in the gold-mining and interstate slave-
trading businesses. Both endeavors were unprofitable,
and Lamar and Trowbridge became deeply indebted
to him. Unlike his two partners, Gardner did not
invest in the illegal international slave trade.
(Allen D. Candler and Clement A. Evans, eds.,
Cyclopedia of Georgia [Atlanta, 1906]; courtesy of the
Georgia Historical Society, Savannah, Ga.)

Howell Cobb (1815–68), who married Gazaway Lamar's first cousin, served as Georgia governor and a congressman. In 1857 President James Buchanan appointed him treasury secretary. Cobb rejected all three of Charles Lamar's applications for customs clearance to import African "apprentices" into the United States, Cuba, and an unnamed destination. In return, Charles called Cobb's stand "the work of a little man to a little object" and taunted his cousin by declaring, "I will reopen the slave trade to foreign countries. Let your cruisers catch me if they can." Near the end of the Civil War, Colonel Charles Lamar served as Major General Cobb's aide.

(Georgia Historical Society Collection of Photographs, MS 1361-PH; courtesy of the Georgia Historical Society, Savannah, Ga.)

James Moore Wayne (1790–1867) of Savannah was
appointed associate Supreme Court justice by President
Franklin Pierce in 1855. He presided over the *Wanderer*
trials with U.S. District Court judge John C. Nicoll,
Charles Lamar's father-in-law. Wayne delivered several
charges to juries admonishing the slave trade, but
the government prosecutors never gained a guilty
verdict related to the *Wanderer* importation. When
the War Between the States erupted, Justice Wayne
opted to remain in Washington with the Union.
(Photo taken from the Alexander Atkinson Lawrence
Papers, MS 2019; courtesy of the Georgia
Historical Society, Savannah, Ga.)

The *Wanderer* anchored on the western shore of Jekyll Island
on November 29, 1858. Only 409 of the 487 Africans survived
the transatlantic crossing known as the Middle Passage, and
more died from sicknesses contracted on the voyage. Charles
Lamar, who did not go on the expedition, traveled from
Savannah to Jekyll as soon as he heard of the yacht's arrival,
picked up three hundred slaves, and shipped them to the South
Carolina plantation of his friend John Montmollin, on the
Savannah River. From there they were distributed further.

(Map designed by Paul F. Rossmann of James Island, S.C.)

The *Wanderer* was built for John D. Johnson of Islip, Long Island, in 1857. In December of that year Johnson took the ship on a cruise to New Orleans, arriving on March 1, 1858, when Charles Lamar happened to be in town. In April 1858 the yacht returned to New York in nine days, a record time. Within a month Johnson sold the vessel to William C. Corrie, who was part of an eight-man syndicate headed by Charles Lamar. In November 1858 the *Wanderer* completed the first known successful landing of Africans on U.S. soil in almost four decades.

(*Harper's Weekly*, January 15, 1858; courtesy of V & J Duncan Antique Maps, Prints & Books, Savannah, Ga.)

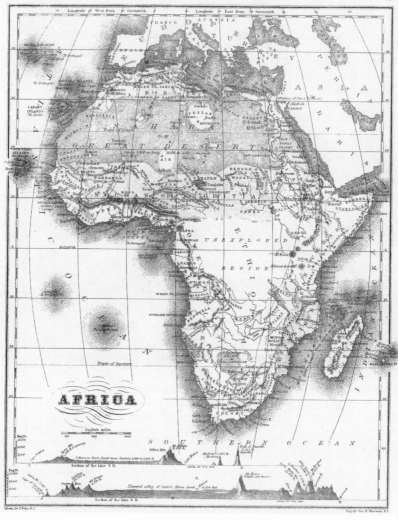

On September 16, 1858, the *Wanderer* reached the coast of Africa.
The yacht sailed thirty miles up the Congo River, and Captain
William C. Corrie placed an order for five hundred Africans with a
slave dealer. In mid-October he and his crew packed 487 captives
into the hold of the ship, whose bulkheads had been removed
and a slave deck installed, and headed back to Georgia.
(McNally's System of Geography, Map No. 32, Africa, 1859; courtesy
of V & J Duncan Antique Maps, Prints & Books, Savannah, Ga.)

Letters of the
Slave-Trader's Letter-Book

PART A

*Letters Concerning Filibustering
and Slave Trading*

Letter no. 2

Confidential
Savannah Feby 12th 1855
J. S. Thrasher, Esq., New Orleans[1]

Dr Sir,

I am in rec't of both of your favors of the 2nd & the 5th. I will not notice the offensive part of the first as it was written under a misapprehension. I will proceed to answer your interrogatories in the order in which they are put.

1st then, "Do you find any ground in Georgia favorable to our wishes"? Our people all favor the acquisition of Cuba & would favor any movement having for its object the taking of it, but it is almost impossible to convince them that a properly organized expedition can be gotten up. They have heard so much talk & little else, that they think it will either end that way, or as did the López[2] trip did [*sic*], & hence are unwilling to go themselves or invest their monies. If you will take the *say so* of some of the very men whose names you have mentioned to me as being in correspondence with you, they'll tell you men & money are abundant, get any quantity of either at any moment etc. etc. For instance Dr. Ramsay[3] of Atlanta, came all the way down to see me on the subject (being a dead head on the Rail Roads) & told me men & money we could get to an unlimited extent in his portion of the state. When I commenced to pin him down I found he did not believe himself what he had said for "grandeur." He said we could get 15,000 men & all the money we wanted. I asked if he was willing to guarantee 100, he said NO, 50, NO, 25, NO. I asked then if he could get 5,000, 4, 3, 2, 1—NO. 500$. "Oh yes." Will you bind yourself to me for 500$. NO, but I will write you when I get home *exactly* what we can do. He did write & he found out he could do exactly *nothing* in any way. I have cited *him*, as you appeared to have some confidence in him & to show you that you can't rely upon all that is said and written.

[2nd interrogatory] "Can you name a Gentleman who would like to go who is capable of taking a high position in the Ga. contingent?" To that I can't reply even to my satisfaction. Captain Nelson[4] has been spoken of & he was at one time anxious to go & *I am told* he is thoroughly fitted for a high position, but Dr. Ramsay told me he was disgusted with the procrastination & had determined to have nothing to do with [him.] You must see that we get such a man as would answer. Inducements would have to be held out to him such as the position he was to occupy, and what his reward in case of success etc. etc. I am not authorized to say or to act in those matters.

[3rd interrogatory] "What number of men (if less than 500) can be raised in Georgia upon the terms sent you?" I answer *very few indeed*. I have had some applications, say half dozen at outside, but no one of them had the 50$, & each & every one wanted to know the *day* he was to be called for. If you would write me & say—have 100 or more men ready by 1st day of any month, that they would *be called* for, I think if I had the authority of the signing the posts of honor, that at least 100 men could be raised *here*, but not upon the 50$ principle.[5] On the contrary, money would have to be expended upon them.

I know I don't give very flattering a/cs [accounts], but I give the true state of affairs. I know the men, their dispositions, tastes & feelings & what is of more importance, their *reliability*. Take the common men & there is not one in ten that it would do to trust. By the by while I think of it, suppose half dozen men should want to go from Geo—that amt enough to induce a call for them. Can you take them & how & on what terms? I have at last succeeded in getting a meeting of the "Lone Star"[6] & got them to agree to give us their funds—which only amts, the tr [treasurer] says, to some 500$, the exact amt he has not given me. When I am enabled to say with certainty that the Expedition will sail on a certain day, *no matter what happens*, I think *then*, under such an excitement, Bonds can be sold. I have seen several Parties to whom Mr. Macias[7] entrusted Bonds, & they are still *unsold*. For instance, there is Mr. Trowbridge[8] of Augusta & Col Sorrel[9] of Americus. Mr. Jones[10] of Columbus *returned his*, not being able to effect a sale of *any* of those I gave him.

I don't think Mr. Macias could have recd money for many of those he got from me—if any. He is here, & I have had a long conversation with him. He is on his way to N. Orleans. I told all the Gents to whom he gave the Bonds that he was no longer connected with Gen'l Q.[11] It was upon that subject he called, stated he had been much mortified by being told he was not worthy of confidence etc. I told him Gen'l Q distinctly said he imputed to him no bad motives but simply that his connection with *him* had *ceased.*[12]

I am so engrossed with my business that I am unable to give the matter as much attention as I would wish, but you can rest assured I will do all in my power for the good cause. There is no use in indulging in vain regrets. I can't go myself, if I could, I could raise the men—any number. When I apply to a man to know whether he would like to go, he asks at once, "Are you going?" & it appears to me, he thinks I am willing to send *him*, where I am unwilling myself to go.

I have done nothing towards raising any more than the 2,000$ I offered to guarantee, but if you get *hard up* you may go 500$ or in case of emergency 1,000$—but say to Gen'l Q—draw at 10 to 15 *days sight*—exclusive of the 500 from the "L. S." [Lone Star] and 500$ (but I'll make him go 500$ more). From Trowbridge I haven't the hope of a dollar. Of course if Gen'l Q does not go, the money to be refunded.[13] With the hope that I'll soon hear something from you that will verify things with us.

I am Very Truly yrs etc.

C. A. L. Lamar

NOTES

1. John Sidney Thrasher was born in Maine in 1807 and moved to Havana in 1836 for his health. He developed commercial interests there and in 1849 bought a local newspaper, the *Faro Industrial.* He was the only non-Cuban member of the Havana Club, a group of influential white Cubans who wanted to overthrow Spanish rule of the island. Thrasher could only allude to his views in his paper, as the government censored the press and demanded that he publish in Spanish. *NYT,* October 29, 1851. Soon after General Narciso López, the leader of three failed filibustering expeditions, was executed in Havana on September 1, 1851, the government closed Thrasher's paper, seized and destroyed his property, and arrested him. He was charged with forwarding a copy of a Cuban declaration of independence written by a revolutionary group from Principe to a New Orleans newspaper, as well as possessing some letters written in cipher and others containing revolutionary doctrine. *NYT,* October 25, 1851, and January 1, 1852. On December 1, 1851, a military commission found him guilty and sentenced him to eight years of hard labor, in irons, in Africa. *NYT,* January 1, 1852. A few months later, the U.S. minister in Madrid gained his release. Thrasher returned to the United States and took up residence in New Orleans, where he became involved in the Cuban filibuster movement and served as one of General Quitman's aides, trying to raise men and money for the 1855 expedition. For Thrasher's explanation of the benefits of annexation, see *NYT,* May 23, 1854.

Lamar started writing to Thrasher in 1854, expressing an interest in the expedition, and wanting to communicate directly with Quitman. One month before Lamar penned this letter to Thrasher, Quitman had written to Charles, explaining that the movement on Cuba would proceed "with from three to four thousand well armed and well provided men, embarked in swift and safe steamers. To avoid a breach of our neutrality laws, the organization and arming will not take place in this country. We must move within sixty days or forfeit a half million already invested. To complete this formidable enterprise, we want yet about $50,000. . . . The want of money is the obstacle in the way of prompt and quick action. . . . Will you help us? If so act at once." John A. Quitman to C. A. L. Lamar, January 5, 1855, John Quitman Collection, Houghton Library, Special Collections, Harvard University, Cambridge, Mass.

2. Narciso López, a native-born Venezuelan who adopted Cuba as his homeland, organized and led three failed filibustering missions to Cuba. The last two in 1850 and 1851 landed men on the island. The final attempt resulted in López's capture and execution.

3. Dr. Henry A. Ramsay is one of the intriguing fringe characters that pop up in Lamar's schemes. He graduated from the Georgia Medical College and was reputed to be Atlanta's first doctor. Frank Boland, "Atlanta's First Physician," *Atlanta Historical Bulletin*, June 1933, 17–18. He once edited the *Daily Atlanta Examiner* and published his own medical journal, the *Georgia Blister and Critic*. Thrasher referred Lamar to Ramsay for help in raising men and money. Lamar, however, considered Ramsay to be a blowhard and unreliable. He was right. Not long after Charles met with him, the federal pension office in Washington detected a large number of claims for revolutionary war pensions from persons around Columbia County, Georgia. A special agent found evidence of a large fraud and arrested two men, one being Dr. Henry A. Ramsay. The doctor posted five thousand dollars bail for his court appearance and promptly disappeared. Ramsay was captured several months later and jailed in Sparta, Georgia, where he poisoned himself. *DMN*, May 30, 1856.

4. Allison Nelson (March 11, 1822–October 7, 1862) was a native Georgian, lawyer, states' rights Democrat, member of the Georgia House of Representatives, and a veteran of the Mexican-American War. At the time Lamar wrote this letter, Nelson was the mayor of Atlanta. Soon afterward he resigned and moved to Texas, where he served in the state legislature and, eventually, in the Confederate army. *Washington City Evening Star*, January 25, 1855; *Texas State Gazette*, September 17, 1859; Thomas W. Cutrer, "Nelson, Allison," Handbook of Texas Online, http://tshaonline.org/handbook/online/articles/fne13 (accessed April 27, 2014).

5. Quitman required volunteers to pay fifty dollars for the privilege of enlisting in the expedition. In exchange, each recruit would receive Cuban bonds at a face value of three to one. However, the notes would have value only if the filibusters were victorious. Quitman to Lamar, January 5, 1855, John Quitman Collection.

6. Americans dedicated to the liberation of Cuba formed the Order of the Lone Star in 1851 after the death of Narciso López. John Quitman became the first president and Ambrosio José Gonzales the chief military officer. The group formed lodges in cities in eight southern states, including two in Savannah. It appears as if Lamar belonged to one of them as he was able to call a meeting of members. *DMN*, September 8 and 13, October 22, and December 31, 1852.

7. Juan Manuel Macias was a Cuban living in the United States who became one of Narciso López's first aides, along with Ambrosio José Gonzales and José Sanchez Ignaza, when López arrived in New York in 1848. Basil Rauch, *American Interest in Cuba, 1848–1855* (New York: Columbia University Press, 1948), 110. He remained active in the liberation movement after López's death and spent time in Savannah trying to raise men and money for the 1855 expedition, but he lost the trust of Quitman, who terminated their association. Quitman to Lamar, January 5, 1855, John Quitman Collection.

8. Nelson C. Trowbridge of Augusta was a constant presence in Charles Lamar's adult life. He was born in Vermont in 1816 and can be traced to Augusta as early as 1841. He did some trading in cotton but devoted most of his efforts to buying, selling, and renting out slaves. *AC*, December 24, 1841, August 23, 1843, and September 29, 1843. He and Charles shared a passion for horses, and both men had entrants at the Augusta track in January 1846. *AC*, January 29, 1846.

9. Colonel Sorrel of Americus could not be identified.

10. Mr. Jones is John Abraham Jones, a lawyer living in Columbus, Georgia, and a close friend of Charles Lamar. *DMN*, April 6, 1884.

11. "Gen'l Q" is John A. Quitman, former governor of Mississippi and leader of the Cuban filibuster movement of 1853–55.

12. Quitman told Lamar that Macias was sent to Savannah to aid the expedition. "At length I learned that he had been induced to lend himself to a petty scheme of counter-movement inconsistent with the trust which he had undertaken in our enterprise. Since then I have had no connexion with him." Quitman to Lamar, January 5, 1855, John Quitman Collection.

13. Charles's understanding that the two-thousand-dollar investment was predicated on Quitman leading the expedition would be the basis of a heated disagreement between the two men, as revealed in later letters.

Letter no. 3

Savannah, Feby 12th 1855
John M. Dow Esq.[1]

Dr John,

Don't you want some Cuban Bonds?[2] Trowbridge can give you all the information you want on the Point. I am in $1000, Trow $1000 & I want you in 1,000$. It is a good Egg. How is our land speculation coming on? Can you sell & at what? Come down & see me. I will try & get up next Saturday. I told my Bookkeeper to send yr a/c.

I am Truly yrs etc.

C. A. L. Lamar

NOTES

1. John Dow owned a dry-goods business and worked as a general commission merchant in Augusta. The two men had common commercial interests, as Lamar refers to a statement of account and a joint land investment. *AC*, September 13, 1841, November 6, 1845.

2. Filibuster expeditions were often financed in part by selling bonds. In this case they were issued at the rate of three dollars face value for every dollar invested, with nominal interest at 6 percent, for an effective rate of 18 percent. Principal and interest would be paid from the spoils of victory. C. Stanley Urban, "The Abortive Quitman Filibustering Expedition, 1853–1855," *Journal of Mississippi History* 18 (February 1956): 179. For the wording of a Cuban bond, see *AG*, October 1, 1851. Dow did not purchase any bonds.

Letter no. 4

Savannah Feby 25th 1855
J. S. Thrasher Esq. New Orleans

My dear Sir,

I write to acknowledge the rct of yours of the 20th & 21st. I have nothing *new* nor interesting to communicate—all the monies *I have as yet recd,* has been a Rail Road Bond for 500$ worth yesterday 88 on the 100, which was handed me by Tr [treasurer] of the "Lone Star." There are monies due the order, but owing to the want of efficiency of the officers, I have little hope of getting any more from *that* quarter. I remitted to Capt. Lovell[1] (through his brother here) my 500$ & obtained from him a Bond for 1500$. I shall make up the deficiency, viz 1500$ & remit Capt. Lovell at N.Y. by all *this week,* which will make good my *guarantee* of 2000$. I *hope* to get from 2 @ [to] 3000 more in the close of 30 days—but won't guarantee it. If my friends can raise the money conveniently they promise to subscribe—otherwise not. Mr. Valiente[2] passed through & I had a conference with him Thursday night of last week. He had authority to collect any monies I had on hand for the cause, but of course he got none. He spoke to me of the probability of a second expedition moving in support of the first & asked my opinion of this point for it to start from. I gave him my views, which he will communicate in full to you—better than I can by letter. Suffice it to say, if the [*sic*] every thing else suits—this is of all others the very best place. But men & money will have to come from some other sources than here. I mentioned "Montgomery," a small summer retreat 11 miles back from Savannah on the Vernon River. The *largest* frigate U.S.N. can pass in & out with perfect safety—but if such a thing should be decided on give me timely notice that everything may be in readiness—such as coal for Strs [steamers] etc. etc. The Collector of this Port is a "Lone Star" man & can be sent away for a few days.[3] The Judge, Circuit Court U.S. will not *trouble* himself nor do anything than his duty requires of him.[4] I have no fears *myself* of the consequences of an Infringement of the Neutrality Laws.[5] Gen'l [President Franklin] Pierce & his whole cabinet, were they *here,* could not convict me or my friends— that is the great advantage of a small place—a man of influence can do as he pleases. Had Sigur taken *my advice* & brought the "Pampero" here, he would not have lost her.[6] I could have managed that for him, & I think his friends are convinced of it, if he is not.

After the 1st movement is made, if Gen. Q will give the *written instructions* to raise men & will furnish the means to equip them, I can by *giving the thing publicity* & assigning the Post of honors to individuals get men enough, *I think* to be of some assistance. The excitement will be immense, after it is known that Americans have landed on the Island & that is the time to move. I will enclose a letter with this to Captain [Woodson] Smith.

I am in haste, Truly yrs etc.

C. A. L. Lamar

I should have mentioned before that I have no feelings against you & that *under the circumstances*, I would have been a d—— sight more severe on you, had I been in your place & viewed things as you did.

NOTES

1. Mansfield Lovell (1822–84) graduated from West Point in 1842 and served in the Mexican War as an aide to General Quitman. He resigned from the army on December 18, 1854, the same day as his good friend Gustavus Woodson Smith, to join the Quitman filibustering expedition. He served as the deputy street commissioner in New York City before the outbreak of the Civil War. *NYTR*, April 28, 1862. Lovell is best remembered as the major general in charge of the Confederate defenses at New Orleans when the U.S. navy attacked in April 1862, and he ordered its evacuation. *AC*, May 4, 1862. Two of Lovell's brothers married daughters of Quitman. *CM*, May 3, 1862.

2. Porfirio Valiente was a Cuban living in New York and a member of the Cuban Council, an organization of Cuban expatriates headquartered there who wanted to overthrow Spanish rule of the island. Urban, "Abortive Quitman Filibustering Expedition," 179; *WDNI*, October 22, 1852. He knew Lamar (or of him) well enough to visit him in Savannah and discuss the strategy of the planned invasion, indicating Lamar's importance in the scheme.

3. John Boston was the port collector for Savannah at the time. Lamar said that Boston could be manipulated, but in that same position during Lamar's slave-trading ventures, Boston showed dedication to his job.

4. The judge of the U.S. circuit court in Savannah was John C. Nicoll, Charles's father-in-law. Lamar apparently did not have a high opinion of Nicoll's work ethic.

5. The Neutrality Act of 1818 prohibited any person residing in the United States from participating in any hostile action against a country with which America was at peace.

6. Laurent Sigur (1816–58), the owner and editor of the *New Orleans Delta*, actively supported Narciso López in his last two filibustering expeditions. *NYT*, November 5, 1851. When a ship was needed in 1851, Sigur purchased the *Pampero*. After dropping off López and his army on the Cuban coast on August 13, the captain returned to Florida and Georgia to pick up more men. But between taking on fuel, loading arms, getting the engine repaired, and sailing along the coast to take on volunteers, the captain was not ready to return to Cuba until September 6, five days after López had been executed. By that time, the U.S. district attorney had learned of the movements of the *Pampero* and sent a revenue cutter after her, seizing her in the Saint Johns River. Sigur could not have left the vessel near Savannah, as Lamar suggested in this letter, without abandoning the effort of returning to Cuba. For a description of the *Pampero*'s movements in Florida and Georgia, see Antonio Rafael de la Cova, "Cuban Filibustering in Jacksonville in 1851," *Northeast Florida History* 3 (1996): 16–34.

Letter no. 5

Savannah Feby 25th 1855
G. W. Smith Esq.[1]
New Orleans

I am in rect [receipt] of yours of the 21st this morning. I have not at *this time* any moneys in my hands. I have a Muscogee Railroad Bond for 500$ worth 88 on the 100, but I will make good my Guarantee for 2000$ *in all the ensuing week*—say on or before the 3 day of March & remit Captain Lovell. I shall telegraph him tomorrow, to draw at 5 days sight for $500 (I remitted already 500$) if he can do so. If he can't *to advantage*, I'll remit by Saturday the 3rd. If our money matters were easier, I could raise 8 @ 10,000, but men who have an abundance of Property, can't raise any more money than they want for immediate necessities. *I hope* to raise 2 to 3000 more, but there is *no certainty* about it. If I do, what disposition shall I make of it? Capt. L [Lovell] writes his brother he will leave *shortly*.[2]

I am Truly yrs etc.

C. A. L. Lamar

NOTES

1. Gustavus Woodson Smith (1822–1896) graduated West Point in 1842, the same year as his friend Mansfield Lovell. Like so many of the filibusters, he fought with distinction in the Mexican-American War. After the war he returned to a teaching position at West Point. In December 1854 he resigned, as did Lovell, moved to New Orleans, and joined John Quitman's expedition. *National Cyclopedia of American Biography* (New York: James T. White, 1892), 7:515–16; *NYT*, April 21, 1858.

2. Captain Mansfield Lovell had two brothers, William Starrow Lovell (b. 1818) and Joseph Lovell Jr. (b. 1824). It could not be determined to whom Lamar was referring.

Letter no. 7

Savannah Dec 9th 1855
Gen'l John A. Quitman[1]
Washington City, D.C.[2]

Dr Sir,

I am in rect of yours of the 9th November. I penned my last to you, under the impression that you had determined to reply to no letters, from any quarter in reference to your connection with Cuban affairs. I was so informed by Mr. Macias & as I had before addressed two letters to you without receiving replies, I was confirmed in that opinion. I am glad of the opportunity to make the amends & withdraw all of an offensive nature contained in my last—as it was written under a misapprehension. As I mentioned in a former letter, I positively declined having anything to do with the movement until I was satisfied of your connection with it & had mentioned you [_?] to act in the premise to that end. Mr. Macias presented your letter of the 29th of Feby 1855 to one [_?] of which I positively desire, to call your attention. It read thus: *"And if a sufficient amount of funds should not be collected for a reasonable enterprise, or if the plan of calling a revolution in Cuba should from any inexcusable circumstances fail then the funds shall be returned to the owners."* The amount paid by me, 2000$ is small, it is true, but I am responsible to the subscribers, for I assured each & every one of them, that their monies should be refunded in case the Expedition did not move under yr command.[3] Mr. Macias also pledged himself to the same effect, but of course, I can't look to him, as you dissolved his connection with the movement months ago—a year at least. I have all the proper vouchers, such as orders to pay Captain Smith, his drafts etc. etc. I would like to know what disposition I am to make of the Bonds I have & would be obliged for information on that point.

    I am Very Respectfully Yr Obt. Servant,

    C. A. L. Lamar

NOTES

1. This is Lamar's first letter-book entry to Quitman, although Charles says he wrote several times before to him. By this time Quitman had cancelled his planned invasion of Cuba and tendered his resignation to the Cuban junta on April 30, 1855. *Illinois Journal,* May 16, 1855; *Daily Commercial Register* (Sandusky, Ohio), May 11, 1855.

2. Before Quitman withdrew from the mission, he won a seat in the U.S. House of Representatives from the Fifth Congressional District in Mississippi and took office in early March 1855, which accounts for his presence in Washington, D.C. J. F. H. Claiborne, *Life and Correspondence of John A. Quitman* (New York: Harper & Brothers, 1860), 2:210–15.

3. According to Basil Rauch, *American Interest in Cuba,* no accounting for the funds has ever been found, and it is unknown what happened to the $500,000 raised.

Letter no. 11

Savannah Dec 4th 1856[1]
Gen'l John A. Quitman
Washington City

Sir,

   I have addressed you time & again through the mails of the U.S., but have recd no replies. I therefore send this by the hands of my friend, Honl Robert Toombs, that I may have some assurance that you have received it.[2] The object is simply to call your attention again to the 2,000$ advanced by me towards the Expedition that was envisioned against Cuba under your Command, & the *terms upon which that advance was made* which were simply these, if the Expedition moved under your Command & was unsuccessful all moneys invested were to be considered *lost*, but if the Expedition did not move under your Command, the moneys were to be refunded, in other words, it was upon your standing and character by which we were to rely & to look for justice. I now call upon you for that justice & the fulfillment of your obligation to refund in case the Expedition did not move. You have treated me, to say the least of it, with great want of consideration, by not replying to my letters. I beg now to give you final notice, that unless I get a reply to this, that is satisfactory, & that will enable me to place myself in proper position with those who subscribed the money, I will be under the painful necessity of publishing in the Papers of the day your whole correspondence to me, though the same be marked "Strictly Private & Confidential." It will be my only remedy.

   I am Respectfully etc.
      C. A. L. Lamar

NOTES

   1. One year had elapsed since Charles recorded the first letter to Quitman in this volume, but apparently he had written several others, to which the general had not replied.
   2. See the next letter for biographical information on Mr. Toombs.

Letter no. 12

Savannah Dec 4th 1856
Honl Robert Toombs[1]
Washington City

My dear Sir,

I beg to trouble you with the delivery of the enclosed communication for Genl John A. Quitman, which please read, seal & hand him. I am determined to place *myself right*, & unless I get a satisfactory answer, I shall do exactly what I have told him I would do—viz, Publish his personal correspondence. I am very sorry to trouble you with this, but I want to know from a responsible party, that he received the letter. You can send it by one of the Pages of the Senate, telling him to deliver it to Gen'l. Quitman *in person*. You will see something *rich* if he don't reply. Hoping you will not consider that I have taken too great a liberty with you,

I am Very Truly yrs etc.

C. A. L. Lamar

NOTES

1. Robert Augustus Toombs (1810–85) was one of the most renowned of all Georgia antebellum and Civil War politicians. He was born in 1810 in Wilkes County and attended Franklin College (University of Georgia) and Union College in Schenectady before studying law at the University of Virginia. After a successful law career, at the age of twenty-seven he turned to politics and was elected to the Georgia legislature. He served until 1844, when he was elected to the U.S. House of Representatives as a member of the Whig Party. In 1853 the state legislature appointed him to the U.S. Senate, and he had been a member of that body for three years when he received this request from Lamar. Toombs became an advocate for states' rights and secession and received the appointment of secretary of state in the first Confederate cabinet under President Jefferson Davis. He escaped to Havana after the war and traveled to France and England before returning to Georgia in 1867. *NYT*, December 16, 1885. Charles was not reluctant to ask any acquaintance, no matter how significant, to do favors for him.

Letter no. 13

Savannah Jany 12th 1857
Honl Robert Toombs
Washington City, D. C.

My dear Sir,

I have to thank you for yours of the 8th recd today. I am pleased to hear that Genl Quitman has determined to reply to my letters. I certainly don't want this money unless I am, under the agreement, entitled to it. The amt I am individually in is a mere trifle $500, but others are in, whom I induced to go in, under the assurance that Genl Quitman said the money would be refunded in case the Expedition did not move. I wrote the Genl time & again & could get no answer. My only alternative was to publish his letters to show the Public I acted in good faith. If he had replied to my letters & given me any kind of an excuse for not sending, I would have been inclined to have let the matter slide, but he had not the courtesy to do even that. I owed it to myself & those of my friends who went in, to show how I stood in the matter. The fact of his occupying a prominent position, was no reason why I should treat him any differently from others. I care not for his position or his reputation as a "fire eater," all I want is simple justice.[1] I am perfectly willing to submit the question between us to any disinterested person or persons—all the evidence is here with me & I would prefer it being arbitrated here than elsewhere, & am willing if he is, to allow you to select one or two gentlemen of your acquaintance in this city to decide the question & you are authorized to say so to him. I can't imagine why he refused to answer my letters—they were respectful both in language & style. Excuse me for troubling you & believe that I fully appreciate your action in this matter.[2]

    I am Truly Yrs etc.
      C. A. L. Lamar

NOTES

1. Fire eaters were southerners who advocated seceding from the Union to preserve the institution of slavery.

2. No record could be found explaining the resolution of this matter, but as Lamar never published the correspondence, it can be assumed that Quitman paid him or that a mediator came up with a compromise. Quitman died one and a half years later on July 17, 1858, on his plantation in Mississippi. For an obituary, see NYT, July 19, 1858.

Letter no. 14

Savannah April 1st 1857
George N. Sanders Esq.[1]
Navy Agent, N.Y.

Dr Sir,

Let me congratulate you, & Fowler[2] too, upon your appointments. I am glad to see it, independent of any selfish motives, and I am glad on *that* account too. I want none of the offices of "Honor & Trust," but want a contact for making money. You have the power of disposing of the contract for the supplying of Timber & Lumber at the Navy Yard, & I have the means & ability of supplying. Will you give me the points to enable me to get it? I have 115000 acres of Pine Land, which is just the "ticket."[3] Trowbridge suggested the above to me, by way of making my lands yield me something, & it is needless for me to say, he will be interested in any contract I may get. He wants a little help just now from his friends & I am doing all I can for him.[4] Won't you help?

I am Truly yrs, etc.

C. A. L. Lamar

NOTES

1. George N. Sanders is one of a number of minor politicians and government officials with whom Lamar had an association. Born in Lexington, Kentucky, in 1812, Sanders reportedly called for the first meeting held in the United States (at Ghent, Kentucky, in November 1843) to debate the admission of Texas into the Union. In 1848 he went to Europe as an agent of Samuel Colt to sell muskets to revolutionary groups, and apparently he got caught up in their causes. He returned to the United States and in 1852 purchased the *Democratic Review*, a political journal that he used to support, among other things, the filibusters and the presidential campaign of Stephen A. Douglas. Perhaps Sanders's association with the filibuster movement accounted for his acquaintance with Lamar. In 1853 President Franklin Pierce appointed Sanders to serve as the American consul to London, under James Buchanan, the U.S. minister to Great Britain. Sanders drew suspicion from Washington by holding meetings at his residence with the leading radical European revolutionaries who had fled their countries for London. The U.S. Senate refused to confirm his appointment and he was recalled in 1854. In 1857 President James Buchanan appointed him the navy agent for the Port of New York. He assumed office on April 1, 1857, and Lamar didn't waste a moment contacting him. No documentation could be found showing that Sanders gave Lamar a contract. Sanders was removed from the post in 1860 by President Buchanan. He died in August 1873. See Merle E. Curti, "George N. Sanders—American Patriot of the Fifties," *South Atlantic Quarterly* 27 (January 1928): 79–87; Rauch, *American Interest in Cuba: 1848–1855*, 214–28; *NYT*, August 10, 1860, and August 13, 1873; *Richmond Enquirer* as reprinted in *AG*, January 9, 1854; *Albany Evening Journal*, April 15, 1860.

2. Fowler is Isaac Vanderbeck Fowler, appointed postmaster of New York City by President Pierce and reappointed by President Buchanan. For much of the 1850s, Fowler was the leader of Tammany Hall, the political organization that controlled New York City. In 1860 he was accused of embezzling $155,000 and fled to Mexico and Cuba. He returned to the United States after the Civil War on learning that the government had no intention of prosecuting him. See *New York Ledger*, June 9, 1860, *New York Herald-Tribune*, October 1, 1869, *NYT*, October 1, 1869.

3. According to available tax rolls, Gazaway Lamar owned considerable tracts of land in southwest Georgia, especially Early, Baker, and Irwin Counties. See Chatham County Tax Digests, 1855, Drawer 69, Box 48, Georgia Archives, Morrow. Charles had sold lumber previously. See *AC*, February 20, 1855.

4. By April 1857 Lamar had money problems as well, and perhaps he requested the business from Sanders for himself as much as for Trowbridge.

Letter no. 15

Savannah April 23 / 57
H. D. Leitner Esq.[1]

Dear Sir,

Mr. B. H. Broomhead[2] is here and has asstounded [*sic*] me by a disclosure to the Effect that he holds from you a Bill of sale of one half the negroes, machinery nearly 16 MM and that the same is not in any manner or shape Responsible for his Indebtedness to the Columbia Mining Co. Can this be possible. Please let me know at once and oblige. Mr. Lamar will be at home soon & will correspond with you in reference to this matter If the above be true.

 Respectfully,
  N. C. Trowbridge[3]

NOTES

1. Henry D. Leitner of Brezelia, Georgia, near Augusta, invested in the gold mines with Lamar. It appears that he sold some assets of the mining company and did not use the funds to pay off his debt to the company. This letter is indicative of the many problems the business was experiencing.

2. B. H. Broomhead of Augusta was also an investor in the mines and took an active role in managing them.

3. For an unknown reason, Nelson Trowbridge recorded this in Charles's letter-book. As the letter is addressed to one of their partners in the gold mines, it is likely that Lamar wanted a copy of it.

Letter no. 16

Savannah, July 27th 1857
Honl. Howell Cobb[1]
Washington City

Dr Sir,

I am lothe [*sic*] to trouble you again but your damned "sap head" of a collector refuses to do anything, & compels me to do so. He detained my vessel eight days after she was ready for sea and after she had applied for her clearance papers. Mr. Boston[2] said she was not "seized" but merely "detained"—said the Department would respond to any demand I might make for damages etc. The District Attorney[3] & all the lawyers to whom he applied for advice, told him, that there was nothing to cause suspicion to attach to the vessel, & he had best discharge her. He said the manifest was an "*unusual* one"—so it was—but he was the occasion of it. He directed me to put on it, the ship stores, & the Captain & officers' private stores, & to attach to each & every article, its cost. I protested against it, as unusual—but he insisted and I did it—and he then makes *that* a justification for his proceedings. I claim 150$ per day damages for said detention—that I did not expect him to pay without referring it to the Department—but then I have a claim for wharfage & storage of the Cargo, made out in accordance with the Port charges, & he declined to pay it—the amount is 120$. I told his officer, Mr. Davenport,[4] that the vessel should not be discharged at my wharf, nor the goods stored in my stores unless he would agree to pay the customary charges. He said they would be paid—the collector refuses—I appeal to you for both claims, viz:

8 days detention @ 150 pr day	$1200.00
Wharfage landing & shipping & storage	120.00
	$1,320.00

Will you please give the matter your attention. I want nothing but what is *right* & *proper* & if you think I am entitled to nothing for detention, why I must submit.

I did not in my other communications disclaim any intention of embarking in the Slave Trade, nor did I say anything to warrant you supposing I would not engage in it. I simply declared there was nothing aboard except what was on the manifest & that I thought there was nothing suspicious on it. I will now say, as the vessel is 1,000 miles from here, that she was as unfit for a voyage to import negroes, as any vessel in port—she was not fitted up *in any way* & there was nothing on board to warrant the suspicions. What she may hereafter do is another matter, which don't concern the present issue.[5]

John Boston had her detained because he said he knew she would be engaged in the trade, & he heard that from men who confessed that they were eavesdroppers who hung around my windows to listen to all communications that took place. I applied to Ward[6] to write you—he says Boston is unfit for the office & ought to be turned out, but the question with him is, who would do to put in. He says he is afraid of Dr. Wayne,[7] who would of all others be the man if he could be relied on. I told him, I would guarantee Wayne & I think he will yet *urge* you to do it. He has the matter under consideration. It is a notorious fact that Boston is a natural "Know Nothing" & has improved vastly his natural advantage. He knows nothing of what is going on in the office—leaves everything in the hands of John Postell[8] who is an "acquired" K N—and still hangs on, notwithstanding the abolition tendency of the party North. Politics as dull as business—it will be a tight race between Brown & Hill[9]—I shall vote for Hill—won't vote for any S. Carolinian for Gov. I am coming on to *bore* you in person unless you will yield to my *short* epistles.

I am Truly yrs etc.

C. A. L. Lamar

NOTES

Note: This is the first letter in the book to mention the slave trade and refers to Lamar's first attempt at it. After Charles purchased and brought the *E. A. Rawlins* to Savannah in late June 1857, he loaded it with stores and supplies and filed a manifest for a commercial voyage to Africa. The port collector, John Boston, considered the cargo suspicious as many of the items were typical supplies for a slaving expedition, such as 13,000 feet of lumber (which could be used for the construction of a slave deck), 200 bricks (possibly to build an oven on deck to cook large quantities of food), 115 barrels of pilot bread (hard tack) and 40 tierces or large barrels of rice (to feed a large number of people), and two cases of firearms and cutlery. Boston seized the ship, which caused Lamar to incur $1,320 for wharfage.

1. Howell Cobb emerged as one of the South's most influential politicians in the antebellum years. In 1835 he married Mary Ann Lamar, Gazaway Lamar's first cousin, making Cobb Charles's cousin once removed. Cobb attended Franklin College, now the University of Georgia, became a lawyer, and was elected by the legislature the solicitor-general of the Western Circuit of Georgia. In 1843 he won the first of three elections to the U.S. House of Representatives. In 1849 he became the Speaker of the House and helped pass the Compromise of 1850. He was elected governor of Georgia in 1851 and served one term before returning to the practice of law. In 1855 he again won election to the House. In 1857 President James Buchanan appointed him secretary of the treasury, making him responsible for the customhouses and port collectors of the country, and placing him in the way of his cousin's plans. See *NYT*, October 10, 1868.

On July 16, on hearing from Charles of the detention of the *Rawlins*, Cobb wired John Boston, ordering him to "lay the papers & facts before the district attorney" to determine probable cause to institute legal proceedings, and if none existed, to release the vessel. See Howell Cobb to John Boston, July 16, 1857, File 2, Box 29, Howell Cobb Folder, Georgia Archives, Morrow, Ga. The U.S. marshal overhauled the cargo the following day and found nothing suspicious, resulting in the ship's clearance. See *DMN*, July 18, 1857. The marshal happened to be Daniel Stewart, a friend of Lamar who would provide valuable assistance in the *Wanderer* venture.

2. John Boston was a longtime Savannah resident and businessman before being appointed collector of the Port of Savannah in March 1853. He knew Lamar well as they both served on the Chatham County Fair Committee and the committee for the sale of stock of the Merchants and Planters Bank. Also, Charles's ships regularly applied for clearance from Boston. It is not known if Boston saw this letter or knew of Lamar's attempts to have him fired, which all failed. For Boston's background, see *SG*, January 25, 1842, and June 28, 1847, *DMN* May 8, 1850, November 2, and December 22, 1855.

3. The district attorney at the time was Joseph Ganahl, who would prosecute the first *Wanderer* cases.

4. H. M. Davenport was an inspector for the Port of Savannah.

5. Lamar felt comfortable enough with Cobb to taunt him. Charles's statement that he never denied an intention to participate in the slave trade—that he only claimed his ship was unfit for a slaving expedition—reveals a cockiness that will reappear during subsequent escapades.

6. John Ward was an influential Savannah lawyer who served as mayor in 1854.

7. Dr. Richard C. Wayne was a six-term mayor of Savannah. In 1857 he served as the president and chairman of the Chatham County Democratic Party, which Charles had rejoined after the collapse of the American Party. Wayne sat on the board of the Savannah Gas Company along with Charles's father-in-law, John C. Nicoll, and he was also a director of the Savannah, Albany, and Gulf Railroad, which Charles had business dealings with and would later serve as a director.

8. John Postell was the deputy collector for the Port of Savannah.

9. Georgia's election for governor in 1857 pitted American Party candidate Benjamin H. Hill against Democrat Joseph E. Brown, who won easily. Brown was born in 1821 in South Carolina but was raised in Georgia.

Letter no. 17

Savannah Oct. 31st 1857
G. B. Lamar Esq.

Dr Father,

I have yours of the 30th. Times are not, nor are they going to be, as bad as you *divine*. Nor are you the Prophet you take the credit of being. I am not broke, nor do I intend to be. I am pressed for ready means, not so much on my own a/c as on others.[1] It will be all right in time. I can only come to the same condition the banks are in viz; Suspension.[2] You say you are not secure in what securities you have. I could have put my Press into a company *certainly* at 100,000$ & *I think* 150,000$ two years ago. I don't consider I owe you the 27,000$ or 37,000$, (I don't know the amt, as I never determined it) for *that*. As I have told you 1000 times, I never intended to pay. I have said I only wanted my share and say so still. I am entitled *to all* my mother's portion certainly, as they are to theirs.[3] I will do what *is right* in settlement of all claims for or against me in the present *crisis* and all others that may arise.

You need give yourself no uneasiness about the Africans and the Slave Trade. I was astonished at some of the remarks in your letter. They show that you have been imbued with something more than the "Panic" by your association north and with Mrs. Fowle.[4] For example, you say "*an expedition to the moon would have been equally sensible, and no more contrary to the laws of Providence and of the Seward doctrine.* May God in his mercy forgive you for all your attempts to violate *his will and his laws.*" Following out the same train of thought where would it land the whole Southern Community? Did the negroes not all come originally from the coast of Africa? What is the difference between going to Africa & Virginia for Negroes and if there is a difference, is not that difference in favor of going to Africa?[5] You need not reproach yourself for not interposing with a stronger power than argument & persuasion to prevent the Expedition. There was nothing you or the government could have done to have prevented it. Let all the Sin be on *me*. I am willing to assume it all.

You have one thing to learn, if you will not think it amiss in my telling you. You view me as a mere child and want to treat me as such, that I won't permit. You came very near causing an explosion when here last, by your manner when you came in to see me about Patten.[6] I am willing to do anything I can, consistent to please & satisfy you *at any sacrifice*, but I am not to be bullied into terms. I am in no fix or humor now to be taunted & found fault with. I am fool enough to think my judgment upon something, as good [as] any body's. And upon the African question, had I had a reliable man, I am satisfied I would have been successful & had a plenty. I had every testimony as to the honesty & nerve of the man from those who knew him from childhood. They were fooled, & so was I. I knew him to be a wild, reckless fellow without any knowledge of the value of money.[7]

I have written & telegraphed Johnston at N.O. and he will attend to the vessel & cargo, if any, upon arrival. I think by a suit I can make Grant liable, or send him to penitentiary, or make his Father settle for him, who is a man of large fortune.[8] I have written no plainer than I was *forced to do*. I think the sooner we understand each other the better. I have written the above with no ill feeling but to prevent it and hope it will be so perceived.

At last account from Charleston, say the 29th, Lafitte & Co. had done nothing for the *Cobden*.[9] If you want her to come here, she can be towed around for 200$. If you can obtain a freight for her in Augusta, let it come or go immediately down, and if you can luggage [sic] 1000 or 1500 bales for *W. Van Guard*, Mr. Phillip's ship, *daily expected*, please do so. Everything is getting on finely. Our Banks are getting in better spirits and the Rail Road Bank discounting *all good paper freely*. Mr. Cuyler says he will *force* other banks to a liberal policy, for he will disct [discount] & the other Banks can take his bills & seal them up & he will pay 7% on them.[10] Some such action on the part of all would relieve the community & benefit Savannah very materially and ease up the action of the Legislature.

I am Truly Yrs. etc.

C. A. L. Lamar

NOTES

Note: Three months have passed since Charles's last letter. The *Rawlins* mission failed when Captain Grant got cold feet at the sight of the squadron cruisers on the African coast. Grant returned the ship to New Orleans in October, handed to Trowbridge the remainder of the money he had been given to purchase Africans, and disappeared. Gazaway heard about the expedition and offered his opinion about the matter to his son, to which Charles is responding.

1. When Charles says "times are not as bad as you divine," he is commenting on the "financial panic" or recession gripping the country in 1857. Charles's claim that his problems are all caused by others is a common refrain, one that he repeats later in this letter by pointing the finger at Captain Grant. Charles also states that he isn't broke, but less than a week later, in Letter no. 18, he wrote, "I never was so hard up in my life."

2. Banks suspended when they could no longer exchange their bank notes and paper currency for specie (gold and silver).

3. Charles is talking about a share of a distribution of his mother's assets. It can be assumed that he is referring to his stepmother, as his biological mother died nineteen years earlier. However, Gazaway's second wife was still alive as of the writing of this letter.

4. Mrs. Fowle is Paulina Cazenove Fowle, Gazaway's sister-in-law through his marriage to his second wife, Harriet Cazenove. Paulina married Colonel John Fowle in 1831. The couple had one daughter, Pauline Fowle, born in 1832. Pauline, with husband Henry Durant, founded Wellesley College in Massachusetts in the early 1870s.

5. Charles argues that there is no difference between buying slaves from other slave states and Africa. In doing so, he ignores the deaths that result from tribal wars fought to procure the slaves and the horrors of the Middle Passage. The Seward Doctrine originated in a speech in 1850 by Senator William Seward, who claimed that the issue of slavery in the territories was governed by a higher law than the Constitution.

6. Patten might be George Patten, a Savannah cotton factor.

7. Charles contradicts himself. He claims that he was fooled by the captain's qualifications but also knew him to be wild and reckless without any knowledge of the value of money.

8. Grant was the captain of the failed *Rawlins* voyage.

9. E. Lafitte and Company was Charles Lamar's shipping agent in Charleston. The Lamars owned the mercantile ship *Richard Cobden*.

10. R. R. Cuyler was the president of the Central of Georgia Railroad and Banking Company, and a longtime associate of Gazaway.

Letter no. 18

Savannah November 5th 1857
N. C. Trowbridge Esq.[1]
New Orleans

Dr Trow,

Your dispatch of the 4th came to hand about bed time last night. It is the only glimpse of sunshine I have had, since my return from the North. I have just Telegraphed you to remit me by *Bank check* on N. York for the amt of the coin.[2] Sight, I see quoted, *at 5% disct.* I am truly glad to find that Grant is at least honest. He has acted *badly* & sacrificed our interests *most shamefully*. His clearance papers would have taken him any where he wanted to go, unmolested. Why did he not return directly to Savh? What took him to the West Indies? Why did he sell any of the outfit? He knew the vessel was fitted for nothing else but *the trade*, & ought to have known we would want to send her back. Port her up for freight for Savannah and send her here. I will send her [on] a trip to Cuba, & in the mean time consummate arrangements for another go. Grant ought to receive no pay—refund what he got & make good all the deficiencies. He had 18000$ in American coin—Whitney says he sold the cargo and used 1800$ of the gold up to the time he left. Whitney is still here.[3] Something is wrong, what & where is it? What excuses does Grant make? Why did he not go to the Coast. He knew, before he undertook the command that there were armed vessels on the coast, and a number of them. He ought have known, that *he was running no risk*, that the Captain & crew are always discharged.[4] The Captain of the "Albert [Abbott] Devereux" was here the other day. The Brig Cruiser even let him take his Gold.[5] If Grant had been equal to the Emergency, we would all have been Easy in money matters. You and Johnston must arrange for the Paper laying over & falling due.[6] I have drafts coming back from the North for cotton bought!! I never was so hard up in my life. I enclose a letter for you. Attend promptly to the vessel, the drafts due & falling due.

I am Truly yrs etc.
C. A. L. Lamar

NOTES

1. Nelson Trowbridge was in New Orleans, attending to the *Rawlins* after it had returned from its failed mission.

2. The coin is the money that Grant returned to Trowbridge after the aborted trip.

3. Whitney's identity could not be determined.

4. At the time, when British cruisers seized U.S. merchant ships suspected of being slavers, which they had no legal right to do, the officers gave the crews a choice: throw the U.S. flag and ownership papers overboard and be put on shore in Africa, or be turned over to a U.S. squadron cruiser and be tried in U.S. court as a pirate and face the death penalty. Most captains chose the former.

5. The *Abbott Devereux* cleared Havana on May 9, 1857, and was captured off the coast of Africa by the HMS *Teazer* in early August with 235 slaves aboard. See *American Traveller*, October 17, 1857, and *CC*, November 5, 1857. Lamar's claim that the British released the captain with his gold could not be verified.

6. Charles is referring to notes Johnson and Trowbridge signed to borrow money or pay for supplies. It appears that Charles endorsed the notes to provide additional security to the lender. They were due for payment, and if Trowbridge and Johnson didn't honor them, the lender would go after Charles.

Letter no. 19

Savannah, Dec 23, 1857
Theodore Johnston Esq.[1]
New Orleans, La

Dr Sir,

I am in rect of yours of the 15th. Mr. Woolhopter wrote you in full yesterday in reference to the different drafts drawn on you.[2] One for 10,000$ was for Trow's and my a/c, & should never have been drawn. It was an error of Mr. W's at the time. The balance was all on a/c of the purchase of negroes, and you & Trow got the money.[3] I knew nothing more than that. I am very much obliged for the pofer [*sic*] of the use of your name [_?] I may be enabled to get along without it.[4] I wish you would advise me in time always, for what renewals you may want. Let me know the particular Bills you want renewed next month & I will do all I can to get them renewed. What Bank or Banks in Charleston did you get the money from? Let me know & I will write them.

In reference to Grant, discharge him. Pay him nothing & hope with me that he will speedily land in Hell. If you think it best to start her [the *Rawlins*] from New Orleans to the Coast, & can make the necessary arrangements for her outfit & the procurement of a cargo *without the money*, I am unwilling to trust any more money in the hands of irresponsible hands.[5] If you think you can recover anything from Grant you can commence the action in my name.

I don't care a Continental about it being used in connection with an enterprise that the intelligence of the country must recognize sooner or later. The Legislature of Carolina has commenced a movement calculated in time, say at its next session, to startle the opponents of the measure. The Committee to whom was referred so much of Gov. Adams' message as related to the Slave Trade, made a very able report in favor of it.[6] It was recd, printed & laid over till the next session, to enable the masses to digest it.

Something ought to be done & done *at once* with the Rawlins. If you can't do anything with her, send her here at once in ballast. I have been expecting L. Viana.[7] He wrote me he would be here to [_?] & make arrangements for carrying out our plans. He has not as yet made his appearance. Is he in New Orleans?

I am Truly Yrs etc.

C. A. L. Lamar

NOTES

1. Theodore Johnston owned the Gros Tete plantation in Iberville Parish and worked as a slave broker in New Orleans. *NOTP*, February 24, 1858; *NYT*, September 10, 1858. Trowbridge made his acquaintance and included him in his and Lamar's slave trade deals, both legal and illegal. Johnston turned out to be a clone of Trowbridge—incompetent, unreliable, and broke. In 1857 Trowbridge delivered to Johnston a gang of slaves that the Lamar-Trowbridge-Gardner partnership had purchased in Beaufort, South Carolina. Johnston sold them without distributing all of the proceeds. This caused Lamar and Gardner to make a trip to New Orleans in late February 1858 to try to collect the debt. Despite Johnston's financial situation, Lamar still included him in the *Rawlins* and *Wanderer* partnerships.

2. Philip Woolhopter was Lamar's bookkeeper.

3. Apparently, Lamar's bookkeeper accidentally credited Johnston and Trowbridge's partnership account (perhaps at a bank) $10,000. The funds should have gone to Lamar and Trowbridge. It could not be determined how the error was resolved.

4. Johnston offered himself as an endorser of Charles's notes. Charles sarcastically declined, as Johnston was in debt to him.

5. Lamar gave his approval to Johnston, a partner in the *Rawlins* slaving expeditions, to send the ship on another mission, but it is unclear what he means by "without the money."

6. In November 1856 Governor James Adams called on the South Carolina legislature to pass a law to reopen the African slave trade. The legislature never did.

7. Lima Viana headed a slave-trading syndicate headquartered in New York. He arranged slaving voyages, including chartering ships, and owned a barracoon in Africa. A barracoon is a holding pen for captured Africans, maintained by a slave dealer, and typically located on the coast to supply slave ships. See Letter no. 20 for more information on Viana. Charles tried to enlist his services, but without success.

Letter no. 20

Savannah Dec 26th 1857
L. Viana,[1] Esq
158 Pearl Str., N.Y., 3rd Floor

Dr Sir,

I am this morning in rect of yours of the 22nd of December. I have been expecting you here daily since the 15th and it was only on the 24th that I wrote Messrs. Johnston & Trowbridge at New Orleans, to send the Bark E. A. Rawlins here, in case you were not there, or if you were, and they failed to make satisfactory arrangements with you.

I am anxious to have you interested in the next expedition & wld [would] be pleased to have you say what interest you would like, & give your views generally as to the manner the whole should be conducted. I would like you to say too, what number you would contract to land at a designated point by your own or other's vessels, the price per head and the time of probable delivery—I to take all the trouble, expense and *risk* after they are safely landed[2]—or, if you would prefer it, make some proposition of the nature of the joint a/c speculation. I think I can manage two or three cargoes to much profit. I have been agitating the subject of re-opening the trade & in connection with others, think there is a marked difference of opinion in the public mind.[3]

Of course great prudence & caution is necessary for though the authorities will take no particular pains to look after anything of the kind yet, if it is brought to their attention, they will be bound to notice & prosecute. I can show you when we meet, the place or places I propose to land them, where you can go in & out *by one tide,* the bar straight & deep, and no [_?] or other persons about—and the [_?] men, [_?] in reference to standing in the community and reliability in case of difficulty who own the [_?].[4]

One thing is certain, nothing can be done in the way of *conviction* if the *worst* should happen, we could only lose the cargo. I would be pleased to hear from you at your earliest convenience.

I am Respectfully yrs etc.
C. A. L. Lamar

NOTES

1. Warren Howard, in describing the offices of Portuguese slave-trading companies in New York, writes, "One belonged to Jose da Costa Lima Viana, an old hand well known on the African coast. He could be found at 158 Pearl Street, hard at work dispatching vessels . . . to his agents at Punta da Lenha and Banana Point in the Congo River." See Warren S. Howard, *American Slavers and the Federal Law, 1837–1862* (Berkeley: University of California Press, 1963), 50, 229. Not all of Viana's expeditions were successful. In July 1857 he sent the bark *William G. Lewis* to the African coast. It was seized in late September at Punta da Lenha on the Congo River. Viana was tried but not convicted. See William Mc-Blair to Isaac Toucey, November 13, 1857, *Message of the President of the United States*, Senate Exec. Doc., 35 Congress, 1 Session, No. 49.

2. Lamar wanted to subcontract the pickup and delivery of the Africans to the United States. From there, Lamar would sell them. No deal between the two was made.

3. Charles believed that much progress had been made in changing public opinion on the slave trade since Governor Adams's speech and the Southern Commercial Convention in Savannah in 1856. At the 1857 convention held in Knoxville, a delegate called for the repeal of the eighth article of the Webster-Ashburton Treaty, which established the joint United States–Great Britain squadron off the coast of Africa. It passed by a vote of 66 to 26. And Leonidas Spratt's resolution to form a committee to study the feasibility of reopening the African slave trade cleared by a vote of 52 to 40. These votes split the attendees. See Barton J. Bernstein, "Southern Politics and Attempts to Reopen the African Slave Trade," *JNH* 51 (January 1966): 25.

4. Lamar could be describing Jekyll Island, Georgia, owned by the Dubignon family, and the location where the *Wanderer* landed her slaves.

Letter no. 22

Savannah Feby 2nd 1858
N. C. Trowbridge Esq. or Theodore Johnston Esq.
New Orleans

Dr Sir,

This will be handed you by Captain Wm Ross Postell whom I have engaged to go out as Supercargo of the Bark "E. A. Rawlins" to the coast of Africa.[1] He is a Gent, reliable in every way & a thorough Sailor & Navigator & understands our coast most thoroughly. He is promised two negroes out of every One Hundred that the vessel may land and $80 per month to his family during his absence for four months. I think now there will be no further delays, but that the vessel will go immediately to sea to return with the full cargo in 90 days.

   I am respectfully yours,
      C. A. L. Lamar

NOTES

1. Lamar finally has everything organized for the second expedition of the *Rawlins*, including a supercargo from Savannah. See Letter no. 23 for biographical information on Postell.

Letter no. 23

Savannah, Feby 2nd, 1858
Captain Wm Ross Postell[1]

Dr Sir,

I desire to give you in a very concise manner a few instructions as to your duties as Supercargo[2] of the Bark E. A. Rawlins. 1st—you will go to New Orleans & report yourself to either N. C. Trowbridge or Theodore Johnston, or in their absence, Capt Gilley[3] at the Bark. 2nd—Captain Gilley is to have as Commander the full control of the Bark as Master, in the general [_?] of the word. 3rd—You, as Supercargo, are to take charge as such of money & cargo, & see that it is properly and [_?] applied to such purposes as intended. 4th—to see that she returns to the coast of Georgia as instructed after she gets her cargo on board. 5th—to represent us & our interests in the best manner you are capable of doing. With the above hastily drawn up & I will leave the rest to your own good judgment.

I am Truly Yrs etc.
C. A. L. Lamar

NOTES

1. At the time of this letter, William Ross Postell was a forty-two-year-old merchant sea captain. He served as a midshipman in the U.S. navy in 1832. Around 1840 he joined the Republic of Texas navy and was given the command of a ship, serving under Commodore Edwin Ward Moore, who would later have a duel with Charles Lamar during one of the *Wanderer* trials. After leaving the Texas navy, Postell returned to work in commercial shipping. In the 1850s he took a job in the U.S. Lighthouse and Buoy Service and charted sections of the Georgia coast, including the Wassaw Sound near Savannah. As Postell had lived in Savannah and was involved in shipping, he and Lamar undoubtedly knew each other, although there is no documentation that he was ever involved in the slave trade. See Carol Wells, "William Ross Postell, Adventurer," *GHQ* 57 (Fall 1973): 390–405.

2. A supercargo is responsible for the commercial aspects of a voyage, including holding, disbursing, and accounting for funds, and managing the cargo.

3. No information could be found for Captain C. W. Gilley, which was most likely a fake name.

Letter no. 24

Confidential
Savannah May 24th, 1858
Thomas Barrett Esq[1]
Augusta

Dr Sir,

I have in contemplation if I can raise the necessary amt of money, the fitting out of an Expedition to go to the coast of Africa for a cargo of African Apprentices, to be *bound for the term of their natural lives* and would like your co-operation.[2] No subscription will be received for a less amt. than 5000$—the amt to be raised is 300,000$. I will take 20,000$ of the stock *& go myself.* I propose to purchase the "Vigo" an Iron Screw Str [steamer] of 1750 tons now in L'pool for sale at 30,000£ cash.[3] She cost 75000£. G. B. Lamar can give you a description of her etc. etc.[4] She is as good as new, save her boilers, and they can be used for several months. If I can buy her, I will put six Paixhan guns on deck and man her with as good men as are to be found in the South.[5] The fighting men will all be stockholders & gentlemen, some of whom are known to you, if not personally, by reputation. My estimate runs thus:[6]

Str., 150,000, Repairs, Guns, Small arms, coal, etc.	$200,000
Supplies 25,000 money for purchase of cargo 75000	100,000
	300,000

I have as you know a vessel now afloat, but it is to my mind extremely doubtful whether she gets in safely, as she had to wait on the coast until her cargo could be collected.[7] If she ever gets clear of the coast, they can't catch her. She ought to be due in from 10 to 30 days. I have another now ready to sail which has orders to order a cargo of 1000 @ [to] 1200 to be in readiness the 1st Sept but to be kept, if necessary, until 1st Oct, which I intend for the Str so that no delay may occur.[8] With her I can make the voyage there and back including all detentions, bad weather if I encounter it etc. in 90 days certain & sure, and the negroes can be sold as fast as landed, at 650$ per head. I can contract for them "to arrive" at that figure, *cash.* The Vigo can bring 2000 with ease and comfort, and I apprehend no difficulty or risk, save ship wreck, and that you can insure against. I can get one of the first lieutenants in the Navy to go out in command & we can whip anything if attacked, that is on that station, either English or American. But I would not propose to fight, for the "Vigo" can steam 11 knots, which should put us out of the reach of any of the cruisers. If you know of anyone who would be likely [to] take an interest, mention it to them *confidentially* & let me know who they are. I want none but reliable men, & men who will have the money the moment it is called for. I can raise 100,000 *here*. What can I raise in & about Augusta?

Truly yours,

C. A. L. Lamar

If the Rawlins gets in with her cargo, I shall want very little more money, for I will take all that is wanting myself.

NOTES

Note: This is Charles Lamar's first entry in the letter-book since February 2, 1858, a period of almost four months. After the British banned slavery in their colonies in the West Indies in 1834, the planters faced a critical labor shortage. The French experienced the same problem after 1848. To solve this problem, the countries imported "African apprentices," hired as free men for a specified number of years, with the option of returning to their homeland after the expiration of the contract. Charles Lamar thought that he could use this policy to bring Africans into the United States.

1. Charles had written previously to Thomas Barrett, the Augusta banker, on January 6, 1856, asking him to invest in a bank. See letters in Part B.

2. Lamar's plan of holding Africans for an indenture lasting the rest of their natural lives clearly makes them slaves.

3. An iron screw steamer is a steamship powered by a propeller as opposed to side paddle wheels.

4. Charles mentions that his father is familiar with the ship, raising the possibility that Gazaway may have been part of the plan. This is unlikely because Gazaway constantly criticized his son for participating in the slave trade. More likely, Gazaway, who dealt with cotton buyers in Liverpool, knew the *Vigo* from legitimate business connections.

5. Paixhans guns fired explosive shells. That Charles seriously considered sending a vessel to Africa prepared to do battle with the superior British or American cruisers of the African squadrons illustrates his recklessness.

6. Charles's estimates of the costs of a slaving voyage were general and unrealistic. For example, he doesn't state an amount for crew wages or bribes, two significant and necessary expenses for any slaving expedition. They may be included in the $25,000 for supplies, or he may have overlooked them. He gives an estimate of revenues and profits in the next letter.

7. Charles is referring to the second voyage of the *E. A. Rawlins*, which left New Orleans on February 11, three and a half months before the date of this letter.

8. It is unclear which ship Lamar has in mind to place the order. His only other ship, besides the *Wanderer*, was the *Richard Cobden*, which was docked in Charleston harbor, awaiting clearance to sail to Africa to pick up a cargo of African emigrants. A review of the "Marine Journal" column of the *Savannah Daily Morning News* and *Charleston Mercury* revealed no other ship owned by Lamar at that time.

Letter no. 25

Confidential
Savannah May 24th 1858
Wm Roundtree Esq.[1]
Nashville Tenn

Dr Sir,

I had a conversation with John A. Chambers this morning, in reference to the purchase of the track in Augusta by himself & yourself.[2] I suggested to him that he should postpone all action in the premises & join me in a speculation which I named, & which he readily assented to. He then begged me to communicate with you, & said he thought you would go 10,000$ and *go along*. It is simply this—I propose to get up an expedition to go to the coast of Africa for a cargo of Negroes. I have the plan and specifications for a steamer iron propeller of 1750 tons 2 years old, now in Liverpool England which costs 75,000£ and which is now offered for 30,000£. She steams without sail 11 knots an hour, is bark rigged & capable of bringing *comfortably* 2000 Negroes. But say we only get 1000, which I have ordered to be in readiness by 1st day of September. We can sell them at 650$ each. I propose to mount Six Paixhan Guns on deck which will enable me to whip any cruiser, English or American on the coast, but I think there would not be a chance in 100000 for a fight in the first place. Such a vessel would not be suspected, & if [_?] did attack, she can outrun them all. The voyage could be made in 60 days from the time of sailing. My estimate runs thus[3]

1st Cost of steamer	150,000
Repairs, Guns, Small arms, Coal etc.	50,000
Provisions, outfits etc.	25,000
Money for purchase of cargo	75,000
Cost of the expedition	$300,000
Say we bring but 1200 Negroes at 650	$780,000
Deduct 1st cost	300,000
Leaves nett profit & steamer on hand	$480,000

If you want to go in, say so at once. If you have any friend who would take a chance, mention it to him, *confidentially* & let me hear from you at once.

I am respectfully yours,

C. A. L. Lamar

NOTES

1. William Roundtree, of Nashville and Memphis, owned the Memphis racetrack and ran his horses there. Like Charles, he had a reputation as a heavy gambler. See the *Cleveland Plain Dealer*, December 31, 1861, and *NOTP*, September 22, 1858.

2. John A. Chambers lived in Savannah and was the first foreman of the Young America Fire Engine Company. See *CC*, April 27, 1855.

3. Charles calculated a respectable $480,000 profit. Although he stated in the letter that he would import only 1,000 Africans, he based his revenue projections on 1,200, costing $75,000, or $62.50 each. Lamar did not provide for any deaths during the Middle Passage, which would assuredly occur. If 15 percent were lost, his estimated profit would be reduced by $117,000. Still, there is no question that a successful slaving expedition could be very lucrative.

Lamar's claim that he had preordered a thousand Africans to be ready by September 1 was unlikely, as there is no record that he ever sent a ship to pick them up. He probably mentioned it to entice Roundtree to invest in the scheme.

Letter no. 26

Savannah May 24th 1858
Seaborn Jones Esq.[1]

My dear Sir,

I have yours of the 21st handed me by your father this morning. I will send the money as directed by the Swan.[2] I can make the bank discount the Note I took for the timber & stop yours, after this next renewal. Mr. Woolhopter says he sent you up a Note. I am glad to hear of your fine prospect in the way of a crop. I hope they will be more than realized. "Black Cloud" has had quite as many mares as I cared him to serve.[3] He won't be 12 years old until 26th June. If you will send your mares down, it shant [_?] you as [_?]. I will feed them & care for them, until they are satisfied.

I am expecting my vessel with the negroes every day now.[4] If she comes in, I will have a lot to send you to work as you proposed some time ago. I have another vessel which sails tomorrow,[5] and am trying to raise stock to send a steamer.[6] Don't you want to invest 5000$? I think it a sure trick with a steamer.

I am truly yours etc.
          C. A. L. Lamar

NOTES

1. Seaborn Jones, a close friend of Charles, practiced law in Augusta. He was the son of Augustus Seaborn Jones, a planter who owned Millhaven plantation in Sylvania, Screven County, and lived in Savannah. After Charles's wife Caro was evicted from her house by Union troops in April 1865, and while Charles served in the state military in Columbus, Georgia, she and her six daughters went to live with Seaborn at Millhaven.

2. The steamer *Swan* traveled the Savannah River route, indicating that Seaborn was in Augusta at that time. The *Swan* did depart from Savannah on May 29, 1858. See *DMN*, May 29, 1858.

3. Black Cloud was Lamar's favorite horse.

4. The vessel was the *E. A. Rawlins*.

5. As explained in the previous letter, the name of the vessel cannot be determined.

6. This would be the *Vigo* as referred to in the two previous letters. There is no record that Jones invested in any of Lamar's slave ships.

Letter no. 27

Savannah May 25th 1858
L W Spratt Esq[1]
Charleston S.C.

Dr Sir,

It has been some time since I have had the pleasure. I was in hope of being able to meet you at Montgomery, but was disappointed.[2] The object of this is simply to inquire if you, or any of your friends or acquaintances, would like to take stock in an expedition such as some of my friends & myself are attempting to get up. It is simply this—to fit out an expedition to go to the coast of Africa for a cargo of African Apprentices. I propose to purchase an Iron Screw Str of 1750 tons. I have my eye on one at this time that will bring comfortably 2000. She is now in L'pool and all ready for sea. She cost in 1856 £70,000 & is now offered for 30000£ cash. I will have an able man, an ex Lt. of the Navy, who stands socially as high as anybody to take command. She will be provided with six Paixhan Guns & manned, the fighting portion of the crew, by gentlemen of birth, education and means. I think the whole can be set on foot for *300,000$* & there is nothing short of an interposition of Divine Providence that can prevent her success. All the Negroes can be sold at 650$ a head as fast as landed. You can thus see the immense profit in the undertaking. What is to be done must be done quickly, for the vessel ought to be underway out by the 1st day of August. I have had some little experience in this matter, & have acquired some little information, at considerable cost, & think I can put it through successfully.

I have a vessel out now, & has been 4 months but I am afraid she may have been captured on the coast as no provision had been made for a cargo & she would have to remain until one was collected, subject to all the risks of detention etc. etc.[3] I have one that is to sail today, & which will take out orders for 1000 to be in readiness by the 1st day of Sept. next, which I intend for the Str, if not the one I have mentioned—a cheaper one. If you or any of your friends want to invest say the word.

I have in your port the ship "Richard Cobden" that is represented by Messr. E. Lafitte & I applied for a clearance for her & declared on the manifest the intention of the voyage was, to go to the coast of Africa for a cargo of Apprentices & return to some port in the U.S. or the island of Cuba. The application was made nearly *two months ago.* Mr. Colcock said as a lawyer he admitted my right, but as a government officer he would have to report it to Washington. I have written twice to the Treasury Department on giving a prompt decision & if a refusal, the reason for such refusal. But though I have been promised that I should have it in a day or two, it is not yet in hand. I know the Secy [Secretary] will refuse it—if he does, he will have many a battery opened on him. Pardon me for troubling you—I am determined to have the trade opened.[4]

I am respectfully etc.

C. A. L. Lamar

NOTES

1. Leonidas Spratt of South Carolina led the movement in the 1850s to reopen the African slave trade. He was born near Fort Mill, South Carolina, in 1818 and attended South Carolina College. After living in Florida during the 1840s, he returned to South Carolina and practiced law in Charleston. In 1853 he became the editor of the *Southern Standard* newspaper. He was elected to the state house of representatives from 1858 to 1860. Although he didn't own slaves, Spratt campaigned tirelessly for the South's right to import Africans. See John Amasa May and Joan Reynolds Faunt, *South Carolina Secedes* (Columbia: University of South Carolina Press, 1968), 213. For a northern commentary on Spratt and his efforts, see *NYTR*, November 30, 1857. There is no evidence that Spratt invested in any of Lamar's slaving expeditions.

2. Charles is referring to the Southern Commercial Convention held in Montgomery, Alabama, which commenced on May 10, 1858. Spratt had issued a report on the reopening of the African slave trade, but it was tabled until the next meeting at Vicksburg. The use of the convention to promote the slave trade movement angered many in the South. The *Richmond Enquirer* editorialized: "The subjects lately discussed at Montgomery changed as much as the times and men who formerly struggled for Southern interest and sighed for brighter days of Southern enterprise. In Montgomery, 'direct trade' was forgotten; 'foreign

capital' ignored; 'commercial capital and credit' never mentioned; 'commercial education and Southern literature' never thought of. The 'slave trade' absorbed the entire time . . . to the distraction of the councils of the South, and the division of her unity; crimination and recrimination were indulged in by one Southern State against another Southern State until . . . the Convention had been turned into a political debating club." See *CM*, June 2, 1858. For a review of Spratt's involvement at the conventions between 1855 and 1859, see Barton J. Bernstein, "Southern Politics and Attempts to Reopen the African Slave Trade," *JNH* 51 (January 1966): 24–29.

3. Lamar seems convinced that the *Rawlins* has failed and attributes it to having to wait at the coast while the Africans were gathered. This assumption turned out to be incorrect.

4. In late February and early March, Charles was in New Orleans trying to collect money from Theodore Johnston. While there, he learned of a debate taking place in the Louisiana legislature about passing a law to allow the importation of African apprentices. Charles was so moved by the concept that on his return to Savannah, he asked his shipping agent in Charleston, E. Lafitte and Company, to apply for clearance for his ship the *Richard Cobden* to sail to the coast of Africa to pick up a cargo of apprentices and return to an unnamed U.S. port. Lamar knew that Charleston port collector William F. Colcock forwarded the highly problematic application to Secretary of the Treasury Howell Cobb for approval. During the long wait for a reply, Charles wrote a private and confidential letter to Cobb, his cousin by marriage, explaining the true purpose of the voyage—to land the Africans on a levee in New Orleans and let the courts decide on the legality. As of the writing of this letter, Lamar still hadn't received an answer.

Letter no. 28

Savannah June 6th 1858
Messrs. E. Lafitte & Co.

Gents,

I have read your reply to Mr. Cobb & wish you had not decided upon suppressing it. You will see that I have used a portion of it in my remarks to him. I think it but right that I should relieve you of all responsibility in the premise & therefore have declared as you see that I was the principal & you the agents. Have it published—if there is any charge made, charge it *to me*.[1] Get Spratt & other Southern men to toast him up. I have not had the time to prepare anything myself but will & open upon him then in the papers.[2]

I am truly yours etc.
C. A. L. Lamar

NOTES

Note: On May 22, Cobb finally sent his decision regarding the application for clearance of the *Cobden* for Africa to port collector William F. Colcock, who forwarded it to E. Lafitte and Company. The lengthy rejection was published in the *Charleston Mercury* on June 1. Although Cobb knew that the application was made on behalf of Lamar, he treated Lafitte as the responsible party. Cobb said that a cargo of African apprentices could only be disposed of in one of two ways: as slaves bound to labor or as emigrants entitled to all the rights and privileges of freemen. He explained that the first was clearly illegal and the second was a ruse to import slaves under another name.

Cobb also used the opportunity to take a swipe at Charles, who had used him for getting clearance for the *Rawlins* in July 1857 and then sent her on a slaving expedition. "To believe . . . that there is a bona fide purpose on the part of Messrs. Lafitte & Co. to bring African emigrants to this country to enjoy the rights and privileges of freemen, would require an amount of credulity which would justly subject the person so believing to the charge of mental imbecility." Lafitte and Lamar were incensed by Cobb's letter.

1. Edward Lafitte wrote a response to Cobb's rejection for the *Charleston Mercury* and sent it to Lamar for review but then changed his mind about sending it to the newspaper. Lamar asked him to reconsider, which he did. The next day, June 7, the letter appeared in the *Mercury*. It objected to Cobb's condescending tone and his disingenuousness, as he knew the application really came from Lamar and not from Lafitte.

2. No documents authored by Spratt and other southern men "toasting up" Cobb on this issue were found. While Spratt continued to campaign for the reopening of the slave trade, the fight with Cobb was Charles's alone. He continued it in his next letter.

Letter no. 29

Savannah June 4th 1858

Messrs. Editors[1]

The application made to W. F. Colcock Esq., Collector of the Port of Charleston, S.C., by Messrs. E. Lafitte & Co., for the clearance of the ship "Richard Cobden" for the coast of Africa for the purpose of taking on board African Emigrants in accordance with the United States passenger laws, and of returning with same, to some port in the United States was made by them as my agents, & in accordance with my instructions. I am alone responsible for any outrage that has been committed upon Public sentiment in Charleston & elsewhere, & I have no apologies to make. I was simply exercising a legal right, and a right which I am still insisting upon, for I am now applying for almost a similar clearance, the difference being to return to a port in the island of Cuba instead of a port in the U.S.[2]

I should have assumed all the obligations of a principal before but Messrs. E. Lafitte & Co. proposed to answer Mr. Cobb, & had my authority to declare me the principal & begged that I would give them the lead off. They having changed their determination, I have thought proper to say a word or two.

To Mr. Secretary Cobb:

Your objection to the form of the application, as involving the subject in some embarrassment, is groundless. Viewed as a matter of legal right, the question is simply this; has anyone the right to land African Emigrants *bond or free* at any port in the United States? If this question is answered in the affirmative, the right of the applicant to such a clearance is clear and indisputable. *You virtually admitted* the right to land such emigrants in some of the non-slaveholding states, but added that "you were not aware of a single state where these newcomers would receive a tolerant much less a cordial reception." Has Northern Public opinion then acquired the force of law? It certainly appears to have attained that force with you, for after stating the object must be to introduce slaves or persons held to service or labor or else to bring them in as other immigrants, entitled to all the rights & privileges of free men, you adduce a formidable array of legal enactments to prove the illegality of the first proposition. To the second, you appease the public opinion of the North unsupported by a single quotation from the law, either State or Federal. Nay, you admit that no law exists by which they can be excluded. The mere omission of the name of the port to which the Cobden would return, does not constitute an objection to the granting of the clearance as it is usual to clear vessels for various ports of the world without naming any particular port. The assumption therefore that it was intended to return to a port which she had no rights to enter in preference to a port she could lawfully enter, is not warranted by anything upon the face of the application & was a conclusion to be arrived at only by an interpretation of the motives of the applicant which interpretation you had no right to make. The ship was therefore by your own admission entitled to a clearance, unless indeed Northern Public opinion is entitled to prevail over the legal right of Southern Citizens. Upon the return of the ship to the United States, the status of the Africans on board, & all other matters affecting the legality of the voyage could have been held in the Federal Courts. You have undertaken to condemn the proposed voyage as illegal, and have closed the courts of the country against me, by depriving me of the only possible means of obtaining a hearing upon the merits of the question. I proposed to you *in writing* that if you would grant the vessel protection on the coast of Africa from molestation that I would land the cargo on the levee in New Orleans & that the legality of the matter [would be determined] in the courts of the United States.[3]

You stated that "ordinarily it would be an unsafe rule for a public officer to act upon a suspicion of a purpose on the part of another to violate the laws of the country." From your course it would appear that the exception to the rule should exist only as a bar to Southern Enterprise, as

Northern vessels are constantly employed in the transportation of coolies who are persons of color held to service or labor.[4]

The application which is now before you for a clearance for the same vessel for almost a similar voyage is not amenable to the objections urged against the other & I am in hopes you will give an immediate answer to it & let the South know whether she has any rights in the Union or not.[5]

Respectfully etc.

C. A. L. Lamar

NOTES

Note: This letter appeared in the letter-book after the letter to Lafitte, but is dated two days earlier. It was published in the *Charleston Mercury* on June 8, 1858, the day after E. Lafitte's letter.

1. The editors of the *Charleston Mercury*.

2. Charles did submit this second application, which Cobb also rejected. See note 5 below.

3. When Lafitte and Company did not get a timely response to the first application for clearance, Lamar wrote to Cobb privately—the letter was never published—asking him to expedite his decision, and he admitted his plan to land Africans on a levee outside of New Orleans and let the federal courts decide the matter. Charles even asked Cobb for U.S. naval squadron protection for his slave ship. Cobb ignored this letter when writing his rejection to Lafitte and Company.

4. Charles is referring to the trade in Chinese "coolies." Although Chinese immigrants to the United States in the 1840s and 1850s entered the country as free people, the ones carried to the West Indies, chiefly Cuba and Peru, were tantamount to slaves. They were coerced or lied to when recruited; shipped in conditions mirroring those of the African slave trade; sold to the highest bidder at the destination port; and made to work as indentured servants in the sugar fields alongside African slaves for terms of eight years at compensation of four dollars per month. Shippers from the United States, mostly of northern origin, freely participated in this trade. Lamar questioned why Cobb held southern shippers in violation of the law for transporting "African apprentices" to Cuba, and not northerners for transporting Chinese "contract laborers." For the number of ships, their nationalities, and the number of Chinese coolies sent to Cuba between 1847 and 1858, see *NOTP* as reprinted in *AC*, October 16, 1859. For some tales of horror of the coolie trade and their treatment on plantations, see *NYTR*, February 18, 1859; *Washington Constitution*, July 30, 1859; *WDNI*, August 1, 1859.

5. Cobb soon rejected Charles's second application for a clearance "for the coast of Africa, to take on board African apprentices and return with the same to a port in Cuba." He explained, "It would seem that the present application is made upon a supposed difference between the slave trade . . . and the slave trade under the name and form of apprenticed Africans. This government does not recognize that distinction." Charles then made a third application for clearance without naming a final destination. Port collector Colcock rejected that one on his own. Lamar was furious. He wanted to make his case to the South—and exact revenge on Cobb—in print, but he waited until the departure of another of his slave ships, the *Wanderer*.

On July 5, Lamar published an eleven-page manifesto attacking Cobb's interpretation of the slave trade laws and abuse of his office. Then Charles got personal. He said the way Cobb handled the response, to dance around the issue and to conciliate the North by taking a stand against slavery, was "the work of a little man to a little object." Lamar informed Cobb that while he didn't intend to engage in the slave trade with the *Cobden,* he would with other ships, and he laid down a challenge. "I intend to violate [the law,] if that shall be the only way by which the South can come to right upon this question, and I will re-open the trade in slaves to foreign countries, let your cruisers catch me if they can." See Charles A. Lamar, *The Reply of C. A. L. Lamar of Savannah, Georgia to the Letter of Hon. Howell Cobb, Secretary of the Treasury of the United States, Refusing a Clearance to the Ship Richard Cobden* (Charleston, S.C., 1858).

Letter no. 30

Savannah July 22nd 1858
John Cunningham Esq.[1]
Charleston S.C.

Dr Sir,

In your review of my letter to Mr. Secretary Cobb, you used the following language: "But his appeal to the passions of sympathy, show, that in case he is caught, he had rather be regarded as a martyr than a convict, as a hero than a freebooter."[2] The above is offensive, & the object of this is to inquire if you intended it to be so, & if you intended, either directly or indirectly, to reflect upon me personally. Your early attention will much oblige.[3]

Very Respectfully
Your Obt [Obedient] Servt
C. A. L. Lamar

NOTES

This is Charles's first letter since June 6, and the first since the *Wanderer* departed Charleston.

1. John Cunningham was the editor of the *Charleston Evening News.*

2. A freebooter is one who pillages and plunders, such as a pirate.

3. Lamar was following the formal rules of the duel. He felt that his honor had been maligned and asked Cunningham if his remark was meant to offend. Cunningham's response would dictate Charles's next step. Lamar's letter of July 28 revealed the editor's response.

Letter no. 31

Savannah July 22nd 1858
L. W. Spratt Esq.

My Dr Sir,

Yours of the 18th with enclosures of articles clipped from the Evening News at hand only this morning. I am much obliged for your kind attention. Ordinarily, I would not consider it necessary for me to notice such articles, but coming from the source it does, from one who sets himself up as the fire Eater of the Editorial Corps of S.C., I am constrained to notice it. I have this moment penned him the following of which this is a copy. [Lamar repeats his letter of July 22nd to Cunningham.]

I am not disposed to make myself any more notorious & conspicuous than I can avoid. I think the above will meet the cause. If his object is a difficulty, he shall have it.

I am Truly yrs etc.

C. A. L. Lamar

Letter no. 32

Savannah July 28th 1858
John Cunningham Esq.
Charleston, S.C.

Dr Sir,

I am in rect of yours of the 26th, in reply to mine of the 22nd and must thank you for the frank & manly disavowal of any intention to wound or offend.[1] Permit me to express the hope, that I may yet see you a convert to our cause & assisting to accomplish that which alone can regenerate our section & make it what God & nature intended it—the garden of the world, & we, the freest, happiest & most prosperous of people. I write you the [_?] calmly & without prejudice & I am satisfied you will be one of the warmest advocates for the reopening of the African Slave Trade.

I am very respectfully yours,

C. A. L. Lamar

NOTES

1. Since Cunningham made his original comment in his newspaper, he would be expected to withdraw it in the same forum. It is unclear whether he did this. In any case, Lamar forgave him.

Letter no. 33

Savannah July 28th 1858
L. W. Spratt Esq.

My dear Sir,

I received this morning a very handsome letter from Col. Cunningham, disavowing any intention to wound or offend, to which I replied, thanking him for the frank & manly tone of the letter. That ends what I at one time thought would be a very unpleasant business. I may have been too thin skinned, but will in future try and avoid interpreting generalities with specialties. I am constantly receiving from different gents of prominence & influence throughout the states, letters approving of my course & denunciation of Cobb. He is a gone sucker in this State. His chance at the Presidency is gone—certain.[1]

I am writing from New Orleans.

I am truly yours etc.

C. A. L. Lamar

NOTES

1. Some observers thought Cobb wanted the Democratic Party nomination for president in 1860. Lamar believed that Cobb's handling of the *Cobden* incident doomed his chances.

Letter no. 34

Savannah August 14th 1858
Messrs. Marez, Otero & Co.[1]
Enclosed to Henry C. Hall Esq.[2]
Care of Messrs. Gorcouria, Pedroso & Co.
Matanzas, Cuba

Gents,

Mr. Horner[3] of your city has been in to see me, & has requested me to open a correspondence with you in reference to the importation of Africans to this country. We have had a very full & confidential conversation & he informs me that you are willing to contract to deliver any number of negroes at a designated point upon our coast, if we can agree upon the terms. The price he named to me he admitted, was very much too high, viz: 500$, in view of the risks to be taken here after they are delivered. I would be willing to give 300$ provided they were sound & free of all marks such as tattooing etc., etc. I am willing to make a joint a/c speculation of it. I have a very fine and fast Bark, the "E. A. Rawlins"[4] home just from the coast and am ready to send her out again as soon as some repairs are met after her if you will [_?] an equal division, after they are disposed of, charging only the absolute expenses incurred & a commission at 10% for attention to the business here & taking all the risks of prosecution etc. etc. Or, I will furnish the vessel & her outfit, & have her at a designated point at a given time to receive a cargo, provided you will agree to have the Negroes ready at that time and as soon as I have notification of their being safely on board, I am willing to pay you the current price of them on the coast. In taking all the risks incident to their transportation, landing, selling etc. etc. Or if neither of the above will suit you, I am open to receive any proposition you may think proper. [The next three lines are unintelligible, but it appears as if Charles is saying that he wants the deal to be done quickly.]

C. A. L. Lamar

NOTES

1. Charles Mares moved from Cuba and established himself in Savannah just weeks after this letter, in September 1858, as Lamar mentions in Letter no. 35. Mares would be tried in Savannah in 1859 for fitting out the bark *Angelita* as a slaver and, with codefendant Joachim Selvas, found not guilty.

2. Henry Cook Hall worked in the U.S. Foreign Service during the Civil War as the consul in Matanzas and afterward as the consul-general in Havana. See *NYH*, December 2, 1869. Little information could be found on him before the war, but he clearly had an interest in the African slave trade. For his obituary see the *Boston Journal*, October 30, 1901.

3. The identity of Mr. Horner could not be determined. James Hervey Horner served as the U.S. consular agent at Sagua la Grande, Cuba, in 1869 but was the consul to Sabanilla, Colombia, in 1858. For James H. Horner's obituary, see *Portland Daily Press*, August 19, 1876.

4. The *Rawlins* returned to Savannah from her failed second slaving expedition on August 2, 1858.

Letter no. 35

Savannah Sept 14th 1858
H. C. Hall Esq. Matanzas, Cuba
Care of S. S. Mares, Otero & Co.

Dear Sir,

I am in rect of yours of the 21st of August & would have replied by the last steamer but thought I would await an answer to mine of the 14th of August written at the instance of M. Horner, which stated my willingness to receive another class of laborer & the terms upon which I would receive them.[1] If that letter miscarried, I will repeat in substance what it contained. I will contract with the party I found for a given number of Africans, delivered at a given point on the coast at 300$ per head, I to take all the risks after they are landed. The negroes to be free of marks, such as tattooing, etc. etc. Or I am willing to make a joint a/c speculation of it. I have a very fast & superior Bark of 273 tons capacity—the E. A. Rawlins—now undergoing repairs & being re-coppered that I am willing to send out to the coast for a cargo. If your friend will furnish her with a cargo I will then receive the Negroes & dispose of them charging you my service a commission of 10%. I would have all the *risks to* [_?] *of a prosecution* in case I were found with them and I think the commission of 10% but a fair commission, when all the trouble, labor & risks are taken into consideration. Or, I will furnish the vessel and her outfit, & send her to a designated point on the coast for a cargo, if your friend will have a *Cargo in readiness* for her upon her arrival out. So soon as I have notification from my Captain, that the negroes are on board, I will pay for them *in cash*, the prices current upon the coast at the time of shipment, taking all the risks from the moment they are on board. If neither of the above suit you, I would be pleased to receive a proposition from you.

Mr. Mares has presented your letter, & has established himself in an office on the Bay.[2] It will afford me pleasure to be of any service to him & I have so signified to him.

I am respectfully etc.

C. A. L. Lamar

NOTES

1. It is not clear what Lamar means by "another class of laborer," as the rest of the letter deals with African slaves. Even if he is referring to African apprentices, they would have to be acquired, shipped, and distributed like slaves.

2. Savannahians referred to Bay Street as "the Bay."

Letter no. 36

Savannah Dec. 18th 1858

Dear Trow,[1]

I returned this morning from Augusta. I distributed the negroes the best I could but I tell you things are in a hell of a fix.[2] No certainty about anything. The Government has employed H. R. Jackson to assist in the prosecution, & are determined to press matters to the utmost extremity.[3] The yacht has been seized, the examination commenced today, & will continue for 30 days, at the rate they are going on.[4] They have all the pilots and men who took the yacht to Brunswick here to testify. *She will be lost certain and sure*, if not the negroes. Dr. Hazlehurst, the brother-in-law of Dubignon, testified today to the fact that he attended to the negroes on Jekyl, & swore they were Africans, & of recent importation.

You must not *deliver a single one of the notes I gave you*—if you pay them what they put in, I think they will be doing well under the circumstances.[5] I don't calculate to get a new dollar for an old one—all of the men must be *bribed.*[6] I must be paid for my time [,] trouble & advances. I think they have 100 witnesses subpoenaed—and one still issuing them. Ganahl is doing his damndest, but I keep pretty well posted as to what he is doing.[7]

You must do the best you can with these parties. Six of those left at Monts, who were sick, died yesterday.[8] I think the whole of them will die that are now sick. They are too enfeebled to administer medicine to. I am paying 50c per day each for all those I took up the country—it was the best I could do.[9] It won't take long at that rate for a large bill to run up.

You see how matters stand & *you must do the best you can.* If they won't *sell* for the original money *in cash,* let them slide.[10] I think I must be paid for all the advances made—don't use one dollar of the money, unless for the purpose you took it for. I tell you Hell is to pay. I don't think they will discharge the men, but turn them over for trial. If so there's no telling when we can dispose of the negroes.[11] If Danese had gone away as I told him to do all would have been well now.[12] Let me hear from you.

Yours,

C. A. L. Lamar

NOTES

1. This is the first entry in the letter-book since September 14, a period of three months, and the first since the landing of the *Wanderer* Africans on November 29. Lamar did not record Nelson Trowbridge's location, but it was probably Jekyll Island. As of the writing of this letter, the news of the crime had been reported in newspapers around the country, three crewmembers had been arrested in Savannah, and Lamar was frantically trying to sell his share of the human cargo.

2. Lamar is referring to the estimated 270 Africans who were taken to a woodyard owned by his cousin Thomas Lamar in Hamburg, South Carolina, near Augusta, Georgia, to be sold.

3. Attorney General Jeremiah Black assigned Henry Rootes Jackson of Savannah as a special prosecutor to assist District Attorney Joseph Ganahl in the *Wanderer* case. Jackson had graduated Yale College in 1839 and practiced law in Savannah until he was appointed U.S. district attorney for Georgia in 1843. He served in the Mexican-American War as colonel of the First Georgia Regiment. Soon after his return he was appointed the judge of the superior court of Chatham County and held that position until he was appointed U.S. minister to Austria in 1853. Jackson returned to Savannah in 1858 and became a partner in the law firm of Ward, Jackson, and Jones, where he was working when asked to participate in the *Wanderer* case. See Kenneth Coleman and Charles Stephen Gurr, eds., *Dictionary of Georgia Biography*, 2 vols. (Athens: University of Georgia Press, 1983), 1:513–14.

4. The examination was the hearing in front of U.S. commissioner Charles Seton Henry to determine if enough evidence existed to send the *Wanderer* case to a grand jury.

5. It is difficult to understand what Lamar means here. Each partner received a portion of the Africans. Lamar may have purchased some of them and planned to pay with notes but changed his mind because the partners owed him money.

6. Lamar is referring to the witnesses who had been subpoenaed by the district attorney.

7. Joseph Ganahl was the thirty-year-old son of one of the first German cotton buyers to settle in Savannah. He originally studied medicine but soon turned to the practice of law. In October 1857 he was appointed the U.S. district attorney for Georgia, and he certainly knew of Lamar's undisguised public attempts to engage in the international slave trade.

8. John Montmollin's South Carolina plantation, where an estimated thirty Africans were left for distribution.

9. Lamar said several times that he could sell Africans "as fast as landed." This wasn't the case with the *Wanderer* victims. He hadn't planned for the expense of feeding and otherwise maintaining them for any length of time.

10. Lamar is probably referring to the thirty-six Africans left on Jekyll Island and in Trowbridge's control. They would eventually be shipped west in March 1859.

11. It is unclear why Lamar and Trowbridge couldn't sell some Africans if Danese, Rajesta, and Arguirvi were held over for trial. If the slaves belonged to Danese, Lamar could sell them and pay him at a later date.

12. Danese is the real name of Captain Nicholas Brown. Lamar claimed to have told him to leave Montmollin's plantation by some route other than Savannah, where Danese and the two crewmembers were arrested.

Letter no. 37

Private & Confidential
Savannah Jany 12th 1859[1]
John Scott Esq.[2]
Warrenton VA

Dr Sir,

Yours of the 5th Jany reached me this morning. I agree with you in all the positions assumed. I am the man you were looking for. I am willing to join any party of responsible Gents, and fit out an Expedition & go and get all we want.

Those that were landed on the island of Jekyl were the likeliest gang I ever saw—40 boys, between the ages of 12 & 15 can't be beat for intelligence & fine appearance, by the same number, from any dozen plantations in Georgia.

I would be unwilling to attempt a landing North of S.C. but would be willing to land anywhere from there to Texas. It would require a large outlay of money to get up an Expedition to insure success. I have bought & paid largely for the experience I have, having made two unsuccessful attempts.[3]

It will require a *cash* capital of 200,000$. I can raise 100 @ 150 m here & in Carolina & the vessel of the size I would have would bring 1000 *comfortably* & without crowding as much as is now done on the Liverpool packets[4]—for you must bear in mind, that she will have no cargo *other than provisions & water for the passengers*. My estimate for the voyage is this summer.

Say we land 1000, which we can do *safely and comfortably* at
500$ each, and they will bring 900$ in Cuba or 750 in La[,]
Miss or Texas. —— $500,000

Put the cost of Str [steamer] at   100,000
Advances to officers & crew
Provisions, outfit etc. etc.   50,000
Coin for purchase of cargo
Say 1000 at $50   50,000
                                                                    ─────────
                                                                     200,000
Nett profit of the voyage $300,000

The above I think a fair & liberal calculation of the outfit, but not of
the price for which they would sell. But I know 300,000$ can be made by
a voyage of the kind if successful.[5] I know all the ins & outs of the matter
& if you or any of your friends want to go in, just see the amt you can raise,
& I can get the balance here & in Carolina. Of course I shall expect a
comm of 5% for my services in getting it up & for my knowledge & experience which has cost me some $80,000 by making two unsuccessful trips.

   I am respectfully yours,
   C.A.L. Lamar

NOTES

   1. Lamar is attempting to organize another slaving expedition only six weeks after the
landing of the *Wanderer*, even as the federal government pursued him and the sales of the
Africans in South Carolina were going poorly.
   2. John Scott, born in 1820, gained admittance to the Virginia Bar in 1841. He practiced
law until 1850, when he became the editor of the *Richmond Whig*. In 1851 he retired to
his plantation near Warrenton, Virginia, which he inherited from his father. He helped
found the Black Horse Cavalry in 1859 and became its first captain. Based on the wording
of Lamar's letter, Scott made the initial contact. No record could be found showing that
Scott had previous involvement in the slave trade, and nothing came of this inquiry. Horace
Edwin Hayden, *Virginia Genealogies: A Genealogy of the Glassel Family of Scotland and Virginia*
(Baltimore: Southern Book Company, 1959), 655–57.
   3. The two unsuccessful attempts were the *Rawlins* expeditions, as Charles admitted in
his letter to R. L. Gamble dated June 20, 1859.
   4. Lamar is referring to the ships that carried cargo and passengers between Liverpool
and the United States.
   5. Lamar's estimate ignored the death rate during the Middle Passage, which was generally 15 to 20 percent, and that held true for the *Wanderer*. If he had included this factor, the
proposed expedition would net $75,000 less. Charles also omitted three major expenses
that he incurred in the *Wanderer* expedition: bad debts, pilferage (the stealing of the Africans), and feeding the Africans until they were sold. These would surely occur again with
Lamar running the operation.

Letter no. 38

Savannah January 13th 1859
Theodore Johnston Esq.[1]

Dr Sir,

I have yours of the 11th & regret you did not get one. I am astounded at what Gov Phinizy has written me & must believe, until it is confirmed that he has been misinformed.[2] The idea of a man's taking Negroes to keep at 50c a head per day, and then refused to give them up when demanded, simply because the law does not recognize them as property is worse than stealing. I thought them all secure up there.[3] I can get nothing from anyone. I have yet to receive a dollar for the sale of those left in & about Hamburg. Trowbridge has sold 24 of those at Benton.[4] Those that Mr. Brailsford had, & which he has sent off 10—I intend to keep myself to reimburse myself for outlays of moneys, if I can get those near Hamburg.[5]

I will send you Woolfolk's [slaves] by Gilbert but is it not passing strange that you refuse to pay his proportion of the outlay when you were here & had the money in your pocket.[6] I had taken the risk for 40 days then, & you wanted me to take it for a still longer time, until you were safe beyond [_?] adventure. Was this right? I offered you the negroes & would have gone up & seen them delivered had you paid the amt due. You have seen how matters stand & how many have died & can judge therefore of the number [_?] the 400. There [can] be [many] and if it as reported by Gov Phinizy and yourself I am very much afraid the ¹⁄₁₆ths nor the ¹⁵⁄₁₆ths would not get a new dollar for an old one.[7]

All this, if it is so, has been caused by the conduct of those interested in not coming forward and claiming and taking away their property. I could have saved mine and one or two others, but I did not like to throw myself open to the charge even of selfishness. The consequence has been, I shall not only lose the original investment, but the most, or at least a part of, the advances I have made.[8] The yacht is gone I think. The law requires that the libel shall be answered by Corrie under oath, denying the accusations.[9] I shall do all that can be done, but my attorneys say it is a bad showing, even if they have nothing but circumstantial evidence. They are examining the laws to see if they want to be admitted as her attorneys: to see that the examination of witnesses is conducted according to the laws of evidence.

If things are as you state in and about Hamburg, you can see as well as I can that there is no use in sending Gilbert. If things on the contrary are right you can get the ¹/₁₆th interest. When here you said you would pay up in 4 or 5 days at outside. That was Sunday, this Thursday and no money—yet.

Yours respectfully,

C. A. L. Lamar

NOTES

1. Theodore Johnston of New Orleans, involved with Lamar's legal (interstate) and illegal (foreign) slave-trading ventures, was the only *Wanderer* partner not charged by the prosecutors, probably because he lived out of state and was unknown to District Attorney Joseph Ganahl.

2. Gazaway Lamar was related to the Phinizys of Augusta through his first marriage to Jane Meek Cresswell. Her sister, Martha, married John Phinizy (1793–1884), and Gazaway and John became brothers-in-law. John had seven sons. James Hamilton Phinizy, born in 1833 and twenty-five years old at the time, was nicknamed "Gov." Dr. Ferdinand Phinizy Calhoun Jr., *Grandmother Was a Phinizy: A Registry of the Descendants of Ferdinand Phinizy and Margaret Condon and Allied Families* (Atlanta: Darby, 1991), 109.

3. Charles had entrusted the care of the Africans taken to Hamburg to his cousin Thomas Lamar. When Thomas had to leave town for a few days, he placed the unsold bondsmen in the hands of another man, who charged Charles Lamar fifty cents a day each for upkeep, and then refused to give them up when Thomas returned. The name of the man is revealed in Letter no. 39.

4. Benton might be Benton County, Alabama (renamed Calhoun County in January 1858), southwest from Rome, Floyd County, Georgia, or a small village in Floyd County, Georgia.

5. William Brailsford was a planter from McIntosh County and a longtime friend of Lamar. Like Charles, he raced horses and belonged to the Savannah Aquatic Club. *DMN,* December 7, 1853.

6. Woolfolk is likely John, of Columbus, Georgia, a large plantation and slave owner, or one of his two sons, Joseph or William. Charles Lamar refers to Gilbert here and in the last paragraph. Gilbert was a clerk of Theodore Johnston and is mentioned in a newspaper article about the *Rawlins* after the ship's second failed mission. "On board the *Rawlins* is a tall wiry-looking fellow . . . called GILBERT. He says that he merely went to the Coast of Africa as a 'passenger,' but he forgets to tell that he is chief clerk to one of the largest negro traders in the city of New-Orleans, named Johns[t]on. This Mr. Gilbert is here still, awaiting the fitting out of the ship, when he will no doubt take another trip to Africa." *NYT,* September 10, 1858. Gilbert was apparently in Georgia and South Carolina helping distribute *Wanderer* Africans. One wonders why Lamar thought it was "passing strange" that Johnston didn't pay him moneys owed in light of Lamar's history with him.

7. Lamar suggests that there were sixteen shares among the eight partners. If four hundred Africans survived the voyage and the first few days on Jekyll Island, as Lamar states, then each ¹/₁₆ share equals about twenty-five Africans. (As Lamar paid some of the crew in slaves, a share might be somewhat less than twenty-five.)

8. Lamar admits that he will lose money on the *Wanderer* expedition, making him zero

for three in the African slave trade, counting his two failures with the *Rawlins*. Charles never reveals the amount of the *Wanderer* loss.

9. Lamar is referring to the libel of information issued in the admiralty court by Judge John C. Nicoll on January 8. Corrie would not appear because the district attorney for South Carolina refused to extradite him. However, he answered the libel from jail through his Georgia attorney. Admiralty Court Journal, January 8 to February 25, 1859, U.S. District Court, Savannah, Georgia, Federal Records Center, Morrow, Ga.

Letter no. 39

Savannah January 15th 1859

Dr Tom[1]

Don't sell any of the Negroes for anything but money. I would not give a damn for all the Notes that have been sent me. I want the money— *money* alone will pay my obligations. Keep the Negroes if they can't be sold for cash, & I will send them West.[2] Settle the business with Tillman *at once*.[3] Delays are dangerous—get the money from him or the negroes. I paid in cash myself 400 for a portion of the crew's negroes & 450 for the balance. You can thus see, after adding expenses, how I am off. Don't let another go without the money, & at fair prices too. I would rather lose the whole than get but a mite of the investment back. Don't let my interest suffer in the hands of these men—look after them.

  I am truly yrs etc.

   C. A. L. Lamar

    Thos. G. Lamar Esq.

    Hamburg S.C.

NOTES

1. Charles's cousin, Thomas G. Lamar of Hamburg, South Carolina, had the responsibility of managing the distribution of the Africans sent to Hamburg after Charles left the area on December 17.

2. Notes in combination with cash were commonly used to finance the purchase of slaves, but Tom Lamar had been selling the Africans for notes alone. Although slaves were in great demand and commanded high prices throughout the South, Charles was unable to sell them profitably for cash. For example, in a recent transaction in Washington County, Georgia, forty-two slaves brought prices averaging $860. *DMN*, January 17, 1859.

3. When Tom Lamar had to leave town for a few days, he transferred the care of the remaining Africans to a man named Tillman, who was undoubtedly one of the sons of Benjamin Ryan Tillman and Sophia Ann Hancock Tillman. Sophia inherited her husband's plantation and slaves in the Edgefield district of South Carolina after her husband's death in 1849. Of her seven living sons in early 1859, only George Dionysus (b. 1825), John Miller

(b. 1833), or Oliver Hancock Tillman (b. 1835) would have been old enough to be entrusted with the Africans. The most famous of the Tillman boys, Benjamin Ryan Jr., or "Pitchfork Ben," so named because as a U.S. senator in 1896 he promised to stick President Grover Cleveland in the derriere with a pitchfork, was only eleven years old at the time. Sophia eventually gained possession of thirty *Wanderer* slaves, though it is unknown if she purchased them or, through her son, confiscated them. Francis Butler Simkins, *Pitchfork Ben Tillman, South Carolinian* (1944; Columbia: University of South Carolina Press, 2002), 28–30.

Letter no. 40

Savannah, Jany 28th 1859[1]

Dr Sir, [Capt. N. D. Brown][2]

I paid Frank 575$.[3] Messrs. T. & J are neither of them here.[4] Mr. T. passed through here disguised, day before yesterday, but I did not see him. Mr. J was here 3 weeks ago, & remained but 1 day—he came to pay up & take his portion, but when he saw the situation of affairs, he went off & refused to pay even his proportion of the amount I had advanced. No one has yet paid one cent.

The Packages that went up the River have all been sold, save 38 that Corrie took, & sold for 300$, the most of them, and for Notes at 12 months, that are not worth a damn.[5] I limited them at 600$ *cash*, but my relative [Tom Lamar] who had the general superintendence of them, was compelled to go away from home & the Party left in charge [Tillman] sacrificed them. If I can do anything with the Notes, I can pay up, otherwise I cannot.[6] It has been a most disastrous business to me. I have done all the work, taken all the responsibility & paid all the money, & shall make nothing, but on the contrary, shall lose a large portion of that I advanced for the Parties.[7]

Your attys. will visit you before the trial.[8] If a true bill be found by the Grand Jury against you, it will be done upon the evidence of Club[b] & Harris—& of course they will, upon the trial, testify to the same thing. In that event, I think all of you ought *to leave*, & I will make arrangements for you to do so, if you agree with me. I have offered Club[b] & Harris 5000$ not to testify, but gov'mt is also trying to buy them.[9] I don't think you will have much difficulty in getting out, if matters take the course I think they may take.[10]

I am afraid they will convict me, but my case is only 7 years & a fine. If I find they are likely to do so, I shall go to Cuba, until I make some compromise with the gov'mt. Matters look badly enough just now but everything in your case depends upon Club[b] & Harris. In time, they can prove I was in charge of the property which will be enough—and they can, I am afraid, prove it by a member.

I am Respectfully yrs

C. A. L. Lamar

Capt. N. D. Brown

NOTES

1. Thirteen days had passed since the previous entry in the letter-book. During that time, Charles dealt with his legal problems. On January 17 he wrote to his father in New York that District Attorney Ganahl was "making a great ass of himself," and that he had no fears, "so far as trials are concerned." However, Charles admitted that all profits from the *Wanderer* were being stolen, that cousin Tom Lamar was selling Africans for nothing "merely to manufacture public opinion with him," and that Tillman still withheld some of the Africans. C. A. L. Lamar to G. B. Lamar, January 17, 1859, Charles A. L. Lamar Papers, Emory.

2. The letter is addressed to "Dr Sir," but Lamar records "Capt. N. D. Brown" at the bottom. As previously mentioned, Brown's real name is Nicholas Danese.

3. The identity of Frank is unknown.

4. Mr. T is Nelson Trowbridge and Mr. J is Theodore Johnston.

5. Lamar referred to the Africans as packages, probably because they were sold in groups. When the *Wanderer* was about to be seized in Brunswick, Corrie made his way to Hamburg, sold his slaves for an extremely low price, and then went to Charleston or Edisto, South Carolina.

6. Lamar had agreed to pay Danese thirty dollars per African, but they disagreed over whether it was per slave landed or slave sold. See Letter no. 55. Lamar's ability to pay depended on the liquidity of the notes he had received for selling his share of the Africans.

7. Lamar's failure to sell his Africans for good prices and cash, or collect advances he made on behalf of the partners, indicates that the *Wanderer*, just like his previous slave-trade ventures, was a losing affair.

8. Brown's attorneys were Lloyd and Owens, arranged and paid for by Lamar.

9. James Clubb piloted the *Wanderer* with the Africans across Saint Andrews Sound and witnessed the unloading of the slaves. Horatio Harris was a pilot who happened to be on Little Cumberland Island when the *Wanderer* arrived on November 28 and saw the landing of the Africans the next day. Both men originally refused to testify at the commissioner's hearing on the grounds that they might incriminate themselves. They did eventually testify in great detail at the *Wanderer* trials, but they would not swear to the identity of the defendants. It is not known if Lamar paid them the five thousand dollars.

10. Danese never tried to escape from jail.

Letter no. 41

Savannah Jany 28th 1859

T. G. Lamar Esq.

Dr Tom,

I have yours of the 25th. I have never thought otherwise, than that you did *for the best*, & as you would under the circumstances, have done for yourself, but the effect has been most disastrous to me. I never for one moment intended Spires should have control of any of them, than those I left with him.[1]

I am sorry indeed you gave up yours, *if you wanted them*, and particularly *the boy I gave you.* Corrie was very wrong, & must have been drinking, or he never would have taken them. I must insist upon paying you what *you are out of pocket*, only asking a little time to do so in, that is but right. If I ever go into another speculation, I will have nothing to do with drinking men.

You can come & go as you please—no one can molest you. If the warrant is served on you, you can refuse to obey it, & go to Carolina. If you come here, you can refuse to testify upon the ground of criminating yourself. Judge McGraw [Magrath] won't give you up, for you have committed no offense against *Georgia.*[2] I am much afraid the way things are going they will convict me of having had one, if not two, in *possession.*[3] If they do hell will be to pay sure.[4]

I am truly yrs etc.

C. A. L. Lamar

NOTES

1. Spires is most likely William, a planter in Hamburg, South Carolina.

2. Charles is probably correct in this assumption, as Judge Magrath wouldn't extradite Corrie to Georgia. No one from the Hamburg-Edgefield, South Carolina, area was arrested or charged with any offense related to the *Wanderer* Africans.

3. Charles is referring to the two African boys, the one that was taken from George Wylly's office and the one Lamar gave Captain Hillary Fraser, who returned him to Lamar.

4. At this point in the saga, Charles Lamar appears worried, if not frightened, about his legal prospects. This attitude would soon change.

Letter no. 42

Savannah Feby 15th 1859
Wm H. Cuyler[1]
Foreman of the Grand Jury
U.S. District Court

I am induced to believe from the action of your Body yesterday, in finding "True Bills" against Messrs. Selvas & Mares, that Capt. Ariel of the Bark Angelita has *perjured* himself, & my reasons for thinking so are these.[2] Before the Bark arrived here, I recd. letters from my correspondents in Matanzas stating she was coming here to go into Dock, & desiring me to take an interest, and go hence to the coast of Africa for a cargo of Slaves, docking at Porto Rico *to complete her outfit*.[3] Shortly after her arrival here, the Captain called upon me with letters of introduction. I declined taking an interest when the Captain told me he was authorized to contract for the delivery of say 800, if we could agree upon terms. *I offered him one price*, & he asked more. I met him once or twice subsequently, when the matter was incidentally referred to, but nothing done of a positive nature when he commenced to act badly & the consignees of the vessel turned him out. It is due to Mess. Selvas & Mares to say, up to the first interview I had with the Captain, that they knew nothing of the objects of the voyage, and would not have known them had I been enabled to have understood *fully*, all the Captain said, for the house in Cuba had written me, that the consignees here *knew nothing*, & begged that I would impart no information to them.

The object I have in making these disclosures, is simply to bring the Captain to punishment for his rascality & *traitorous action* in the premises. The Bark never fitted out here—she has nothing aboard now, that she had not when she came in (of a suspicious character) her object being, to fit out at Porto Rico. Had Selvas & Mares permitted the Capt. to have continued his reckless career, he would never have testified against them. If any act has been committed against the laws of the U.S. the Captain is certainly the guilty party.[4]

Sworn to before me

I am Respectfully etc.,

C. A. L. Lamar

NOTES

1. William H. Cuyler was a physician, former Savannah mayor and alderman, judge of the inferior court of Chatham County, director of the Planters Bank, and a leader of the local Democratic Party. He was also a member of the grand jury that returned true bills against Corrie, Danese ["Brown"], Rajesta, and Arguirvi. For the grand jury, see *DMN*, February 14, 1859. It appears as if Lamar wrote this letter unsolicited.

2. The bark *Angelita* arrived in Savannah on October 30, 1858, and was detained by port collector John Boston on January 19, 1859. Joachim Selvas, Charles Mares, and J. G. Cassimeras were charged with fitting her out for the slave trade. On February 14, 1859, a grand jury found true bills against the defendants based on the testimony of Captain Avriel, the former master of the vessel. *DMN*, February 15, 1859; *NYTR*, January 21, 1859.

3. Slave ships embarking from an American port for Africa often avoided detection of carrying slaving supplies by taking them on board at Cuba or Puerto Rico, where obtaining port clearance from American consuls and local customs officials was easier.

4. A petit jury found the defendants—Selvas and Mares—not guilty on May 6, 1859. *NYT*, May 7, 1859. Cassimeras was not mentioned in the verdict.

Letter no. 43

Savannah April 4th 1859[1]
Mr. Raymond[2]
Editor of N.Y. Times

Sir,

My prolonged & continued absence from home, taken in connection with the fact that I received your Editorial of the 21st March, as having been written by an irresponsible party, who did not recognize that responsibility which attaches to gentlemen, is the excuse I have to offer for not having before noticed your remarks which were personal and offensive to myself.[3] I hope the above will satisfactorily account for any apparent neglect. I have been informed by friends, that I have been mistaken in my estimate of your character (& they derived their information from personal friends of yours) & that you would respond to any call made upon you.[4] The object of this is, to inquire if you have been properly represented by your friends. It is my purpose to go to Cuba next week, unless circumstances should arise to prevent, and a telegram, which will be paid for here, announcing your decision, will much oblige.

Respectfully yrs etc.

C. A. L. Lamar

NOTES

1. This is the first entry recorded in the letter-book in six weeks, although Lamar did write other letters during this time.

2. Henry Jarvis Raymond (1820–69) founded the *New York Daily Times* in 1851 and used it to voice his Whig, and then Republican, political views. Raymond was raised in Livingston County, New York, and attended the University of Vermont. He made his way to New York City and while studying to become a lawyer began writing articles for Horace Greeley's weekly paper, the *New Yorker*. He then wrote for Horace Greeley's daily *New York Tribune*. In 1843 he worked for the New York–based *Courier and Enquirer* before founding the *Times*. Raymond could not resist the lure of politics and in 1849 was elected to the New York state legislature representing the Whig Party. He won reelection and gained the appointment of speaker of the assembly. In 1854 he was elected lieutenant governor. When the Whig Party broke up in 1854, he became a Republican. See his obituary in *NYT*, June 19, 1869. While Raymond repeatedly attacked Lamar in his newspaper, he also criticized the New York authorities for clearing so many slave ships. See *NYT*, April 1 and May 7, 1859.

3. The *Times* began its coverage of the landing of the *Wanderer* Africans on December 16, 1858, when it commented on a charge leveled by another New York paper, the *Journal of Commerce*, that the voyage was made to test the constitutionality of the laws against the slave trade, recalling the exchange of letters between Lamar and Howell Cobb in May and June 1858. The *Times* called on the *Journal* to verify its statements and seemed more concerned

about Cobb's supposed knowledge of the venture. After that, the *Times* ran articles from other newspapers covering the hearings held by U.S. commissioner Charles S. Henry and the various sightings of Africans, but Charles Lamar was hardly mentioned, other than his involvement in taking Africans from Jekyll Island up the Savannah River. On March 21, 1859, the *Times* ran an editorial on Lamar titled "Chivalric Swindling," sparked by the events at the auction of the *Wanderer*. Raymond claimed that "the 'gentlemen of Georgia' seem to take a special pride in being gazetted as knaves and liars; and after stealing the honorable flag of an honorable association [the New York Yacht Club] to cover the most dastardly tricks of the piratical peddler . . . by open and riotous violations of the laws even of their own peculiar society." Charles considered this an assault on his character.

4. True to the code duello, as Charles had done with Mr. Cunningham the previous July, he asked Raymond if he wished to withdraw the offensive remarks, and if not, would he answer Charles's call for a duel.

Letter no. 44

Savannah April 9th 1859
Messrs. Horace Greeley & Co.[1]
N.Y. Tribune

Gents,

Will you favor me with the name and whereabouts of your correspondent, who writes from "Georgia" under date of the 25th March, & published in your issue of the 1st April.[2] It is customary with the Press of this section, to surrender the name of the author of any communication, when it is applied for with the assertion, that the party is to be held legally or personally responsible which I hereby declare to be my intention. I hope the same custom prevails with you.

I am Respectfully etc.

C. A. L. Lamar

NOTES

1. Horace Greeley (1811–72) was born on his father's farm in Amherst, New Hampshire. Greeley, who had been taught to read by his mother, spent his teenage years employed as an apprentice typesetter. In 1831 he moved to New York City and worked at printing jobs until 1834, when he became the editor of the *New Yorker*, a literary journal. In 1841 he founded and edited the *New York Tribune*, which he used to express his Whig ideology. In 1854 he turned to the fledgling Republican Party and editorialized against slavery and the slave trade.

2. Like the *New York Times*, the *New York Tribune* did not focus on Lamar as a main character in the *Wanderer* affair until the edition of March 14, 1859, after the auction of the yacht. It asked, "Who is he? A speculator who wished to fit her out for another voyage?" The next day the paper began answering its own questions. It reported that Lamar was the same

man who had previously asked the State Department (actually, the Treasury Department) for clearance to the coast of Africa.

On March 17 the *Tribune* reported on the auction of the *Wanderer*, including the challenge by Charles Van Horn, the winning bid by Lamar, and Lamar's knockout blow. It concluded by stating, "The whole matter was pre-constructed so that no bidder should be allowed against Lamar. . . . This Lamar is the person who took the wild Africans from the prison here last week, also the owner of the fifty [actually, thirty-six] captured in Telfair County. No doubt he will get possession of these in the same manner."

On March 21 the paper presented more information on Lamar, "thought to have prodigious business talent—for Savannah; and is believed to carry pretty much the whole of that place in his breeches pocket." If Charles had seen this edition, he probably would have approved. The article claimed that the courts had enough evidence to convict Lamar based on his own statements at the event.

On March 23 and 29 the paper ran other articles on Lamar, but it was a report from "Georgia," dated March 25, 1859, and published in the April 1 issue that forced Charles to ask Greeley for the author's real name. "Georgia," in referring to the article of March 21, stated that Lamar "does not, in a money sense, carry the whole city of Savannah in his breeches pocket . . . for he has been considered as insolvent in pocket as he is in character for some time past." The author went on to state, "It is greatly to be feared there is no truth in the oft-repeated assertion that the people of the Southern States are opposed to the reopening of the African slave-trade, else they would be more inclined to assist in bringing to punishment the vile wretches living among them, and boasting of their nefarious traffic." Charles sought redress for the insult.

Letter no. 45

Savannah April 11th 1859
Editor of the Times N.Y.

Sir,

I have yours of the 7th inst. this morning, enclosing your article in the "Times" of the 22nd.[1] Had you closed your remarks with the first paragraph the retraction would have been complete & satisfactory, but you take occasion to remark that my conduct at the sale of the Wanderer was "insolent", a breach of chivalry, "law & decency", and inconsistent with the character I am represented to bear & you go on to say that "whatever he may think of the Slave Trade in the abstract, he knows it is in flagrant violation of law. If he wishes to be engaged in it, his course as a high minded honorable gentleman is first of all, to seek a repeal of the laws which forbid it & brand it as piracy. Instead of this he entered upon it not openly, or even in frank defense of the law but in a clandestine manner, possessing himself of the flag of an honorable association for the prosecution of a criminal traffic, and resorting throughout to subterfuge & concealments utterly at variance with the character he is reported to bear."[2]

In reply to the above I have simply to say that had I waited for the repeal of the Laws, I should have waited in vain, the North having control of the legislation of the country. I deny in toto the truth of the remainder of your article. If you will refer to my letter of the 5th July / 58 to Secy. Cobb which was published in all the principal newspapers of the day & in addition, was put in pamphlet form (a copy of which I sent you in the mail) for more thorough distribution & circulation, you will find I declared that I would re-open the trade in Slaves with foreign countries & defied the Government & its cruisers. The only "subterfuge", if such it can be called, that was resorted to, was the not declaring the intention of the voyage of the Wanderer, which would have prevented her leaving port. I had proposed in my unpublished correspondence with Secy. Cobb to go with an officer of the Navy on board my vessel & get a cargo of Africans & land them publicly on the levy in New Orleans, & test the constitutionality of the laws of Congress. This he declined.

In reference to concealments etc. etc. I have to say since the Slaves were landed there have been no concealments *on my part*. I took them on board a Steam Boat from Jekyl Island & took them to a plantation 15 miles above this city on Savannah River, declared publicly they were there, sent some to Hamburg S.C. & made that public.[3]

I have retaken all that the U.S. officers arrested—have two of the boys at my house in the city—have taken them around & introduced them as young wanderers to all or most of the Federal Officers—and have traveled them from one end of the State to the other, *literally*—declaring them to be portions of the cargo of the "Slaving Yacht Wanderer".[4]

In regard to the Yacht Flag I had nothing to do with its violation—nor was it done with my knowledge or approbation, yet in as much as it was done (or so reported) & I was a party in interest, I am prepared to settle with any one of the Officers of the Club who may think me *any way* amenable.

When the Yacht was first purchased, it was not the intention to have had her bring Slaves, but simply to visit the coast, with the view of making engagements of Slaves for other vessels. About the time she sailed, I gave orders for her to bring as many Slaves as she could do comfortably, simply to show Secy. Cobb that mine were not vain, empty threats, as many were induced to believe.[5]

I have been by the temper of your Note induced to explain my [_?].

I hope you will now make a full & free withdrawal of all your charges. I am amenable for my conduct of the sale of the "Wanderer", to Mr. Van Horn & I signified my willingness at the time to respond to any call he might make—& were you acquainted with all the "*circumstances*" connected with the knocking of him down, I venture the assertion, that you would have "sympathized" with me. I await your determination & action in the matter. I am not satisfied with the article of the 22nd for the reasons assigned.

I am Respectfully etc.

C. A. L. Lamar

NOTES

1. On March 22 Henry Raymond published another article on Lamar in response to a letter he received from a person he did not name. The writer criticized the *Times*'s editorial of March 21 and asked that the remarks be withdrawn to "repair the injuries you have done [Lamar]." The author reasoned, "You may search the country in its whole length and breadth, and you cannot find one who stands higher in estimation of those who know him, as a high-minded, frank and fearless gentleman. His opinions on the Slave-trade may be wrong, but he honestly entertains them. They are the same that were generally entertained in Great Britain and America half a century ago."

2. Raymond recognized that the author of the letter deserved respect and admitted "that the epithets employed in our article . . . yesterday were not designed to have any application to Mr. Lamar's general character, or to be used towards him in any way outside of his connection with this specific transaction." Charles found this sentence acceptable, but not the comments that followed.

3. No public declaration by Lamar could be found of the transport of the Africans from Jekyll Island to Montmollin's plantation and then to Hamburg, South Carolina.

4. Lamar did retake all the captured Africans: the teenage boy who had been captured on Jekyll Island and taken to a holding cell in Savannah; the boy whom Lamar had given to Captain Hillary Fraser but was returned to him; the two men who were taken into custody after being found in the Macon train station; and thirty-six Africans who were being transported across Georgia when seized by a local marshal. A local newspaper reported that Lamar did escort one African boy—not two—around Savannah in a buggy. See *DMN*, March 28, 1859.

5. Lamar had previously mentioned the idea of sending a vessel to Africa to place orders for slaves for another vessel to pick up. See Letter no. 27. That Lamar originally planned for the *Wanderer* to place orders is questionable in light of the fact that the ship had been outfitted with huge water tanks soon after purchase and manned with an experienced captain, sail master, and crew of twelve foreigners.

Letter no. 46

Savannah April 19th 1859
Messrs. H. Greeley & Co.
New York

Gents,

I have your very unsatisfactory Note of the 12th in reply to mine of the 9th, & beg to say in reply that the article referred to was, as a whole, offensive, it being filled with falsehood and misrepresentations, and was written with the view of creating prejudice against me. I beg to return you my thanks for the proffered use of your columns, but, as it is not my habit, nor is it in accordance with my taste, to settle such matters by a newspaper controversy, I must decline it. I beg therefore to renew the request I made in mine of the 9th & hope you will see the propriety of complying with it.

I am Respectfully etc.
C. A. L. Lamar

Letter no. 48

Savannah April 20th 1859
H. J. Raymond, Esq.

Sir,

Your favor of the 16th has reached me on the eve of my departure for the Havana—a trip that I cannot now delay. Your letter of the 16th is entirely unsatisfactory. Allow me to repeat the inquiry made in my previous letter—do you hold yourself responsible for the offensive matter published in your columns? As you decline further explanation, my future course will depend & be governed entirely by your response to the above Enquiry. I shall return in 20 @ 30 days when your reply to this will receive prompt attention.

Very Respectfully etc.
C. A. L. Lamar

Letter no. 49

Savannah May 7th 1859
H. J. Raymond Esq.

Sir,

I recd yours of the 4th this morning. You have taken the usual refuge of a coward, who, afraid to fight, undervalues his adversary. Common as is this course in your meridian, *the boast of your friends induced me to believe* that you would hold yourself responsible to those whom you had offended.[1] But for this and the previous impression I had formed of your character, I would have had no correspondence with you. When we meet I have determined upon my course.[2]

Respectfully etc.

C. A. L. Lamar

NOTES

1. Charles Lamar never revealed the names of Raymond's friends.
2. Lamar explains his course in Letter no. 51.

Letter no. 50

Savannah May 12th 1859
Messrs. Boykin & McRae[1]
Mobile, Ala.

Gents,

I have yours of the 5th inst. I left for Havana but returned to repair damages done to sails etc. etc. I shall go again in a few days. The Str. [steamer] Ship project was one of some magnitude, but it was & is, an easy matter to put it on foot successfully. I can raise the necessary means in Geo & Ala in 60 days, if I would assume the task of soliciting subscribers etc. I think I have had letters enough soliciting the privilege of taking stock, which at 1000$ only pr letter, would put afloat two Str. Ships. I would be pleased to hear from you as to the exact amount of stock you & your friends would take. All of it however to be represented *by you*—the other subscribers to know nothing—not to have a word to say.

I would have taken 10,000$ myself in the Wanderer's Expedition which

I proposed, but she must go to Havana where I am assured I can get 30,000$ for her. In case I sell her, I would be willing to take 10,000$ each in 3 other suitable vessels, but she is the vessel of all others in the world, but I am unable at this time to fit her out & put funds aside for her cargo & I am unwilling to have any interested who cannot be of some service upon the return of the vessel and who are not willing to stand up and defend his property.

Upon my return from Havana I will be better prepared to say what I will do in the premises. If I cannot get at least 30,000 cash for the Wanderer I shall return with her & then start her on. If you want an interest for yourself & friends just say how much.[2]

I am Respectfully etc.

C. A. L. Lamar

NOTES

1. Colin J. McRae and James Boykin were partners in a cotton factoring firm in Mobile, Alabama. In early January 1859 the Washington correspondent of the *Philadelphia Gazette* wrote, "To the credit of the South, it may be said that there is but one member from that section who openly avows himself in favor of the reopening of the slave-trade. Mr. McRae of Mississippi occupies that 'bad eminence.'" See reprint in *NYTR*, January 17, 1859. It is hard to believe that the correspondent hadn't heard of Charles Lamar, Leonidas Spratt, or William Gaulden, to name but a few other vocal advocates for reopening the trade.

2. Lamar did not sell the *Wanderer* in Havana and returned to Savannah with the ship.

Letter no. 51

Savannah May 19th 1859
B. R. Alden Esq.[1]
No. 5 West 14th Street

My dear Sir,

I am in rect of yours of the 16th this morning. Permit me to thank you for the kind feelings which prompted it, as well as for the actual part you took in bringing about such explanations & retractions as appeared in the "Times" of the 22nd March. I have had a long correspondence with Mr. Raymond, which has just been closed, in which he refuses to meet me upon my terms. I had made up my mind not to notice any attack coming from any Paper whose head was not a recognized Gentleman, and judging from the scurrilous article in the "Times" of the 21st March, that its Editor was not a Gentleman, I determined to let him pass—but some of his friends sojourning here remarked at the Table of the Public House in presence of friends of mine that Mr. Raymond was Ex Lt Gov. of the State of NY, a Gentleman of chivalry, & one who recognized personal responsibility for offensive articles that appeared in the columns of his Paper & that "if Mr. Lamar wanted a fight he could be accommodated upon application to him."

I wrote him immediately, apologizing for any apparent neglect & asking him the direct question if he would respond to my call made upon him. He evaded a reply to that question, but wrote, enclosing the article of the 22nd which he said was or ought to be satisfactory to any Gentleman & expressing the hope that it would so prove in my case. He said it was unnecessary he thought to answer the question relating to personal responsibility etc.

I wrote him a very civil reply, giving him some particulars in reference to my connection with the Wanderer, stated his Explanations & Retractions were not satisfactory & hope with the light before him he would do the needful. He declined. I then renewed my first inquiry. He still evaded the question, but replied that no matter how he would be inclined to act under ordinary circumstances, he would not consent to meet me upon terms of equality as I had avowed my connection with a traffic which the laws of this country denounced as Piracy & the civilized nations of the world looked upon as odious.

I replied to that by denouncing him as a coward & closed by saying when I met him, my mind was made up as to how I should act. I shall simply put an indignity upon him in a public moment such for instance as slapping his face and if he don't resent it, why I shall take no further notice of him. I hope your letter proposed to be written the 21st day will reach me tomorrow as I go to Havana with the Wanderer at 10 tomorrow.

I am dear Sir

Very truly yours etc.

C. A. L. Lamar

NOTES

1. This correspondence reveals that Bradford R. Alden was the man who wrote the letter to the *New York Times* defending Lamar from the paper's March 21 editorial. Alden was born in 1811, the son of Revolutionary War hero Major Roger Alden. He entered West Point in 1827 and graduated in 1831 as a second lieutenant. He served as an aide-de-camp to General Winfield Scott from September 1840 to January 1842 and as an instructor at West Point, where he ultimately became commandant of cadets. In 1853, while commanding a fort in northern California, Alden suffered a severe wound in a battle in Oregon against a

tribe of Native Americans and soon resigned from the military. He then got involved in oil drilling in western Pennsylvania. George W. Cullum, *Biographical Register of the Officers and Graduates of the U.S. Military Academy at West Point, New York*, vol. 1, 1802–1840 (New York: D. Van Nostrand, 1868), 393–94. It is not known how Lamar made the acquaintance of Alden, but it was probably through Charles's father Gazaway, who lived in New York between 1846 and 1861 and held a high-profile position as a bank president.

Letter no. 52

Private & Confidential
Savannah June 20th 1859
C. C. Cook Esq.[1]
Blakely, Ga.

Dr Sir,

I have yours of the 9th only this morning. I returned home only on Friday night & have been sick abed ever since. Your letter though ought to have reached me before I left for Milledgeville, which was only last Wednesday. In writing me in future write "private" across the seal. I have for a long time suspected that my letters have been opened by the Post Office Department.

In reply to your direct inquiry—I have the Wanderer now almost ready for a cruise & will put her into a company at a less figure than she cost the old one, viz at 25,000$. She requires no fitting out, having all her ballast room filled with iron water tanks, which are under the main floor. No suspicion can attach to her until she takes on board a cargo, & then unless there be a [_?], nothing that goes by sail or steam can catch her. All she wants is a new main sail & provisions for the voyage. I have the Am. Capt. & mate now on board & have my eye on a Spanish Capt.[2]

Everything can be ready by the 4th to 5th July to sail now upon one condition alone—can you & your friends come in & that is this: if they will subscribe the money, say 25,000 @ 30,000$ & put it in your hands in cash to you & you alone for its investment & they to know nothing of the plans until they are summoned to look after their property. You & I alone are to arrange matters—if you don't consent to my [_?] no harm can be done, you can take your money & return with it. I want to be responsible to no one, but to myself & my personal friends. If every subscriber were to know the full bill of particulars, I would much sooner put it in the newspapers at once.

You are aware that it is a risky business. I lost two out of 3.[3] To be sure at

first I knew not of the business. I have learned something since & I hope
I can put my information to some a/c. I have been in for "grandeur" &
been fighting for a principle, *now* I am in for the dollars.[4] If you want
stock upon the terms proposed let me hear or see you at once. She will
go the 1st July sometime with or without the cooperation of friends. I am
waiting for a main sail & a Spanish Capt—that is all. What you intend
doing must be done at once.

    I am Truly yrs etc.

      C. A. L. Lamar

        I have no fear as to the result of the trials here in my case.

NOTES

1. C. C. Cook is William C. Cook, a lawyer from Blakely, Early County, Georgia. Gazaway Lamar owned property in Early County, which might explain the connection between
Charles and Cook.

2. Many slave ships carried two sets of ownership papers (one illegitimate) and two
captains, one American and one Spanish. If a squadron cruiser from any country other
than the United States approached the slaver, the crew ran up the Stars and Stripes and
the U.S. captain took command, as the United States gave no right of search to any nation.
However, if a U.S. squadron cruiser approached, the slaver would fly the Spanish flag and
the Spanish captain would take the helm, knowing that the American naval captain would
let a foreign ship pass.

3. Charles is claiming that he lost money only on the two *Rawlins* ventures, but he admits
several times in subsequent letters that the *Wanderer* expedition was unprofitable as well.

4. On Charles Lamar's motivation for entering the slave trade, see the commentary in
chapter 20.

Letter no. 53

Savannah June 20th 1859
R. L. Gamble Esq.[1]

Dr Sir,

    Yours of the 14th was laid before me this morning. The objects we had
in view was the proposition of a cargo of Africans. The Bark E. A. Rawlins
went twice to the coast but owing to the dishonesty of her officers she
brought none, but the last time came back very much damaged & requiring much repairs. Had I supplied it would have cost ¼ of what it did. I
should have sold her in her crippled condition. I consulted with those of
the stockholders who were here & they agreed with me, viz to have her
repaired, send her to Havana & sell her—which was done. Her a/c was

never made up until after the sale for I had no idea myself of the amt I had advanced. I was so much lugaged [*sic*] with matters connected with the Wanderer & her cargo, & was so much away from home during the whole season, that the matter escaped my attention.

There were no new stockholders & consequently no others than the originals could have shared any of the profits had there been any. What I did was done by the concurrence of the majority of the stockholders. You were in the N. West & could not be consulted. D. Williamson is the only one who declines or rather takes the view you do.[2] The Parties in interest were myself, N. C. Trowbridge, Theo. Johnston, W. W. Cheever,[3] Dr. Williamson, Jno. S. Montmollin, & yourself.[4]

However, it matters not—I was not as prompt in making out my a/cs as I should have been & though I can show vouchers for everything I shall claim nothing. You can examine the a/c and if you are *not perfectly satisfied* that the balance against you is *justly* due, I would not have a cent of it. I have put it to each & every one the same way, that I have seen—just put it in the way to yourself—had the Rawlins brought in a cargo would I or would I not have been interested. Your decision which I know will be in accordance with your honesty, connections, will satisfy me. The subject will never be alluded to again [_?].

Very Respectfully,

C. A. L. Lamar

NOTES

1. Roger Lawson Gamble II, born in 1829, practiced law in Louisville, Jefferson County, Georgia. He was the son of Roger Lawson Gamble Sr., who was elected to the state legislature and U.S. House of Representatives for Jefferson County, and served as the judge of the Middle Circuit of Georgia. The younger Gamble was the captain of the Jefferson County Guards, though he did not follow his father into politics. In 1848 Charles sailed to New York on the same ship as R. L. Gamble and likely made his acquaintance during the five-day trip. For Gamble's background, see Marion Little Durden, *A History of St. George Parish, Colony of Georgia, Jefferson County, State of Georgia* (Swainsboro, Ga.: Magnolia, 1983), 39, 71, 206. For the trip to New York, see *CC*, August 7, 1848.

2. Dr. Eldridge C. Williamson II, originally of Jefferson County, settled in Bibb County, participated in state politics, and supported secession. For politics, see *AC*, July 20, 1849. For support of secession, see *Macon Telegraph*, December 11, 1860.

3. W. W. Cheever had been Gazaway Lamar's agent in Albany, Georgia, for several years and continued to act in that capacity until his death in 1863. He also partnered with Gazaway and Charles in cotton purchases during the Civil War. See G. B. Lamar to W. W. Cheever, January 25, 1855, G. B. Lamar letter book, GHS.

4. Trowbridge, Johnston, and Montmollin, all partners in the *Wanderer*, complete the seven-man partnership. Their individual shares are not known, although Lamar admitted to losing $80,000 on the two expeditions.

Letter no. 54

Savannah July 13th 1859[1]
Jas. H. Brigham Esq.[2]
Bastrop, Morehouse Parish La:

Dr Sir,

I have an expedition all ready to sail—only awaiting a suitable Captain who has experience on the coast. I have the Am. Captain & mate *now* on board, & the vessel all ready to sail tomorrow, if her provisions & Captain were on board.[3] I have written to Havana for a Captain & expect to hear or see him by 1st August. If you want for self & friends 15000$ stock, you can have it, by replying at once. If you will come here, I will lay the whole thing before you. The Parties subscribing must agree to lose their interest if they, *after due notice be given them,* fail to be on the ground to take their property.

I have lost money by the last voyage simply by my co-partners failing to come up & get, & [_?] the negroes falling into the official's hands, which cost money to get them out, but worse than all, in falling into the hands of damned rascals, who will give but a meager account of them. I think I have everything fixed so that no capture can take place until the cargo is on board and [_?] if the wind blows—nothing that goes to sea can catch her. The items foot up as below.

The vessel	25,000.00
Outfit	5,000.00
Advance to officers and crew for the trip	5,000.00
Money on board for purchase of cargo	15,000.00[4]
	$50,000.00

The above approximates to the figures. They may be less or they may be more, but won't vary but a few thousand dollars either way. I would much prefer to land them in the Gulf, but am not particular where. If you want the interest come or write. Move quickly—for she will sail early next month anyhow.

I am Respectfully etc.

C. A. L. Lamar

NOTES

1. This is Lamar's first letter-book entry in more than three weeks. His efforts to raise funds for another slaving venture did not appear to be successful.

2. James Brigham was the man named to receive the contract to import 2,500 African apprentices by the Louisiana House of Representatives in March 1858. See *NYTR*, March 26, 1858.

3. The ship must be the *Wanderer*.

4. At a cost of fifty dollars per African, Lamar is planning on bringing back three hundred. As with the other expeditions, his cost estimates are incomplete and appear low.

Letter no. 55

Savannah July 20th 1859
W. C. Cook Esq.

Dr Sir,

I have yours of the 14th this morning enclosing check for Five Hundred Dollars for which I herewith enclose you a receipt. The amts you refer to have never been received. The two thousand Dollar draft I have heard nothing of.[1]

It is irresponsible for me to say when the W[anderer] will sail. I have had nothing from my correspondence in Havana in reference to a Captain & the mail facilities are so few & irregular now with the Island, I can make no calculations. I have had numberless applications from men who come well recommended to take command but as much depends upon the man I want to know something of his antecedents before putting him in charge. Everything is ready save the supplies & the Capt.

We need be in no hurry, for this is not *the time* for leaving. She sailed last year 5th July & went to Trinidad & had to throw away six weeks of her time, to avoid the rainy season there. If I don't hear from Havana soon I shall write to N.Y. for a Capt.

    I am Truly yrs etc.

    C. A. L. Lamar

The man who went in her before would like to go again but he made an extraordinary claim the last time, and it of course was not settled in full and he might take some advantage and throw us, to pay off any feeling he might have against the old Company. For instance he claimed he was to have received $30 a head for every one who had life in him, that was landed, independent of his condition, even though he might die before he could be housed. Such was not the contract.[2] If you think he will do again we can try him—what say you? He is anxious to go and he is a smart fellow—but he might, though I hardly think he would sacrifice us for he and I have never had any misunderstanding—always got along well.

NOTES

1. Of all the men from whom Charles Lamar solicited funds for a slaving expedition, it appears as if Cook was the only one who invested. According to this letter, Cook claimed to have sent Lamar $2,500, which represented only a small portion of the total amount needed.

2. Charles is referring to Nicholas Danese, who at that time was sitting in the Savannah jail. As 409 Africans were landed on Jekyll beach, Danese's claim totaled $12,270. At least nine Africans died on Jekyll Island after the landing, and an unspecified number perished at Montmollin's plantation in South Carolina.

Letter no. 56

Savannah July 20th 1859

Dr Sir [Nicholas Danese[1]],

I have not been to see you for some time & for several reasons. The 1st is, I was advised as it was your intention to leave, not to be seen with you for some time before you left or I would be suspected of getting you out.[2] The next is, I heard you thought I had not treated you well etc. etc. when I was the only one of the Eight who were interested in the Enterprise who did anything for you & all that you have recd has been through my personal Exertions.[3]

I have not yet recd back the money I invested & paid out since the return of the vessel—but all I have heard may have been as great *lies* as were told you of me & which Capt Lambert[4] informed me of, & which I satisfied him were *lies*—so I have concluded to make good my word to you, given last winter, viz to give you a showing in the next Expedition. The vessel is all ready for sea, only wants a new main sail & *her provisions*, to sail next week for *China*, & I have a first rate captain aboard. If you would like to go to *China* in her in the same capacity as you went there the last time, say so, & we will put it into writing.[5]

No one of the old party is interested, and everything that is agreed upon will be fulfilled. I can give you in detail all the arrangements, if you *want to go*. If you do not, it is all right. There is a Party in Cuba who has just made the voyage and who is anxious to go. I shall have to send to N.Y. for a new main sail & jib—all of the above is confidential—Destroy this.

I am etc.

C. A. L. Lamar

Let me hear from you at your earliest convenience. If you think it prudent I can come out to see you, if we can talk the matter over without interruption—or maybe it would be better to wait until after your release.

NOTES

1. This letter was addressed to "Dr Sir." Someone, probably the author of the article in the *North American Review*, wrote on the top of the page, "Nicholas Denese." The proper spelling is "Danese."

2. In his letter to Nicholas Danese of January 18, 1859, Lamar recommended escaping from jail as an option. It seems as if Danese was considering it. John Boston, the port collector, also heard the rumors and posted a revenue cutter in the Savannah River to prevent the *Wanderer* from carrying away Danese.

3. Charles again admits that there were eight partners in the *Wanderer* venture, but he doesn't name them. They are likely himself, William Corrie, Nelson Trowbridge, Theodore Johnston, John Tucker, Richard Akin, John Montmollin, and William Brailsford, as they are mentioned by Lamar as having received Africans.

4. The identity of Captain Lambert could not be determined.

5. Lamar states that China is the destination for the *Wanderer*. He repeats this in the next letter to Trowbridge, although he told W. C. Cook in the previous letter that the ship was going to Africa. Charles never revealed his real intention—he may not have known. The *Wanderer* would go to neither place.

Letter no. 57

Savannah July 21st 1859

Dr Trow,

I have yours of the 15th. You did right in saying to Farnum I would pay him nothing more, I owe him nothing, & if I did, the course he has thought proper to pursue in reference to his claim, would decide me not to pay him. He has been threatening for some time to publish his journal, giving in detail all the incidents of the voyage, & I wish he would do so, if he does, purchase and send me a copy, for I have no doubt it would while away a weary hour. I would like to see it anyway. Why did he not come out & get his proportion of the negroes, as he said he would do *& as I wrote him to do?*[1]

I saw [Danese] this morning [_?] here every day. He says nothing can be done before the month of October—it won't do to *leave here before that time.* The Wanderer is going to China, & may return with coolies. They are worth from 340 @ 350$ each in Cuba & cost but 12$ & their passage.[2]

I told you, Tucker returned one of the boys sold in Columbus—sent him to Akin's for *my* a/c!!! He is in Joe Bryan's, & has had a number of fits—has the itch, and Joe wants him removed.[3] I don't know what to do with him—no one will take him. He is a dead Expense to me. I never see Akin—he never comes to town. When I was at his place last, the negroes were improving.[4]

How fast can your ponies go? Are they handsome? What do you ask for them? I do not want them to keep—I am too poor for that now but if I can make anything off them, I would be willing to take them. I go to Warm Springs 1st of August.[5]

If you order the sails for the Wanderer, viz main sail, big foresail & jib, let the big foresail be made *larger* than the old one was. I should think you could run up to Port Jefferson & see the sail maker there, who made the sails & order them. I'll pay the cash for them, but they must be guaranteed to fit.

Nothing new—the weather has been very warm for nearly a week, but yesterday & today, it is delightful.

I am Truly yrs

C. A. L. Lamar

How fast is your horse? Has the man, Capt Harden, ever been to the coast & made a voyage with negroes.[6] If he has you might write him to call by here on his way North & see me, *leaving me free to accept him or not.*

NOTES

1. Farnum was to be paid in Africans, but he left Charleston on December 11 and didn't collect his share, much less sell them. Lamar doesn't reveal who sold them, or who received the proceeds. If Farnum did keep a journal, it has never been found or published.

2. Again, Lamar states the yacht is going to China, as opposed to Africa.

3. Joseph Bryan was a slave broker in Savannah and likely had a holding cell for slaves. The "itch" might have been epilepsy, as Charles said that he had the fits.

4. In March 1858 Richard Akin was transporting thirty-six of the *Wanderer* Africans westward across Georgia when a deputy marshal seized and detained them, first in the jail in Jacksonville, Georgia, then at the farm of Mr. Woodson Wilcox. All the Africans were eventually released to Akin, except two, who been incapacitated during the journey and were in no condition to continue. Mr. Wilcox agreed to look after them while Akin completed his trip. These are probably the two "Negroes" to whom Lamar is referring. See *DMN,* April 12, 1859.

5. Lamar and his family frequently vacationed in Warm Springs, near Columbus, for the soothing mineral springs. The town would become the Little White House for President Franklin D. Roosevelt.

6. Captain Harden could be Captain Hayden, who is mentioned in Letter no. 62 as captain of the *Rawlins* in another fiasco involving that ship.

Letter no. 58

Savannah July 21st 1859
Wm. C. Cook Esq.

Dr Sir,

I wrote you yesterday & I write now to say that the *Captain* says it is useless to leave here before the 1st Oct. or the middle of September at *the earliest*—that the rainy season will set in 1st August & continue till Oct., & unless we *happen to catch a lot of negroes in the baracoons* on the coast, it will be very risky to try to bring them to the coast for shipment, as a great many will necessarily be lost.[1] *Now* this is very unexpected, so much so, that I feel it is but due, that you should have the money subscribed, refunded, if you desire. It was deposited *specially* & a certificate of deposit taken for it, so if you do not feel disposed to await the time, say so, & I will send it to you. If however you are disposed to let it go, it can remain as originally agreed upon. I regret this as much as any one can, as I want the Negroes *now*, but all my best informed men, my old Capt. too, says 1st Oct. is plenty of time to go & the best time too. If you still want it invested, you can send the balance along as you get it & the fitting out can continue at leisure.[2]

I am truly yrs etc.
C. A. L. Lamar

NOTES

1. Lamar continued to tell Cook that the next expedition would be to Africa, despite informing Danese and Trowbridge it would go to China.
2. It could not be determined if Cook sent more funds to Lamar.

Letter no. 59

Savannah July 30th 1859
B. R. Alden Esq.

My dear Sir,

I am in receipt of both your favors of the 25th & 27th. I regret that my letter of May did not reach you in time to enable you to settle matters with Raymond. I have never yet seen his article commenting upon my difficulty with Dubignon,[1] & would be obliged for a copy of the Paper containing it, if you have one or can without much trouble, procure one.

It matters not to me, what your views & sentiments are in reference to the African Slave Trade—though I would like you to be right. We shall never quarrel on that subject. Many of my best friends differ with me, & among them, my Father. I know that I am right, & that the sentiment of the people of the South is fast making that way—even the Politicians, & those too who have been in that corrupting atmosphere of Washington City are coming to us. I have sacrificed for time, a large & profitable business & still larger Expectations, & meet the opposition of friends, and the denunciations of Enemies & of the Entire Press of the North, & I am determined not now to give it up. I am going to make what I have lost out of it, benefit my state & section, and let the U.S. do their best to put the consequences upon me.

In treating with Raymond demand nothing but what is *right* and then yield nothing. I am opposed to compromises. He shall make the amends, or he shall fight me. I will put it upon him in such a way that to get out of it, without a fight, will bring upon him the contempt of even his friends. He will have to fight me or my friends and their friends. He will frankly object to [_?] upon grounds of "inequality", for he stands at least as high as does himself Socially or Politically & is too opposed to the reopening (or was) of the Slave Trade. However, the matter is now in your hands, and there I am willing to leave it, until you abandon all hopes of a settlement, when of course it reverts again into mine.[2]

I am Truly yrs etc.

C. A. L. Lamar

NOTES

1. The *New York Times* article on the Dubignon incident, assuming it appeared in print, could not be found.

2. Charles didn't hesitate to ask others to act as middlemen in his disputes. He asked the same of his cousin and member of the House of Representatives, L. Q. C. Lamar, in his disagreement with Henry Raymond. See Letter no. 67.

Letter no. 60

Savannah Oct 6th 1859
L Viana Esq.

Dr Sir,

I am anxious to make up some of my heavy losses in the trade, & write to know if you can furnish me say in 90 days with a cargo of 300 delivered free on board & the vessel safely at sea.[1] I would like much if you would recommend to me a suitable man to put in command, as a man of your selection could co-operate much better with your people on the coast. I want your No. 1 man who is thoroughly acquainted on the coast—none other. I have a Captain who is a thorough navigator, who has never been on such a cruise before, who would like to go 2nd in command.[2] An early answer will much oblige.

Truly yrs etc.

C. A. L. Lamar

P.S. The money will be paid you in cash before the starting of the vessel on this side. Of course, you giving the usual obligations to comply with yr agreement.

NOTES

1. Reeling from losses in the slave trade—compounded by bad investments in legitimate businesses—Lamar reached out to Luis Viana to partner in an expedition to Africa. Nothing resulted from this proposal.

2. The man might have been William Black, a Savannah resident who once captained the *Richard Cobden* for the Lamars. In January 1857 the Philadelphia Underwriters Association gave Black a gold watch for his efforts bringing the *Cobden* safely into a port despite her being in a seriously disabled condition. See *DMN*, January 8, 1857. However, Gazaway thought Black did not control expenses on freight runs and relieved him of his duties. See G. B. Lamar to C. A. L. Lamar, October 16 and December 3, 1858, G. B. Lamar Estate letter book. Soon after these letters were written, Black became involved in the theft of the *Wanderer*. See Letter no. 65.

Letter no. 61

Savannah Oct. 6th 1859
W. C. Cook Esq.
Blakely Geo.

Dr Sir,

I have been home for a week & am at a loss to know how to act for the want of a proper man, *one who is acquainted on the coast* to take command. Placed as I am, I would like much to see you & confer upon the point, for though I have told you time & again I would assume no responsibility beyond others, yet it wld [would] be best I think that you should assist in the formation of our plans. The vessel's duplicate set of sails *are here* & every thing in readiness. She is closely watched by the Revenue Cutter. Boston[1] has recd information from your neighborhood of her intended cruise, but I care not for that. I can send her to sea at any moment.

I have this morning written to N.Y. to a House[2] to know if they can give me in 90 Days on the Coast 300 & guarantee me with them to sea. If so the money would be paid them in cash *here*, before the sailing of the vessel. I can get 1000 men to go in Command but to get one that *I know* is reliable is the thing. I do not want this to fail under any circumstances.

I would like much to confer with you. I have seen the other parties & *they want to leave it to me,* but I am determined to make them assume their portion of the responsibility—it is too much for me to take.[3] There has been much delay, but it has all been for the best. Vessels that went out, at that time, have been compelled *to wait* on the coast or at sea. I think now we could lose nothing by waiting a month or two longer, but of that I want your views.

None of the money has been touched save 375$ to pay for the new suit of sales [*sic*] & remains as *a special deposit* in the Bank still.[4] When can you come down. I shall be compelled to be at Worth Court on 17th I think.[5]

　I am Truly yrs
　　C. A. L. Lamar

1. John Boston, the port collector for Savannah.
2. Charles is referring to his letter of the same date to Luis Viana.

3. If Lamar had other investors for this expedition, he didn't write to them as he did to Cook.

4. Lamar never revealed the amount of Cook's investment.

5. Lamar is referring to his court date for the trial of the Telfair County posse.

Letter no. 62

Savannah Oct 10th 1859
Messrs. Hamel & Co.[1]
Havana

Dr Sirs,

I am in rect of yours of the 29th September. I wrote you full particulars as reported to me by Capt. Markham, of the sale of the Bark E. A. Rawlins.[2] I presume you have that letter on this. The collector of the Port[3] was the purchaser, though a Dr. Spencer was the one she was knocked off to.[4] I have written Mr. Mallory[5] who is asking for Mr. Davis,[6] that I had information that no money has yet been paid for her & that if it be possible, I wanted him to contest the sale. If she comes to Havana have her arrested, even though you may not be enabled to hold her & I think they may be induced to give her up. I have sent them word such a course would be pursued in every Port she may enter. They are much alarmed & I think ready to treat for terms. I did all I could for your interest & could I have reached Apalachicola might have been of assistance.[7] I rode 42 miles in the heaviest rain you ever saw to reach Columbus, & when I got there, found there was no conveyance by land or water & even the wires were down, doubtless cut for the occasion. Mr. Marsden[8] can tell you what Capt. [_?] undertook in going down the River upwards of 300 miles in an open two oared boat.

I am anxious to get a suitable man for the Wanderer. A Capt. D. S. Martin is here, wanting to become interested & go in command.[9] He refers me to the House of [_?], Rosell & Co. of Havana[10]—says he was mate & subsequently in command of [the Haidee and] made a successful landing of a cargo in the Niagara.[11] Will you do me the kindness to make the necessary inquiries concerning his capabilities, character etc. etc. Your attention will much oblige me. I would like to hear by return mail. If I can be of any service to you in any way, command me.

I think the sale of the Bark ought to be contested, she was sold before she was condemned & at a time too, when very few persons were in Apalachicola & of a time too that the usual facilities of getting to the place [_?] cut off.

I am Truly yrs etc.

C. A. L. Lamar

NOTES

1. Hamel and Company was Lamar's shipping agent in Havana and handled the *Wanderer* when it arrived in March 1860. See G. B. Lamar to Charles Lamar, May 5, 1860, G. B. Lamar Estate letter book.

2. The *E. A. Rawlins* became involved in another mysterious voyage in early 1859. In mid-December 1858 the ship left Savannah for Havana with a cargo of rice, under the command of Captain Horace H. Hayden and a supercargo named Delamayer. After leaving Cuba, the ship was spotted in early March in Saint Joseph Bay, near Apalachicola, Florida, by the U.S. surveying steamer *Vixen*. Captain J. K. Durr boarded the *Rawlins*, found its papers to be irregular, and on seeing a large number of casks of water, he determined that it was a slaver and towed it to Apalachicola harbor. Authorities interviewed the crew and learned of another crime. The ship had been sold in Cuba, supposedly by agents of Charles Lamar. The new owner put a Spanish captain in command. After the ship left Cuba, the new captain told Captain Hayden and his crew that they were going to Africa for slaves. Hayden and the crew refused. A fight broke out, the Spanish captain was killed, and his body was thrown overboard. Hayden had the name *Rosa Lee* painted over *Rawlins* and sailed to Saint Joseph Bay. Hayden and supercargo Delamayer took a rowboat to Apalachicola; after staying several nights, they headed to Pensacola. By that time the news of the *Rawlins* had reached the town, and the authorities arrested Hayden and Delamayer. However, they soon escaped. The rest of the crew remained as prisoners on board the ship. The *Rawlins*'s three officers were charged with murder and manslaughter. The second officer was tried first, convicted of manslaughter, and sentenced to three years in prison and charged a thousand-dollar fine. In separate trials, the first and third officers were acquitted. See *NYT*, June 11 and 13, 1859. For a variation of this story, see *AC*, April 8, 1859. The ship was condemned as a slaver and auctioned on August 27 for $5,250 to Dr. S. W. Spencer. See *Columbus Daily Enquirer*, September 6, 1859. According to this article, "C. A. L. Lamar's agent was on hand, having made a somewhat hasty trip down from Columbus in a yawl boat." No reference could be found for Captain Markham.

3. The Port of Apalachicola, where the *Rawlins* was towed and auctioned.

4. "Knocked off" refers to the winning bid at an auction.

5. Lamar is referring to Stephen Russell Mallory, U.S. senator from Florida at the time. Charles's connection to Mallory is unknown, but Gazaway corresponded with Mallory, who became Confederate secretary of the navy during the Civil War.

6. The identity of Mr. Davis could not be determined.

7. This suggests that Hamel and Company had an interest in or perhaps even owned the *Rawlins* and that Lamar attempted to attend the auction on the firm's behalf but was thwarted by the weather.

8. This is likely George Marsden, whose steamboat *Massachusetts* was seized in January 1855 on the grounds that it was about to participate in the 1855 filibuster expedition against Cuba—the same one in which Charles Lamar was involved. See *WDNI*, January 27, 1855; *NYEP*, March 9, 1855. Also, a Geo. Marsden traveled with C. Lamar from Havana to New Orleans in June 1860. See *NOD*, June 5, 1860.

9. David S. Martin came to Savannah in early October and asked Lamar if he could cap-

tain the next *Wanderer* voyage and purchase a 75 percent share in the yacht for $20,000. It is not known if Charles received a reply from Hamel.

10. No information could be found on Rosell and Company of Havana.

11. The slave ship *Haidee* was rumored to have landed nine hundred slaves at Cárdenas, Cuba, in mid-1858 before being scuttled off Long Island. See *NYT*, October 5, 1858. No record could be found of a slave ship named *Niagara*.

Letter no. 63

Savannah Oct. 10th 1859
Addison Cammack Esq.[1]

My Dr Sir,

Will you be kind enough to make inquiries for me of the character & standing of a Captain D. S. Martin. He refers me to Wm Jerough, 32 Custom House Street, N.O.[2] He wants the command of one of my vessels— says he has just landed a cargo from the Schr [schooner] Niagara in Cuba—that he was 1st mate aboard the Ship Haidee, that landed a cargo in Cuba, & was scuttled off N.J. about one year ago.[3] Make all the inquiries you think necessary.

I have been very badly swindled by getting into the hands of rascals & vagabonds. I am out of pocket on the Wanderer—had to assume all the responsibility, pay all the money & do all the work.[4]

Trow is in N.Y. I can't say when he will be out.

Our cotton market dull at 10 ¾ for Mids [middling cotton]: Frts [freight], [_?] at ⅜th to L'pool—some asking ¹⁄₃₂ more.

I am Truly yrs etc.,
C. A. L. Lamar

NOTES

1. Addison Cammack headed the shipping company Cammack and Converse in New Orleans. He gained fame as a blockade runner during the Civil War and as a Wall Street trader afterward. See *NYT*, February 6, 1901. From the wording of this letter, he knew of Charles's slave-trading activities. There is no record that Lamar received a reference on Martin from Cammack. In 1863 Nelson Trowbridge wrote to Lamar in London from Glen Cove, New York, and mentioned that Cammack was with him, indicating that the three men had a close relationship. See Trowbridge to Lamar, August 20, 1863, in "The Lamar Correspondence," *NYT*, January 16, 1864.

2. No information on William Jerough of New Orleans could be found.

3. As mentioned in the previous letter, the slave ship *Haidee* was rumored to have dropped off nine hundred slaves at Cárdenas, Cuba, in mid-1858 before being scuttled off

Long Island—not New Jersey. In an article about the *Haidee,* the first mate's name is given as Macomber, which was most likely fictitious. See *NYT,* October 5, 1858.

4. Lamar's admission of losing money on the *Wanderer* voyage yet again confirms that all three of his slaving ventures were unprofitable.

Letter no. 64

Savannah Oct 11th 1859
Francis S. Bartow Esq.[1]

Dr Sir,

I address you as the agent of Jno. S. Montmollin's Estate to claim from said Estate, the value of 27 Negroes which were left with him on his plantation in the month of December last, & which are unaccounted for, & which I have evidence of, were shipped by him to Florida & there disposed of.

His sudden & unexpected death, occurring just at the time I was arranging a settlement with him, has caused all matters appertaining to the Negroes, to be much mystified & confused. Mr. Jno. F. Tucker who attended to the business of that department after the death of Mr. Montmollin, says he knows nothing of the balance of the Negroes—the difference between the number left on the Plantation & the number accounted for.

I have letters from Florida going to prove, that 27 were sent there & disposed of—how many more may have gone the same and other ways I can't assume. I only claim what I can show he disposed of & never accounted for.[2]

Mrs. Montmollin who is well acquainted with all the details of Mr. M's business, doubtless knows of the shipment to Florida, & when she is made acquainted with the facts that they have not been settled for—as can be shown by the a/c current rendered by Jno. F. Tucker, I think she would recommend a prompt payment, for had her husband lived, I am satisfied he would have adjusted everything to the satisfaction of all interested.[3]

I am very Truly yrs etc.

C. A. L. Lamar

NOTES

1. Francis Stebbins Bartow (1816–61) was one of Savannah's most revered war heroes. He was born in Savannah and attended the University of Georgia and Yale Law School but never received a degree. Bartow returned to Savannah to practice law and soon became

involved in politics. He served in both houses of the state legislature and became a member of the American Party along with Charles Lamar during the mid-1850s. Bartow also held the rank of captain of the Oglethorpe Light Infantry militia unit. He was an ardent secessionist and campaigned for Georgia to leave the Union after Lincoln's election in November 1860. See Kenneth Coleman and Charles Stephen Gurr, eds., *Dictionary of Georgia Biography*, 2 vols. (Athens: University of Georgia Press, 1983), 1:64–65. Bartow handled the estate of John Montmollin after he was killed in July 1859 when a boiler on the ship on which he was riding exploded. For more information on Bartow's military career and death, see Letter no. 70.

2. A review of the shipping records for the Port of Savannah for the months of December 1858 and January 1859 revealed no shipment of slaves to Florida.

3. There is no record that Lamar collected from Montmollin's estate.

Letter no. 65

Savannah Oct 19th 1859
Wm C. Cook Esq.[1]

Dr Sir,

The Wanderer is off. She went to sea this morning with a full complement of men, provisions & munitions of war etc. etc. But alas! She went without my knowledge or consent. A Captain Martin called on me some two weeks ago & wanted the Command & offered to put in 20,000$ in cash. He brought letters, but they were from parties in Havana whom I *did not know*, & I told him he would have to await answers to my letters I wrote there concerning him. He expressed himself perfectly satisfied, & asked permission to remain on board & he would look after matters etc. I consented. I started for Worth Court on Saturday night, got as far as Albany & found that in consequence of the sickness of Judge Lamar, there would be no court.[2]

I left & came home arriving here yesterday (Tuesday) morning. I was not exactly satisfied with the complexion of things, as I found he had in my absence taken all the sails out of the warehouse, stating *I had given him authority to do so*. I tried all day to find him & being unable to do so I went to Jno. Boston, the Collector, last night about 7 o'clock & told him I was afraid some thing was wrong etc. & requested him to keep an extra look out & to send an officer to her—she was then lying off my Press. He said she could not get down, but this morning I found she had gone. He got his crew & provisions on board at night & put out. The Cutter had gone from her station. He has undoubtedly gone to the Coast of Africa for a cargo of negroes & if he is as smart there, as he has been here he will get one.

This is all I can give you. I have gotten Mr. Boston to write to every part of the country & to request our Gov'mt to notify our vessels & ministers *every where* & if possible to have her retaken. We must at some time get the vessel—she is without papers. He must have had his plan well laid & for some time, so bold & daring & [an] act has never before been committed.[3] I hope to hear of her in the future. I am out 25,000$ as he not only took what belongs to her that was in the W[are] House but *lots of other things.* He *may* land a cargo & [_?] fair, but I have serious doubts.

I am Truly yrs etc.

C. A. L. Lamar

NOTES

1. This is the fifth letter to William Cook, the one man known to have invested in Lamar's next slaving expedition.

2. Judge Henry G. Lamar was Charles's distant cousin.

3. David Martin (probably not his real name) mysteriously arrived in Savannah, offered to invest in the *Wanderer*, outfitted the ship, then absconded with it and a hijacked crew for a slaving expedition to Africa, all under the nose of Charles Lamar. It raises the question: Was Lamar part of the scheme? The wording of this letter is totally out of character for Lamar, as he actually praises the boldness and daring of the man who stole his ship.

Letter no. 66

Savannah May 13th 1860
Miss Bessie Williams[1]
Stonington, Conn.

Dear Miss Bessie,

I am in rect of your Note of the 9th this Sunday morning. I am confounded. I do not know what to say. It is impossible for me to say anything, in justification of the course Billy[2] has pursued towards you, which is entirely unjustifiable, & which he himself would be the first to condemn in others, & yet I cannot be expected, friend that he has always been of mine, to take up the "cudgels" in open warfare against him, no matter how much I may & *do* condemn him in his treatment of you.

I can, if you will permit, offer a few suggestions, as to the causes that have brought about such results, & as you *requested* that I should, I will do so. At the same time, I do not desire you for a moment to suppose, I am an apologist for any of his acts. That he *loved* you, I do not think

you will doubt, even in the face of the unkind and uncalled for letter he
sent you. That he intended to have complied with his engagements, to
the strictest letter, I feel that I can assure you, knowing him as I do, but
I saw a manifest change in his feelings, upon my return from New Orleans, & when I questioned him upon the subject, he said, he had been
badly treated by your father[3] who had written unkindly of him, making
accusations against him & declined to reply to any of the many inquiries
he had made of him etc. He was much annoyed and very much outraged
in feeling, & wanted to go immediately to Stonington, and for me to ac-
company him, to have matters cleared up & his character, which he said
had been assailed, vindicated. He was beside himself, & could I have left
home at that juncture, & gone with him, all would have gone well, I am
satisfied, but I could not, & *just then*, at the most critical moment, when
he thought, by the interference of others, he had *lost you*, Miss Joe[4] made
her re-appearance upon the stage, and going directly to his house, took
complete possession of him & it. He has become so much enamored of
her, & she exercises such influence over him, that she alone can do anything with him. He heeds nothing I can say to him, which has any bearing
directly or indirectly upon Miss Joe, hence, it has been some time since I
broached the subject of your affairs. I do most sincerely sympathize with
you Miss Bessie, & there is nothing I *could* do for you, that I am not willing to undertake. If I can serve you in any way, please command me. You
requested the return of the letter of Billy's—with your permission I will
return it, & if you say so, *destroy* it, it can in no possible event, do you any
good, & will only tend to open the wounds afresh every time it is read. I
would like on his account to put it out of sight for ever. May I do it? I hope
to see you again one of these days when I'll be most happy to renew my
acquaintance with you, provided yr father does not object to an association with one who was so intimately connected with the Wanderer[5]—of
which he has [_?].

I am truly yours,
C. A. L. Lamar

NOTES

1. Bessie Smith Williams Sherman (1832–1915) would have been twenty-seven years
old and unmarried at the writing of this letter. It is not known how she and Billy met, but
her father reportedly owned land in Georgia and perhaps took Bessie on a trip to the state.
This letter shows a softer side of Charles Lamar. It also highlights another social issue of the
time, geographically "mixed" couples.

2. William Brailsford (1826–1887) of McIntosh County, a good friend of Charles and

a fellow member in the Savannah Aquatic Club and Savannah Jockey Club, was a cotton planter and factor. Lamar mentions Brailsford as having received *Wanderer* Africans in his letter to Theodore Johnston of January 13, 1859. District attorney Joseph Ganahl indicted Brailsford for "holding and aiding and abetting in the holding of African Negroes" but the grand jury returned "No Bill." However, in May 1859 he received a true bill in the U.S. Circuit Court in New Orleans for holding and selling Africans, probably from the *Wanderer*. *New Orleans Daily True Delta*, May 11, 1859. At the start of the war, Brailsford served as a first lieutenant in Lamar's Mounted Rifles and succeeded Charles as captain.

    3. Charles Phelps Williams (1804–79) was a ship owner, businessman, and investor. Bessie's father apparently did not approve of Brailsford because he owned slaves and was charged, though not indicted, in the *Wanderer* trials, thus causing Brailsford to terminate their engagement.

    4. Miss Joe could not be identified.

    5. Charles couldn't resist getting in a dig at Bessie's father, who no doubt didn't approve of him, either.

Letter no. 67

Savannah June 12th 1860
L. Q. C. Lamar Esq.[1]

Dr Lucius,

    I wrote you sometime during the winter, requesting you to telegraph me when Raymond of the N.Y. Times, arrived in Washington, that I might go on & meet him. You never replied, & I therefore feel some resistance in again addressing you, but I'll try it *once* more.

    I received the Enclosed through the mail this morning, & being unable to decipher the name of the M. C. who franked it, though I sent it to the P.O. [post office] & made the request of them to give me the name, I send it to you, with the request that you will find out who sent it to me, & demand of him, *in my name*, if he intended in any way to reflect on me by addressing it "In Jail." If he did, *challenge him peremptorily in my name*, & telegraph me, & I will be there to meet the appointment.[2]

    I am not in Jail, & the damned Government has not the power to put & keep me there. I am in my own rooms over my office, & go home every night & live like a fighting cock at *the expense of the Government*, for we notified the Marshal, at the beginning, unless he furnished us we would not stay with him, but dissolve all connection that exist or might exist between us. He submitted the same to the Judges, & they told him to supply us.

    I can *whip* the Gov'mt any time they make the issue unless they raise a few additional regiments. Attend to this—act promptly & decisively. If I go out on the field, the result will be on a very different one from the one I had with Commodore Moore, against whom I had no feelings. If you feel any hesitancy in acting in accordance with the within, turn it over to my friend Jack Jones.[3] He will do the needful.

I am Truly yrs etc.

C. A. L. Lamar

NOTES

1. Lucius Quintas Cincinnatus Lamar Jr. (1825–93) was the son of Gazaway's first cousin Lucius Quintas Cincinnatus Lamar Sr. He attended schools in Georgia and moved to Mississippi at age twenty-four to practice law and teach mathematics at the University of Mississippi. At the time of this letter, Lucius was a member of the U.S. House of Representatives from Mississippi. Over the span of his career he served the federal government as a member of the U.S. House and Senate, secretary of the interior (1885–88), and associate justice of the U.S. Supreme Court (1888–93).

2. It is not known if Lucius pursued this matter for his cousin, but Charles never did go to Washington to confront Raymond.

3. Jack Jones was Charles's friend from Columbus, Georgia. Jones must have been in Washington at the time.

Letter no. 68

Savannah June 18th 1860
Matthew H. Hopkins Esq.[1]

Dr Sir,

I have your note of this morning. My reply to your first Note was Severe, as it should have been under the circumstances, you having struck my boy, whom I know to be respectful & polite, as avowed in your Note, without provocation. You now declare distinctly & positively that the boy *was* "impertinent in manner" & impeded your passage through the street. I am glad you have placed yourself in such position, as to enable me to withdraw language, which, according to your own statement of the facts, was unjust. It is not my desire to put an indignity upon anyone, particularly one so young as yourself, & for whom I have always entertained friendly feelings. I cheerfully withdraw the offensive letter. I think you would have done better to have put the boy out of the way & made complaint to [me.][2]

Respectfully yrs etc.

C. A. L. Lamar

NOTES

1. Matthew Hopkins was born in Savannah in April 1837 and was thirteen years younger than Lamar. He worked as a clerk with the firm of Boston and Villalonga and served as a member of the Savannah Volunteer Guards militia company. In 1861 the company members elected him second lieutenant of Company B. He was part of the garrison that defended Fort Pulaski in April 1862 when it was captured by Union forces. He was imprisoned at Fort Columbus on Governors Island and Johnson's Island, Lake Sandusky, Ohio, before being exchanged at Vicksburg. He also fought in North Georgia, confronting General William T. Sherman's army. See *Confederate Veteran*, January 1917, 132.

2. Generally speaking, a white person did not strike someone else's slave, other than on his own property or in self-defense. If a white found the behavior of another's bondsman objectionable, he or she would lodge a complaint with the owner, who would render punishment if he thought it warranted. As Hopkins struck Charles's slave on the street, Lamar demanded an explanation. Hopkins gave an acceptable one, avoiding a possible challenge to a duel. That Lamar, a slave trader responsible for the deaths of around one hundred innocent Africans, would risk a fight over the mistreatment of one of his slaves presents an interesting dynamic in the slave-master relationship.

Letter no. 69

Savannah Jany 20th 1861[1]
Wm. C Cook Esq.

Dr Sir,

I have at last something definite to report concerning the Wanderer. She has been detained in Havana by the Deputy U.S. Consul, upon some technicality, & it was only late in December that I got an order from Mr. Cobb as Secy of the Treasury to him, to give her her clearance.[2] I then sent an agent, Mr. Trowbridge, there to pay up her Bills & to save her. He has made the arrangements & she will come here to have her Register changed. As it now stands, if she were taken, she would go to Boston, as her Register is issued from there. I am expecting her daily. She will then go immediately to the Coast—every thing being arranged as far as can be, & I do hope we shall have no more troubles but land safely a cargo.[3]

I have the rascal who stole her, in Jail here. How he got away from L'pool, when I had a requisition there in the hands of Beverly Tucker, our consul, I can't imagine.[4] He went to Key West & there stole the Bark William & had gotten 20 miles at sea, when he was overtaken & brought back by the U.S. steamer *Crusader*.[5] Hearing of him there, passing as a relative of mine, I sent a requisition from the U.S. District Court for Geo & got him. He was tried there first, but owing to the present state of political excitement, he was acquitted—he claiming the vessel *William* as his property, having been taken with Slaves aboard by U.S. vessel, & that he was only trying to recover his own property. The real owners, fearing to make themselves known, did not interfere & he thus got clear. I shall give him a benefit here.[6]

I am Respectfully etc.

C. A. L. Lamar

NOTES

1. This letter was written the day after Georgia seceded from the Union.

2. Gazaway Lamar took ownership of the *Wanderer* in early 1860 and had it taken to Havana in the spring for Charles to sell. Charles never sold the ship, which remained in Cuba. Lamar claimed that he received an order from Howell Cobb in late December giving the *Wanderer* clearance from Havana. If true, this must have been one of Cobb's last acts, because he resigned from his post of secretary of the treasury on December 8, 1860, in light of Abraham Lincoln's election. Gazaway Lamar probably secured the clearance as he remained on speaking terms with his cousin.

3. The *Wanderer* never went on another slaving expedition.

4. Nathaniel Beverly Tucker (1820–90) was a Virginian who worked as a journalist and founded the *Washington Sentinel* newspaper. The U.S. Senate elected him as their printer in 1853, and four years later Tucker received the appointment of American consul to Liverpool, where Gazaway Lamar had many contacts through his cotton trading. Tucker sided with the Confederacy and spent most of the war years in England, France, and Canada, trying to garner support for the South's cause. After the war he was accused of belonging to the group that assassinated President Lincoln, but he was never charged. David Martin likely hitchhiked by ship to Liverpool and then Key West.

5. The bark *William* was seized by the uss *Wyandotte* off the coast of Cuba on May 9, 1860, with 570 of an estimated 744 Africans originally boarded. The ship was taken to Key West. See *NYT*, July 12, 1860; Howard, *American Slavers and the Federal Law*, 220, 238, 248, 297n8.

6. Charles was able to obtain a warrant for Martin's arrest in Key West because a grand jury in Savannah had found a true bill against him on November 15, 1859, for "feloniously running away with a vessel." If Lamar indeed was part of the scheme to steal the *Wanderer*, he might have had Martin arrested afterward if Martin broke their agreement after he ran away with the ship.

Letter no. 70

Savannah September 3rd 1861

My dear Mrs. Bartow[1]

Many, many thanks to you for the present today, of Frank's Uniform Hat.[2] You know full well the love I bore him. I wish I had the power of language, to express to you all the emotions of my heart, or that Frank had left me as a legacy, his ability & eloquence, to do justice to myself, in thanking you for the compliment you have paid me in selecting me out of the host of his admiring friends, as one, worthy to wear that, which he has made illustrious. I can only promise, with the help of God, to do nothing that will ever cause you to regret the preference thus shown. I will wear it, & if I go into action, I hope I may be actuated by the same high and patriotic emotions that animated him, and that I may be equally as fortunate in my efforts to illustrate, my native state—Georgia. With many kind wishes for your health & happiness, I am, as I ever have been, the true friend of yourself and poor Frank.

    C. A. L. Lamar

NOTES

1. Louisa Greene Berrien Bartow was the wife of Francis Stebbins Bartow (1816–61). See Letter no. 64 for details on Bartow's early career. After Abraham Lincoln's victory in November 1860, Bartow was elected to Georgia's secession convention, which voted to leave the Union on January 19, 1861. He was then elected to the Confederate Congress. After the bombardment of Fort Sumter, Bartow offered the Oglethorpe Light Infantry to Governor Joseph E. Brown to serve in Virginia, certain to be the first battleground of the war. Brown declined, claiming that the company would be of greatest value defending their native Savannah should the city be attacked. Thirsting to defend the South from the Yankees, Bartow helped pass an act in Congress allowing state militia companies to tender their services directly to the Confederacy if they committed to duty for the remainder of the war, thus circumventing the governor's authority. The Oglethorpes voted to take advantage of the law, and the secretary of war ordered them to Virginia. An incensed Brown demanded that they not go and ordered any company with arms issued by the state to return them to the Augusta arsenal before leaving Georgia. He also accused Bartow of disrespecting the authorities of Georgia. Bartow ignored the order, claiming that he would not send one hundred men into battle with no means of defense. He wrote to Brown, "I go to illustrate, if I can, my native state; at all events to be true to her interests and her character." *Southern Recorder* (Milledgeville, Ga.), July 9, 1861.

Bartow left Georgia on May 21 as a captain of a company. Two months later he charged into the fray at Bull Run as the brevetted brigadier general of the Eighth Georgia Regiment. Bartow was killed and his body was shipped back to Savannah and lay in state before being buried with full military honors in Laurel Grove Cemetery. Today, his bust is part of the monument to Confederate soldiers in Forsyth Park, Savannah.

2. Mrs. Bartow's gift of her husband's hat to Charles Lamar attests to the high regard that some Savannahians held for him as a patriot of the southern cause.

Letters of the
Slave-Trader's Letter-Book

PART B

*Letters Concerning
Miscellaneous Subjects*

Letter no. 1

Savannah Feby. 2nd 1855
Messrs. Jas Ashburner & Jessey Miller
Committee Timber Cutters Convention

Gentlemen,

Mr. Burns of this city handed me your letter of the 19th Jany only this morning, or I should have given an earlier reply. It will be out of my power to attend your adjourned meeting on the 1st Monday in Feby, as my business arrangements won't allow my being absent from the city at that time.

I must beg to decline the honor you propose to confer upon me & thank you for the compliment of having singled me out to act as your Agent. I appreciate it, & will lend my feeble aid to further the views of the association. Command me. Let me give you briefly & in a friendly manner some of the reasons which actuated me in declining the Trust.

The 1st & most important one is, I am satisfied that I (nor no one else) could ever give satisfaction to so large a body of men, whose interests, though apparently the same, would be forever clashing. The matter of *advancing* alone, would produce difficulty the first week. Most views would be regulated on their *demands* for an advance, not by the quality & quantity of the Timber, but by their *wants*, & most men's wants are *greater* than *prudent* men are willing to gratify. But being their agent, they would *claim* the right to *demand* what they considered a fair advance, indeed a man under such circumstances would be unable to say to whom he belonged. He certainly could not claim himself.

Truly I have no place [_?] for the keeping of any quantity of timber, nor can a suitable one be had without involving the expenditure of a larger amount of money than I am willing to invest *that way*, at *this time.*

It was my intention to have gone into the business in connection with a cousin of mine but *he* subsequently determined to settle elsewhere, & I abandoned the idea *for the present.*

What I may do, I am not *now* prepared to say. If I should determine to go in next season, I'll be glad to have the patronage of each & every one of you, but only so long as I can give satisfaction and do justice to both—as you requested.

I'll now give you my views of the different localities, etc. 1st in order then—Fig Island or more properly speaking, the river between Hutchinson & Fig Islands. That is the best place as things now are in the vicinity of the city, but that has its objections, which I'll state. 1st then, there are too many who own (& a great many more who claim) an interest in said River (or Bay since Government has stopped the open end of it). There are, Maj. Starke, Robt A. Allan, P. K. Shields (the honest man) & the city of Savannah who own Fig Island. Maj. Starke owns all that portion of Hutchinson Island that borders on that River. It would be next to an impossibility to rent all those interests, particularly as *they* are all more or less in the timber business themselves. I know nothing of Rabbitt Island, but it would labor (as does Fig Island) under the disadvantage of having to be approached by water. On windy, cold, or hot days, *merchants won't expose themselves* when they can buy by not doing so from Robt. A. Allan & P. K. Shields & the O'Byn's *on this side of the river*, & who adjoin the city.

I have a creek running through my lands & coming out at Quantock (now Robert's Mill) & it is the place of all others that would make a suitable place by the expenditure of 6, 8, or 10,000$—that is by widening it to 100 feet through the whole of my land. You may think I am actuated by selfish motives in this, but not so. Come down and look for yourselves & if you agree with me, you may select a Gentleman & I another & let them say what it is worth for 5 or 10 yrs. You do the work necessary—I have a number of applications for it, if the association wants it & *can do no better after looking around*, they shall have it on reasonable terms.

In haste Truly yrs etc.

C. A. L. Lamar

Mr. Burns who takes this can explain everything I have said which is not plain. I have written in a great hurry.

NOTES

Author's note: This, the first recording in the letter book, shows Charles turning down an offer to be the agent of the Timber Cutters Association and giving advice on the best place in Savannah to build a mill and warehouse. There are no signs of nefarious motives, money problems, or seething anger.

Letter no. 6

Savannah March 4th 1855
G. B. Lamar Esq.

Dear Father,

I had yours of the 28th this morning and was glad to hear that the express was all ready. Hope she will be home by the last of the week.

I was surprised to hear of any complaint from Mr. Buck. The Captain could not have explained things properly. I have no more to do with his loading up a [_?] than you had. The Captain determined to do so merely asking me if it was prudent to do so to which I replied "yes" and gave him [_?] because what Captain Gilmer had me. [_?] ran vessels going out and coming in drawing more [_?] than his [_?] called for. Now to the particulars the afternoon he was to have left the steamer came along side to take him, but the Harbormaster was not there and never [_?] ahead of him and the Captain refused to do anything without the Harbormaster. The consequence was he lost that tide. The Captain was so distressed that to relieve him I paid the [_?] of the boat myself and at his request engaged another boat to come after him the next morning (4 a.m.). The boat so then had being [sic] engaged to another vessel the next morning I was not there but then went alongside and there remained inactive until the tide had exhausted itself all of an hour and a half when according to the captain of boat and steamers a very feeble effort was made to go ahead. The pilot then informed them it was needless to try. She could not and should not go. When I went down after breakfast the Captain then for the first time told me of the threats made by the pilots to the effect if he had loaded down to over 15½ he should not go, unless he unloaded. His statement was corroborated by other captains. I then announced my intention of dismissing the pilot and putting on board one of my steamship pilots to carry her down. I went to the chairman's (at board commission of pilots) house to get the necessary authority but he was not to be found. I then looked after him or three of the members, but could not see them. I ascertained afterwards they were dodging me, and they were waiting to come in collision with the pilots [_?] not [_?] was to be lost. I took the responsibility and told the pilot I did not want his services. He told me the law gave him the authority and he would take her down. He was [_?] by [_?] of friends and pilots had threatened to kill any pilot and me with personal violence. The Captain then begged me to allow the pilot to try again, though he said that there was no use trying that tide as all the pilots in the pilotage could not get her out. I went aboard with Mr. Craig and announced I would kill the first man who laid hands on either of us. Mr. Craig took charge and got everything in readiness when low and behold the steamer the Captain lugaged was not there. There was a steamer alongside lugaged to the inside ship and it was necessary for us to move to enable her to get out. To do so we took her boat, the tide then had fallen 3 or 4 inches, we got her out into the stream and by my guaranteeing the inside ship a boat the next morning, I got the consent to go along. We went until we got to the wrecks—it was then 8½ o'clock and very thick when she took the bottom. The next morning's tide I could not lugage a boat for her. The only one I could get I was bound to give the ship whose boat we had taken the evening before and to get that in I rode to all the grog shops and two or three whore houses until after 11 o'clock to find the Captain. Well there was a tide lost—during that day it blew a gale from the west and of course we had no tide of consequence, yet contrary to my advice the Captain engaged a boat to go to him. His efforts were vain and there he remained until next morning when he got off and went down. Now let me add a few facts more and I'll close. The first afternoon two vessels went down each drawing upwards of 16 feet. The next morning (with 18 inch more tide though) the "George Evans" went down drawing 16.5. The afternoon or evening we left the wharf, with a tide not so high by 12 inches and upwards 16 feet went down again. The next morning there was a good tide and two or three went down (that's the morning we were without a boat). The morning we got off the Br. ship Warbler went down from the hydraulic wharf drawing 17.2!!! When the bark got down off Tybee (the wind being ahead) the mate and pilot hooked the keel and measured her draft it was 16.9—her marks called for 16. The Captain accounts for it by the fact of his having a new keel put in since his marks were regulated. Who is at fault? I would not have same trouble again for 10 times the comms. I acted throughout with as much enthusiasm and I to the interest of the owners as if those owners had been yourself and myself. The Captain did me great injustice if he did not give an account of the whole to Mr. B. He expressed his thanks to me proffering his services and assuring me he should ever in coming here consign his vessel to me. The vessel Mr. B. is now sending me I chartered to the parties here at ⅜—he to have consignment on other side. No commission on this. I allowed him 1% of my commission in the "Sarah Park's" case, except on disbursements of course. Where is the "Cobden"? What are you going to do with her? I made this agreement with Mr. Buck.

I am to allow him a return at 1% if I don't retain consignment for him on the other side, for all ships he sends to me.

I think it would be best for the owners to send word to Captain of the "Crowel" to pay me here the 3 [_?] on his frt. Otherwise he won't do it. Did you arrange with them about the consignment on other side? All well with me. I have rheumatism in the knees and a very bad cold.

Is Mr. Church to have 2½% commission as you wrote no mention of it is made in charter or [_?] to have the consignment on either side— which if even?

    Love to all
      C. A. L. Lamar

NOTES

Author's note: Charles's explanation of problems with loading and unloading a ship in Savannah.

Letter no. 8

Savannah Jany 6th 1856
Thomas Barrett Esq[1]
Augusta, Ga

Dear Sir,

Where money is necessary to accomplish anything, I must confess, I have little, if any confidence in you, but as you replied to me yesterday, when I remarked—you had no idea of taking any stock in the bonds, that you did intend so to do and would take $10,000. I have concluded to comply with yr request and write you my views, plans etc., etc. and in doing so, let one premise by saying, you are the only man I have *limited* it to, the intended directors don't dream of it—so what I write is *strictly confidential.* I may fail, if I do I want no one to know it.

To begin then with first principles. I am going to establish a bank *anyhow.* I have already enough to start the one, the charter of which I control.[2] It is an excellent charter & if I don't succeed in what I propose I shall have the name changed & go to work with it. The directors in either case will be myself, Wm Battersby,[3] Octavus Cohen,[4] Thomas Holcombe,[5] Joseph Burke,[6] John H. Davis[7]—it [_?] necessary at this time. Now to the development of my plan. The Exchange Bank charter suits me *quite* as well as mine & requires no alterations.

The capital can be raised to $1,500,000 commencing operations when $100,000 shall have been paid in—the amount I must have to commence mine with. Old Hutchison[8] won't open the bank until the last moment, when he will put down in connection with me or two friends the $100,000. He is afraid of me, hence, I start mine with the view of putting him *easy*. When his books are opened, I propose subscribing the full amt of all my subscriptions to his stock, if I find I can get control (of course with consent of directors with whom I'll confer at the proper time). But here comes the *bug*—it will require $187,750 to control matters—that is, to pay 25% of the amount of subscriptions—each share having a vote. I would have to take 7,500 shares and pay $25 per share. Well, we need not call in any more and if we deem it necessary we can, after putting in *our own directors*, reduce the stock back to $200,000. Of course it would be best to let it all remain in, *which we* must try to do. I make the two hundred thousand in this way. I preassume (*sic*) Hutchison will have ready his $100,000 and then our $100,000 would make the $200,000. To plan the handout successfully, would be worth $1,000 and I would give that myself. Another very important item too, is this—we control and can keep others from putting into operation our present bank—reducing competition and our having the value of the other stock. Can you raise $100,000 *in cash* in Augusta? If so *go to work & do it*. I will attend to the $100,000 here—then we have the thing dead *I think*. If I have the understanding so you are to have control in Augusta of not less than $500,000 after all is paid in. Now let me see what you can do. *It must be done at once*. If you can't do anything, *say so at once*—don't keep me waiting. *Now*, suppose I am foiled, are you willing to go into the present one? I'll have the name changed either to the Bank of Commerce or the Bank of the South—*immediately*[9]—then after that is done, at the heel of the session, I will apply for an extension of capital—say to $2,000,000.[10] The weather is dreadfully cold but clear and beautiful. Let me hear at once. *Write nothing you aren't going to stand to by the letter*.

I am truly yours,

C. A. L. Lamar

NOTES

1. Thomas Barrett (1808–65) was an Augusta commission merchant and banker who had business dealings with Gazaway Lamar.

2. The bank would become the Bank of Commerce in Savannah. It received its charter from the Georgia legislature in 1856 and was organized in May of that year with the election of a board of directors. *DMN*, May 12, 1856. They in turn elected Gazaway Lamar as president and John C. Ferrill as cashier. The bank operated successfully for years. This letter is notable because it shows that Charles Lamar came up with the idea for establishing the bank, one of his few business successes. However, there can be little doubt that the institution thrived because of the management of his father and others. The original directors were Gazaway Lamar, Charles Lamar, Charles Green, Thomas Holcombe, Joseph Burke, and John H. Davis.

3. William Battersby was a Savannah commission merchant.

4. Octavus Cohen was a Savannah commission merchant.

5. Thomas Holcombe was a wholesale grocer. He had served as an alderman on the city council and would become the mayor of Savannah in 1862.

6. Joseph Burke was a Savannah commission merchant and general exchange broker.

7. No background information on John H. Davis could be found.

8. Old Hutchison was R. Hutchison, a Savannah shipping agent and commission merchant.

9. The bank was to be called "The Mechanics and Traders Bank" but the General Assembly, with the sanction of the governor, approved changing the name to the Bank of Commerce.

10. The capital stock was indeed limited to $2,000,000.

Letter no. 9

Savannah May 17, 1856

My dear Father,[1]

I have yours of the 16th this morning. I don't think either Caro[2] or myself are amenable to the charge made against us. Upon your arrival in Augusta, I wrote more than once requesting you and your family to come down. I dealt as frankly as this with you. I requested you to come *before* the month of April, at which time Caro was engaged to go in the country with Mrs. Anderson.[3] Just before our return from the country Caro wrote Ma[4] telling her when she would expect her, etc. I did not see the letter and therefore know nothing of the "peculiar nature" of it. On my part I know there was not even an omission and I don't *think* there was in Caro's. I did not want Ma to come at a time to interfere with Caro's visit to the country and so told you. She could have come at any time before or after and we fully expected her. Caro was unwilling to allow them to be here without her (though I urged her to do so). I thought she was right for it would have excited remarks—you and your family in town and me and mine in the country. I regret exceedingly that you should have put such a construction upon the matter. You are the last person in the world I should offend, neglect or slight in any way, and if my relations with your family[5] were other of the most pleasant kind, I would on your a/c endeavor to do nothing that they would construe into a slight. I am sorry you have determined to give us the go by. I expected you & *wanted* you—I was not aware you were anything of a stickler for etiquette and am sorry you have turned such a leaf—for I am an outsider and know, or more properly speaking, think very little of it. Hope you will yet come this way—must consider the amends made and everything settled.

You can accommodate your friends in the way of stock—plenty of it yet unsold—25% is called for on the 31st.[6] Nothing new.

I am Truly Yours, etc.

C. A. L. Lamar

NOTES

1. In 1839, one year after Gazaway Lamar lost his entire first family, except Charles, in the ss *Pulaski* disaster, he married Harriet Cazenove. The couple lived in Alexandria, Virginia, and Savannah before moving to New York City in 1846. Gazaway, a native of Augusta, maintained close ties with the town throughout his life and was in the process of building a house there when this letter was written.

2. Caro is Caroline Nicoll Lamar, Charles's wife.

3. Most likely Mrs. Edward C. Anderson.

4. Harriet Cazenove Lamar, Gazaway's second wife and Charles's stepmother.

5. At the writing of this letter, Gazaway's children with Harriet were Charlotte, born 1840, Gazaway DeRossett or Derry, born January 1842, Anthony, born 1844, Annie, born 1846, and Harriet, born 1853.

6. Charles is probably referring to the Bank of Commerce stock.

Letter no. 10

Savannah May 19th 1856
Gazaway B Lamar Esq., Augusta[1]

My dear Father,

Mr. Cuyler[2] informed me this morning—requesting me to communicate the fact to you—that Mr. Holford[3] had written him, that the Pres't. of the Kanawha Co., Va,[4] had called upon him to pay over the balance of the money rec'd on a/c of Texan bonds for a/c Gen'l. Hamilton[5] to him—he holding the first lien on them. He, Mr. Holford declined, showing his obligations to pay them over to the court here. The Pres't. then threatened a caveat but had not as to date of the letter executed his threat. Pierce Butler[6] has engaged [_?] & Bartow[7] to defend his claim, and I presume the Kanawha Co. will employ counsel, so there is no telling when the amount will be determined.

I should like to know how Caro or myself gave offense. She says there was nothing peculiar in her letter that she was aware of. I know I have been guilty of the sin of omission or commission. *(Next sentence unreadable)*
[_?] to [_?] have to matter [_?] at once for if [_?] commence and get [_?] way, there is no telling where it will [_?] shall as I write before [_?] to do [_?] to retain your affection and good opinion—but I must confess, that notwithstanding I have tried to disabuse my [_?] of the impression, it will often recur—that this imaginary slight and want of attention would never have been thought of by you unless ingested by another. Now I have thought a great deal upon the subject matter of your letter, and have come to the conclusion that I and Caro too, have done more than I think would have been done in case my own mother had been in the like position—for I have no idea of treating you as stranger, certainly not you. If Ma desires all the courtesies and etiquette of fashionable life attended to her, say so, and it shall be done. I have been in the habit of going to your house in Brooklyn without any hesitation from either of you. Certain it is, Ma has never given Caro an invitation—you have. I wrote you time and again to come and bring your family and I generally mean what I write. I know Caro expected you before she went in the country—and since. I don't think now that bad feelings on Ma's part caused the suspicion of want of attention on ours—but I know she is and has been for years in bad health and is very changeable, wanting to go today and changing her mind tomorrow. I shall stop writing for I find the more I write the warmer my feelings become. There is always mutually a kind of jealous feeling between stepmothers and stepchildren. I have felt it, and I have [_?] out. I want to be able to satisfy myself, yourself and the world. It was not my work.

I am truly yours,
C. A. L. Lamar

NOTES

1. Gazaway was in Augusta preparing to move into a house he had just built.
2. Richard R. Cuyler was a friend and business associate of G. B. Lamar. At the time of this letter he was president of the Central of Georgia Banking and Railroad Company.
3. James Holford was a British banker.
4. Kanawha Company is the James River and Kanawha Canal Company.
5. James Hamilton of South Carolina was a longtime business associate of Gazaway

Lamar and a fervent supporter of the Texas territory in its struggle to become independent of Mexico and then the Republic of Texas in its quest to become part of the United States. See *CM*, December 25, 1857.

 6. Pierce Butler owned plantations on Saint Simons Island.

 7. Francis Stebbins Bartow was a lawyer in Savannah in 1856. He would become one of Savannah's most revered Civil War casualties. See Letter no. 70.

Letter no. 21

Savannah, Dec 26th 1857
John Campbell Esq.[1]

Dr Sir,

 To prevent anything like misunderstanding on either side, I desire to submit to writing our agreement entered into this morning. If I am correct in stating it, you will be pleased to signify your assent by a communication in writing to me. You are to have what is known as the Sporting Privilege at the Ten Broeck Race Course[2] the coming meeting, commencing the 5th January next, at Two Thousand Dollars—$2000—the sporting to be confined to what is known as the Citizens' Stand and I had agreed to your proposition in reference to the Privilege next year— viz: You to have the whole known as Eating, Drinking and Sporting for the meeting in Jany 1859 at Twenty five Hundred dollars—2,500$—the same to be confined to the Citizen's Stand—it being understood however, that I am not to [_?] If any sporting in any other horse or [_?] on along the track.

 Respectfully etc.

  C. A. L. Lamar

NOTES

 1. The identity of John Campbell could not be determined.

 2. The Ten Broeck Race Course was located three miles west of Savannah. Charles purchased the track in 1857 and served as the president of the Savannah Jockey Club in 1859 and 1860. The "sporting privilege" is the right to use a sporting facility.

Letter no. 47

Savannah, April 20th 1859
H. J. Raymond, Esq.
New York

Sir,

Your letter of the 16th is before me and is unsatisfactory. I must therefore repeat the inquiry made of mine of the 4th to this effect. Do you
hold yourself personally responsible for articles that appear in the columns of the "Times"? If you do, will you name someone out of the state of
New York or who will go out, to receive from me such a communication
as the nature of the case demands. You are doubtless aware of the existing statutes of N.Y. against dueling. I am unwilling at this time to incur
the risk of coming before a Northern Jury and hence the above request.

　　Respectfully,
　　　　C. A. L. Lamar

NOTES

"Void" is written vertically across the lower portion of this letter, in Lamar's handwriting. A
new letter (no. 48) replaced this one.

Notes

1. For about twelve years after the ban of the importation of Africans into the United States, effective January 1, 1808, slave traders and pirates snuck their cargoes into the country through territories bordering the states, such as Spanish Florida and Texas, and even through portions of Louisiana, which became a state in 1812. See David Head, "Slave Smuggling by Foreign Privateers: The Illegal Slave Trade and the Geopolitics of the Early Republic," *Journal of the Early Republic* 33 (Fall 2013): 433–62. However, the author found no record of a slave ship successfully landing Africans on the shores of the United States between 1820 and 1858, when the *Wanderer* completed its mission.

Historians and other observers have debated the existence of illegal slave importations into the United States, particularly Florida and Texas, whose thousands of miles of desolate, unguarded coastline were so close to slaveholding islands in the West Indies. Florida, which became a U.S. territory in 1819 and a state in 1845, is only ninety miles from Cuba and the journey was relatively easy for slave smugglers. But only one documented landing of slaves in Florida from Cuba between 1819 and 1858 can be found; that 1837 voyage brought only eight enslaved humans, not the hundreds who were regularly landed in Cuba and Brazil. See Dorothy Dodd, "The Schooner Emperor: An Incident of the Illegal Slave Trade in Florida," *Florida Historical Quarterly* 13 (January 1935): 117–28. Also see Kenneth F. Kipple, "The Case against a Nineteenth-Century Cuba-Florida Slave Trade," *Florida Historical Quarterly* 49 (April 1971): 346–55, and a reprint from the *New York Evening Post* (hereafter cited as *NYEP*) in the *Globe* (Washington, D.C.), June 8, 1843. For an example of two newspapers of the time debating the existence of the slave trade to Florida, see the Washington *Daily National Intelligencer* (hereafter cited as *WDNI*), May 30, 1843.

Texas, which became an independent republic in 1836, entered the United States as a slave state in 1845. Many newspapers reported rumors of illegal landings of slaves, from both Cuba and Africa (*Massachusetts Spy*, June 27, 1849). However, Eugene C. Baker, in "The African Slave Trade in Texas," *Quarterly of the Texas State Historical Association* 6 (October 1902): 145–58, claims, "There is no available evidence that this desultory traffic continued after annexation," although "many old Texans remember that Africans were frequently sold in the state, even down to the late fifties." If a ship successfully landed slaves in Texas between 1846 and 1858, it was never reported.

Lamar pleaded guilty to freeing from jail a member of the *Wanderer* crew, John Egbert Farnum, so that he could attend a party. Lamar served a thirty-day sentence in rooms above his office and went home at night. The incident is discussed in chapters 16 and 17.

2. "A Slave-Trader's Letter-Book," *North American Review* 143 (November 1886): 447–61 (hereafter cited as "Slave-Trader's Letter-Book," *NAR*). Because the article refers to Lamar's "letter-book," this volume uses the same spelling. According to the Society of American Archivists, letter-press copybook technology, first patented in 1780, allowed people to make copies of letters for their own records: "A screw-powered letter press was used in conjunction with a press book, a bound volume of blank, tissue paper pages. A letter freshly written in special copying ink was placed on a dampened page while the rest of the pages were protected by oilcloths. The book was then closed and the mechanical press screwed down tightly. The pressure and moisture caused an impression of the letter to be retained on the underside of the tissue sheet. This impression could then be read through the top of the thin paper." The Society of American Archivists cites JoAnne Yates, *Control through Communication: The Rise of System in American Management* (Baltimore: Johns Hopkins University Press, 1989), 26–28.

3. Ronald T. Takaki, *A Pro-Slavery Crusade: The Agitation to Reopen the African Slave Trade* (New York: Free Press, 1971), 202–4; Don E. Fehrenbacher, *The Slaveholding Republic: An Account of the United States Government's Relations to Slavery*, ed. Ward M. McAfee (New York: Oxford University Press, 2002), 182; Tom Henderson Wells, *The Slave Ship Wanderer* (Athens: University of Georgia Press, 1967), 4.

4. Harvey Wish, "The Revival of the African Slave Trade in the United States, 1856–1860," *Mississippi Historical Review* 27 (March 1941): 583n60; Warren S. Howard, *American Slavers and the Federal Law, 1837–1862* (Berkeley: University of California Press, 1963), 320–21; Wells, *Slave Ship Wanderer,* 97–98.

5. "Slave-Trader's Letter-Book," *NAR,* 447.

6. In September 1872 Lamar made his last will in New York (Will of G. B. Lamar, Box 9, File 3, G. B. Lamar Papers, Special Collections, Hargrett Rare Book and Manuscript Library, University of Georgia, Athens, hereafter cited as G. B. Lamar Papers, UGA). Lamar named his son DeRosset and two other men as co-executors: Robert Soutter, his son-in-law who died in 1873, and Timothy H. Porter, a friend. Apparently, the probate court named DeRosset as sole executor as he took care of the liquidation of the estate.

7. Box 2, Folder 6, James Jordan Collection of Lamar family papers, MS 2549, Georgia Historical Society, Savannah, Ga. (hereafter cited as G. B. Lamar Papers, GHS).

8. The Montclair Public Library provided copies of the available town directories for the period. Frank Jones was not listed in the 1920 issue, but he lived at the address in 1923. The 1949 directory lists "Helen G [Helen Griffith Jones] wid [widow] of Frank C" living at the address. In 1951 a new resident is listed.

9. The best accounts of the *Wanderer* saga are a three-part article published in 1904 by Winfield M. Thompson in *The Rudder* titled "Historic American Yachts: The Slave Yacht Wanderer"; and Tom Henderson Wells's *Slave Ship Wanderer,* In 2006 Eric Calonius wrote *The Wanderer: The Last American Slaver and the Conspiracy That Set Its Sails in Motion,* but the book is so factually flawed and contains so many questionable references that it is difficult to view it as a nonfiction work. This author wrote "Charles Augustus Lafayette Lamar and the Movement to Reopen the African Slave Trade," published in 2009 in the *Georgia Historical Quarterly* (hereafter cited as *GHQ*), before finding the Slave-Trader's Letter-Book.

10. C. A. L. Lamar to G. B. Lamar, November 5, 1860, Charles A. L. Lamar Papers, Stuart A. Rose Manuscript, Archives, and Rare Book Library, Emory University (hereafter cited as C. A. L. Lamar Papers, Emory).

CHAPTER 2. "You Are a Noble Boy"

1. For a history of the Lamar family, see Harold Dihel LeMar, *History of the Lamar or Lemar Family in America* (Omaha, Neb.: Cockle, 1941). Some of the more renowned Lamars living around that time were Lucius Quintus Cincinnatus Lamar, one of Georgia's most prominent judges before he committed suicide in 1834, and Mirabeau Buonaparte Lamar, the second president of the Republic of Texas. For Charles's baptism, see Parish Register 1822–1851, Roll C-0978–05, p. 8, Christ Church Manuscript Collection, MS 978, Georgia Historical Society, Savannah (hereafter cited as GHS). The oft-repeated tale that Lafayette held Charles in his arms and stood as his godfather is false. For example, see Tom Henderson Wells, *The Slave Ship Wanderer* (Athens: University of Georgia Press, 1967), 3. One of Charles's classmates at the Chatham Academy in Savannah would remember his distinct Augusta accent and readiness to fight anyone who mocked it. *Savannah Morning News* (hereafter cited as *SMN*), April 6, 1884. The friend's comment suggests that while Gazaway lived in Savannah in the 1820s, Charles spent his early years in Augusta.

2. Gazaway Lamar's business interests are discussed in more detail in chapter 3.

3. For the company's charter, see *The Statutes at Large of South Carolina,* vol. 8, ed. David J. McCord (Columbia, S.C.: A. S. Johnston, 1840), 430–31; and *Acts of the General Assembly of the State of Georgia Passed at an Annual Session in November and December, 1836* (Milledgeville, Ga.: P. L. Robinson, 1837), 260–61. For Lamar's attempt to sell the *Pulaski,* see G. B. Lamar to M. B. Lamar, April 15, 1838, in Adam Gulick Jr., ed., *The Papers of Mirabeau Buonaparte Lamar,* 6 vols. (Austin, Tex.: A. C. Baldwin, 1921), 2:140–41. For ship dimensions, Robert Walker Groves, "The Wreck of the Steam Packet 'Pulaski,'" read before the Cosmos Club, Savannah, Georgia," November 9, 1955, Cosmos Club papers, MS 974, Box 2, Folder 1, GHS.

4. The description of the ship is taken from Gazaway's sister, Mrs. Hugh McLeod (Rebecca Lamar), "The Loss of the Steamer Pulaski," *GHQ* 3 (Summer

1919): 63–95; James Hamilton Couper (although an author is not named, this is Couper's account), "Loss of the Steamer Pulaski," *The Historical Collections of Georgia* (New York: Pudney & Russell, 1855), 353–64; Groves, "Wreck of the Steam Packet 'Pulaski'"; and a visual inspection of a model of the ship on display at the Ships of Sea Museum in Savannah. The narrative descriptions are not always consistent. Couper noted that he slept in a berth next to Colonel and Mrs. Dunham, indicating that men and women shared the cabin on the bottom deck. Slaves who were not nurses taking care of children would have slept in cabins separate from the whites on the lower deck, although no account mentions them. No account states where Gazaway and the oldest boys, Charles and Thomas, slept, but, as it wasn't in a stateroom, it was probably in the men's cabin on the main deck. For Rebecca's initial hesitance going on the ship, see McLeod, "Loss of the Steamer Pulaski," 65–66.

5. For the *Home* disaster, see *Albany (N.Y.) Argus*, October 27, 1837.

6. Several firsthand accounts of the *Pulaski* disaster exist. Gazaway Lamar wrote of his experience in a letter dated July 6, 1838, to Sarah Mackay, whose brother lost his wife and two children. Caroline Lamar Woodbridge Papers, MS 0878, Folder 3, item 3, GHS. Other accounts include McLeod, "Loss of the Steamer Pulaski" (the longest and most detailed); Peter Lawson (second mate of the ship), *Daily Georgian* (hereafter cited as *DG*), July 3, 1838; B. W. Fosdick, *Portland (Maine) Weekly Advertiser*, July 3, 1838; Captain Hubbard, *New York Commercial Advertiser* (hereafter cited as the *NYCA*), June 27, 1838; and Couper, "Loss of the Steamer Pulaski," 353–64. The description of the explosion and the days following the disaster are taken primarily from the accounts of Gazaway Lamar, Rebecca Lamar McLeod, Peter Lawson, and Captain Hubbard. Hubbard praised Rebecca for her actions during the disaster. "She was our preserving angel."

7. The man who commandeered the lifeboat was Captain S. Hibbert, the first mate of the *Pulaski*. See Hibbert's account in the *Charleston Mercury* (hereafter cited as *CM*), June 20, 1838. As it turned out, this boat leaked badly and was soon abandoned by the crewmen. Under the weight of the Lamar and Mackay families, it probably would have sunk. The two larger lifeboats on hoists and covered with tarp were boarded by James Hamilton Couper and twenty-two others, including men, women, and children, several crewmen, and two female slaves. Five of those twenty-three, including the two slaves, died while trying to land on the North Carolina coast.

8. McLeod, "Loss of the Steamer Pulaski," 72.

9. Rebecca Lamar McLeod calls the child Connie, but her real name was Corinne.

10. McLeod, "Loss of the Steamer Pulaski," 77.

11. Lawson's account doesn't mention the entire group leaving the raft, but he does say that the rowboats had no oars. It is not known how the people propelled the boats in this attempt.

12. McLeod, "Loss of the Steamer Pulaski," 82.

13. Ibid., 89.

14. The seven survivors from Rebecca's raft were the older Mrs. Smith, Mr. Hutchinson, Charles, an unidentified white man, two female slaves, and herself. Twenty-three occupants on Pearson's raft survived, and one man died.

15. Gazaway Lamar named his first son by his second wife Gazaway DeRosset and one of his steamboats the *DeRosset* in honor of Dr. Armand John DeRosset Sr.

16. Lamar described his experiences once he reached land in two letters to the *Charleston Courier* (hereafter cited as *CC*), June 27 and July 7, 1838. An unsigned letter to the *Charleston Mercury*, June 27, 1838, also describes the landing at New River Inlet. Second mate Lawson's account differs from Lamar's. He claimed that he and another man walked to New River Inlet as Lamar and the others were too exhausted to make the trip. He also stated that Lamar authorized him to offer one hundred dollars for every person saved from the raft. Lamar contested Lawson's account, claiming that Lawson was a Dane and had limited command of the English language.

17. For the count of dead and survivors, see Groves, "Wreck of the Steam Packet 'Pulaski,'" 18. For the mood in town, see G. B. Lamar to Sarah McKay, July 6, 1838. For the public meeting, see *CM*, June 28, 1838.

CHAPTER 3. "Young as You Are, You Are Failing Already in Mind"

1. For the history of the Savannah Fire Department, see Thomas Gamble Jr., *A History of the City Government of Savannah, Georgia from 1790 to 1901* (Savannah, Ga.: under direction of the city council, 1900), 50–51, 150–53, 196–97, 236–39; John E. Maguire, comp., *Savannah Fire Department* (Savannah, Ga.: Firemen's Relief Fund Assoc., 1906). The other event that residents feared as much as if not more than a fire was a slave revolt.

2. For accounts of the fire, see *Savannah Daily Morning News* (hereafter cited as *DMN*), April 12, 13, 17, and 19, 1852.

3. For Basil Lamar's family, see Harold Dihel LeMar, *History of the Lamar or Lemar Family in America* (Omaha, Neb.: Cockle, 1941), 93–95; Cazenove Lamar Miller Helm, "The Record of My Ancestry, The Frank H. Miller Family, 1972," Special Collections and Institution Archives, Augusta University, Augusta, Collection 94–10, Box 2. Basil's activities were deduced from the assets he owned at his death on November 5, 1827. Will of Basil Lamar, Probate Record Books, Richmond County, Book 2 (1798–1839), 272–73, Richmond County Courthouse, Augusta, Ga. For the Steam Boat Company charter and history, see Charles Colcock Jones Jr. and Salem Dutcher, *Memorial History of Augusta, Georgia: From Its Settlement in 1735 to the Close of the Eighteenth Century* (Syracuse, N.Y.: D. Mason, 1890), 469–74.

4. No public schools existed in Augusta in the early 1800s. If Gazaway Lamar went to a private institution, it might have been the Richmond Academy. For his job as an assistant bank clerk, see *Milledgeville Reflector*, December 2, 1817. For

his job as an agent for the Steam Boat Company, see *Augusta Chronicle* (hereafter cited as *AC*), July 22, 1818, and February 20, 1819.

5. For notices of Lamar as a consignee, see *Columbia Museum and Savannah Daily Gazette*, February 10 and April 15, 1820. For announcement of the partnership, see ibid., October 21, 1820, and *AC*, November 27, 1820. For the dissolution, see *AC*, May 28, 1823.

6. For marriage date, see Helm, "Record of My Ancestry," Collection 94–10, Box 2. Jane Creswell was the daughter of Robert Creswell, who moved to Augusta in 1795 and became a member of the first Augusta City Council in 1798. See *AC*, March 22, 1935. In marrying Jane, Gazaway gained five brothers-in-law and sisters-in-law. He developed business relationships with the husbands of two of Jane's sisters: John Phinizy, who married Martha Creswell, and William Sims, who married Ann Creswell.

7. For Lamar's commercial activities, see *Savannah Daily Georgian* (hereafter cited as *SG*), April 4, May 6, September 28, and November 17, 1824. For shipping agent activities, see ibid., November 12, 1824, and April 7, 1825. For the *Enterprise*, see ibid., December 9, 1825. For freight services to Macon and Milledgeville, see *Savannah Republican* (hereafter cited as *SR*), September 22, 1825.

8. For Planter's Bank, see *SG*, December 20, 1825. For the Bank of Macon and the Mechanic's Bank of Augusta, see *AC*, October 18, 1826, and *SG*, July 16, 1831.

9. Chatham County Superior Court Deeds, Microfilm Rolls 2P, 446, 452, 455, and 2R, 483, Chatham County Courthouse, Savannah, Ga.

10. Alexander Crosby Brown, "The *John Randolph*: America's First Commercially Successful Iron Steamboat," *GHQ* 36 (March 1852): 32–45. Lamar convinced Congress to lift the import duty on iron, which saved him about $4,000. *SG*, February 12 and August 28, 1834.

11. For the launch of the *John Randolph*, see *SG*, July 10, 1834. In February 1834 Lamar became one of nine members of the Corresponding Committee of the State Rights Association of Chatham County. See *SG*, February 18, 1834. That September he ran for city alderman on the State Rights ticket. Although he lost, he remained devoted to the agenda and one of its main principles: the right of nullification. *SG*, September 3, 1834. For Lamar's belief in nullification, see *New York Times* (hereafter cited as *NYT*), January 28, 1866.

12. *Acts of the General Assembly of the State of Georgia Passed in November and December 1835* (Milledgeville, Ga.: John A. Cuthbert, 1836), 271–75; Jones and Dutcher, *Memorial History of Augusta*, 474–76.

13. *SG*, December 30, 1835, January 9 and March 29, 1836.

14. Minutes of City Council (1832–1837), City Hall, Savannah, 327–28.

15. Richmond County Superior Court Deeds, Book Y, 509–22, Richmond County Courthouse, Augusta, Georgia. Lamar sold a one-seventh interest in the bridge to Paul Fitzsimons. Gazaway Bugg Lamar daybook 1836–1848, Vol. 1, G. B. Lamar Papers, GHS (hereafter cited as G. B. Lamar daybook), 165. During

this period Lamar also served as a director of the Savannah Insurance and Trust Company, which specialized in fire insurance and exchange transactions with other banks. *SG,* June 11, 1838.

16. For Gazaway's payment to A. Bolmar, see G. B. Lamar daybook, 176. For Gazaway and Charles's stay in Virginia, see G. B. Lamar to M. B. Lamar, September 30, 1840, in Adam Gulick Jr., ed., *The Papers of Mirabeau Buonaparte Lamar,* 6 vols. (Austin, Tex.: A. C. Baldwin, 1921), 3:455. Each page in Gazaway Lamar's daybook from mid-1839 to mid-1840 is headed with the location "Savannah," indicating that he kept residences there and Alexandria during this time. A newspaper reported that Gazaway and Charles, after the sinking of the *Pulaski,* were taken to the house of a Mr. Cazeneau [Cazenove] near Wilmington to recover, and during the following year, Gazaway returned to marry Harriet, the man's daughter. As there are many inaccuracies in this account, one cannot be certain if this is how Gazaway met Harriet. *New York News* as reprinted in the *Baltimore Sun,* January 5, 1866. For Gazaway's payment to Hallowell's School, see G. B. Lamar daybook, 223, 225.

17. *SG,* June 8, 1841, and December 3, 1844.

18. For Charles at Charlottesville, see G. B. Lamar daybook, 266. For the grocery business, see *SG,* September 21, 1841, and December 11, 1842. For towing services, see *SG,* January 3, 1844. For dissolution of the grocery inventory, see *SG,* February 21, 1844.

19. For commission merchant, see *SG,* March 21 and June 25, 1845. For trip to Liverpool, see Passenger Lists, *American and Commercial Daily Advertiser* (Baltimore), June 20, 1844, and the *New York Spectator* (hereafter cited as *NYS*), September 28, 1844.

20. In December 1845 Gazaway advertised that he would soon leave the state. See *SG,* December 16, 1845. He and Harriet would have two more daughters, Harriet and Annie. LeMar, *History of the Lamar or Lemar Family,* 112–13. Anthony died in 1862 at the age of eighteen and Annie in 1870 at the age of twenty-four, both from unspecified illnesses.

21. Charles, at age twenty-two, took over the responsibility of paying taxes on much of Gazaway's Savannah property, including the Eastern Wharves and buildings, the family house on Broughton and Habersham, sixteen slaves, a carriage, saddle horses, and dogs. Tax Digests, Savannah, Georgia, microfilm 1844–1848, drawer 72, Box 2, Municipal Records, Georgia Archives. The deed of sale for the wharves was not recorded until May 1855. Chatham County Superior Court Deeds, microfilm Roll 3Q-511, Savannah. For the description of the cotton press, see *DMN,* April 19, 1850. For plank roads, see *DMN,* June 7, 1851, and March 17, 1852. For steamship agent, see *DMN,* January 2, 1854. For commission agent, see *DMN,* June 13, 1854.

22. Born in 1793, John Cochran Nicoll trained as a lawyer and served in many prestigious positions, including representative in the Georgia legislature, mayor of Savannah, judge of the superior court of the state of Georgia, and, starting

in 1839, judge of the U.S. district court. Warren Grice, "The Confederate States Court," *GHQ* 9 (Summer 1925): 144n27. Caro, as Charles's wife was known, gave birth to Eliza Anderson on January 12, 1847, Jane Cresswell on March 14, 1848, and William Sims on July 24, 1850. The ages of Charles Lamar's daughters are taken from the Lamar family Bible as supplied by a descendant of Charles Lamar. In 1852 his fourteen-month-old son William Sims Lamar died in Brooklyn, New York, while the family visited Gazaway. *DMN*, October 13, 1852.

23. For the rifle club, see *SG*, January 7, 1845, and February 25, 1846. For horse racing, see *DMN*, March 22, 1848. For health officer, see *SR*, May 21, 1850.

24. For Georgia Hussars, see *Roll of Officers and Members of the Georgia Hussars* (Savannah, Ga.: Morning News, 1906), 36. For parades, see *DMN*, February 22, 1853, and *Savannah Evening Journal*, May 3, 1853. For the Aquatic Club, see *DMN*, February 8 and December 6–7, 1853. For agricultural fairs, see *DMN*, October 19, 1852, and November 2, 1855.

25. For election results, see *DMN*, December 7, 1852. For the vote on black seamen, see Minutes of City Council (1853–1855), 61, and for the vote on Catholics, 87.

26. *DMN*, April 12, 13, and 17, 1852.

27. For the first case, see Minutes of City Council (1853–1855), 46, and Civil Minutes, Book No. 21 (January 1853–May 1855), Superior Court of Chatham County, Savannah, 89, 133, 199. The Minutes of City Council of May 5, 1853, mention the first charge of assault and battery but do not state the name of the man attacked. No reports of the incident were published in the local newspapers. For the second case, see Civil Minutes, Book No. 21 (January 1853–May 1855), Superior Court of Chatham County, Savannah, 260, 303. The minutes do not provide the name of the person assaulted.

28. For resignation from the militia, see *Roll of Officers and Members of the Georgia Hussars*, 36. For Gazaway's criticisms, see G. B. Lamar to C. A. L. Lamar, December 28, 1854, January 6 and 9, 1855, G. B. Lamar Estate copy correspondence December 1854–1860, 1860–1878, Vol. 19, G. B. Lamar Papers, GHS (hereafter cited as G. B. Lamar Estate letter book).

CHAPTER 4. "I Have No Fears of the Consequences"

1. *Easton (Md.) Star*, September 16, 1851.

2. For early U.S. concerns about English or French control of Cuba, see Basil Rauch, *American Interest in Cuba: 1848–1855* (New York: Columbia University Press, 1948), 11–47; Lester D. Langley, "Slavery, Reform, and American Policy in Cuba, 1823–1878," *Revista de Historia de America* 65/66 (January–December 1968): 72–73; Thomas M. Leonard, *James K. Polk: A Clear and Unquestionable Destiny* (Wilmington, Del.: Scholarly Resources, 2001), 183; Robert Granville Caldwell, *The Lopez Expeditions to Cuba, 1848–1851* (Princeton, N.J.: Princeton University Press, 1915), 28–29.

3. Rauch, *American Interest in Cuba*, 16.

4. Because of incomplete or nonexistent records, it is difficult to obtain accurate statistics on the number of Africans imported into Cuba, especially after 1820 when the trade became illegal. Several historians have come up with estimates. Particularly helpful is D. R. Murray, "Statistics of the Slave Trade to Cuba, 1790–1867," *Journal of Latin American Studies* 3 (November 1971): 131–49. According to customhouse records, 240,721 Africans were imported through Havana between 1790 and 1821, when the trade was legal. Afterward, Murray estimates 47,272 imports between 1821 and 1829 and another 107,438 between 1830 and 1838. He reports that the official Cuban census for 1841 presents a white population of 418,291, an enslaved population of 436,495, and a free colored population of 152,838.

5. For a letter requesting David Turnbull's recall, and Secretary of State for Foreign Affairs Lord Palmerston's reply, see Boston *Liberator* (hereafter cited as *BL*), October 28, 1842. See also Rauch, *American Interest in Cuba*, 38–40. In 1791 slaves revolted in the French colony of San Domingue (now Haiti). Several thousand whites were slaughtered and thousands more fled the island for safety, some to the United States. The uprising, which eventually led to the independence of San Domingue in 1804, instilled a fear in white southerners and Cubans that the same could happen to them.

6. For origins of the Havana Club, see Rauch, *American Interest in Cuba*, 51–52. Rauch explains that the planters were annexationists for economic reasons. They were joined by an unlikely ally, the liberals, who supported annexation for patriotic reasons—to overthrow colonial rule.

7. The president of the Cuban community in New York, known as the Cuban Council, was Cristobal Madan, who traveled frequently between New York and Havana and coordinated the efforts of the dissidents. Rauch, *American Interest in Cuba*, 51–52. For Polk's role and the attempt to purchase Cuba, see Leonard, *James K. Polk*, 184. The British denied having any intentions of annexing Cuba and accused the United States of extreme hypocrisy. See *The Times* (London) (hereafter cited as *LT*), December 14, 1852, as reprinted in *NYT*, January 3, 1853.

8. For the importance of Cuba to the South, see Ray Boussard, "Governor John A. Quitman and the Lopez Expeditions of 1851–1852," *Journal of Mississippi History* (hereafter cited as *JMH*) 28 (May 1966): 103–4.

9. *DMN*, May 27, 1850.

10. For the aborted uprising, see *New Orleans Delta*, July 23, 1848, as reported in *Boston Herald*, August 3, 1848. For meeting the Cuban community in New York, see Robert E. May, *Manifest Destiny's Underworld: Filibustering in Antebellum America* (Chapel Hill: University of North Carolina Press, 2002), 22; Rauch, *American Interest in Cuba*, 108–9.

11. See Ambrosio José Gonzales's obituary in the *Columbia (S.C.) State*, August 2, 1893.

12. See *Boston Daily Bee*, December 7, 1849. It is unclear whether Lopez and the men officially formed the junta before or after the Round Island affair. For the Round Island fiasco, see Boussard, "Governor John A. Quitman," 105–7; May, *Manifest Destiny's Underworld*, 22. For Commodore V. M. Randolph's threat to blockade the filibusters, see *Mississippi Free Trader*, September 5, 1849. For the Neutrality Act, see Caldwell, *Lopez Expeditions to Cuba*, 57.

13. For Sigur's relationship with Lopez, see *NYT*, November 5, 1851. For the Lopez-Quitman meeting, see J. F. H. Claiborne, *Life and Correspondence of John A. Quitman: Major-General, U.S.A., and Governor of the State of Mississippi* (New York: Harper & Brothers, 1860), 2:57–58; Boussard, "Governor John A. Quitman," 107–9.

14. For the text of the Cuban bonds, see *Alexandria (Va.) Gazette* (hereafter cited as *AG*), October 1, 1851. For notice from the Spanish minister and Taylor's order to stop the expedition, see *DMN*, May 23 and 25, 1850.

15. For the Cardenas expedition, see *DMN*, May 27, 28, 29, 1850; Caldwell, *Lopez Expeditions to Cuba*, 57–74.

16. For the three trials of Henderson, see *Trenton (N.J.) State Gazette*, December 28, 1850; *NYEP*, January 16, 1851; *Boston Daily Bee*, January 27, 1851; *New London (Conn.) Daily Chronicle*, January 29, 1851; *Mississippi Free Trader*, February 12 and March 19, 1851; *New Orleans Times-Picayune* (hereafter cited as *NOTP*), March 7, 1851. See also Boussard, "Governor John A. Quitman," 113–16.

17. A. J. Gonzales to M. B. Lamar, March 14, 1851, in Adam Gulick Jr., ed., *The Papers of Mirabeau B. Lamar*, 6 vols. (Austin, Tex.: A. C. Baldwin, *1921*), 4:282–4.

18. For Lopez's final invasion of Cuba, see the statement of Lieutenant Van Vechten in the Washington (D.C.) *Daily Union* (hereafter cited as *WDU*), September 17, 1851, as reprinted from the *New York Herald* (hereafter cited as *NYH*), and Caldwell, *Lopez Expeditions to Cuba*, 91–113. The rest of Lopez's men, captured in the final days of the assault, eventually were pardoned by the queen of Spain. For the movements in Florida to support Lopez, Antonio Rafael de la Cova, "Cuban Filibustering in Jacksonville in 1851," *Northeast Florida History Journal* 3 (1996): 16–34; *NOTP*, May 11, 1851.

19. For Order of the Lone Star, see *AG*, December 29, 1851, and August 27, 1852; *NYT*, March 13, 1855; Rauch, *American Interest in Cuba*, 228–39. Two Savannah divisions formed: Washington Division No. 2 and Angela Division No. 5. Daniel H. Stewart, Lamar's friend and future city and U.S. marshal, belonged to the Washington Division. *DMN*, September 8 and 13, October 22, and December 31, 1852; Gordon B. Smith, *History of the Georgia Militia, The Companies*, (Milledgeville, Ga.: Boyd, 2001), 4:325–27. For Gonzales's campaign to keep U.S. interest in Cuba alive, see *WDU*, September 24, 1852, and April 25, 1854.

20. In January 1854 Captain General Pezuela started instituting reforms. He liberated all *emancipados*—Africans who were captured on slave ships after 1835, when the last Spanish slave trade treaty was signed, but were still sold into slavery. He legalized the importation of African apprentices to Cuba. In March

1854 the Spanish government gave Pezuela the right to search plantations for smuggled slaves. The captain general even announced his intention to arm free blacks to help defend the island against attack. C. Stanley Urban, "The Abortive Quitman Filibustering Expedition, 1853–1855," *JMH* 18 (February 1956): 175–196; C. Stanley Urban, "The Africanization of Cuba Scare, 1853–1855," *Hispanic American Historical Review* 37 (February 1957): 29–45. While Pezuela frightened southerners, his actions were mocked as insincere by Jamaican planters, who wanted Cuba to end slavery so that the cost of raising sugar crops in both countries would be based on free labor. *NYT*, June 27, 1854. In late February 1854 another affair strained American-Spanish relations even further. Breaking the policy of allowing American merchant ships sailing from one U.S. port to another to stop in Havana without paying duties on their cargoes, Cuban authorities seized the *Black Warrior* and didn't release her until the owners paid a $6,000 fine. American businessmen and politicians both in the North and South were outraged over the violation of a long-standing commercial agreement. Henry Lorenzo Janes, "The Black Warrior Affair," *American Historical Review* 12 (January 1907): 280–98; *NYT*, May 29, 1854.

21. For Quitman and the Cuban Council coming to terms, see Urban, "Abortive Filibustering Expedition," 178–79. On May 30 the U.S. president made any future vote on accepting new slave territory into the Union more contentious by signing into law the Kansas-Nebraska Act. This act effectively repealed the Missouri Compromise of 1820 by splitting the Nebraska territory—all of which was north of the 36/30 line—in two and giving the new territories the right to vote on their status. This victory for the South came after a bitter debate that split Congress along sectional lines. Rauch, *American Interest in Cuba*, 286.

22. For Pierce's proclamation, see *WDU*, June 1, 1854. For posting bond, see Claiborne, *Life and Correspondence of John A. Quitman*, 2:196–206. President Pierce and Secretary of State William L. Marcy, still concerned about the British and French designs on Cuba and the Africanization of the island, asked the ministers to Spain, Great Britain, and France (Pierre Soule, James Buchanan, and John Y. Mason, respectively) to review the condition of affairs regarding the island. On October 18 they issued the Ostend Manifesto, which implied that the United States would be justified in taking the island by force if Spain refused to sell Cuba to the United States. As Pierce had made clear that America would only acquire the island by purchase, the report created anger and scorn in the cabinet and Marcy repudiated it. Sidney Webster, "Mr. Marcy, the Cuban Question and the Ostend Manifesto," *Political Science Quarterly* 8 (March 1893): 1–32.

23. John A. Quitman to C. A. L. Lamar, January 5, 1855, John Quitman Collection, Houghton Library, Special Collections, Harvard University, Cambridge, Mass.

24. C. A. L. Lamar to John Thrasher, February 25, 1855, Charles Lamar letter book 1855–1863, Vol. 24, G. B. Lamar Papers, GHS (hereafter cited as Slave-Trader's Letter-Book, GHS).

25. John Quitman to C. A. L. Lamar, January 5, 1855, John Quitman Collection; C. A. L. Lamar to John Thrasher, February 12, 1855, Slave-Trader's Letter-Book, GHS.

26. C. A. L. Lamar to John Thrasher, February 12, 1855, Slave-Trader's Letter-Book, GHS.

27. C. A. L. Lamar to John Thrasher, February 25, 1855, Slave-Trader's Letter-Book, GHS.

28. For de la Concha's declarations, see *WDNI*, February 26, 1855. For the failed plot, see *WDU*, June 1, 1855. For Quitman's resignation, see *Daily Illinois State Journal*, May 16, 1855, and *Daily Commercial Register* (Sandusky, Ohio), May 11, 1855.

29. C. A. L. Lamar to John A. Quitman, December 9, 1855, and December 4, 1856, Slave-Trader's Letter-Book, GHS; C. A. L. Lamar to Robert Toombs, December 4, 1856, ibid.

30. C. A. L. Lamar to Robert Toombs, January 12, 1857, ibid.

CHAPTER 5. "I Never Was So Hard Up in My Life"

1. G. B. Lamar to Charles Lamar, January 9 and 31, February 1, 14, and 22, 1855, and January 4, 1856, G. B. Lamar Estate letter book.

2. G. B. Lamar to Charles Lamar, January 25, 1855, G. B. Lamar letter book 1854–1858, V. 20, Box 15, G. B. Lamar Papers, GHS (hereafter cited as G. B. Lamar letter book). For Gazaway's financial statement, see G. B. Lamar to Charles Lamar, August 1, 1855, Box 1, Folder 4, G. B. Lamar Papers, UGA. For the deed of sale of the Eastern Wharves, Chatham County Superior Court Deeds, Roll 3Q-511.

3. For sending DeRosset to Savannah, see G. B. Lamar to Charles Lamar, November 19, 1855, G. B. Lamar letter book. Dates of birth of Charles's children are taken from the Lamar family Bible.

4. G. B. Lamar to Charles Lamar, November 30, 1855, and G. B. Lamar to Thomas B. Lamar, October 24, 1855, G. B. Lamar letter book. For election results, see *DMN*, October 2, 1855. For the platform of the American Party of Georgia, see *CC*, July 2, 1855.

5. Trowbridge was born in Vermont in 1816 and can be traced to Augusta as early as 1841. He and Charles shared a passion for horses, and both men had entrants at the Augusta track in January 1846. *AC*, January 29, 1846. For Trowbridge's dealing in slaves, see *AC*, December 24, 1841, August 23, 1843, and September 29, 1843. For James Gardner's background, see Russell K. Brown, "Augusta's Other Voice: James Gardner and the *Constitutionalist*," *GHQ* 85 (Winter 2001): 592–607. For problems with the mines, see Nelson Trowbridge to James Gardner, December 19, 1855, Box 2, Folder 37, James Gardner Papers, Georgia Archives, Morrow (hereafter cited as Gardner Papers). For Charles's investment in the mines, see Lamar to Gardner, April 6, 1859, Box 2, Folder 27, Gardner Papers.

6. G. B. Lamar to Charles Lamar, October 22, 1855, G. B. Lamar letter book. During this time Charles also served as a director on two bank boards, and sold insurance and portable gas machines. See *DMN*, February 16, May 12, and August 5, 1856, and January 3, 1857. At night Charles attended public meetings to raise funds for slave-holding settlers in Kansas. *DMN*, March 26, 1856.

7. Nelson Trowbridge to James Gardner, January 21, 1857, Box 2, Folder 37, Gardner Papers.

8. C. A. L. Lamar to James Gardner, February 28, 1857, Box 2, Folder 27, Gardner Papers.

9. G. B. Lamar to Charles Lamar, October 14, 1856, G. B. Lamar letter book.

10. Lamar was not a delegate to the Savannah meeting, but he undoubtedly knew of its proceedings. The proponents of the slave trade continued to press the issue for the next three conventions. For the 1855 Southern Commercial Convention, see *Debow's Review* 18 (May 1855): 628. For the 1856 Savannah convention, see ibid., 22 (January 1857): 89, 91–92, and (February 1857): 216–24; Barton J. Bernstein, "Southern Politics and the Attempts to Reopen the African Slave Trade," *Journal of Negro History* (hereafter cited as *JNH*) 51 (January 1966): 24–29; Herbert Wender, "The Southern Commercial Convention at Savannah, 1856," *GHQ* 15 (Summer 1931): 173–91.

11. For Adams's speech, see *NYT*, November 28, 1856.

12. For the origins of the use of Africans as slaves by Portugal and Spain and the start of the Atlantic slave trade, see *United States' Telegraph* (Washington, D.C.), September 6, 1833, and Massachusetts Spy (Worcester), December 17, 1834; for the distribution of slave imports to the Western Hemisphere, see Philip D. Curtin, *The Atlantic Slave Trade: A Census* (Madison: University of Wisconsin Press, 1969), 88–89; and the Emory University Trans-Atlantic Slave Trade Database at slavevoyages.org. During the era of the Atlantic slave trade, legal and illegal, Curtin estimates a total of 9,566,000 Africans landed in the West, with 427,000 or 4.5 percent going to British North America and the United States, while the Emory Slave Trade Database puts the numbers at 10,703,000 and 389,000 or 3.6 percent, respectively. The overwhelming majority disembarked in Brazil: 38 percent according to Curtin, and 45 percent estimated by Emory.

13. For the origins of British involvement in the Atlantic slave trade, see W. E. B. Du Bois, *The Suppression of the African Slave Trade* (Baton Rouge: Louisiana State University Press, 1896), 2–5. For the first landing of slaves in Virginia, see ibid., 17. (Other sources mark the year as 1820. See *United States' Telegraph* [Washington, D.C.], September 6, 1833). For early slave-trade statistics to North America, see "The African Slave Trade," *Debow's Review* 18 (January 1855): 16–17. The estimate of slave imports of 250,000 before the American Revolution is taken from the count of 229,000 imported by 1770 and 263,000 by 1790. See also Curtin, *Atlantic Slave Trade*, 72, 87. The Emory University Trans-Atlantic Slave Trade Database puts the number at 280,000. The last cargo of slaves before the Revolution landed at Savannah in July 1775. James A. McMillin, *The Final Victims:*

Foreign Slave Trade to North America, 1783–1810 (Columbia: University of South Carolina Press, 2004), 5. During the war the British army commander in America, General Henry Clinton, issued the Philipsburg Proclamation offering bondsmen freedom if they escaped to British lines. The royal governor of Virginia, the Earl of Dunmore, issued a similar proclamation in 1775 to the slaves of Virginia. For slave losses during the war, see McMillin, *Final Victims*, 8. The British resettled some of the freed slaves to Nova Scotia, and many of them eventually moved to the British colony of Sierra Leone in Africa. For resumption of the trade, see Du Bois, *Suppression of the African Slave Trade*, 50. For the number of imports, see McMillin, *Final Victims*, 48.

14. *Notes of Debates in the Federal Convention of 1787 Reported by James Madison* (Athens: Ohio University Press, 1966), 502–8.

15. As of October 1, 1798, with the passage of the Georgia state constitution nine years before the federal ban, the slave trade to the United States had been outlawed due to individual state action, although none had a navy to combat it. DuBois, *Suppression of the African Slave Trade*, 51–52, Appendix A, 222–29, and Appendix B, 230–40. For South Carolina legislation against importation and acts extending the ban, see David J. McCord, ed., *The Statutes at Large of South Carolina* (Columbia, S.C.: A. S. Johnston, 1840), 7:431–32, 433, 434, 436. For the Georgia state constitution, Article IV, Section 11, see http://georgiainfo.galileo.usg .edu/topics/government/related_article/constitutions/georgia-constitution-of -1798 (accessed January 10, 2014). For the number of slaves imported from 1804 through 1807, see "The African Slave Trade," *Debow's Review* 18 (January 1855): 17. For the states of embarkation of the slave ships, see *DMN*, January 13, 1859. Of the 202 arrivals in Charleston, seventy ships were British, sixty-one embarked from Charleston, and fifty-nine embarked from Rhode Island.

16. Fearful of an influx of free blacks and mixed-race individuals fleeing Saint-Domingue (Haiti) after Napoleon retook the island from black revolutionaries, Congress passed the Act of 1803. This prohibited the captain of any ship from entering any U.S. port where slave importation previously had been abolished with any blacks who were not residents, citizens, or registered seamen of the United States. Still, some made it to the United States. For the acts of 1794, 1800, and 1803, see http://avalon.law.yale.edu/subject_menus/slmenu.asp (accessed April 25, 2017).

17. Matthew E. Mason, "Congress Debates Prohibiting the Atlantic Slave Trade to the United States, 1806–1807," *Journal of the Early Republic* 20 (Spring 2000): 59–81. The most contentious issue concerned the disposition of Africans illegally landed in the country. The sides finally agreed to turn over the Africans to a person appointed by the state to receive them—a victory for the South.

18. For the British abolition of the slave trade, see Louis Taylor Merrill, "The English Campaign for Abolition of the Slave Trade," *JNH* 30 (October 1945): 382–99.

19. Thomas, *Slave Trade*, 575–79.

20. For a discussion of British policy against the trade, see Bernard H. Nelson, "The Slave Trade as a Factor in British Foreign Policy: 1815–1862," *JNH* 27 (April 1942): 195–98. All of the treaties are referenced in Lewis Hertslet, comp., *Treaties and Conventions and Reciprocal Regulations at Present Subsisting between Great Britain and Foreign Powers* (London: Henry Butterworth, 1835–64): British treaty of 1817 with Portugal, 2:81–93; Treaty of 1815, 79–80; Treaty of 1817 with Spain, 2:273–85 (this treaty was replaced by another dated June 28, 1835; see 4:440–49); Treaties of 1814 and 1818 with the Netherlands, 3:270–71, 272–84; Treaty of 1826 with Brazil, 3:33. See also Wilbur Devereux Jones, "The Origins and Passage of Lord Aberdeen's Act," *Hispanic American Historical Review* 42 (November 1962): 507–9. For the treaty of 1831 with France, see Hertslet, *Treaties*, 4:112–21. In 1815 Napoleon outlawed the slave trade from any port in France or its colonies. On November 30, 1831, the British and French entered into a treaty agreeing to the mutual right of search, but only in certain waters along the African coast. In 1845 Great Britain and France signed a treaty replacing the prior treaties. This document maintained the right of search and stipulated that each country would maintain a naval force of at least twenty-six cruisers on the coast of Africa. The treaty had a term of ten years and was not renewed. Hertslet, *Treaties*, 7:338–42.

21. For treaties with African tribes, see Hertslet, *Treaties*, 12:2–13, 31–52.

22. For a discussion of the British navy impressing British-born crew members of U.S. vessels in the early nineteenth century, and that policy's relationship to the slave trade, see *NYT*, May 20, 1858. For the slave trade acts of 1818, 1819, and 1820, see Du Bois, *Suppression of the African Slave Trade*, 118–23. For the effectiveness of the American ships on the African coast, see the report from the committee on the suppression of the slave trade in *Boston Repertory*, April 20, 1822.

23. For Parliament's efforts to abolish slavery in the British colonies, see Izhak Gross, "The Abolition of Negro Slavery and British Parliamentary Politics," *Historical Journal* 23 (March 1980): 63–85. Slavery in England was abolished in 1772 as a result of a court ruling. Daniel J. Hulsebosch, "Nothing but Liberty: 'Somerset's Case' and the British Empire," *Law and History Review* 24 (Fall 2006): 647–57.

24. The Portuguese so openly violated their treaty of 1817 that in 1839 the British Parliament passed an act that authorized their navy to seize Portuguese ships fitted out for the slave trade and bring them to British vice admiralty courts instead of mixed commission courts. The pressure led to the two countries signing a new, stricter treaty in 1842. "Failure of Efforts to Suppress the Slave Trade," *African Repository* 16 (January 1840): 7–9. For the new treaty with Portugal, see Hertslet, *Treaties*, 4:625–35; Leslie M. Bethell, "Britain, Portugal and the Suppression of the Brazilian Slave Trade: The Origins of Lord Palmerston's Act of 1839," *English Historical Review* 80 (October 1965): 761–84. On June 28, 1835, Great Britain and Spain signed another treaty in which the latter pledged to abolish the trade totally and finally in all parts of the world and gave both nations the mutual right of search. Hertslet, *Treaties*, 4:440–60.

25. It was illegal for a ship to have two sets of "papers"—especially the ship register, which established the nationality of the vessel, and stamped clearance papers from the port collector of the last port called. One set was obtained illegally, usually through forgery or bribery. A captain might proceed on his slave voyage with just U.S. papers, as most of the cruisers were British and French and wouldn't usually stop any ship flying the U.S. flag.

The slave trade was dominated by Spanish and Portuguese men who ran clandestine companies in New York, New Orleans, Havana, and various Brazilian cities. These people needed U.S. ships with related papers and U.S. flags. Accordingly, they recruited U.S. citizens—preferably naturalized—to purchase the ships.

For ships departing from a U.S. port, the sham American owner, who usually went as the captain on the voyage, filed a manifest with the port collector and a request for clearance to Africa. Although there was an active trade with Africa for products such as palm oil and various nuts, any commercial ship headed there would draw the interest of the port collector, and the manifest would be carefully scrutinized for items used in the slave trade. However, accommodating custom inspectors and other port officials still approved many such ships.

Often, ship captains of slavers, to avoid suspicion, requested clearance to a port in Cuba or Brazil and then sailed directly to Africa, or they traveled to the destination port where they outfitted the slaver. (For a list of eighty-five slavers flying under the U.S. flag from February 1858 to July 1860 and their port of embarkation, see *NYEP*, July 28, 1860.) Regardless of the port of embarkation, these ships eventually went to Africa, picked up their human cargoes, and returned to Brazil or Cuba.

Slave trade syndicates in Brazil were greatly aided by American-issued documents called "sea letters." The U.S. government determined that Americans in Brazil who wanted to buy a ship from another American shouldn't have to travel all the way to the United States to obtain a new ship register. So the American consul in the Brazilian city, usually São Paulo or Rio de Janeiro, was authorized to issue sea letters, which served as temporary registers and allowed the ship to travel to any port, including one in Africa. Thus, a Brazilian slave trader could pay an American captain to purchase a ship from another American and go on a slave run under U.S. colors. The trader might charter the ship from the American but keep him on as captain and proceed on the trip. Slave traders in Cuba were aided by dishonest captains general and, in some years, lenient American consuls.

For a description of slavers leaving New York for Africa, see *Debow's Review* 23 (July 1857): 51–54, and *Debow's Review* 18 (February 1855): 223–28. For an example of a slaver leaving New Orleans, see *Debow's Review* 25 (August 1858): 241–42. For slave ships clearing from Brazil and the use of sea letters, see *Boston Recorder*, January 23, 1851; Lawrence F. Hill, "The Abolition of the African Slave Trade to Brazil," *Hispanic American Historical Review* 11 (May 1931): 169–97; *Boston Daily Bee*, December 25, 1849; *NYS*, January 23, 1851. For the slave trade from

Cuba, see Frederick C. Drake, ed., "Secret History of the Slave Trade to Cuba Written by an American Naval Officer, Robert Wilson Schufeldt, 1861," *JNH* 55 (July 1970): 218–35; *NYEP*, February 7, 1861.

26. Lieutenant Charles Fitzgerald of the British brig *Buzzard* shocked New Yorkers when he escorted two slavers, the *Eagle* and the *Clara*, into New York harbor in June 1839. Two weeks later, another British cruiser guided the *Wyoming* into the harbor, followed in two months by a British man-of-war herding in the *Butterfly* and the *Catharine*. New York district attorney Benjamin F. Butler did not try the *Eagle* and *Clara* cases because the ships were owned by Spaniards. Lieutenant Fitzgerald escorted the ships to Africa for hearings. Butler did confiscate the three other ships, but all the prisoners jumped bail. See *NYCA*, November 15, 1839; Warren S. Howard, *American Slavers and the Federal Law, 1837–1862* (Berkeley: University of California Press, 1963), 37–39; Thomas, *Atlantic Slave Trade*, 661. The British pursued their diplomatic offensive and hosted a slave trade convention in London in December 1841 with four other nations—France, Austria, Russia, and Prussia, the last three of which had little to do with the odious commerce. The United States was invited but didn't attend and pressured France not to ratify the resulting Quintuple Treaty, which granted a mutual right of search to the signatories. For Minister Lewis Cass's letter to French minister of foreign affairs M. Guizot regarding his objections to the treaty, see *NYS*, June 8, 1842. See also Robert Vincent Remini, *Daniel Webster: The Man and His Time* (New York: W. W. Norton, 1997), 544–55.

27. Remini, *Daniel Webster*, 560–62.

28. For the mutiny and trip to Long Island, see *Hampshire (Mass.) Gazette*, September 4, 1839; for a discussion of the legal issues involved, see *New York Emancipator* (hereafter cited as *NYE*), September 12, 1839; for the decision handed down by the U.S. District Court in Connecticut, see *AG*, January 18, 1840; for the Supreme Court decision, see *WDNI*, March 15, 1841, as reprinted in *NYCA*, March 16, 1841; for John Adams's argument to the Supreme Court, see *NYS*, March 20, 1841.

29. For the mutiny, the events in Nassau, and the return to New Orleans, see *NYE*, January 7, 1842. For the ruling, see *NYCA*, May 24, 1842. For Webster's letter to Lord Ashburton, see *WDNI*, November 26, 1842.

30. For a description of the Brazilian slave trade in the 1820s, see Dinizulu Gene Tinnie, "The Slaving Brig Henriqueta and Her Evil Sisters: A Case Study in the 19th-Century Illegal Slave Trade to Brazil," *Journal of African American History* 93 (Fall 2008): 509–31. For commentary on the Brazilian slave trade in the early to mid-1840s, see *Trenton State Gazette*, December 3, 1847. Edward Kent, U.S. consul at Rio de Janeiro from 1849 to 1853, described a major reason for the large importation of slaves in a letter to Secretary of State Daniel Webster. "But there are facts not generally known . . . one, and the most important, is, that it has been found here more profitable to exhaust slaves by long continued and severe labor for eight or ten years, and then supply their places by new im-

portations, than to raise children. . . . The mortality rate among adult slaves and children is truly astonishing. So long as the trade continues, there will be a very large demand annually to supply the void made by death and disability alone." Edward Kent to Daniel Webster, April 10, 1852, *Message from the President of the United States*, 34 Congress, 1 Session, Senate Exec. Doc. No. 99 (Washington, D.C.: A. O. P. Nicholson, 1856) (hereafter cited as *Message from the President*, No. 99), 74–75. For the Aberdeen Act of 1845, see Jones, "Origins and Passage of Lord Aberdeen's Act," 508–18; Leslie Bethell, "The Mixed Commissions for the Suppression of the Transatlantic Slave Trade in the Nineteenth Century," *Journal of African History* 7 (1966): 91–92.

31. For Brazil banning the trade, see *New London (Conn.) Daily Chronicle*, December 2, 1850; Jane Elizabeth Adams, "The Abolition of the Brazilian Slave Trade," *JNH* 10 (October 1925): 607–37; Dale T. Graden, "An Act 'Even of Public Security': Slave Resistance, Social Tensions, and the End of the International Slave Trade to Brazil, 1835–1856," *Hispanic American Historical Review* 76 (May 1996): 249–82. For slave importations to Brazil, see *Report from the Select Committee on Slave Trade Treaties*, ordered by the House of Commons to be printed August 12, 1853, iv.

32. For slave imports to Cuba, see Curtin, *Atlantic Slave Trade*, 234. For the decrease in slave trade activity due to declining coffee exports and the transfer of slaves to sugar fields, see *LT*, June 1, 1850. For testimonials to Concha's honesty, see *The Thirteenth Annual Report of the American and Foreign Anti-Slavery Society, 1853* (New York: American & Foreign Anti-Slavery Society, 1853), 168. For the reduction of the West Africa Squadron, *Message of the President of the United States*, 35 Congress, 1 Session, Senate Exec. Doc., No. 49: 28 (hereafter cited as *Message from the President*, No. 49), 28.

33. Rauch claims there were 70,000 cholera deaths in 1854. Basil Rauch, *American Interest in Cuba: 1848–1855* (New York: Columbia University Press, 1948), 277–78. An article in *Debow's Review* put the number at 20,000. "Cuba," *Debow's Review* 18 (February 1855): 164. For observations on the increase in the slave trade to Cuba, see John F. Crampton to W. L. Marcy, May 27, 1854, *Message from the President*, No. 99, 56–57.

34. For British accusations of Spanish officials in Cuba, see "Suppression of Slave Trades," *African Repository* 30 (December 1854): 370–71; *NYT*, June 27, 1854. For Spain's dependence on Cuba, see "Cuba," *Debow's Review* 18 (February 1855): 164.

35. For the slave trade flourishing in New York, see *Albany (N.Y.) Evening Journal*, January 22, 1855, and July 12, 1856; *NYH*, July 14, 1856, and April 1, 1857. See also a reprint from the *New York Journal of Commerce* (hereafter cited as *NYJC*) titled "The Slave Traffic," *African Repository* (August 1856): 241–42. For foreigners buying U.S. ships for the trade, see Crampton to Marcy, February 16, 1854, *Message from the President*, No. 99, 56. For a Portuguese syndicate operating in New York, see Howard, *American Slavers and the Federal Law*, 49–50.

36. For reports of British warships harassing U.S. merchant ships in the waters around Cuba, see *NYCA*, May 20, 1858, and *Message from the President of the United States*, 36 Congress, 2 Session, House of Representatives Exec. Doc. No. 7, 132–34. For the increase in vessels flying the U.S. flag, see Lord Napier to Lewis Cass, December 24, 1857, *Message from the President*, No. 49, 11–16. During this period the British said they had a right of visit that allowed them to establish a ship's status by examining its papers. If the captain could not prove its U.S. bona fides, then the British navy could search and seize it. For a discussion of the rights of search and visit, see *NYT*, May 20, 1858.

37. C. A. L. Lamar to R. L. Gamble, June 20, 1859, Slave-Trader's Letter-Book, GHS. For Theodore Johnston's activities in the 1850s, including ownership of a plantation, see *NOTP*, January 3, 1852, and February 24, 1858. According to a report in the *NYT* of September 10, 1858, he was one of the largest slave traders in the city of New Orleans. For Gazaway Lamar's early association with Cheever, see G. B. Lamar to W. W. Cheever, January 25, 1855, G. B. Lamar letter book. Roger Lawson Gamble II, born in 1829, practiced law in Louisville, Jefferson County, Georgia. He was the captain of the Jefferson County Guards. In 1848 Charles Lamar sailed to New York on the same ship as R. L. Gamble Jr. and probably met him during the five-day trip. *CC*, August 7, 1848. For Gamble's background, see Marion Little Durden, *A History of St. George Parish, Colony of Georgia, Jefferson County, State of Georgia* (Swainsboro, Ga.: Magnolia, 1983), 39, 71, 206. Dr. Eldridge C. Williamson II, originally of Jefferson County, settled in Bibb County, participated in state politics, and supported secession. For his political activity, see *AC*, July 20, 1849. For his support of secession, see *Macon Telegraph* (hereafter cited as *MT*), December 11, 1860.

38. For the *Rawlins* calling at Savannah on a coffee run, see the *Boston Traveler* (hereafter cited as *BT*), October 10, 1856.

39. For the ship's arrival in Savannah after Lamar's purchase, see *BT*, July 6, 1857; for its manifest, see *DMN*, July 17, 1857; for the ship's seizure, see *CC*, July 16, 1857. John Boston was a longtime Savannah resident and businessman before being appointed collector of the Port of Savannah in March 1853. He knew Lamar well as they both served on the Chatham County Fair Committee and the committee for the sale of stock of the Merchants and Planters Bank. Also, Charles regularly applied to Boston for clearance of his ships. For Boston's background, see *SG*, January 25, 1842, and June 28, 1847; *DMN*, May 8, 1850, November 2 and December 22, 1855.

40. C. A. L. Lamar to Howell Cobb, July 27, 1857, Slave-Trader's Letter-Book, GHS, emphasis in original. Cobb (1815–68) was seventeen years younger than Gazaway, and nine years older than Charles.

41. Howell Cobb to John Boston, July 16, 1857, Record Group 4-2-46, File 2, Howell Cobb Folder, Georgia Archives, Morrow, Ga.; *DMN*, July 18, 1857.

42. For Stewart's involvement in committees, see *DMN*, March 26 and November 15, 1856. Stewart was appointed U.S. marshal for the district of Georgia in

June 1855. *DMN*, June 20, 1855. He also served as city marshal from 1849 to 1851 and again from 1857 to 1859.

43. C. A. L. Lamar to Howell Cobb, July 27, 1857, Slave-Trader's Letter-Book, GHS.

44. Ibid., emphasis in original.

45. For the *Rawlins* in Funchal, see Consular Letters, Funchal, "Quarterly Account of American Trade—Return of the Arrival and Departure of American Vessels and Statement of Fees Received," T205, Roll No. 3, National Archives, Washington, D.C.

46. C. A. L. Lamar to Nelson Trowbridge, November 5, 1857, Slave-Trader's Letter-Book, GHS, emphasis in original.

47. Ibid.

CHAPTER 6. "An Expedition to the Moon Would Have Been Equally Sensible"

1. C. A. L. Lamar to G. B. Lamar, October 31, 1857, Slave-Trader's Letter-Book, GHS, emphasis in original.

2. Ibid.

3. For the flour mill and bank director, see *DMN*, September 4, 1857, and January 13, 1857. For Charles's recommendation to found the bank, see C. A. L. Lamar to Thomas Barrett, January 6, 1856, Slave-Trader's Letter-Book, GHS. For the agricultural fair, see *DMN*, October 27, 1857.

4. C. A. L. Lamar to L. Viana, December 26, 1857, Slave-Trader's Letter-Book, GHS, emphasis in original.

5. C. A. L. Lamar to James Gardner, January 18 and 20, 1858, Box 2, Folder 27, Gardner Papers. An endorser of a note guarantees payment of it.

6. Ibid., January 20, 1858. Although the nature of the deal with Lewin could not be determined, Gazaway Lamar introduced the man to Charles. He told his son, "Mr. Lewin will send you an order. He is not wealthy but he is honest." G. B. Lamar to C. A. L. Lamar, January 9, 1855, G. B. Lamar Estate letter book.

7. C. A. L. Lamar to James Gardner, January 25, 1858, Box 2, Folder 27, Gardner Papers. In the early 1850s Major Henry C. Wayne of Savannah, son of associate Supreme Court justice James Moore Wayne, petitioned Secretary of War Jefferson Davis to fund the importation of camels to determine if they were adaptable to the harsh terrain of Texas for military purposes. In 1855 a grant of $30,000 was approved and Wayne began shipping camels from the Middle East to Texas, but the experiment eventually died. Charles never mentioned the camels again. A description of the camel experiment can be found in the e-book by Henry C. Wayne, David D. Porter et al., *Camels for Texas* (Seattle: Mockingbird Books, 2011).

8. For the loan from the Marine Bank, see Superior Court of Chatham County, Civil Minutes, Book 24, September 1859–November 1862, 29. For the loan from Merchants and Planters Bank, see ibid., 400.

9. Charles Lamar to Caro Lamar, January 10, 1858, Charles Lafayette Lamar

Papers, Georgia Archives, Morrow, Ga. (hereafter cited as Charles Lamar Papers, G.A.).

10. For instructions, C. A. L. Lamar to Captain Wm. Ross Postell, February 2, 1858, Slave-Trader's Letter-Book, GHS. For Postell's salary, see C. A. L. Lamar to N. C. Trowbridge or Theodore Johnston, February 2, 1858, ibid. For the departure of the ship, see *NOTP*, February 12, 1858.

11. C. A. L. Lamar to James Gardner, February 27 and March 3, 1858, Box 2, Folder 27, Gardner Papers.

12. For sugar production of the British colonies in the West Indies, see Noel Deerr, *The History of Sugar* (London: Chapman & Hall, 1949), 1:193–203. For freed slaves leaving the plantations, see G. W. Roberts, "Immigration of Africans into the British Caribbean," *Population Studies* 7 (March 1954): 235. For planters importing East Indian workers, see Deerr, *History of Sugar*, 2:388–90. For the ban on Indian emigration to the West Indies, see Roberts, "Immigration of Africans," 237n4.

13. Sierra Leone was founded by the British in 1787 to relocate displaced blacks living in London and Nova Scotia who had joined the British cause during the American Revolution. For the operations of the mixed commission courts, see Christopher Fyfe, *A History of Sierra Leone* (London: Oxford University Press, 1962), 137–38; Leslie Bethell, "The Mixed Commissions for the Suppression of the Transatlantic Slave Trade in the Nineteenth Century," *Journal of African History* 7 (1966): 79–93. A few slave ships were captured by British cruisers in the seas around the West Indies, and the Africans were delivered directly to British colonies. Also, mixed commission courts operated in Havana and Rio de Janeiro, and Africans liberated by them were sent to British colonies. William A. Green, *British Slave Emancipation: The Sugar Colonies and the Great Experiment, 1830–1865* (London: Clarendon, 1992), 261.

14. William A. Green, "The West Indies and British West African Policy in the Nineteenth Century: A Corrective Statement," *Journal of African History* 15 (1974): 248–49.

15. Roberts, "Immigration of Africans," 236, 243; Green, "West Indies," 251; *LT*, July 16, 1857.

16. Roberts, "Immigration of Africans," 239–41; "The Ordinances of British Guiana Relative to the Emigration of Africans," *Accounts and Papers, Papers Relative to the West Indies 1841* 16 (Session 26, January–June 1841) (London: William Clowes & Sons, 1841), 264–67. Emigrants had to be residents of Sierra Leone for at least six weeks to discourage traders from using the system to send slaves to the colonies. One female was required for every two males. At first the Africans were transported in privately owned ships with their fares or "bounties" paid by the colony receiving the immigrants. Several "headmen" or scouts also made the voyage to evaluate the conditions in the colonies and report back to residents of Sierra Leone. Starting in 1843, at the request of the planters, the British government took control of the transportation and chartered three ships, one for each

colony. Recaptives no longer received support from the British in Sierra Leone; they either had to support themselves or emigrate. Also, the Colonial Land and Emigration Commission relaxed the rule controlling the ratio of men to women, as well as the six-week residency requirement. Due to the continued disappointing recruitment numbers, in 1845 the British government cut the number of transport ships and emigration agents to one, which served all three colonies. Despite these efforts, Africans still signed up in relatively small numbers. Roberts, "Immigration of Africans," 245–47; Green, "West Indies," 255.

17. At one point in the late 1840s four thousand liberated slaves resided in the government facility in Sierra Leone. In 1849, in an effort to avoid supporting so many of them, the British government offered to pay for the recaptives' transportation to the West Indies. The planters eagerly accepted and in the years 1848 through 1850, twelve thousand Africans relocated to the West Indies, the highest number for any three-year period since the plan's inception. For the Sugar Duties Act, see Deerr, *History of Sugar*, 2:430–38. For emigration to Brazil after the Sugar Act, see Roberts, "Immigration of Africans," 249–50.

18. Roberts, "Immigration of Africans," 251.

19. For the announcement of France's plan, see *LT*, July 1, 1857.

20. Ibid.

21. *LT*, July 16, 1857.

22. *LT*, July 6, 1857.

23. *LT*, July 18, 1857.

24. *LT*, July 7, 1857; *London Post*, July 15, 1857, as reprinted in the *NYT*, August 3, 1857.

25. *New Orleans Bee* (hereafter cited as *NOB*), March 4, 1858; James Paisley Hendrix Jr., "The Efforts to Reopen the African Slave Trade in Louisiana," *Louisiana History* 10 (Spring 1969): 99–103.

26. C. A. L. Lamar to James Gardner, March 4, 1858, Box 2, Folder 27, Gardner Papers.

27. *NOTP*, March 15, 1858.

28. Charles A. L. Lamar, *The Reply of C. A. L. Lamar of Savannah, Georgia to the Letter of Hon. Howell Cobb, Secretary of the Treasury of the United States, Refusing a Clearance to the Ship Richard Cobden* (Charleston, S.C.: Steam Power Press of Walker, Evans & Co., 1858), 1, Special Collections Division, Hargrett Rare Book and Manuscript Library, University of Georgia.

CHAPTER 7. "Let Your Cruisers Catch Me If They Can"

1. Cobb refers to Colcock's letter of April 20 in his letter of May 22, 1858. *CM*, June 1, 1858. Lamar claimed that he wrote to Cobb before Cobb's official reply of May 22 and explained his real intentions with the *Cobden*. This letter was confidential and never published. Lamar to Messrs. Editors, June 4, 1858, Slave-Trader's Letter-Book, GHS.

2. Charles Lamar to Thomas Barrett, to William Roundtree, and to Seaborn Jones, all dated May 24, 1858; and to L. W. Spratt, May 25, 1858, Slave-Trader's Letter-Book, GHS.

3. Lamar mentions installing Paixhan guns in his letters to Thomas Barrett and William Roundtree, May 24, 1858, and L. W. Spratt, May 25, 1858, Slave-Trader's Letter-Book, GHS. Other slave ships had been known to carry heavy guns, such as the *Clara B. Williams*. *New York Weekly Herald*, December 12, 1857.

4. *CM*, June 1, 1858. For Cobb's views on the African slave trade before the incident with Charles Lamar, see the *Savannah Georgian* as reprinted in the *CC*, October 28, 1854.

5. *CM*, June 1, 1858.

6. Ibid.

7. *Charleston News*, June 7, 1858.

8. C. A. L. Lamar to James Gardner, June 2, 1858, Box 2, Folder 27, Gardner Papers; C. A. L. Lamar to Lafitte & Co., June 6, 1858, Slave-Trader's Letter-Book, GHS.

9. C. A. L. Lamar to Messrs. Editors, June 4, 1858, Slave-Trader's Letter-Book, GHS.

10. Ibid.

11. Ibid. The British attempts to stop the illegal African slave trade created a severe shortage of field hands in Cuba. Planters turned to a relatively new source: China, with the assistance of British and U.S. shippers. Both countries were able to gain footholds in China by signing treaties with the Chinese government in 1842 and 1844, respectively, which gave them commercial access to five Chinese ports and the right to govern the areas allotted to them. The coolie trade started soon afterward, in 1847, but sputtered, only to be renewed in earnest in 1853. Chinese workers sent to the West Indies were bonded to labor. Although they signed contracts (often under the threat of violence), typically for a period of eight years at a salary of about four dollars a month, and were guaranteed food, shelter, and medical treatment, they were shipped under conditions akin to those of the African slave trade. They were sold to the highest bidder in Cuba and worked alongside Africans in the oppressive sugar fields. Soon after arriving in China in 1855, U.S. consul to China Peter Parker issued a public notification to all U.S. citizens to desist from engaging in the trade on account of the atrocities, immoralities, and illegalities associated with it. *AG*, April 25, 1857; *NYT*, April 17, 1860.

Massachusetts U.S. representative Thomas D. Elliot said in a report to the House of Representatives, "It is a mortifying fact that American ship-masters and Northern owners are found willing to connect themselves with a trade in many respects as barbarous as that of the African Slave-trade." In 1859 Attorney General Jeremiah S. Black ruled that the current laws did not prohibit U.S. shippers from participating in the coolie trade and that Congress had to act to make it illegal. *NYT*, April 17, 1860.

Chinese citizens also started to emigrate to the United States around this time, but as free persons, their movements were not in violation of any slave-trade laws.

For a history of the coolie trade in the 1840s and 1850s, see *NYT*, April 17, 1860; Evelyn Hu-Dehart, "Chinese Coolie Labor in Cuba in the Nineteenth Century: Free Labor or Neoslavery," *Contributions in Black Studies* 12 (1994): 38–54; Renee C. Redman, "From Importation of Slaves to Migration of Laborers: The Struggle to Outlaw American Participation in the Chinese Coolie Trade and the Seeds of United States Immigration Law," *Albany Government Law Review* 3 (2010): 1–55; Arnold J. Meagher, *The Coolie Trade: The Traffic in Chinese Laborers to Latin America, 1847–1874* (Bloomington, Ind.: Xlibris, 2008).

12. Lamar to Messrs. Editors, June 4, 1858, Slave-Trader's Letter-Book, GHS.

13. Lamar, *Reply of C. A. L. Lamar*, 4.

14. Ibid., 7–8.

15. Lamar to John Cunningham, July 22 and 28, 1858, Slave-Trader's Letter-Book, GHS. For Lamar's commentary on the matter, see Lamar to L. W. Spratt, July 22 and 28, 1858, ibid.

16. Lamar, *Reply of C. A. L. Lamar*, 10.

CHAPTER 8. "As Near Perfection as Anything of the Kind"

1. For the ship's arrival in New Orleans, see *NOB*, March 1, 1858, and *NOTP*, March 1, 1858; for descriptions of the yacht, see *NYT*, June 11, 1858, and *Boston Herald*, August 14, 1857. For the *Wanderer*'s itinerary from New York to New Orleans, see *NYH*, April 13, 1858.

2. Lamar doesn't reveal when he first saw the *Wanderer*, but New Orleans is the first documented instance when he and the ship were in the same place together. The yacht didn't stop at Savannah on its trip from New York to New Orleans, although it is possible that Lamar might have been visiting Charleston or Brunswick when it docked at those sites. Lamar claimed there were eight partners but never named them. Lamar to Danese, July 20, 1859, Slave-Trader's Letter-Book, GHS. William Corrie claimed that he had a one-eighth interest in the yacht. Admiralty Court Journal, January 8 to February 25, 1859, U.S. District Court, Savannah, Georgia, Federal Records Center, Morrow, Ga., 173. The eight partners apparently split sixteen shares, but the size of each partner's holdings could not be determined. Lamar states, "I am very much afraid the $\frac{1}{16}$ths nor the $\frac{15}{16}$ths would not get a new dollar for an old one." Lamar to Theodore Johnston, January 13, 1859, Slave-Trader's Letter-Book, GHS. For guests visiting the yacht in New Orleans, including General William Walker, the leader of the filibuster movement in Nicaragua, see *NOTP*, March 6, 1858, and *Brooklyn Eagle*, March 8, 1858.

3. For the hotel registration, see *Washington Evening Star*, July 21, 1857. For sale of the flour mill, see Superior Court Deeds, Chatham County, microfilm roll 3R, 207, Chatham County Courthouse, Savannah, Ga. One local merchant described

Lamar's credit as entirely dead in Savannah. W. R. Fleming to James Gardner, June 14, 1858, Box 1, Folder 12, Gardner Papers.

4. See Corrie's obituary, *Charleston Daily News*, December 28, 1870. For honor guard and the Southern Rights Association, see *CC*, April 20, 1850, and August 28, 1851.

5. Laura A. White, "The United States in the 1850s as Seen by the British Consuls," *Mississippi Valley Historical Review* 19 (1933): 525. Corrie was also involved as a second in several duels. One made national headlines in early 1858. A disagreement originated between two well-known naval officers, Commander E. B. Boutwell and former lieutenant A. C. Rhind. When Boutwell refused to retract certain statements made against Rhind and also refused Rhind's call for "satisfaction," Rhind had his second, William Corrie, post a notice near the entrance to the Navy Department calling Boutwell a coward and a liar. The duel never took place, but Corrie and Rhind spent a short time in jail for violating Washington City's antidueling laws. *NYT*, February 23, 1858, and *NOTP*, March 2 and 4, 1858.

6. *NYT*, June 11, 1858. The assertion that Corrie won "a $200,000 judgment in favor of his family upon some revolutionary claim" could not be substantiated after a review of the following records: Records of the Accounting Officers of the Department of Treasury, Record Group 217; Register of Letters and Accounts Received, Entry 284, Volume 3, 1851–1859; Letters Sent by the Miscellaneous Claims Division, Entry 256, Volume 18, March 22, 1817–August 12, 1885; Claims Division Correspondence, Miscellaneous Letters and Papers Received, Entry 601, August 20, 1810–January 8, 1900, National Archives, Washington, D.C.

7. *NYT*, June 11, 1858. According to the newspaper, after Johnson returned to New York, he received a letter from Corrie offering to buy the ship, but this is only conjecture. It is possible that arrangements for the sale were made in New Orleans. According to an article in *Porter's Spirit of the Times*, as reprinted in *CC*, June 14, 1858, "This celebrated yacht, which has caused so great a sensation in the Southern waters . . . has been purchased by Captain W. C. Corrie, of South Carolina—the price given, we learn, being $12,000." No bill of sale could be found to establish the correct sales price. An "L. Lamar" sailed from New York to Savannah on April 19. For the passenger list, see *NYT*, April 19, 1858. It was common for passengers on ships or guests at hotels to alter their names to avoid detection. Lamar usually signed letters and documents with "C. A. L. Lamar" and could have left off the "C. A."

8. For the $6,000 check, see *NYT*, June 11, 1858. For Trowbridge buying the outfit for the schooner, see *NYT*, June 12, 1858. For the arrival of Briggs ("Brooks"), see *NYH*, June 17, 1858. While many slave ships cleared New York for Africa with the help of corrupt officials, Sidney S. Norton was praised as one man who faithfully performed the responsibilities of his office and caused more than twenty vessels to be stopped. *New York Tribune* (hereafter cited as *NYTR*), March 28, 1861.

9. Passport Application No. 7889, Records of the U.S. Department of State,

Record Group 59, National Archives, College Park, Md. The passport age of thirty-five is different than the age of forty-one as calculated based on his reported year of birth of 1817.

10. The events leading up to and including the seizing of the *Wanderer* are taken from *NYH*, June 10 and 11, 1858; *NYEP*, June 10 and 11, 1858; and *NYT*, June 11 and 12, 1858. Farnum is sometimes spelled Farnham, but the former is correct.

11. For Farnum's background, see his obituary in *NYTR*, May 17, 1870; for Farnum in New Orleans, see Thomas Fleming Day, ed., "Author's Notes," *The Rudder* 15 (1904): 60. For Farnum and the Worth Legion, see *CC*, May 8, 1855.

12. Corrie registered as the sole owner of the ship. Antonio J. Waring Collection, MS 1287, Box 4, Folder 51, GHS. For clearance, see *NYCA*, June 8, 1858. For Corrie's plan of loading provisions at Port Jefferson, see *NYH*, June 11, 1858. A letter published in the *New York Times* tells a different version of the seizure. On Tuesday morning, June 8, with the tide low, Corrie realized that he couldn't load the provisions from the *Charter Oak* and get out of the harbor. He decided to send the *Charter Oak* to New York and follow in the *Wanderer* and take on the provisions there. Because there was no wind, Corrie had to wait a day. When he went to sea the next day, the *Harriet Lane* flagged him down and towed the two vessels to New York. *NYT*, June 12, 1858.

13. *NYEP*, June 11, 1858. See also the statement of Sydney S. Norton, *NYH*, June 17, 1858.

14. *NYH*, December 13, 1858. In an explanation for the trip per the *New York Times*, June 11, 1858, Corrie said that he had plantations in Trinidad and needed to visit them as problems had arisen since the introduction of the apprentice system. Captain Hawkins, the designer of the yacht, said that the water tanks were installed on his recommendation for ballast and should be filled with water. *NYH*, June 11, 1858.

15. *NYT*, June 11, 1858; *N.Y. Express* as reported in *CC*, June 15, 1858; *NYEP*, June 12, 1858.

16. *NYT*, June 11, 1858.

17. *NYT*, March 18, 1861. Rynders was one of the colorful characters in New York City in the mid-nineteenth century. He became involved in New York politics in 1844 when he helped form the Empire Club, an organization devoted to garnering votes for Democratic candidates by various forms of intimidation, often physical. *NYH*, February 2, 1845. The man could influence elections and was rewarded by party officials for his efforts. In 1845, after the election of James K. Polk to the presidency, he was given a job in the New York customhouse. *NOTP*, July 3, 1845. In 1857, after the election of President James Buchanan, he was appointed the U.S. marshal for the southern district of New York. *Albany Evening Journal*, July 13, 1857. Rynders was sympathetic to the South; during his tenure as U.S. marshal, many ships bound for Africa were cleared by him or his department, only to be seized months later as slavers. Rynders was linked by one

newspaper to the founding of the Worth Legion, and he may have known John Farnum at the time of the seizure of the *Wanderer*. *WDNI*, April 28, 1855. For a list of slave ships sailing under the U.S. flag from February 1859 to July 16, 1860, and the ports from which they cleared, *NYEP*, July 28, 1860. About thirty-five of the eighty-five ships listed were cleared from New York. For an obituary of Rynders, see *NYH*, January 14, 1885.

18. *NYT*, June 12, 1858.

19. *NYEP*, June 11, 1858. Briggs probably assisted in hiring the crew as he had hands-on experience with slavers. He was the sail master on the *Clara B. Williams*, which was owned by Nicholas Danese, who served on the *Wanderer* under the name Nicholas Brown. Mr. Brent was identified as being on the yacht when it was seized by the revenue cutter in Port Jefferson, and it is assumed he made the trip to Charleston on the yacht, as he also made the trip to Africa. *NYH*, June 11, 1858.

20. For the *Wanderer*'s arrival in Charleston, see *CC*, June 26, 1858. For the ship's registry, *Wanderer* Folder, Slave Papers, Manuscript Division, Library of Congress, Washington, D.C. (hereafter cited as *Wanderer* Folder). For check-in at the Moultrie House, see *CC*, June 26 and July 1, 1858. Trowbridge sailed from New York on a commercial ship, the *Nashville*, arriving on June 22. *CC*, June 22, 1858. Lamar sailed to Charleston from Savannah on June 21. On the same ship was N. D. Brown, which probably stood for "Nicholas Danese Brown." *CC*, June 21, 1858.

21. *CC*, June 26 and July 1, 1858. On June 27 John C. Pierce "of the *Wanderer*" checked in with Corrie and Farnum. He apparently made the trip from New York, although his name was not on the crew list from either New York or Charleston. A few unflattering references to a man named Captain John C. Pierce of Bedford, Massachusetts, were found, but he could not be connected to any of the *Wanderer* individuals. *Whaleman's Shipping List and Merchant's Transcript*, August 29, 1854; Briton Cooper Busch, *Whaling Will Never Do for Me* (Lexington: University Press of Kentucky, 1994), 69.

22. For Corrie's activities in Charleston, see Nathaniel Levin's testimony in *DMN*, November 18, 1859, and *CM*, November 19, 1859; Henry J. McCloud's testimony in *CM*, November 21, 1859; Captain N. L. Coste's testimony in *DMN*, November 18, 1859, *CM*, November 19, 1859, and *SR*, January 10, 1859, as reported in *WDNI*, January 13, 1859. For the party, see "The Log of the *Wanderer*," *Wanderer* Records, Stuart A. Rose Library, Emory University (hereafter cited as "Log of *Wanderer*"). In October 1859 Hugh E. Vincent helped organize a public meeting in Charleston to draft resolutions calling for the repeal of the laws prohibiting the African slave trade. *DMN*, October 14, 1859. In January 1860 his ship *Jehossee*, which he captained, was seized by the British off the coast of Africa as a suspected slaver. *NYT*, April 5, 1860. Vincent would certainly be sympathetic to Lamar's mission.

23. List of Persons, July 2, 1858, *Wanderer* Folder.

24. Testimony of H. Pinckney Walker, in *CM*, November 21, 1859, and *DMN*, November 19, 1859. The accounts of Walker's testimony in these two papers differ. The former reports that Walker gave "protections" to Farnum, Mr. Brent, and Nicholas Dennis. The latter reports the protections were issued to Mr. Brent, Mr. Beman, and Nicholas Denney.

25. "Log of *Wanderer*."

26. For the *Rawlins's* return to Savannah, see *DMN*, August 2, 1858. For the *Rawlins* in Saint Thomas, see John G. Willis to Lewis Cass, November 19, 1859, Consular Letters, St. Paul de Loando, National Archives, Washington, D.C. For other reports on the *Rawlins*, see *DMN*, August 14, 18, and 24, 1858. On the *Rawlins's* return trip from Africa, the acting captain and supercargo saved a British ship whose crew had been decimated by yellow fever and was adrift at sea off the coast of Cuba. *CM*, September 17, 1858.

27. *CC*, August 30, 1858, as reprinted in *DMN*, August 31, 1858.

28. *CM* as reprinted in the *DMN*, September 1, 1858.

29. Ibid. The article also explains why the federal authorities had jurisdiction and not the state. "If the *Echo* had first come into the hands of the state authorities, the crew, ship and negroes would have been disposed of under the State Act of 1835, which is very severe. But now, although the vessel and Africans are within the waters of the State, they came here under federal capture and authority, and must remain so, subject to federal disposal under federal laws."

30. *DMN*, September 9, 1858.

31. For the voyage of the *Niagara*, see *NYT*, December 13, 1858. The *Echo* crewmen were tried in Charleston in April 1859, defended by Leonidas Spratt. In two separate trials, all were found not guilty. Captain Townsend's trial was transferred from Boston to Key West, where, in May 1859, he was found not guilty. For the *Echo* trials, see Douglas A. Levien, *The Case of the Slaver Echo* (Albany, N.Y., 1859), copy at the GHS.

32. C. A. L. Lamar to Henry C. Hall, August 14 and September 14, 1858, Slave-Trader's Letter-Book, GHS.

CHAPTER 9. "The Degraded Children of Africa"

1. For the *Wanderer*'s record time, see *NYH*, April 23, 1858. For the Baltimore Clipper, see Warren S. Howard, *American Slavers and the Federal Law, 1837–1862* (Berkeley: University of California Press, 1963), 30–32.

2. Nicholas Danese owned the slaver *Clara B. Williams*, which was seized off the coast of Africa by the HMS *Alecto* on October 20, 1857. See Howard, *American Slavers and the Federal Law*, 249. Danese also captained the brig *Globe*, which left New Orleans on May 26, 1856, for the Congo River with a cargo that smacked of a slaver: 200 pipes of rum, 100 barrels of bread, 41 tierces of rice, and 4,500 feet of timber. *New Orleans Price-Current and Commercial Intelligencer*, May 28, 1856. Clearly, Danese was familiar with Africa when he sailed on the *Wanderer*.

3. If the Africans were to be acquired by barter instead of for gold, the ship

would have to carry additional products for exchange, such as muskets, gunpowder, cutlasses, whiskey, and tobacco.

4. For sneaking supplies to a slaver after it cleared customs, see *NYJC* as reprinted in the *African Repository* 32 (August 1856): 243. For auxiliaries, see Howard, *American Slavers and the Federal Law*, 8. For granting clearance to a ship that a port collector had seized, see F. H. Hatch to Lewis Cass, March 18, 1858, in *Message of the President of the United States*, 35 Congress, 1 Session, Senate Exec. Doc. No. 49 (hereafter cited as *Message from the President*, No. 49), 40–41. For bribing port officials, see *NYEP*, February 7, 1861. For Hugh Vincent's involvement in the trade, see *CC*, April 2, 1860.

5. "Log of *Wanderer*." For departure date, see *CM*, July 5, 1858.

6. Lord Napier to Lewis Cass, January 17 and February 28, 1858, *Message from the President*, No. 49, 34–35, 39. For Napier's claim of a right of search, see Cass to Napier, April 10, 1858, ibid., 42–55. For the history of the right of search and the right of visit, see *NYT*, May 20, 1858.

7. Cass to Napier, April 10, 1858, *Message from the President*, No. 49, 42–55.

8. In 1857, 10,436 slaves were landed in Cuba, followed by 16,992 in 1858. The number would climb to 30,473 in 1859. D. R. Murray, "Statistics of the Slave Trade to Cuba, 1790–1867," 147. The French contract with the Regis Company of Marseilles called for twenty thousand Africans to be sent to the Caribbean over three years starting in March 1857. William McBlair to Isaac Toucey, September 23, 1857, *Message from the President*, No. 49, 62–63.

9. Dr. J. W. Lugenbeel, "Five Years Residence in Liberia," *African Repository* 31 (October 1855): 315.

10. *Augusta Daily Constitutionalist* (hereafter cited as *ADC*), as reprinted in *NYJC*, as reprinted in *African Repository* 34 (June 1858): 189–90.

11. For a description of barracoons and their placement, see James Hall, M.D., "Abolition of the Slave Trade of Gallinas," *African Repository* 26 (March 1850): 68–71; for the advantages of placing barracoons at the mouth of the Congo River, see *NYJC* as reprinted in *African Repository* 33 (February 1857): 59. For the belief that the Congo River was the center of the African slave trade, see T. A. Conover to Isaac Toucey, October 13, 1857, *Message from the President*, No. 49, 63–64. In addition to the Congo River, Wydah, a port in the kingdom of Dahomey, served as a major source of slaves. Led by King Gezo and followed by his son Badahung, the country not only dealt heavily in the slave trade but also practiced human sacrifice on a large scale. *CC*, August 30, 1860, and *West African Herald* as reprinted in *NYT*, November 28, 1860.

12. *NYH*, February 7, 1859.

13. For the *Wanderer* arriving in Pont de Lain, see "Log of *Wanderer*." For another account of a slaving expedition in the same location, see *NYEP*, February 7, 1861. The reporter states that "the ship sails unmolested some thirty miles up the river . . . and beats into a pier opposite the 'factory' and warehouse belonging to the Havana Company. . . . The resident agent comes on board, and . . . over their wine, they discuss the price of rum and the price of niggers." See also Lieutenant

T. Lee Walker to Commander William McBlair, November 8, 1857, *Message from the President*, No. 49, 83.

14. "Log of *Wanderer*."

15. Ibid. For Farnum's remark, see "The Yacht Wanderer," *Albany Statesman*, December 15, 1858, as reprinted in *NYH*, December 18, 1858.

16. For the *Bremen* incident, see Lt. Hunter Davidson to Commander William Blair, October 12, 1857; Flag Officer T. A. Conover to Secretary of the Navy Isaac Toucey, October 19, 1857; and Cass to Napier, April 10, 1858, all in *Message from the President*, No. 49, 73, 69–70, 42–55. A reporter sailing with the *Vincennes* and the *Cumberland* reported that he heard the *Wanderer* was picking up slaves. *NYH*, February 7, 1859.

17. "Log of *Wanderer*."

18. For slavers and slave dealers coordinating on the coast of Africa, see *CM*, June 24, 1858; *NYEP*, March 22, 1861. For hearing the construction of the *Wanderer*'s slave decks, see Tom Henderson Wells, *The Slave Ship Wanderer* (Athens: University of Georgia Press, 1967), 14.

19. For loading Africans on a slaver, see *NYEP*, March 22, 1861.

20. For the danger of using chains and cuffs and letting the crew exercise control, see "The Slave Trade in New York," *Debow's Review* 18 (February 1855): 226. Women and children were generally not bound. For using nails, see *NYJC* as reprinted in the *African Repository* 32 (August 1856): 244. For docility of certain Africans, see "How to Ship Slaves," *African Repository* 31 (May 1855): 147. This last account is based on the book by Theodore Canot, *Adventures of an African Slaver: Being a True Account of the Life of Captain Theodore Canot, Trader in Gold, Ivory & Slaves on the Coast of Guinea* (Garden City, N.Y.: Garden City Publishing, 1854). See note 26 for comments on his observations.

21. While most accounts of the Middle Passage state that the slaves were stripped naked, one witness to the landing of the *Wanderer* Africans on Jekyll Island claimed that a few of them wore blankets and various articles of apparel. These items were probably given to the Africans after they had landed. Testimony of Horatio Harris in *DMN*, November 17, 1859.

22. For the *Vincennes* giving chase, see T. A. Conover to Secretary of the Navy, December 13, 1858, Letters Received by Secretary of the Navy from Commanding Officers of Squadrons, National Archives. One cargo of 1,140 Africans took nine hours to load. Using the same size and number of canoes, about four hours would be necessary to load five hundred. *NYEP*, March 22, 1861.

23. For ship measurements, see Winfield M. Thompson, "Historic American Yachts: The Slave Yacht Wanderer," *The Rudder* 15 (February 1904): 53.

24. For spacing slaves between decks, see "Africa and the Africans," *African Repository* 30 (March 1854): 70.

25. For separation of the sexes, see "How to Ship Slaves," 146–47.

26. This account of the Middle Passage is an amalgamation of *NYEP*, February 7 and March 22, 1861; "The Slave Trade in New York," *Debow's Review* 18

(February 1855): 223–8; *DMN*, September 1, 1858; "Horrors of the Slave Trade," *African Repository* 34 (November 1858): 342–44; and Canot, *Adventures of an African Slaver*. While Canot is clearly familiar with Africa, some historians have questioned the accuracy of his book and suggested that he was a fictional character. However, the *African Repository* noted, "The individuality of the man, and of his long connection with the slave trade on the west coast of Africa, we have personal knowledge, and we have no reason to doubt the general truthfulness of the narrative." *African Repository* 30 (November 1854): 327. While the book is informative, Canot made some dubious comments, such as: "These hints will apprise the reader that the greatest care, compatible with safety, is taken of a negro's health and cleanliness on the [slave] voyage." "How to Ship Slaves," 146.

27. For toilets, see *NYEP*, March 22, 1861. For a sample of statistics of slave deaths during the middle passage, see Howard, *American Slavers and the Federal Law*, Appendix D, 238.

CHAPTER 10. "I Tell You Hell Is to Pay"

1. *DMN*, November 23, 1858.

2. Most of what is known about the arrival of the *Wanderer* at Jekyll Island—the encounters among the various individuals, negotiating for a pilot, the landing of the Africans, and the first four days there—is obtained from the testimony of pilot Horatio Harris and lighthouse keeper James Clubb. Their courtroom examinations were recorded by reporters from three newspapers, the *Savannah Daily Morning News*, *Savannah Republican*, and *Charleston Mercury*, and they took notes in varying degrees of detail. In addition, the witnesses participated in many hearings, three of which were covered extensively—the commissioner's hearing in late December 1858, the first *Wanderer* trial in November 1859, and the Farnum trial in May 1860. The testimony of each witness occasionally varied from examination to examination. As a result, some of the primary source material is contradictory, confusing, and vague. The best attempt has been made to present the sequence of events at Jekyll Island as accurately as possible based on the reported testimony of Horatio Harris in *DMN*, November 17 and 18, 1859, and *CM*, November 19, 1859, and May 24, 1860; and James Clubb in *DMN*, November 18, 1859, and *CM*, November 19, 1859, and May 24, 1860.

3. For Danese's trip to Savannah, see testimony of Captain Nicholas King in *DMN*, November 18, 1859. Trowbridge must have left Jekyll for Savannah by some other means, as King identified Danese, who gave his name as Wilson, as the only passenger picked up at Jekyll.

4. John F. Tucker owned Drakies plantation on the Georgia side of the Savannah River, about sixteen miles west of Savannah, with about two hundred slaves. See testimony of Dr. H. W. Duke in *DMN*, January 4, 1859. Tucker also had an office and house in town. He was a director of the Republican Blues Building and Loan Association and, later, the Mechanics Savings Bank. Once a member of

the Know-Nothing Party with Lamar, Tucker was a sitting member of the Savannah city council at the time of the landing. Thomas Burke (alternatively spelled Bourke) was a member of the Savannah Aquatic Club, which Lamar helped found in 1853. *DMN*, December 7, 1853. He and Lamar helped organize the Chatham County Vigilance Association for the preservation of southern rights in 1859. *DMN*, December 22, 1859. For the trip from Savannah to Jekyll Island, see the testimony of Luke Christie in *DMN*, November 18, 1859. Christie was recruited when the original pilot did not appear. For picking up Thomas Burke in Brunswick, see *SR*, December 31, 1858.

5. Testimony of Luke Christie in *SR*, December 31, 1858, *DMN*, November 18, 1859, and *CM*, November 19, 1859, and May 24, 1860. In the November 1859 trial, Christie did not identify Farnum as having boarded the *Lamar* for the return trip to Savannah, but he did during the Farnum (May 1860) trial. He said, "The man called Farnum got on board before the negroes were taken on board of the *Lamar.*" Christie testified that he overheard someone say three hundred Africans had been loaded on the tug, but he didn't take his own count. Farnum, in a subsequent offer through an intermediary to testify in exchange for immunity, said that he could lead investigators to the exact spot where three hundred Africans were landed. See chapter 17. These are the only reported estimates of Africans taken on the *Lamar* on December 3.

6. Testimony of Luke Christie in *CM*, November 19, 1859. There is some confusion regarding the date that the *Lamar* arrived in South Carolina. One newspaper reported Christie as saying that he left Jekyll Island on the morning of December 3. "Nothing occurred on the return trip. . . . Did not stop at Savannah on return, but passed by," indicating that they arrived at Montmollin's plantation that night. *DMN*, November 18, 1859. However, the *Charleston Mercury* of November 19, 1859, reported him as saying that they left Jekyll Island at eleven o'clock on the morning of December 3, got as far as Sapelo Island that night, and anchored. Thus, they would have arrived on December 4. Based on the length of the trip from Jekyll to Montmollin's plantation—about seventeen hours—the December 4 date is more likely. Christie said he dropped off Lamar six miles west of the city at a plantation with a French name. That would have been Coleraine, which was owned at the time by James Potter. No connection between Potter and the *Wanderer* has been found, although it is assumed that Lamar had his permission to use his land.

7. For Montmollin as a private auctioneer, slave broker, and bank president, see *DMN*, July 1, 1856, September 1, 1858, and January 4, 1858.

8. For sighting another steamer, see testimony of Thomas Barnes in *SR*, December 21, 1858, as reprinted in the *NYH*, December 24, 1858. For the account that slaves were sent up the Satilla River, see *SR*, December 11, 1858, as reprinted in *CM*, December 13, 1858. (*Lamar* pilot Luke Christie claimed that he did not see another steamer while at Jekyll Island. *SR*, December 31, 1858.) The number of sixty Africans is a calculation based on known facts. About four hundred

Africans survived the voyage and the first few days at Jekyll Island. The *Lamar* reportedly took three hundred up the Savannah River. In March 1859 thirty-six Africans, who had been hidden on Jekyll Island, were transported across Georgia. That leaves about sixty Africans unaccounted for. It is assumed that the other steamboat took them.

9. Testimony of Dr. Robert Hazlehurst in *DMN*, November 21, 1859. Hazlehurst said he visited the island around December 10, one week after the bulk of the Africans had departed on the steamers.

10. For sinking slavers after a mission, see "Slave Trade in New York," *Debow's Review* 18 (February 1855): 225.

11. Woodford Mabry to Joseph Ganahl, December 8, 1858, Letters Received by the Office of the United States Attorney, National Archives, College Park, Md. (hereafter cited as U.S. Attorney Letters).

12. Ibid.; testimony of Woodford Mabry, *DMN*, December 20, 1858. Reporters for the *Brunswick Herald* went on the ship and wrote that they saw nothing that could be considered legal evidence that it was a slaver, but they saw "a number of primitive looking rough wooden spoons," and they knew persons who went on board who said "that they smelt niggers—and real Africans at that." *Brunswick Herald*, December 15, 1858, as reprinted in *NYH*, January 4, 1859.

13. For the arrival of Danese and the two others in Savannah, see testimony of Michael Cass in *DMN*, November 18, 1859. The name of one of the crewmembers is spelled many different ways in newspaper reports, and as it was a fake name, there is no correct spelling. "Arguirvi" is used here. For the clothing store, see testimony of William O. Price in *DMN*, November 18, 1859, and *CM*, November 19, 1859.

14. For Joseph Ganahl, see Pleasant, Alexander, Stovall Collection, MS 1021, GHS. For interest in the *Georgian* newspaper, see *DMN*, March 10, 1852; for involvement in Democratic party, see *DMN*, June 24, 1853, and September 22, 1854; for the Southern Commercial Convention, see *DMN*, October 29, 1856; for appointment as U.S. district attorney, see *DMN*, October 26, 1857.

15. For the arrest of the three crewmen, see Joseph Ganahl to Junius Hillyer, December 15, 1858, U.S. Attorney Letters.

16. Joseph Ganahl to Woodford Mabry, December 13, 1858, ibid.

17. For the deputy and Mabry searching the yacht, see testimony of Adrian V. LaRoche in *CM*, November 21, 1859. For towing the *Wanderer* back to Savannah, see *DMN*, December 22, 1858. For the search of Jekyll Island, see *CM*, November 21, 1859. Of the confiscated items, only the logbook is known to exist to this day, at the Manuscript and Rare Book Library at Emory University. J. Egbert Farnum spoke of another logbook, and it is possible that two were kept. However, a second one has never been found.

18. For the guard refusing to give up the *Wanderer*, see *SR*, December 13, 1858. For Corrie picking up and selling his Africans, see C. A. L. Lamar to Capt. N. D. Brown, January 28, 1859, Slave-Trader's Letter-Book, GHS.

19. For Farnum's trip from Savannah to Charleston, see *CM*, December 6, 1858. For his journey from Charleston to New York, see *CM*, December 13, 1858. Farnum had no fear of the authorities as he gave his name for the Savannah-to-Charleston leg as J. E. Farnum, and for the New York leg as "Capt. Farnum of the yacht Wanderer."

20. For the party, see *Boston Advertiser* as reprinted in *CM*, December 20, 1858. For the Farnum interview, see *Albany (N.Y.) Statesman*, December 15, 1858, as reprinted in *DMN*, December 23, 1858.

21. Testimony of Hillary B. Fraser in *DMN* and *SR*, December 30, 1858. Fraser didn't mention Lamar by name when he testified about picking up the men at Coleraine, though Fraser certainly would have known him. Ganahl never pressed Fraser to identify the men. Lamar remained on the boat for the trip to Augusta. See C. A. L. Lamar to Nelson Trowbridge, December 18, 1858, Slave-Trader's Letter-Book, GHS.

22. Mr. Mackenzie to Joseph Ganahl, December 14, 1858, U.S. Attorney Letters; *AC*, December 16, 1858, as reprinted in *CM*, December 17, 1858.

23. C. A. L. Lamar to Nelson Trowbridge, December 18, 1858, Slave-Trader's Letter-Book, GHS.

24. Ibid., emphasis in original.

25. Testimony of Hillary Fraser in *DMN*, December 30, 1858. For reporting of African boy, see *DMN*, December 16, 1858.

26. For sightings of Africans, see *DMN*, December 16 and 27, 1858; *CM*, December 28, 1858; *NYT*, December 29, 1858, and January 12, 1859. It is likely that some of these sightings were of the same group of Africans, namely, those taken by steamer up the Satilla River.

27. Testimony of Dr. W. H. Duke in *DMN*, January 4, 1859. The estimate of thirty Africans left at Montmollin's plantation was derived by deducting the 270 reported by an observer to have been dropped off at Hamburg from the 300 Africans understood to have been taken to Montmollin's from Jekyll Island by Captain Luke Christie. Charles Lamar later claimed he had proof that Montmollin sent twenty-seven Africans to Florida. C. A. L. Lamar to Francis Bartow, October 11, 1859, Slave-Trader's Letter-Book, GHS.

CHAPTER 11. "She Could Not Possibly Accommodate More Than Half That Number"

1. Henry Rootes Jackson was born in 1820 in Athens, Georgia. He graduated Yale College in 1839 and moved to Savannah to practice law. In 1843 he was appointed U.S. district attorney for Georgia. He served in the Mexican-American War as colonel of the First Georgia Regiment. He was appointed the judge of the superior court of Chatham County and served in that position until he was appointed U.S. minister to Austria in 1853. On his return to Savannah in 1858 he became a partner in the law firm of Ward, Jackson, and Jones, where he was working when asked to act as special prosecutor in the *Wanderer* case. Kenneth

Coleman and Charles Stephen Gurr, eds., *Dictionary of Georgia Biography*, 2 vols. (Athens: University of Georgia Press, 1983), 1:513–14. For granting power, see Howell Cobb to John Boston; Ward, Jackson, and Jones; and Joseph Ganahl, all dated December 18, 1858, in U.S. Attorney Letters. For Boston becoming temporary special agent, see Howell Cobb to John Boston, December 24, 1858, ibid.

2. For the first two months, Nicholas Danese paid the jail bills. After that a Spanish cigar store owner named Molina settled the account. Testimony of Charles Van Horn in *CM*, January 3 and November 21, 1859. Manuel and Raymond Molina both owned cigar stores in Savannah during this time. It is not known if they were related. Manuel, who was Spanish, served on a committee with John Montmollin to draft recommendations for a new Masonic hall. *DMN*, May 20, 1857, November 4, 1858, February 1 and October 1, 1859. For crewmen and slave-ship owners protecting each other, see Warren S. Howard, *American Slavers and the Federal Law, 1837–1862* (Berkeley: University of California Press, 1963), 21–22.

3. Testimony of Horatio Harris in *DMN*, December 21, 1858.

4. *DMN*, December 25, 1858; testimony of Edward Gordon in *CM*, November 21, 1859. For the difficulty with the captain, see *SR*, December 25, 1858.

5. Joseph Ganahl to Jeremiah Black, December 25, 1858, U.S. Attorney Letters.

6. For theft of the African boy, see *DMN*, December 27, 28, 1858, and January 27, 1859; testimony of George W. Wylly in *CM*, November 21, 1859. Members of the Kroo tribe had a great talent for mimicry. However, it is unlikely that the *Wanderer* Africans were Kroos as they were Mohammedans from the area around Liberia, far north of the Congo region. "Observations in Africa" from the *American Missionary* as reprinted in the *African Repository* 29 (April 1853): 105.

7. H. R. Jackson to Howell Cobb, December 27, 1858, and Joseph Ganahl to J. S. Black, December 28, 1858, U.S. Attorney Letters. For the selection of Spurlock, see note following Jackson to Cobb, December 27, 1858.

8. *DMN*, December 30, 1858.

9. Ibid.

10. For seizing the Africans, see testimony of Thomas L. Ross in *CM*, November 21, 1859; *DMN*, December 29, 1858. For Ganahl's order to Van Horn, see testimony of Charles Van Horn in *CM*, November 21, 1859.

11. For northern condemnation, see *NYCA*, December 16, 1858, *Cleveland Leader*, December 29, 1858, and *NYT*, January 1, 1859. For support of the *Wanderer* in the South, see "A Cargo of Slaves Landed," *Georgia Citizen*, December 17, 1858, as reprinted in *DMN*, December 21, 1858; "A Slaver," *Macon State Press*, as reprinted in *DMN*, December 18, 1858; "The Slave Trade and the South," *DMN*, December 27, 1858.

12. For condemnation of the *Wanderer* in the South, see *AC*, December 16, 1858, as reprinted in *CM*, December 17, 1858; *Montgomery Advertiser*, December 28, 1858; *SR*, December 13, 1858; *NODP*, December 30, 1858.

13. *NYT*, January 1, 1859; *CM*, December 18, 1858.

14. *DMN*, January 14, 1859.

15. *DMN*, January 4, 1859.

16. C. A. L. Lamar to Nelson Trowbridge, December 18, 1858, Slave-Trader's Letter-Book, GHS; C. A. L. Lamar to James Gardner, December 28, 1858, Box 2, Folder 27, Gardner Papers.

17. C. A. L. Lamar to James Gardner, December 28, 1858, Box 2, Folder 27, Gardner Papers; Charles Lamar to Gazaway Lamar, January 9, 1859, Charles A. L. Lamar Papers, Emory.

CHAPTER 12. "I Am Afraid They Will Convict Me"

1. For the warrant, see Admiralty Court Journal, January 8 to February 25, 1859, U.S. District Court, Savannah, Georgia, Federal Records Center, Morrow, Georgia, 172. For Judge Magrath's rejection, see *CM*, January 15 and 18, 1859.

2. Admiralty Court Journal, 173–75.

3. Ibid., 176–77.

4. For having to post bond, C. A. L. Lamar to G. B. Lamar, January 9, 1859, Charles A. L. Lamar Papers, Emory. For Charles's view of the trials, see C. A. L. Lamar to Gazaway Lamar, January 17, 1859, ibid. For Charles's admission to Danese, see C. A. L. Lamar to N. D. Brown, January 28, 1859, Slave-Trader's Letter-Book, GHS.

5. C. A. L. Lamar to James Gardner, January 12, 1859, Box 2, Folder 27, Gardner Papers. For Gardner's pursuit of Lamar, see William R. Fleming to James Gardner, January 13, 14, 20, 22, 1859, Box 2, Folder 12, ibid.

6. C. A. L. Lamar to Gazaway Lamar, January 9, 1859, Charles A. L. Lamar Papers, Emory.

7. For Tillman taking the Africans, see C. A. L. Lamar to Theodore Johnston, January 13, 1859; C. A. L. Lamar to Tom Lamar, January 15, 1859; and C. A. L. Lamar to N. D. Brown, January 28, 1859, all in Slave-Trader's Letter-Book, GHS. Charles also wrote to his father in New York, admitting that all profits from the *Wanderer* were being stolen, that Tom Lamar was selling Africans for nothing "merely to manufacture public opinion with him." C. A. L. Lamar to G. B. Lamar, January 17, 1859, Charles A. L. Lamar Papers, Emory. Tillman was undoubtedly one of the sons of Sophia Ann Hancock Tillman, widow of Benjamin Ryan Tillman. She inherited her husband's plantation and slaves in the Edgefield district of South Carolina after his death in 1849. Of her seven living sons in early 1859, only George Dionysus (b. 1825), John Miller (b. 1833), or Oliver Hancock Tillman (b. 1835) would have been old enough to be entrusted with the Africans. The most famous of the Tillman boys, Benjamin Ryan Jr., or "Pitchfork Ben," was only eleven years old at the time. Sophia eventually gained possession of thirty *Wanderer* slaves, though it is unknown if she purchased them or, through her son, confiscated them. Francis Butler Simkins, *Pitchfork Ben Tillman, South Carolinian* (Columbia: University of South Carolina Press, 2002), 28–30.

8. C. A. L. Lamar to Tom Lamar, January 15 and 28, 1859, Slave-Trader's Letter-Book, GHS; C. A. L. Lamar to Theodore Johnston, January 13, 1859, ibid.

9. C. A. L. Lamar to N. D. Brown, January 28, 1859, ibid.

10. C. A. L. Lamar to James Gardner, January 12, 1859, Box 2, Folder 27, Gardner Papers, and C. A. L. Lamar to N. D. Brown, January 28, 1859, Slave-Trader's Letter-Book, GHS.

11. C. A. L. Lamar to John Scott, January 12, 1859, Slave-Trader's Letter-Book, GHS.

12. C. A. L. Lamar to Wm. H. Cuyler, February 15, 1859, ibid.

13. *DMN*, February 14, 1859.

14. For Akin transporting the Africans by wagon, see Lamar to Gardner, February 20, 1859, Box 2, Folder 27, Gardner Papers. Richardson F. Akin joined Lamar in many civic and sporting activities. He was the clerk of the Savannah city council and sheriff when Lamar was an alderman. *DMN*, January 4 and 15, 1854. They were both members of the Savannah Aquatic Club, the Savannah Jockey Club, and the Chatham Regatta Club. *DMN*, December 7, 1853, September 13, 1855, August 23, 1856, and January 5, 1857. Akin earned a living as a wood vendor. *DMN*, January 19, 1857. His name is alternatively spelled Aikin or Aiken.

15. For the Telfair County posse's account of the capture of the Africans, see *NYT*, April 22, 1859. For Akin's account, see *DMN*, March 22, 1859. There are conflicting reports as to whether three or four domestic slaves accompanied Akin. *NYT*, April 22, 1859. For other news accounts, see *DMN*, March 12, 21, 25, 1859.

16. For release of the Africans, see *SR* as reprinted in *NYT*, March 28, 1859. Two of the Africans became debilitated during the first part of the journey and were unable to continue. A Jacksonville farmer, Woodford Wilcox, consented to look after them for Akin and claimed that after Akin's departure, a man from Savannah claiming to be Mr. Williams came to his residence asking about the blacks. The man turned out to be Officer Gordon of Savannah, but it is unknown who sent him, Stewart or Ganahl. Akin eventually reclaimed the two Africans. *DMN*, April 12 and 22, 1859.

17. For reporting on the Macon Africans, see testimony of Charles Van Horn in *CM*, November 21, 1859, and *DMN*, November 19, 1859, as reprinted in *NYT*, November 23, 1859; testimony of John Staley in *CM*, November 21, 1859, and *DMN*, November 19, 1859, as reprinted in *NYT*, November 23, 1859; testimony of John Tucker in *CM*, November 21, 1859. Daniel Stewart must have been acting in his capacity as a city marshal, as this was a local affair. A reporter for the *New York Tribune* said that Ganahl went out of town purposely to allow Lamar to take the two Africans. There is no evidence that he did leave town, but if he did, Lamar probably learned of it and plotted to reclaim his Africans on that day. See *NYTR*, April 1, 1859. There can be little doubt that Ganahl tried his best to convict Lamar and the others.

18. For coverage and commentary on the auction, see *DMN*, March 14, 1859; *NYT*, March 21, 22, and April 1, 1859; *NYTR*, March 17, 21, 23, and April 1, 2, 1859. One explanation for Van Horn bidding against Lamar had to do with the two Macon Africans, and not because Lamar humiliated Van Horn. After Lamar was awarded Gumbo and Cuffee, Van Horn presented Lamar with the bill for the

board of the Africans while in his custody. Lamar refused, which angered Van Horn so much that he became a bidder for the yacht. *NYTR*, March 29, 1859.

19. *DMN*, March 28, 1859.

20. For the arrest and hearing of the Telfair County posse, see *DMN*, April 15, 1859, and *NYT*, April 22, 1859.

21. *DMN*, April 15, 1859, and *NYT*, April 22, 1859.

22. *DMN*, April 16, 1859.

23. Minutes of the U.S. Circuit Court of Savannah, Georgia, March 1857–November 1860, Federal Records Center, Morrow, Ga., 142–43, 146–47, 150, 152–54 (hereafter cited as Circuit Court Minutes). Randolph Mott was another friend of Lamar and apparently bought or had possession of one or more of the Africans. Theodore Johnston was the only *Wanderer* partner whom Ganahl did not charge with a crime before a grand jury, probably because he was from New Orleans and not identified as part of the Lamar clique. In May 1859 Trowbridge was charged by a grand jury in New Orleans for "holding as slaves persons of color imported into the United States," probably *Wanderer* Africans. *New Orleans Daily True Delta*, May 11, 1859.

24. *CC*, May 13, 1859, as reprinted in *DMN*, May 16 and 17, 1859. James Moore Wayne was born in Savannah in 1790 and attended the College of New Jersey, graduating in 1808. He studied and practiced law in Savannah and after the War of 1812 entered politics. He served in the state house of representatives, as mayor of Savannah, as judge of the Court of Common Pleas and the superior court in Savannah, and in the U.S. House of Representatives. In 1835 he was appointed an associate justice of the U.S. Supreme Court, where he would serve until his death in 1867. When the Civil War began, he remained in Washington, D.C., with the Union. See Robert Manson Myers, ed., *The Children of Pride: A True Story of Georgia and the Civil War* (New Haven, Conn.: Yale University Press, 1972), 1718.

25. Henry R. Jackson, *The Wanderer Case: The Speech of Honorable Henry R. Jackson of Savannah, GA* (Atlanta, Ga.: n.p., n.d.), 40–41. While this document is not dated, in his speech Jackson said that L. Q. C. Lamar was the current secretary of the interior. His term spanned from March 6, 1885, to January 10, 1888. Since Jackson refers to a critique of L. Q. C. Lamar in the *North American Review* of November 1886, his speech would have been given between late 1886 and 1887.

26. Jackson, *Wanderer Case*, 40–41. Farnum's offer to furnish the logbook of the *Wanderer* as part of his immunity deal raises the possibility that the crew kept two logs, as another logbook had been seized with the ship in Brunswick. The logbook that Farnum claimed to possess has never been recovered.

CHAPTER 13. "I Shall Simply Put an Indignity upon Him"

1. *NYT*, March 21, 1859.

2. C. A. L. Lamar to Mr. Raymond, April 4, 1859, Slave-Trader's Letter-Book, GHS.

3. *NYT*, March 22, 1859.

4. Ibid.

5. Ibid.

6. C. A. L. Lamar to Editor of the Times New York, April 11, 1859, Slave-Trader's Letter-Book, GHS. Lamar had previously mentioned the idea of sending a vessel to Africa to place orders for slaves for another ship to pick up. In a letter to Leonidas Spratt he said, "I have one that is to sail today, and which will take out orders for 1,000 to be in readiness by the first day of September next, which I intend for the steamer, if not the one I have mentioned—a cheaper one." C. A. L. Lamar to L. W. Spratt, May 25, 1858, Slave-Trader's Letter-Book, GHS. That Lamar originally planned for the *Wanderer* to place orders is highly questionable in light of the fact that the ship had been outfitted with huge water tanks soon after purchase and manned with an experienced captain, sail master, supercargo, and crew of twelve foreigners.

7. C. A. L. Lamar to H. J. Raymond, Esq., April 20, 1859, Slave-Trader's Letter-Book, GHS.

8. C. A. L. Lamar to H. J. Raymond, Esq., May 7, 1859, ibid.; C. A. L. Lamar to B. R. Alden, May 19, 1859, ibid.

9. George W. Cullum, *Biographical Register of the Officers and Graduates of the U.S. Military Academy at West Point, New York*, vol. 1, 1802–1840 (New York: D. Van Nostrand, 1868), 393–94.

10. C. A. L. Lamar to B. R. Alden, July 30, 1859, Slave-Trader's Letter-Book, GHS.

11. C. A. L. Lamar to L. Q. C. Lamar, June 12, 1860, ibid.

12. *NYTR*, April 1, 1859. For Lamar's letters to Greeley, see C. A. L. Lamar to Horace Greeley, April 9 and 19, 1859, Slave-Trader's Letter-Book, GHS.

13. *DMN*, March 29 and 30, 1859.

CHAPTER 14. "Tell the People of Savannah They Can Kiss My Arse"

1. For Montmollin's death, see *SR*, June 13, 1859, and *Frank Leslie's Illustrated Newspaper*, July 2, 1859, which has a sketch of the recovery of the body.

2. For Lamar's claim on the twenty-seven Africans, C. A. L. Lamar to Francis S. Bartow, October 11, 1859, Slave-Trader's Letter-Book, GHS. There is no record that Lamar ever collected from Montmollin's widow.

3. *CM*, May 10, 1859.

4. *DMN*, May 16, June 13, and July 9, 1859.

5. G. B. Lamar to Charles Lamar, January 12, February 16, and March 30, 1859, G. B. Lamar Estate letter book.

6. G. B. Lamar to Charles Lamar, January 12 and 14, and February 16, 1859, ibid.

7. G. B. Lamar to Charles Lamar, March 2, May 19, and August 3, 1859, ibid. Gazaway's wish for the *Rawlins* case came true, in typical Charles Lamar fashion.

In March the ship sailed to Havana with a cargo of rice, where Charles reportedly sold her to a Cuban commercial house. Shortly afterward the ship embarked on another run, and a dispute arose between the Spanish captain who had boarded at Havana and the American captain and three mates. The Spaniard was killed and thrown overboard. The *Rawlins* was seized by the U.S. steamer *Vixen* and towed to Apalachicola, Florida, where the captain and three mates were tried. *DMN*, March 28 and April 9, 1859; *NYT*, June 11 and 13, 1860; *NYH*, March 28, 1859; *NYTR*, April 19, 1859; *Columbus (Ga.) Daily Enquirer*, September 6, 1859.

8. For the guano agency, G. B. Lamar to Charles Lamar, August 10, 1859, G. B. Lamar Estate letter book. For lectures on running the agency, G. B. Lamar to Charles Lamar, September 16, 24, and October 14, 1859, ibid.

9. Charles had suggested opening a bank, which led to the founding of the Bank of Commerce. C. A. L. Lamar to Thomas Barrett, January 6, 1856, Slave-Trader's Letter-Book, GHS. For the bank presidency and fatherly advice, see G. B. Lamar to C. A. L. Lamar, October 14, 1859, G. B. Lamar Estate letter book.

10. For Charles's praise of the *Wanderer*, see C. A. L. Lamar to Boykin and McRae, May 12, 1859, Slave-Trader's Letter-Book, GHS. For the rumored escape, see *DMN*, October 20, 1859.

11. C. A. L. Lamar to W. C. Cook, June 20, 1859, Slave-Trader's Letter-Book, GHS. Emphasis in original.

12. C. A. L. Lamar to Jas. H. Brigham, July 13, 1859, ibid. Emphasis in original.

13. C. A. L. Lamar to W. C. Cook, June 20, 1859, ibid.

14. C. A. L. Lamar to Nicholas Danese, July 20, 1859; C. A. L. Lamar to Nelson Trowbridge, July 21, 1859; C. A. L. Lamar to William C. Cook, July 21, 1859; ibid.

15. C. A. L. Lamar to L. Viana, October 6, 1859; C. A. L. Lamar to W. C. Cook, October 6, 1859, ibid.

16. Depositions of Gazaway Bugg Lamar Jr. and James H. Phinizy, *The United States of America, by Information, Versus the Schooner* "Wanderer," *and Cargo* (hereafter referred to as *U.S. vs. the* "Wanderer") (Boston: Prentis & Deland, 1860), 174–78.

17. C. A. L. Lamar to Hamel & Co., October 10, 1859; C. A. L. Lamar to Addison Commack, October 10, 1859, Slave-Trader's Letter-Book, GHS. The *Haidee* was rumored to have dropped off nine hundred slaves at Cárdenas, Cuba, in mid-1858 before being scuttled off Long Island. *NYT*, October 5, 1858. For capture of the *Niagara*, see Napier to Cass, February 28, 1858, *Message from the President*, No. 49, 39.

18. For the request to hire a crew, see depositions of William F. Black and Christopher Hussey, *U.S. vs. the* "Wanderer," 26–28, 74–75. For filling water tanks and moving the ship to the river, see deposition of Major T. Donnell, ibid., 55.

19. For removing the sails, see deposition of Major T. Donnell, ibid., 55. For informing Charles Lamar, see deposition of Gazaway Bugg Lamar Jr., ibid., 174–75. For Charles's instructions to the bookkeeper, see deposition of Philip D. Woolhopter, ibid., 178–79.

20. For activities on Monday, see depositions of Thomas J. Murphy and Major T. Donnell, ibid., 106–7, 56. For Martin's failure to pay, see deposition of Philip D. Woolhopter, ibid., 178–79.

21. For Lamar learning of trial postponement and searching for Martin, see Lamar to Cook, October 19, 1859, Slave-Trader's Letter-Book, GHS. For Martin's default, see deposition of Philip D. Woolhopter, *U.S. vs. the* "Wanderer," 178–79.

22. Deposition of John Boston, *U.S. vs. the* "Wanderer," 28–30.

23. For Martin boarding on Tuesday night, see depositions of Thomas King and Henry Welton, ibid., 84, 159–60.

24. See ibid., depositions of Ned Allen, 18–20, Thomas King, 84–85, Henry Welton, 158–61, and Harry Sommers, 141–43. While most of the crew's testimony indicated that William Black was part of the scheme, Black claimed that he was a victim like the others.

25. See depositions in n. 24.

26. Depositions of Gazaway Bugg Lamar Jr., 174–76, James H. Phinizy, 176–77, and John Boston, 28–30, in *U.S. vs. the* "Wanderer."

27. Depositions of William F. Black and Henry Welton, ibid., 27–28, 161–62.

28. *Philadelphia Evening Journal,* November 19, 1859, as reprinted in *CC*, November 26, 1859. Emphasis in original.

29. C. A. L. Lamar to W. C. Cook, October 19, 1859, Slave-Trader's Letter-Book, GHS.

CHAPTER 15. "Such Men as C. A. L. Lamar Run Riot without Hindrance"

1. *CC*, November 18, 1859.

2. For jury selection, see *SR*, November 17, 1859; *DMN*, November 16 and 17, 1859.

3. Testimony of Horatio Harris in *DMN*, November 17 and 18, 1859.

4. Testimony of Luke Christie in *DMN*, November 18, 1859; *CM*, November 19, 1859.

5. Testimony of James Clubb in *DMN*, November 18, 1859.

6. Testimony of Nicholas Coste in *CM*, November 19, 1859; testimony of Michael Cass and William Price in *DMN*, November 18, 1859.

7. Testimony of Charles Van Horn in *DMN*, November 19, 1859.

8. *DMN*, November 21, 1859.

9. *DMN*, November 22 and 23, 1859.

10. Background information on the jurors was obtained from the *Directories for the City of Savannah, 1859 and 1860* (Savannah, Ga.: John M. Cooper, 1859, 1860). Four of the twelve jurors were not listed in the Savannah city directories of 1858, 1859, and 1860.

11. Tom Henderson Wells, in his fine work on the *Wanderer*, claims that there was friction between Joseph Ganahl and Jackson and that Jackson had asked Attorney General Black to inform Ganahl that he was subject to his (Jackson's)

orders. See Tom Henderson Wells, *The Slave Ship Wanderer* (Athens: University of Georgia Press, 1967), 57. Jackson later praised Ganahl's efforts. Henry R. Jackson, *The Wanderer Case: The Speech of Honorable Henry R. Jackson of Savannah, GA* (Atlanta, Ga.: n.p., n.d.), 42.

12. Charles C. Jones Jr. to Rev. and Mrs. C. C. Jones, January 3, 1859, *in The Children of Pride: A True Story of Georgia and the Civil War, ed.* Robert Manson Myers (New Haven, Conn.: Yale University Press, 1972), 469–70.

13. *DMN*, November 24, 1859.

14. *DMN*, November 26 and 29, 1859.

15. *DMN*, as reprinted in *CM*, December 1, 1859.

16. *CM*, December 3, 1859. For granting bail to "Brown," see Circuit Court Minutes, 214. Convictions of men charged with participation in the slave trade in northern courts were rare as well. Northern newspapers of the day constantly complained about the failure of the law in these cases. The *New York Times* of April 1, 1859, in commenting on the upcoming *Wanderer* trials, lamented, "There has always been remissness in regard to vessels fitted out for the Slave-trade in this City, in Boston and in Baltimore. Scores of such expeditions have taken place every year for a long time past,—yet punishments have very rarely been inflicted." The *Albany (N.Y.) Evening Journal* of July 12, 1856, claimed, "Between the skill of lawyers, the looseness of statutes, the doughfacery of Federal judges, the perjury of parties, and the insufficiency of laws, the majority of the cases of alledged [*sic*] slavers adjudicated in the City Hall, fail of conviction, and wholly miscarry." The *New York Herald* of July 14, 1856, reported, "Since 1854 there have been thirty-two persons indicted, and thirteen tried, of whom one was convicted and twelve acquitted; the indictments against the other nineteen are so recent that they have not yet been tried. . . . Thus we see that though vessels have been captured and condemned, there has been but one man convicted of the offence against the statute. Why such a proportion of acquittals?"

17. *CM*, as reprinted in *DMN*, November 2, 1859.

18. *SR*, December 3, 1859.

19. For Price's letter, see *DMN*, December 15, 1859. For the vigilance society, see *DMN*, December 22 and 24, 1859.

20. Jackson, *Wanderer Case*, 42.

21. Ibid., 42–43. Peyton had testified as a handwriting expert at the *Wanderer* trial.

22. *NYEP*, December 10, 1859, as reprinted in *SR*, December 14, 1859. Although Farnum and Rynders might have known each other through the Worth Legion when the *Wanderer* was seized in New York in June 1858, and Rynders may have closed an eye to the evidence against the yacht, the marshal performed his duty here by arresting Farnum.

23. Jackson, *Wanderer Case*, 43–47; *Washington Star* as reprinted in *DMN*, December 26, 1859. On December 17 Farnum, aware that Attorney General Black had told Henry Jackson that he, Farnum, was willing to exchange evidence for

immunity, wrote to Joseph Ganahl demanding that the district attorney produce proof that he offered such a deal. Farnum claimed either Jackson or Ganahl started the lie to turn the people of Savannah against him and make it easier for the government to convict him. *DMN*, December 23, 1859.

CHAPTER 16. "The *Wanderer* Bothers Me to Death"

1. For the Jockey Club, see *DMN*, January 4, 1860. For director of the railroad, see *DMN*, Jan 7, 1860. For Democratic Party, see *DMN*, January 25, 1860. For the Vigilance Association, see *DMN*, December 22 and 24, 1859.

2. Deposition of Harry Sommers, 145–58, and Henry Welton, 158–72, *in U.S. vs. the* "Wanderer."

3. Ibid.

4. Ibid.

5. *U.S. vs. the* "Wanderer," 1–3; *BT*, December 27, 1859, as reprinted in *NYT*, December 29, 1859.

6. G. B. Lamar to Joseph Story Fay, January 5, 1860, G. B. Lamar letter book 1859 August–1860, vol. 21, GHS; *U.S. vs. the* "Wanderer," 5–7.

7. *U.S. vs. the* "Wanderer," 7–9. Gazaway, in his letter to former president Andrew Johnson, written after Lamar's incarceration after the war, explained, "I owned the schooner Wanderer, after she had been condemned by the United States for importing slaves, and after a man named Martin had stolen and run away with her, and after she was returned to Boston. I had taken her for debts due to me [from Charles Lamar], and gave bonds in Boston for the infraction of the revenue laws by Martin when he departed with her." See *G. B. Lamar, Sen. to Ex-President Andrew Johnson* (n.p., n.d.), 15–16, Box 1, Folder 16, G. B. Lamar Papers, GHS. Gazaway, in his letter to Charles of March 3, 1860, writes, "I enclose you a Bill of Sale for the Wanderer." G. B. Lamar Estate letter book.

8. G. B. Lamar to Charles Lamar, February 22, March 3 and 6, 1860, G. B. Lamar Estate letter book.

9. *BT*, April 23, 1860, as reprinted in *NYT*, April 25, 1860. The judge ruled that Welton, as first mate, must have known that the ship was bound for Africa and denied him compensation. One of Gazaway Lamar's lawyers in the case was Albert G. Browne Jr., who would have the elder Lamar thrown in jail in late 1865.

10. G. B. Lamar to Charles Lamar, March 9 and 12, 1860, G. B. Lamar Estate letter book.

11. For Hamilton Couper's background, see Robert Manson Myers, ed., *The Children of Pride: A True Story of Georgia and the Civil War* (New Haven, Conn.: Yale University Press, 1972), 1496.

12. Circuit Court Minutes, 253. Couper also tried to get true bills for the men on the crew list who had left Charleston on the *Wanderer*, which seems odd as Couper had to know those names were fictitious and he didn't have any of them in custody, nor did he know where to find them. The jury returned "no bill" for all of them.

13. For the breakout of Captain Farnum and the subsequent confrontation, see *SR* as reprinted in *CC,* May 4, 1860.

14. *NYT,* May 7, 1860.

15. *DMN,* May 9, 1860.

CHAPTER 17. "The Most Strangely Constituted Piece of Human Nature"

1. Circuit Court Minutes, 267–71; *DMN,* May 15–17, 1860.

2. Circuit Court Minutes, 273–74; *DMN,* May 18, 19, 1860.

3. *DMN,* May 22, 1860.

4. *CM,* May 24, 1860.

5. *CM,* May 26, 1860. Bacon's testimony confirmed Luke Christie's contention that three hundred Africans were taken from Jekyll Island to Montmollin's plantation.

6. Ibid.

7. *DMN,* May 25, 1860.

8. The first formal set of rules for dueling was recorded in 1777 in Ireland and is known as the Code Duello. See https://www.sos.mo.gov/CMSImages/MDH/CodeDuello.pdf (accessed April 15, 2017). In 1838 John Lyde Wilson, former governor of South Carolina, published *Code of Honor; or Rules for the Government of Principals and Seconds in Duelling* (Charleston, S.C.: Thomas J. Eccles, 1838). They are similar but not identical.

9. *DMN,* May 25, 1860.

10. Ibid. If Judges Wayne and Nicoll had heard of the impending duel, they did not comment on it publicly or try to stop it.

11. *DMN,* May 26, 1860.

12. Circuit Court Minutes, 285; *DMN,* May 26, 1860.

13. Circuit Court Minutes, 285. The minutes state that Judge Wayne presided alone.

14. Ibid.; *DMN,* May 26, 1860.

15. Circuit Court Minutes, 286; *DMN,* May 26, 1860.

16. Circuit Court Minutes, 288. One man of note on the Lamar jury was Fermin Cerveau, the artist who in 1837 painted the View of Savannah that now hangs in the Georgia Historical Society in Savannah. For the court proceedings and Judge Wayne's requirement of the prosecution, see *DMN,* May 29, 1860.

17. Circuit Court Minutes, 288–90; *DMN,* May 29, 1860.

18. Circuit Court Minutes, 291–92. The Georgia district attorney would never get his hands on William Corrie as Judge Magrath of the U.S. circuit court for South Carolina ruled in April that importing Africans who were not free in Africa was not in violation of the Act of 1820. *CM,* April 21, 1860; *WDNI,* May 15, 1860.

19. Circuit Court Minutes, 295; C. A. L. Lamar to L. Q. C. Lamar, June 12, 1860, Slave-Trader's Letter-Book, GHS.

20. C. A. L. Lamar to L. Q. C. Lamar, June 12, 1860, Slave-Trader's Letter-Book, GHS.

21. G. B. Lamar to Charles Lamar, May 11, 25, and June 4, 1860, G. B. Lamar Estate letter book.

22. An example of a slave owner confronting a white man over a slave's misbehavior is found in the Slave Narratives, a compendium of interviews with former slaves from the Federal Writers' Project, 1936–38, as maintained by the Manuscript Division of the Library of Congress and accessible online. See the interview of Benjamin Johnson at https://www.loc.gov/resource/mesn.042/?sp=325 (accessed April 25, 2017).

23. C. A. L. Lamar to Matthew H. Hopkins, June 18, 1860, Slave-Trader's Letter-Book, GHS.

CHAPTER 18. "I Want Dissolution"

1. For daily coverage of the convention, see NYT, April 23 to May 5, 1860. For a summary, see "The Disruption of the Democratic Party," NYT, May 4, 1860.

2. NYT, June 25, 1860.

3. NYT, May 11, 1860.

4. NYT, May 19 and 21, 1860. For the negative view of Lincoln, see Albany (N.Y.) Atlas and Argus as reprinted in NYT, May 21, 1860.

5. G. B. Lamar to Charles Lamar, May 29, 1860, G. B. Lamar Estate letter book.

6. C. A. L. Lamar to G. B. Lamar, November 5, 1860, Charles A. L. Lamar Papers, Emory.

7. DMN, November 7, 1860, as reprinted in NYT, November 14, 1860.

8. Circuit Court Minutes, 316–17. Captain David Martin would be tried in the Confederate States Court and sentenced to five years in prison. See Tom Henderson Wells, The Slave Ship Wanderer (Athens: University of Georgia Press, 1967), 81–82.

9. For the celebration, NYT, November 9, 1860. For Charles's letter, C. A. L. Lamar to G. B. Lamar, November 26, 1860, Charles A. L. Lamar Papers, Emory. The Minute Men were a paramilitary organization formed in many of the Deep South states leading up to the election of 1860 to exert influence—such as attending political meetings—to ensure secession. For the constitution of a Minute Man group, see NYT, November 15, 1860. The laws that the South had been calling on the North to repeal were the "personal liberty laws," which were designed to circumvent the Fugitive Slave Act of 1850.

10. DMN, April 16, 1860.

11. For a report that Gazaway had been confronted by a group of citizens on the street in New York and ordered to leave the city, see DMN, May 4, 1861. This account was later denied. NYT, May 19, 1861. For purchasing muskets, see NYT, December 29, 1860. For hostility from other directors, see G. B. Lamar to J. Soutter, May 28, 1861, Personal Press Copy Books of G. B. Lamar, National

Archives, Book 28F, Division of Treasury Department Archives, Civil War Records of the Fifth Special Treasury Agency (hereafter cited as G. B. Lamar Civil War Copy Books).

12. For Gazaway Lamar's comments on his wife's health, see G. B. Lamar to Charles Lamar, March 26 and May 21, 1860, G. B. Lamar Estate letter book. For overextending on guano, see G. B. Lamar to Charles Lamar, June 8, 1860, ibid.

13. For Harriet Lamar's death, see *SR*, May 10, 1861. For Gazaway's return to Savannah, see G. B. Lamar to J. Soutter, May 28, 1861, 28F, G. B. Lamar Civil War Copy Books. One of Gazaway's three daughters was living with an aunt in Massachusetts, and one of his two sons, DeRosset, was attending the University of Virginia. Charlotte, Anthony, and Annie were living with him. Gazaway soon moved into a house he built on Columbia Square.

14. C. A. L. Lamar to Wm. C. Cook, January 20, 1861, Slave-Trader's Letter-Book, GHS. For Martin's capture, see *NYCA*, September 3, 1860. For his acquittal and transfer to Savannah, see *Washington Constitution*, January 8, 1861, and *NYCA*, January 5, 1861.

15. C. A. L. Lamar to Wm. C. Cook, January 20, 1861, Slave-Trader's Letter-Book, GHS.

16. For rumors, see *CM*, January 4, 1861, *Boston Herald*, February 15, 1861, and *WDNI*, May 8, 1861. For the *Wanderer*'s capture, see *Boston Evening Transcript*, May 18, 1861. For the yacht in Union service, see *Boston Evening Transcript*, May 21 and June 22, 1861, *Boston Daily Advertiser*, July 15, 1861, and *NOTP*, October 23, 1861.

17. For drilling the Mounted Rifles, see *DMN*, May 24, 1861. For Bartow's funeral, see *CM*, July 29, 1861. For the hat, see C. A. L. Lamar to Mrs. Bartow, September 3, 1861, Slave-Trader's Letter-Book, GHS.

18. For raising a regiment, see *DMN*, August 10, 1861. For going into camp, see *DMN*, September 30, 1861. For handling business affairs, see *DMN*, October 28, 1861.

19. The letters Charles sent to Gazaway while he was stationed on Jekyll Island reflect his discontent. See C. A. L. Lamar to G. B. Lamar, December 8, 13, 22, 24, and 26, 1861, Charles A. L. Lamar Papers, Emory.

20. C. A. L. Lamar to G. B. Lamar, December 24, 1861, ibid.

21. C. A. L. Lamar to G. B. Lamar, December 26, 1861, ibid. For Charles getting thrown out of the service, see G. B. Lamar to Jefferson Davis, November 27, 1862, Letters Received by the Confederate Secretary of War, 1861–1865, August–December 1862, Roll no. 58, National Archives, Washington, D.C.

CHAPTER 19. "He Was a Prime Mover in Secession"

1. G. B. Lamar to Jefferson Davis, November 27, 1862, Letters Received by the Confederate Secretary of War, 1861–1865, August–December 1862, Roll no. 58, National Archives, Washington, D.C. Lamar regularly communicated his

ideas on how to run the Confederacy to Davis and most members of the cabinet. In September 1862 he wrote the president, "I think the time has arrived for you to offer peace to the government of the U. States." See G. B. Lamar to President Davis, September 5, 1862, Book 28 E, G. B. Lamar Civil War Copy Books.

2. C. A. L. Lamar to Nelson Trowbridge, January 8, 1863, Slave-Trader's Letter-Book, GHS.

3. G. B. Lamar to W. W. Cheever, September 1, 1862, Book 28E, G. B. Lamar Civil War Copy Books. For blockade-running profits, see Stephen R. Wise, *Lifeline of the Confederacy: Blockade Running during the Civil War* (Columbia: University of South Carolina Press, 1988), 70, 115.

4. G. B. Lamar to A. G. Black, April 16, 1863, and G. B. Lamar to Reverend W. B. Yates, April 20, 1863, Book 28E, G. B. Lamar Civil War Copy Books.

5. For interest in the *St. Johns* and the *Charleston*, see C. A. L. Lamar to Nelson Trowbridge, January 8, 1863, and C. A. L. Lamar to William Brailsford, April 9, 1863, Slave-Trader's Letter-Book, GHS. For the capture of the *St. Johns*, C. A. L. Lamar to Hall Haddon, April 20, 1863, ibid. For blaming others, C. A. L. Lamar to L. G. Bowers, April 29, 1863, ibid.

6. C. A. L. Lamar to Capt. Harry Lebby, April 28, 1863, and C. A. L. Lamar to Capt. John Ferguson, April 30, 1863, Slave-Trader's Letter-Book, GHS.

7. For the advertisement, *DMN*, April 28, 1863. For letter to the governor, G. B. Lamar to Governor Joseph E. Brown, May 11, 1863, Book 28E, G. B. Lamar Civil War Copy Books.

8. For the trip to England, see C. A. L. Lamar to Caro Lamar, July 6 and 23, 1863, Charles Lamar Papers, G. A. Henry J. Hartstene, a native of South Carolina, gained national fame in 1855 when, as a U.S. navy officer, he made a voyage to the Arctic to save stranded British scientists. At the outbreak of the war he resigned his commission and joined the Confederate navy. See the *Macon Weekly Telegraph*, April 24, 1868. For instructions to Captain Martin, see G. B. Lamar to Capt. D. A. Martin, June 25, 1863, Book 28E, G. B. Lamar Civil War Copy Books.

9. C. A. L. Lamar to Caro Lamar, July 23, 1863, Charles Lamar Papers, G.A.

10. For Charles in London, see C. A. L. Lamar to William Crowder, July 24 and 28, and August 1, 1863, and C. A. L. Lamar to Gazaway Lamar, August 8, 1863, all in Book 28C, G. B. Lamar Civil War Copy Books. Also see C. A. L. Lamar to Caro Lamar, July 23, 1863, Charles Lamar Papers, G.A.

11. C. A. L. Lamar to Caro Lamar, August 2, 1863, Charles Lamar Papers, G.A.

12. For Gazaway's request to visit Slidell, see G. B. Lamar to H. J. Hartstene and C. A. L. Lamar, July 31, 1863, "The Lamar Correspondence," *NYT*, January 16, 1864. There is no record that Charles met with Slidell. For Charles's visit to Hattie, see C. A. L. Lamar to Gazaway Lamar, September 16, 1863, Book 28C, G. B. Lamar Civil War Copy Books. It was during this trip to Paris that Charles, on learning of the death of General Thomas J. ("Stonewall") Jackson by one of his own men at Chancellorsville, designed and ordered a medal in Jackson's honor. The medals hadn't been produced by the time he left for home and

were shipped to Savannah later, though Charles would never see them. For the discovery of the medals, see *NOTP*, February 3, 1894. For Lamar's involvement, see *MT*, January 10, 1915. Charles doesn't mention ordering the medals in his letters from Europe.

13. C. A. L. Lamar to Gazaway Lamar, September 16, 1863, Book 28C, G. B. Lamar Civil War Copy Books.

14. C. A. L. Lamar to G. B. Lamar, October 18, 1863, ibid. Earl (John) Russell was Great Britain's secretary of state for foreign affairs.

15. Ibid.

16. C. A. L. Lamar to John F. McCauley, October 28, 1863, Book 28C, G. B. Lamar Civil War Copy Books.

17. For recovering the *Ceres*, see *Official Records of the Union and Confederate Navies in the War of the Rebellion* (hereafter cited as *OR-N*) (Washington, D.C.: Government Printing Office, 1899), ser. 1, vol. 9, 336–38. For the published letters, see *NYT*, January 16, 1864.

18. For the Confederate law, see *The War of the Rebellion: A Compilation of the Official Records of the Union and Confederate Armies* (hereafter cited as *OR*) (Washington, D.C.: Government Printing Office, 1900), ser. 4, vol. 3, 187. For Brown's charter and appointment of Lamar as agent, see Allen D. Candler, *The Confederate Records of the State of Georgia* (Atlanta: C. P. Byrd, 1909), 2:581. For the ships operated by the company and their success rate, see Thomas Robson Hay, "Gazaway Bugg Lamar, Confederate Banker and Business Man," *GHQ* 37 (Summer 1953): 119–21, and Robert Neil Mathis, "Gazaway Bugg Lamar: A Southern Entrepreneur" (PhD dissertation, University of Georgia, 1968), 145–47.

CHAPTER 20. A Sad Legacy

1. In 1864, at age forty-one, Charles Lamar was eligible to be drafted into the severely shorthanded Confederate army, but he never was, probably because he had been previously thrown out. According to an obituary for his wife, Charles returned to state service as a "volunteer aide" to General Cobb. See *Columbus (Ga.) Daily Enquirer*, August 22, 1902. His date of entry could not be found. For Confederate conscription laws, see William L. Shaw, "The Confederate Conscription and Exemption Acts," *American Journal of Legal History* 6 (October 1962): 376.

2. For General Geary's pronouncement, see *Memorial of G. B. Lamar to the Honorable the Senate and House of Representatives of the United States*, Box 2, Folder 2, 1–2, G. B. Lamar Papers, GHS.

3. For G. B. Lamar's oath of allegiance, Box 1, Folder 14, G. B. Lamar Papers, GHS. For requesting Charles and DeRosset to stop fighting, see *Memorial of G. B. Lamar*, 2. For Charles's reaction, see C. A. L. Lamar to Caro Lamar, February 14, 1865, Charles Lamar Papers, G.A. Because of Charles's harsh reaction to him taking the oath, Gazaway wrote an explanation to his children. He put it in a sealed envelope with the instructions "to be opened upon my death." Union authorities

confiscated it with his other papers, which resulted in its premature publication. See *NYT*, January 28, 1866.

4. For moving in with Bowers, see C. A. L. Lamar to Caro Lamar, March 1, 1865, Charles Lamar Papers, G.A. For Charles's disgust with superior officers, see C. A. L. Lamar to Caro Lamar, February 14, 1865, ibid.

5. For a summary of the principal events of Wilson's Raid, see *OR*, ser. 1, vol. 49, pt. 1, 339–40, 355–63.

6. C. A. L. Lamar to Seaborn Jones, April 10, 1865, Charles Lamar Papers, G.A.; *AC*, April 11, 1865.

7. See General Emory Upton's report in *OR*, ser. 1, vol. 49, pt. 1, 473–75, and James Pickett Jones, *Yankee Blitzkrieg: Wilson's Raid through Alabama and Georgia* (Athens: University of Georgia Press, 1976), 126–44.

8. General Upton's report, 473–75; Jones, *Yankee Blitzkrieg*, 126–44.

9. For Lamar's death, see *SR*, April 29, 1865. Rebecca Lamar McLeod, Gazaway's sister, heard another version: "He had participated in the defense of Columbus and acted very gallantly but after the retreat commenced he became separated from his friends & was ordered to surrender, which he did. He was then asked for his side arms and he had just replied that he had none when some foolish fellow shot off a pistol near and the Yankee knowing his [gun was] already cocked & supposing that Charles had fired, shot him dead. These particulars we learned through a cousin." Rebecca McLeod to G. B. Lamar, May 1, 1865, Box 1, Folder 11, G. B. Lamar Papers, UGA.

10. For Winslow's comment, *The Last Battle of the Civil War: Paper Read by Charles Jewett Swift at the Organizing of First Meeting of the Columbus Historical Society* (Columbus, Ga.: Gilbert, 1915), 26. For turning over Lamar's body, see George S. Owens to "My dear Sir," undated, Charles Lamar Papers, G.A. For the theft of Lamar's watch, see Howell Cobb to Caro Lamar, January 3, 1866, ibid.

11. Caro Lamar to G. B. Lamar, July 20, 1865, Box 1, Folder 11, G. B. Lamar Papers, UGA.

12. Mrs. [Sarah] Bowers to Caro Lamar, November 2, 1865, Charles Lamar Papers, G.A.

13. *Savannah Daily Herald and News*, June 4, 1866.

14. For Gazaway's obligations, *G. B. Lamar Sr., To the Congress of the United States*, March 22, 1871, 5, Box 7, Folder 6, G. B. Lamar Papers, UGA. For Caro's nightmare, Caro Lamar to G. B. Lamar, December 4, 1866, G. B. Lamar Estate letter book. An inventory of Charles's estate assets totaled $108,000, including $75,000 for the Eastern Wharves and land adjacent to them. There was no comparable listing of debts. See Estate of Chas. A. L. Lamar, Folder L-155, Records Department, Chatham County Probate Court, Savannah, Georgia (hereafter cited as C. A. L. Lamar's Estate).

15. Caro Lamar to G. B. Lamar, December 27, 1867, G. B. Lamar Estate letter book.

16. Ibid.

17. Caro had to file an annual statement of receipts and expenses with the probate court. In the early years she listed the payees, but in 1870 she referred to voucher numbers instead of names, making it impossible to track the amount paid to each creditor over the course of the settlement of the estate. For these and the document dismissing her as administratrix, see C. A. L. Lamar's Estate. It is unclear how much of Charles's debt to Gazaway was paid. It appears that Gazaway forgave some of the liability when he won his cotton case, but Caro eventually was sued by the other beneficiaries of Gazaway's estate. The settlement and legal issues of Gazaway's estate are beyond the scope of this work.

18. Caro Lamar to G. B. Lamar, July 20, 1865, G. B. Lamar Estate letter book.

19. *Columbus Daily Enquirer*, August 22, 1902.

20. *ADC*, April 23, 1865; *SR*, April 29, 1865.

21. For Union confiscation and shipping of captured cotton in Savannah, George Winston Smith, "Cotton from Savannah in 1865," *Journal of Southern History* 21 (November 1955): 495–512. For the estimate of Lamar's cotton, *Memorial of G. B. Lamar*, 2. These numbers vary slightly from estimates given by Lamar in other documents. In one early filing he claimed that the total value of cotton taken from him by the federal government exceeded $1.7 million. See "The United States," undated, Box 1, Folder 9, G. B. Lamar Papers, UGA.

22. For Browne persuading Lamar to leave his books and papers in the bank, see G. B. Lamar to Albert Browne Sr., February 6, 1865, Box 1, Folder 12, G. B. Lamar Papers, GHS. For Browne taking possession of the bank, see Deposition of Albert G. Browne, March 14, 1865, Box 3, Folder 6, ibid. Union agents confiscated more of Lamar's papers when he was arrested in April and December 1865. See *G. B. Lamar, Sen. to Ex-President Andrew Johnson*, G. B. Lamar Papers, GHS, 1, 13, 14.

23. G. B. Lamar to Charles A. Dana, undated, Box 7, Folder 6, G. B. Lamar Papers, UGA. While the copy of this letter is undated, it was written in response to Dana's publication of a letter from Lamar to C. C. Memminger, secretary of the Confederate Treasury, dated April 15, 1861, and would have been written soon afterward. A search of the *New York Tribune*, for which Dana worked as the editor, indicates that the letter from Lamar to Dana was never published. Charles Dana and other U.S. officials would have known of Gazaway Lamar from the other high-profile incidents in which the southerner was involved during the last few months of his residence in New York. See Thomas Robson Hay, "Gazaway Bugg Lamar, Confederate Banker and Businessman," *GHQ* 37 (June 1953): 106–10; *NYTR*, February 11, 1861.

24. *Memorial of G. B. Lamar*, 3–4, G. B. Lamar Papers, GHS.

25. Ibid., 3–5. For requests for an interview, see G. B. Lamar to President Andrew Johnson, June 18 and July 17, 1865, Paul H. Bergeron, ed., *The Papers of Andrew Johnson*, 16 vols. (Knoxville: University of Tennessee Press, 1989), 8:255, 422.

26. Lamar wrote several accounts of his efforts trying to reclaim his cotton.

They are fairly consistent. See *Memorial of G. B. Lamar*, 5–17; *Lamar to Johnson*, 1–17; G. B. Lamar Statement of Facts sent to Governor Charles Jenkins, Box 2, Folder 2, all three in G. B. Lamar Papers, GHS.

27. The trial was covered daily in the *Savannah National Republican* (December 27, 1865, to December 30, 1865) and the *Savannah Daily Herald* (January 1, 1866 to January 11, 1866). See also Richard C. Marsh, "The Military Trial of Gazaway Bugg Lamar," *GHQ* 85 (Winter 2001): 555–91.

28. For the order of confinement, see J. W. B. Johnson to G. B. Lamar, January 12, 1866, Box 1, Folder 12, G. B. Lamar Papers, GHS. For Lamar's account of his incarceration after being found guilty by the military commission, see *Lamar to Johnson*, 15, G. B. Lamar Papers, GHS. For General Brannan's order putting the military commission's sentence on hold, *Savannah Daily Herald*, February 1, 1866.

29. Chief Clerk of War Department (John Potts) to G. B. Lamar, June 5, 1872, Box 1, Folder 12, G. B. Lamar Papers, GHS. Gazaway lost all of his lawsuits against government employees.

30. For Lamar's actions after the seizure of the *Wanderer*, see *Lamar to Johnson*, 15–16, G. B. Lamar Papers, GHS. For the auction of the yacht and its first postwar run, see *Daily Eastern Argus* (Portland, Maine), November 14 and 19, 1865. For its wreck, see *Philadelphia Inquirer*, January 14, 1871.

31. For Lamar's victory in the Court of Claims, see Gazaway B. Lamar vs. the United States, No. 3222, Box 8, Folder 1, G. B. Lamar Papers, UGA. The Supreme Court decisions favoring southerners with confiscated property and who took the oath were *United States v. Padelford* (1869) and *United States v. Klein* (1871).

32. For Gazaway's obituary, see *AC*, October 10, 1874, and *NYTR*, October 7, 1874. For Lamar's bequeath, see *AG*, November 13, 1874.

33. G. B. Lamar to C. A. L. Lamar, January 25 and June 8, 1855, G. B. Lamar Estate letter book. For "Debts Due by Lamar, Trowbridge & Gardner," see Box 2, Folder 37, Gardner Papers. For Lamar's plea for ideas for making money, see Lamar to Gardner, February 28, 1858, Box 2, Folder 27, Gardner Papers.

34. "Slave-Trader's Letter-Book," *NAR*, 454.

Selected Bibliography

NEWSPAPERS

Alexandria Gazette
Augusta Chronicle
Augusta Daily Constitutionalist
Charleston Courier
Charleston Mercury
London Times
Macon Telegraph
New Orleans Times-Picayune
New York Evening Post
New York Herald
New York Journal of Commerce
New York Times
New York Tribune
Savannah Daily Georgian
Savannah Daily Morning News
Savannah National Republican
Savannah Republican

MANUSCRIPT SOURCES

Augusta Genealogical Society, Augusta, Georgia
    Estate of Basil Lamar in Account with G. B. Lamar, Executor, Account
        Book E (1827–1832), Probate Court, Richmond County
Augusta University, Augusta, Georgia
    Cazenove Lamar Miller Helm Collection, "The Record of My Ancestry, The
        Frank H. Miller Family, 1972"
Chatham County Courthouse, Savannah, Georgia
    Superior Court Deeds, Chatham County, Microfilm Rolls
Chatham County Probate Court, Records Department, Savannah, Georgia
    Estate of Chas. A. L. Lamar, Folder L-155
Emory University, Atlanta, Georgia, Stuart A. Rose Manuscript, Archives, and
    Rare Book Library
    Charles A. L. Lamar Papers, 1857–1865
    "The Log of the Wanderer"

Federal Records Center, Morrow, Georgia
    Admiralty Court Journal, January 8 to February 25, 1859, U.S. District
        Court, Savannah, Georgia
    Minutes of the U.S. Circuit Court (Savannah, Georgia, March 1857–November
        1860)
Georgia Archives, Morrow, Georgia
    James Gardner Papers, AC 1951-003M
    Charles Lafayette Lamar Papers, AC 1973-504M
    Tax Digests, Savannah, Georgia, 1844–1860, Municipal Records
Georgia Historical Society, Savannah, Georgia
    James Jordan Collection of Lamar Family Papers, MS 2549, including the
        Slave-Trader's Letter-Book
    Parish Register 1822–1851, Christ Church Manuscript Collection, M5978
    Pleasant, Alexander, Stovall Collection, MS 1021
    Antonio J. Waring Collection, MS 1287
    Caroline Lamar Woodbridge Papers, MS 0878
Library of Congress, Washington, D.C., Manuscript Division
    Wanderer Folder, Slave Papers
National Archives, College Park, Maryland
    Letters Received by the Office of the United States Attorney, December 8,
        1858–April 10, 1860
    Personal Press Copy Books of Outgoing Correspondence of Mr. G. B. Lamar,
        Lamar Records, Records of Civil War Special Agencies of the Treasury
        Department, 5th Special Agency
    Records of the U.S. Department of State, Record Group 59
National Archives, Washington, D.C.
    Consular Letters, St. Paul de Loando, September 28, 1858–November 19,
        1859
    Letters Received by the Confederate Secretary of War, 1861–1865
Richmond County Courthouse, Augusta, Georgia
    Will of Basil Lamar, Probate Record Books, Richmond County, Book 2
        (1798–1839)
Savannah City Hall, Savannah, Georgia
    Minutes of City Council
University of Georgia, Athens, Georgia, Special Collections, Hargrett Rare Book
    and Manuscript Library
    Gazaway Bugg Lamar Papers

SECONDARY SOURCES

Lamar Family and the *Wanderer*

Brown, Alexander Crosby. "The John Randolph: America's First Commercially
    Successful Iron Steamboat." *Georgia Historical Quarterly* 36 (March 1852): 32–45.

Genealogical Committee of the Georgia Historical Society. "Laurel Grove Cemetery, Savannah, Georgia. Volume 1, 12 Oct 1852–30 Nov 1861, Savannah, Georgia."

Gulick, Adam, Jr., ed. *The Papers of Mirabeau Bonaparte Lamar.* 6 vols. Austin, Tex., 1921.

Hay, Thomas Robson. "Gazaway Bugg Lamar, Confederate Banker and Business Man." *Georgia Historical Quarterly* 37 (Summer 1953): 89–128.

Jackson, Henry R. *The Wanderer Case: The Speech of Honorable Henry R. Jackson of Savannah, GA.* Atlanta, Ga.: n.p., n.d.

Jordan, Jim. "Charles Augustus Lafayette Lamar and the Movement to Reopen the African Slave Trade." *Georgia Historical Quarterly* 93 (Fall 2009): 247–90.

Lamar, Charles A. L. *The Reply of C. A. L. Lamar of Savannah, Georgia to the Letter of Hon. Howell Cobb, Secretary of the Treasury of the United States, Refusing a Clearance to the Ship Richard Cobden.* Charleston, S.C., 1858.

Lamar, G. B. *G. B. Lamar to Ex-President Andrew Johnson.* N.p., n.d.

———. *Memorial of G. B. Lamar to the Honorable The Senate and the House of Representatives of the United States.* N.p., n.d.

———. *To the Congress of the United States.* N.p., March 22, 1871.

LeMar, Harold Dihel. *History of the Lamar or Lemar Family in America.* Omaha, Neb., 1941.

McLeod, Rebecca Lamar. "The Loss of the Steamer Pulaski." *Georgia Historical Quarterly* 3 (Summer 1919): 63–95.

"A Slave-Trader's Letter-Book." *North American Review* 143 (November 1886): 447–61.

Thompson, Winfield M. "Historic American Yachts: The Slave Yacht Wanderer." *The Rudder* 15 (February–April 1904): 51–60, 113–16, 238–42.

The United States of America, by Information, Versus the Schooner "Wanderer," *and Cargo.* Boston: Prentis & Deland, 1860.

Wells, Tom Henderson. "Charles Augustus Lafayette Lamar, Gentleman Slave Trader." *Georgia Historical Quarterly* 47 (June 1963): 158–68.

———. *The Slave Ship Wanderer.* Athens: University of Georgia Press, 1967.

White, Laura A. "The South in the 1850s as Seen by British Consuls." *Journal of Southern History* 1 (February 1935): 29–48.

———. "The United States in the 1850s as Seen by the British Consuls." *Mississippi Valley Historical Review* 19 (1933): 509–36.

Georgia

Brown, Russell K. "Augusta's Other Voice: James Gardner and the *Constitutionalist.*" *Georgia Historical Quarterly* 85 (Winter 2001): 592–607.

Coleman, Kenneth, and Charles Stephen Gurr, eds. *Dictionary of Georgia Biography.* 2 vols. Athens: University of Georgia Press, 1983.

Gamble, Thomas. *Savannah Duels and Duelists: 1733–1877.* Savannah, Ga.: Oglethorpe, 1997.

Harden, William. *Recollections of a Long and Satisfactory Life.* Savannah, Ga.: Press of Review Printing Co., 1934.

Jones, Charles Colcock, and Salem Dutcher. *Memorial History of Augusta, Georgia: From Its Settlement in 1735 to the Close of the Eighteenth Century.* Syracuse, N.Y.: D. Mason, 1890.

Jones, James Pickett. *Yankee Blitzkrieg: Wilson's Raid through Alabama and Georgia.* Athens: University of Georgia Press, 1976.

Lawrence, Alexander A. *James Moore Wayne, Southern Unionist.* Westport, Conn.: Greenwood, 1970.

Myers, Robert Manson, ed. *The Children of Pride: A True Story of Georgia and the Civil War.* New Haven, Conn.: Yale University Press, 1972.

Smith, George Winston. "Cotton from Savannah in 1865." *Journal of Southern History* 21 (November 1955): 495–512.

Winslow, Edward F. *The Last Battle of the Civil War: Paper Read by Charles Jewett Swift at the Organizing of First Meeting of the Columbus Historical Society.* Columbus, Ga.: Gilbert, 1915.

African Slave Trade

The African Repository, American Colonization Society, Washington, D.C.

Behrendt, Stephen D. "The Annual Volume and Regional Distribution of the British Slave Trade, 1780–1807." *Journal of African History* 38 (1997): 187–211.

Bernstein, Barton J. "Southern Politics and the Attempts to Reopen the African Slave Trade." *Journal of Negro History* 51 (January 1966): 16–35.

Bethell, Leslie M. "Britain, Portugal and the Suppression of the Brazilian Slave Trade: The Origins of Lord Palmerston's Act of 1839." *English Historical Review* 80 (October 1965): 761–84.

———. "The Mixed Commissions for the Suppression of the Transatlantic Slave Trade in the Nineteenth Century." *Journal of African History* 7 (1966): 79–93.

Brizan, George. "The Colonial Land and Emigration Commission and Immigration to Jamaica 1840–1860." *Caribbean Quarterly* 20 (September–December 1974): 39–58.

Canney, Donald L. *Africa Squadron: The U.S. Navy and the Slave Trade, 1842–1861.* Washington, D.C.: Potomac, 2006.

Canot, Theodore. *Adventures of an African Slaver: Being a True Account of the Life of Captain Theodore Canot, Trader in Gold, Ivory & Slaves on the Coast of Guinea.* Garden City, N.Y.: Garden City Publishing, 1854.

Curtin, Philip D. *The Atlantic Slave Trade: A Census.* Madison: University of Wisconsin Press, 1969.

Deerr, Noel. *The History of Sugar.* 2 vols. London: Chapman & Hall, 1949.

Drake, Frederick C., ed. "Secret History of the Slave Trade to Cuba Written by an American Naval Officer, Robert Wilson Schufeldt, 1861." *Journal of Negro History* 55 (July 1970): 218–35.

Du Bois, W. E. B. *The Suppression of the African Slave Trade*. Baton Rouge: Louisiana State University Press, 1896.

Ettis, David, and David Richardson. *Atlas of the Transatlantic Slave Trade*. New Haven, Conn.: Yale University Press, 2015.

Fehrenbacher, Don E. *The Slaveholding Republic: An Account of the United States Government's Relations to Slavery*, ed. Ward M. McAfee. New York: Oxford University Press, 2002.

Fornell, Earl W. "Agitation in Texas for Reopening the Slave Trade." *Southwestern Historical Quarterly* 60 (October 1956): 245–59.

Fyfe, Christopher. *A History of Sierra Leone*. London: Oxford University Press, 1962.

Graden, Dale T. "An Act 'Even of Public Security': Slave Resistance, Social Tensions, and the End of the International Slave Trade to Brazil, 1835–1856." *Hispanic American Historical Review* 76 (May 1996): 249–82.

Green, William A. *British Slave Emancipation: The Sugar Colonies and the Great Experiment, 1830–1865*. London: Clarendon, 1992.

———. "The West Indies and British West African Policy in the Nineteenth Century: A Corrective Statement." *Journal of African History* 15 (1974): 247–59.

Gross, Izhak. "The Abolition of Negro Slavery and British Parliamentary Politics." *Historical Journal* 23 (March 1980): 63–85.

Hendrix, James Paisley, Jr. "The Efforts to Reopen the African Slave Trade in Louisiana." *Louisiana History* 10 (Spring 1969): 97–123.

Heron, Stella. "The African Apprentice Bill." *Proceedings of the Mississippi Valley Historical Association for the Year* 8 (1916): 135–45.

Hertslet, Lewis, comp. *Treaties and Conventions and Reciprocal Regulations at Present Subsisting between Great Britain and Foreign Powers*. London: Henry Butterworth, 1835–64.

Howard, Warren S. *American Slavers and the Federal Law, 1837–1862*. Berkeley: University of California Press, 1963.

Hulsebosch, Daniel J. "Nothing but Liberty: 'Somerset's Case' and the British Empire." *Law and History Review* 24 (Fall 2006): 647–57.

Jennings, Lawrence C. "French Policy towards Trading with African and Brazilian Slave Merchants, 1840–1853." *Journal of African History* 17 (1976): 515–28.

Jones, Wilbur Devereux. "The Origins and Passage of Lord Aberdeen's Act." *Hispanic American Historical Review* 42 (November 1962): 502–20.

Kipple, Kenneth F. "The Case against a Nineteenth-Century Cuba-Florida Slave Trade." *Florida Historical Quarterly* 49 (April 1971): 346–55.

Levien, Douglas A. *The Case of the Slaver Echo*. Albany, N.Y., 1859.

Madison, James. *Notes of Debates in the Federal Convention of 1787 Reported by James Madison*. Athens: Ohio University Press, 1966.

Mason, Matthew E. "Congress Debates Prohibiting the Atlantic Slave Trade to the United States, 1806–1807." *Journal of the Early Republic* 20 (Spring 2000): 59–81.

McMillin, James A. *The Final Victims: Foreign Slave Trade to North America, 1783–1810*. Columbia: University of South Carolina Press, 2004.

Merrill, Louis Taylor. "The English Campaign for Abolition of the Slave Trade." *Journal of Negro History* 30 (October 1945): 382–99.

Message from the President of the United States, House of Representatives, 36 Congress, 2 Session, Exec. Doc. No. 7.

Message from the President of the United States, Senate, 34 Congress, 1 Session, Exec. Doc. No. 99.

Message of the President of the United States, Senate, 31 Congress, 2 Session, Exec. Doc. No. 6.

Message of the President of the United States, Senate, 35 Congress, 1 Session, Exec. Doc. No. 49.

Mower, J. H. "The Republic of Liberia." *Journal of Negro History* 32 (July 1947): 265–306.

Nelson, Bernard H. "The Slave Trade as a Factor in British Foreign Policy: 1815–1862." *Journal of Negro History* 27 (April 1942): 192–209.

Report from the Select Committee on Slave Trade Treaties, ordered by the House of Commons. N.p., August 12, 1853.

Roberts, G. W. "Immigration of Africans into the British Caribbean." *Population Studies* 7 (March 1954): 235–62.

"Slave Hunts in Central Africa." *Harper's New Monthly Magazine*, April 1874, 710–17.

Spratt, L. W. *Speech upon the Foreign Slave Trade before the Legislature of South Carolina by L. W. Spratt, Esq., of Charleston*. Columbia: Steam-Power Press Southern Guardian, 1858.

Stein, Robert. "Measuring the French Slave Trade, 1713–1792/3." *Journal of African History* 19 (1978): 515–21.

Takaki, Ronald. "The Movement to Reopen the African Slave Trade in South Carolina." *South Carolina Historical Magazine* 66 (January 1965): 38–54.

———. *A Pro-Slavery Crusade: The Agitation to Reopen the African Slave Trade*. New York: Free Press, 1971.

Thomas, Hugh. *The Slave Trade: The Story of the Atlantic Slave Trade, 1440–1870*. New York: Simon & Schuster, 1997.

Van Cleve, George. "Mansfield's Decision: Toward Human Freedom." *Law and History Review* 24 (Fall 2006): 665–71.

Ward, W. E. F. *The Royal Navy and the Slavers*. New York: Pantheon, 1970.

Weatherford, W. D. *The Negro from Africa to America*. New York: George H. Doran, 1924.

Wender, Herbert. "The Southern Commercial Convention at Savannah, 1856." *Georgia Historical Quarterly* 15 (Summer 1931): 173–91.

Wiecek, William M. "Slavery and Abolition before the United States Supreme Court, 1820–1860." *Journal of American History* 65 (June 1978): 34–59.

Wish, Harvey. "The Revival of the African Slave Trade in the United States, 1856–1860." *Mississippi Historical Review* 27 (March 1941): 569–88.

Filibusters and Cuba–United States Relations

Boussard, Ray. "Governor John A. Quitman and the Lopez Expeditions of 1851–1852." *Journal of Mississippi History* 28 (May 1966): 103–20.

Caldwell, Robert Granville. *The Lopez Expeditions to Cuba, 1848–1851*. Princeton, N.J.: Princeton University Press, 1915.

Claiborne, J. F. H. *Life and Correspondence of John A. Quitman*. New York: Harper & Brothers, 1860.

De la Cova, Antonio Rafael. "Cuban Filibustering in Jacksonville in 1851." *Northeast Florida History Journal* 3 (1996): 17–34.

Janes, Henry Lorenzo. "The Black Warrior Affair." *American Historical Review* 12 (January 1907): 280–98.

Langley, Lester D. "Slavery, Reform, and American Policy in Cuba, 1823–1878." *Revista de Historia de America* 65/66 (January–December 1968): 71–84.

Leonard, Thomas M. *James K. Polk: A Clear and Unquestionable Destiny*. Wilmington, Del.: Scholarly Resources, 2001.

May, Robert E. "John A. Quitman and the Southern Martial Spirit," *Journal of Mississippi History* 41 (May 1979): 155–81.

———. *Manifest Destiny's Underworld: Filibustering in Antebellum America*. Chapel Hill: University of North Carolina Press, 2002.

Murray, D. R. "Statistics of the Slave Trade to Cuba, 1790–1867." *Journal of Latin American Studies* 3 (November 1971): 131–49.

Rauch, Basil. *American Interest in Cuba, 1848–1855*. New York: Columbia University Press, 1948.

Urban, C. Stanley. "The Abortive Quitman Filibustering Expedition, 1853–1855." *Journal of Mississippi History* 18 (February 1956): 175–96.

———. "The Africanization of Cuba Scare, 1853–1855." *Hispanic American Historical Review* 37 (February 1957): 29–45.

Webster, Sidney. "Mr. Marcy, The Cuban Question and the Ostend Manifesto." *Political Science Quarterly* 8 (March 1893): 1–32.

Index

In this index, CL refers to Charles Augustus Lafayette Lamar and GBL refers to Gazaway Bugg Lamar.

UnCivil Wars